M. Millioud

AF854930

ELECTRONIC DATA PROCESSING

ELECTRONIC DATA PROCESSING

by Glyn Emery

Lecturer in Computer Science
Royal Holloway College, University of London

AMERICAN ELSEVIER PUBLISHING COMPANY, INC.
New York 1969

First published 1968 *by*
Sir Isaac Pitman & Sons Ltd

American Edition published in 1969 by
American Elsevier Publishing Company, Inc.
52 Vanderbilt Avenue, New York, New York 10017

© G. Emery 1968

Standard Book Number 444–19759–1

Library of Congress Catalog Card Number: 78–75215

Made in Great Britain

To Betty, who bore the brunt of it

Preface

THE student of computer science is generally well enough served in the mathematical aspects of his subject; but there is a shortage of serious works covering the processing of file data. The very assiduous searcher can find the information, of course, if he tries hard enough: several programming books cover commercial programming, and the majority of the introductory works on computers are written from a commercial angle. The best source of information on the commercial application of computers is, of course, the huge volume of manuals and data sheets issued by the computer manufacturers, and there are several privately written books based on particular commercial systems. Unfortunately, if he concentrates unduly on a particular set of solutions to the problems of system design, the student runs the risk not only of ignoring the fact that there may be other, and possibly better, solutions to the same set of problems, but also of losing sight of the existence of the problems themselves.

It is the aim of this book to point out some of the main principles underlying the design of computer systems, and to show how different solutions to the same problems can give rise to different features in assembly languages and operating systems. The book is aimed particularly at students on courses leading to professional qualifications in computing: students working for certificates of the C.G.L.I., the Scottish Diploma in System Analysis, membership of the British Computer Society or the Institute of Data Processing. Students at Technical Colleges studying for HNC or HND in mathematics and computing, and students on various courses in data processing or system analysis should find the book indispensable. It also covers certain sections of University courses leading to diplomas and higher degrees in computer science; indeed the ordinary University mathematics student will find it most useful in dealing with equipment and basic computer science. I hope too that it will be used as background reading by lecturers and teachers who are required to teach something about computers incidental to other disciplines. Those who are already working with computers may also find it useful as a book of reference.

Although I realize that most readers will have a not inconsiderable grasp of mathematics, there will also be many who have not. Consequently I have kept the mathematics in the book as simple as possible, and there is nothing here that should provide difficulties above those of G.C.E. Ordinary Level.

In order to illustrate several basic ideas, I have used an imaginary assembly language. I have turned to this method because there is no existing language that incorporates all the features that I wanted to illustrate. Moreover, to have used the language of an existing system would have been to devote a disproportionate amount of space to describing peculiarities of the language not particularly relevant to the main argument of the book. This quite apart from the impossibility of deciding which language to choose. However, the prospective reader should not fear that he will be expected to learn yet one more computer language here in its entirety. The statements are for the most part self-explanatory and can be thought of merely as shorthand expressions for the operations they represent. The format and syntax of the language have been chosen to permit a natural expression of commercial algorithms. For instance I have chosen a two-address format, and a syntax in which the direct manipulation of sets is possible. Set-manipulation functions can be provided in any assembly language so long as the assembler can attach a set limit or set length automatically (following a dimension declaration) either to the appropriate modifier (codeword) or to the machine-code instructions operating on the set. The distinction between word sets and byte sets can be recorded in a similar way. In the language used here a set name does double duty as the name of the first element in the set, and it can be indexed as such. It depends on the function whether a name is interpreted as that of a set or as that of the first element in the set. Although direct manipulation of sets is not provided in any of the major assembly languages at the present time, I believe that it will be a universal feature soon—perhaps on the next generation of machines.

Only three chapters are concerned with programming in an assembly language, and these are followed by two chapters dealing with assembly, fault diagnosis, and machine operation. A large section of the book is concerned with equipment, both the hardware of the system centre and peripheral equipment. There are also an introduction to floating point, a brief review of the commoner higher-level languages, a chapter on multiprogramming and supervisory systems, and a discourse on the architecture of a computer series.

The reader will find a few exercises at the end of each chapter, and a set of answers to them at the end of the book. Since many of the exercises admit a choice of approach, the answers should be treated as models rather than definitive solutions. The student can use them in one of several ways: the advanced student will be able, if he wishes, to work right through the exercises and compare his results with the answers given; he may even find it instructive to do some of the programming examples in another language. The intermediate student too should find most of the exercises easy enough, though he may occasionally wish to turn to the answers for a hint on how to proceed. The beginner on the other hand may prefer to use some of the model answers as additional illustrative material on the relevant chapter.

I have included an appendix on the City and Guilds code, since this is in quite wide use today in schools and colleges. The appendix gives a summary of the code as it exists on going to press, and many of the worked examples given in the body of the book have been translated into it. Unfortunately several of the facilities described are not provided in the City and Guilds code, so it has not been possible to give a translation in each case, and some of the translations that are provided are inevitably a little circuitous. Nevertheless the appendix should be of value to students studying this code, and it should also be instructive to other students as a typical example of a one-address machine-type code.

Computer science is still relatively new, and there has not yet been time for it to acquire a settled terminology; consequently a single concept may often be referred to by several different names, or worse still the same name may be used to denote two entirely different concepts. In this book I have used the terminology I believe to be most widely current in Britain, though occasionally I have borrowed an American term if by doing so I have been able to avoid confusion. In several cases I have had to give alternative terms for the same idea where they appear to be equally widespread.

Camberley, *July*, 1968. G.E.

Contents

1. *What is Data Processing?*

THE year 1890 was a census year in the United States. The population at that time was 63 million, and collating the returns was going to be an enormous task. It was therefore suggested by a certain Hermann Hollerith that some of the collating should be done by machinery. Hollerith's idea was that the data collected by the census takers should be coded in the form of holes in pieces of pasteboard: a hole in a particular position could represent the information that a citizen was *male*, while its absence would indicate that the citizen was *female;* a group of holes elsewhere on the card would represent the *Caucasian race*, while different patterns would represent *Negro* or *Indian*. Similarly, other patterns of holes could be used to denote different age groups, occupations, and so on. The holes were to be sensed electrically, and mechanical counters would accumulate totals of the various patterns that could appear on the cards.

Between 1890 and the next census, which was in 1900, Hollerith made a number of improvements to his machines. He introduced mechanical devices for feeding the cards, which originally had to be fed into the machines by hand. He also devised an arrangement for sorting the cards into separate pockets according to the patterns of holes. After the 1900 census it was estimated that Hollerith's machines had done in one year and seven months what a hundred clerks would have taken seven years and eleven months to do.

PUNCHED CARDS

Hollerith's work on the American census returns was probably the first example of true mechanical data processing, and it led directly to the complex punched-card data-processing systems that are in use today. Machines are available nowadays not only for collating and sorting but also for merging stacks of cards, for punching new cards from old ones, and for carrying out simple calculations on data read from cards. Tabulating printers are also available, which will produce legible documents from information punched in cards.

With the aid of punched cards it is possible to carry out most of the straightforward *paperwork* in a modern commercial concern.

Jobs such as ledger posting, invoicing, payroll calculation, and even some simple sales analysis, can be performed on punched-card installations by running stacks of cards successively through various machines. Until the electronic computer, punched-card installations were practically the sole form of mechanical data processing in commerce, and even today punched cards usually provide the best answer to the data-processing needs of a small concern with less than a hundred employees.

CHARLES BABBAGE

Punched-card processing was one of the two main streams of development that eventually led to the modern commercial computer; the other was the work of Charles Babbage. Babbage was born in Devonshire in 1792, and he occupied a chair of mathematics at Cambridge from 1828 until 1839. He conceived the idea of a machine that would produce tables of mathematical functions automatically once it had been given the right initial setting. His first attempt to realize this idea he called his Difference Engine. To see how it worked, let us take the example of the cubes of the natural numbers—

1 8 27 64 125 216 etc.

If we take the differences between adjacent pairs of numbers in this series, we form another series, thus—

7 19 37 61 91

By taking differences once more, we get a third series—

12 18 24 30

If we take differences a third time, however, we get—

6 6 6

a repetition of the same constant value. Having discovered the pattern, however, we could go on to extend the original series by building it up from the bottom, so to speak. Thus the next member in the series of second differences is 36, the next member in the series of first differences is 91 + 36, which is 127; so the next cube must be 216 + 127, or 343. Many common mathematical functions have this property, that taking successive differences leads eventually to a constant sequence. In such cases Babbage saw that it would be possible to generate a table of values by following a series of simple rules, rules that could easily be implemented mechanically.

The Difference Engine was never finished. In 1842 the Government, which had been supporting Babbage until then, decided that the project was costing too much and abandoned it.* But by that time Babbage was busy with another idea, his Analytical Engine. The difference method is applicable only to a restricted class of functions; many of the commonest functions cannot be evaluated in this way but can still lend themselves to mechanical methods of evaluation, provided that the method is adjusted to suit the particular function. Such were the considerations that led Babbage to formulate his plan for the Analytical Engine, which was the true precursor of the modern digital computer. Unfortunately this was not completed either. Babbage was unlucky enough to have been born before his time. The ideas he was trying to realize in terms of gear wheels and pinions had to wait another century for the invention of the electronic valve to make their realization possible.

STORED PROGRAMS

Calculating machines had been made before Babbage, of course. One of the first was invented by the French philosopher and mathematician Blaise Pascal in 1642; and, at the same time that Babbage was designing his Analytical Engine, a countryman of Pascal, a certain Charles Xavier Thomas, was enjoying great commercial success with a hand calculator which he manufactured. Babbage's chief contribution to the subject was the concept of the stored program. The Difference Engine operated on a fixed program consisting simply of a sequence of additions. The Analytical Engine, on the other hand, had to perform a different sequence of operations depending on the function it was evaluating. But, if it were to operate at anything like the speed it was capable of, it must have the full set of operating instructions available to it at all times: it must not, like a conventional hand calculator, be made to wait upon a human operator whose function is to control each step. The medium actually used by Babbage to store his program was in fact a set of punched cards. The cards he used were of a type that had been devised by the weaver Jacquard to control the lifting of individual threads of the warp on a loom producing complicated designs.

Stored programs, in modern computer jargon, are referred to as *software*, as distinct from the palpable *hardware* of the machines themselves, since a stored program can be obliterated and replaced by another performing a different task. Program storage is simply a means whereby a sequence of instructions can be carried out in the absence of their originator. Instances of programming occur often

* Peel. A period of declining trade led to a cut in tariffs, and a consequent fall in revenue.

enough in everyday life. A car driver, for example, asking his way, might receive as a reply the following program—

> "Carry on down here until you get to the traffic lights, then turn left. Drive on until you see a turning on the right with a pub on the corner. Turn there. The street you want is the third on the right."

FLOW DIAGRAMS

This set of directions can be expressed diagrammatically in the manner shown in Fig. 1.1, which is an example of what is known as a *flow diagram.* Every one of the operations detailed must have been carried out, consciously or unconsciously, in its proper sequence if the goal has been reached. Figure 1.1 also shows something that must appear in any flow diagram except the most trivial: whatever or whoever follows it must have the option of taking alternative courses of action depending on the conditions at that time. Thus, every time the driver in our example comes to a right-hand turning, he must ask himself if there is a pub at the corner. If there is, he turns: if not, he drives on to the next turning. Similarly, while he is looking for the street he wants, he is obliged to count, turning only after the count has reached three.

From the flow diagram in Fig. 1.1 we can see that there is a choice provided at each branch point whether to go on to the next step in the program or to loop back to an earlier step. Each loop is traversed several times; the second loop twice, and the first loop as many times as it takes to find the pub. By convention we draw diamond-shaped blocks to denote the conditional steps in the process; this is a convenient shape for expressing two-way or three-way choices. Conditional steps in a program are known as jumps or branches.

The idea of looping, or *iteration* as it is called, is fundamental to computer processes. The more iteration a process involves, the more worth-while it is to program it for automatic computation, since the more iteration there is the more work the machine does in relation to the work done by the programmer. This is one of the reasons why the type of data processing known as arithmetic lends itself so well to mechanization. Babbage's original idea for his engines was that they should be employed in calculating tables of mathematical functions, performing the same sequence of operations over and over again until the desired number of values had been calculated. The actual amount of calculation would then be enormous compared with the labour of compiling the program.

Some mathematical processes have to make use of iteration even when they are calculating a single value. Take for instance Horner's method of calculating a square root, for which the flow diagram is shown in Fig. 1.2. By the test *accurate enough?* is meant, "Is the difference between the result of this iteration and that of the last iteration less than the degree of precision we are working to?"*

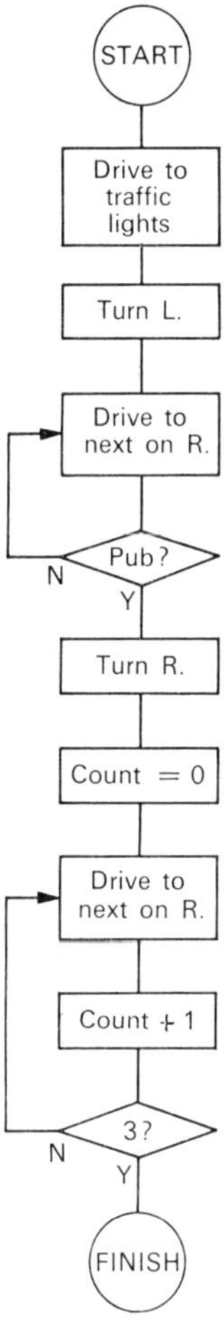

FIG. 1.1.

Commercial jobs as well as mathematical jobs have a basis of iteration. Take for example banking. The main work of a branch

* For the benefit of mathematically inclined readers, the flow diagram represents the formula—

$$R_{n+1} = \frac{1}{2}\left(R_n + \frac{N}{R_n}\right)$$

bank is keeping depositors' accounts. Each depositor must be debited or credited according to the withdrawals or deposits made in his name. The same processes are applied to all the accounts, since the methods of withdrawal and deposit are the same for everyone, and

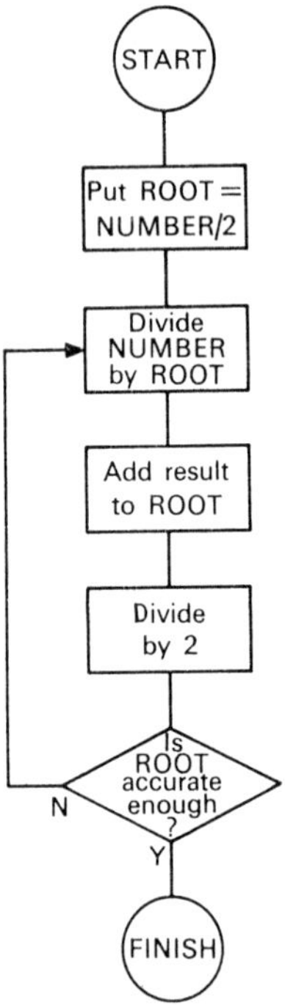

FIG. 1.2.

the same treatment is accorded every account in turn—though naturally not every one of all the operations possible applies to every account, and some accounts may not be operated upon at all on a particular occasion.

FILE UPDATING

It will be convenient at this point to introduce some of the terms used in commercial computer work. All the information that is to be operated on in a particular way is collected together in what is known as a *file*—in the case of a bank, the main file would be the set of all customer accounts. Every file is made up of a sequence of *records*, each one dealing with an individual case, and each record contains a number of separate *items*—name, address, balance of account, overdraft limit, and so on. Operations performed on records are known as *transactions* or *movements*, and when a record is operated upon—perhaps by the debiting of an account, or by a change in the address—it is said to be *moved*. Movements occur in accordance with incoming documents (cheques, deposit slips, credit transfers, etc.) which together are known as the *input;* there is generally also an *output* from a commercial process—in the case of the bank, the output would include statements of account, lists of transactions with other branches, and so on. The process of running through a complete file, carrying out movements as indicated by the input, is known as *updating*.

File updating is by far the most important job in commercial data processing, so it will be worth our while to consider some more examples of it besides banking. Let us take insurance for example: here, the main file consists of policy records. In accident insurance, the main movements are claims, changes, and premium payments; in life insurance a record is moved when a premium is paid, and there is a final movement when the policy matures. Input consists of new policies, changes, claims, and premium payments. The principal output in insurance consists of premium renewal notices and receipts.

In a warehouse or store the main file is an inventory of stock, giving the name of each item, its price, the amount on hand, and the level at which it must be reordered. Movements are issues and deliveries, and of course re-orders. Input consists principally of orders, and output of invoices. In mail-order selling, since a mail-order house is essentially a warehouse, there must also be an inventory file; but just as important as this is the file of customer accounts or agent accounts, giving the individual's name and address and the state of his or her balance. This file has to be debited according to goods sent, and it has to be credited with payments, whether lump sums or instalments. Input therefore consists principally of orders and payments, and output of invoices and statements.

The foregoing is of course a simplification of what goes on in real commercial businesses. In fact there are many exceptions and special circumstances that have to be taken into account, and several subsidiary files that have to be updated periodically—employee files, for instance, and commission files for agents and brokers. No two businesses are exactly alike, even when they are engaged in the same sort of trading. The reader will certainly be able to draw upon his own experience to find other examples of file updating, and will be able to imagine how each one could be analysed for purposes of mechanical data processing.

Simple file-updating procedures can be carried out on punched-card installations. The main file is then a stack of cards, each record occupying one or more cards according to its length. Updating a record involves punching a new card or cards to represent its new state, and eventually destroying the old cards. When a computer is used for file updating, it is usual to hold the file on some magnetic recording medium, for instance magnetic tape. The usual width of computer tape is half an inch, and it comes in reels up to 3,000 feet in length. A single tape 3,000 feet long can hold as much information as thirty books the length of this one. Even so, it is very often necessary for a business to use several reels to accommodate the whole of its main file.

On a medium-speed transport, a magnetic tape takes about five minutes to run through; consequently it is not practicable to refer

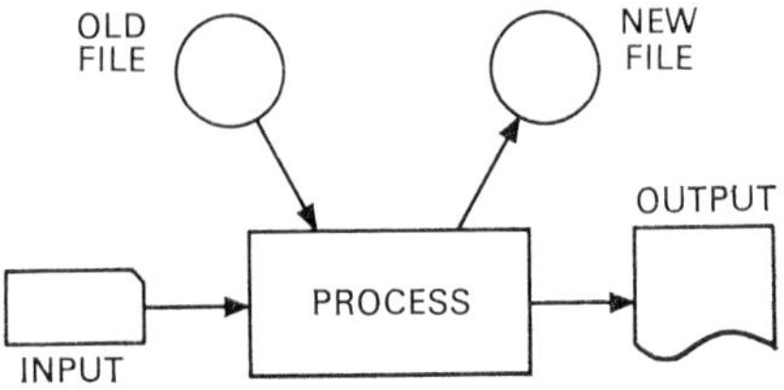

FIG. 1.3. Updating a File

to records in the file at random, as one might do had they been printed records. The best way to work with magnetic tape is to run through the whole file, dealing with records in the order in which they appear on it. Moreover, for reasons we shall discuss later, it is not possible to amend a record on a magnetic-tape file simply by erasing and recording over the top of it; consequently updating has to be done by re-creating an entirely new tape from the old one, amending those records that are moved, and simply copying those that are not. With this way of working, it is quite a simple matter to insert new records in their proper place in the sequence, and to delete records without leaving gaps. Every updating run then produces a new generation of the file. As a safeguard it is usual to keep old files from a generation or so back, so that the current version of the file can be reconstituted if it becomes damaged. Old files kept for security are often moved to another building as a safeguard against damage by fire.

Figure 1.3 shows diagrammatically how a computer can be used for updating a file. The input must be in some form that a computer can read; it is shown in this diagram using the symbol for punched cards. Modern punched cards have one corner cut away to make sure that they cannot be inserted into the reader upside-down or back to front. Output is shown in Fig. 1.3 in the form of a printed sheet; this is its commonest form, since most computer output is destined eventually to be assimilated by human beings. Most printers used for computer output print a line at a time. Such printers require their stationery to be in the form of a continuous strid. and it is usually preprinted as a sequence of forms.

Another common type of computer input is punched paper tape. Fig. 1.4 shows a short length of what is known as 8-hole punchep tape—the small holes near the centre-line are known as *sprocket holes;* they are used simply for location, and do not carry any information. Each row of holes across the tape represents a character—either a letter of the alphabet, a numerical digit, or some other symbol. With the possibility of a hole or no hole in each of eight

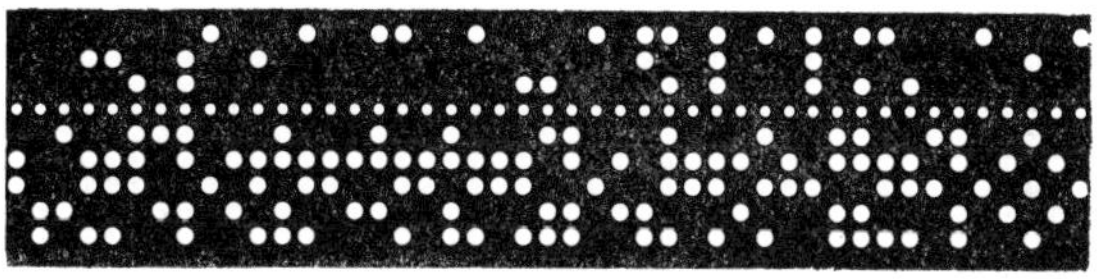

FIG. 1.4. 8-Hole Paper Tape

positions, the number of different characters that can be represented is 2^8 or 256; but it is common practice to do as Fig. 1.4 shows and use only those combinations that have an even number of holes. Then, if some fault develops in the punch or the reader and a hole fails to be read or an extra hole appears, it is detected at once and can be remedied. This type of check is known as a parity check. Even parity is chosen, since this makes blank tape (no holes) acceptable. With a parity check, 8-hole tape allows only 2^7, or 128, different character codes to be punched; but this is enough for all the letters of the alphabet, both capital and lower-case, all the decimal digits, and a good many other characters as well.

There is a great range of computer input devices, from devices for reading pencil marks on specially prepared forms, to devices that can read a normal type face. There is even a device that will, to a limited degree, accept the spoken word. Such things are expensive though, so it is likely that punched cards and punched paper tape will be with us for some time yet. This is in spite of the fact that numbers of girls have to be employed preparing data, that is, transcribing original documents on key punches. Input and output devices and file devices are known collectively as *peripherals.* The electronic unit that stores and obeys the program, controlling the peripheral units in the process, is known as the *processor,* or *system centre.*

SORTING

The items on a file are held in a definite order—the order of the serial number that they are normally referred to by. In order to carry out an updating run in the way that we have described, the input items must be in the same sequence as the file items, for only then can the file be run straight through without a break. Now the input arrives in a completely random sequence, so it must be sorted somehow before the updating run. It would be possible to sort it before presenting it to the computer, either manually or, if it is transcribed on to cards, on a card sorter. But why not sort on the computer itself? Sorting is just the kind of data-processing activity that a computer is ideally suited for.

Data that has to be sorted must be held on some medium that can be written on as well as read from, since sorting involves shunting data backwards and forwards from one place to another. Magnetic tapes will suit very well. To sort properly it is necessary to have at least three tapes: one will be supplied holding the data to be sorted; the other two are tapes that have been made available for general use. Tapes like this are known as *scratch tapes.* We shall be dealing with sorting procedures in some detail in Chapter 13.

SYSTEM FLOWCHARTS

Figure 1.5 shows what is known as a *system flowchart.* It gives a chain of three related activities, or *runs:* transcription of data from cards to magnetic tape, sorting, and file updating. They could be carried out one after the other on the same computer, with magnetic tapes being loaded and unloaded as necessary between runs. In this way, no more than three magnetic-tape units would be needed on the installation. Extra units are particularly useful, however, when there is a multi-reel file, for then a great deal of time can be saved by loading up a new reel while the previous reel is still being processed. Time is of the essence in any computer installation, since there is often not sufficient time to perform all the tasks that have to be done; and, even if there is time to spare, time on a computer is a very saleable item. One of the principal tasks of computer managers is trying to devise ways of getting more data processing done without spending any more money.

Figure 1.5 shows a single *job,* made up of three separate *runs.* The aggregate of all the jobs performed on the same set of files is known as a *system.* Runs are sometimes subdivided further into separate *passes*—sorting runs are an example.

On a single run there are generally several separate processes going on at the same time; thus, on an updating run, such as that shown in the figure, there might be an input file being read, a main

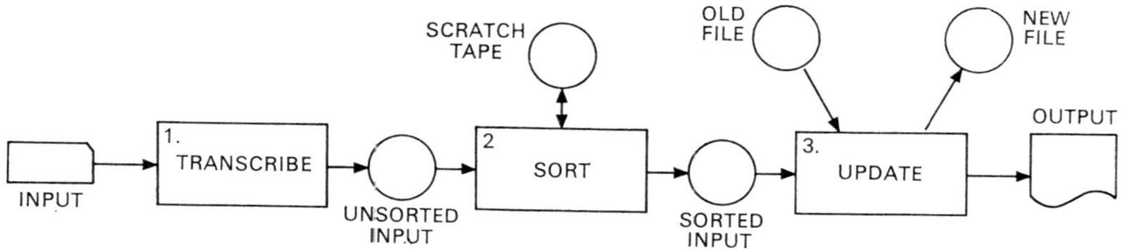

Fig. 1.5. Typical Job

file being copied, some output being printed, and of course some computation, all going on together. If these processes could be allowed to go on independently of the others, they would take different lengths of time; but, because they are interlocked, the fastest process has to wait upon the slowest, and the time that elapses for the whole run is that of the slowest process. We refer to this as *real time*, in contrast to the individual process times (computing time, file-run time, input time, and output time).

We use the term *file activity* to denote the proportion of file records moved during a single run. When a file has a low activity, the slowest process is usually that of copying it. Real time and file-run time are then the same, and the run is said to be *tape-limited*. With higher file activities it is not uncommon to find the run limited by the speed of computation or the speed of the printer. A tape-limited job can be speeded up by using faster tape units, or sometimes by using more of them.

RANDOM ACCESS

The need for sorting can be avoided if a different type of file device is used, one that enables access to be made rapidly to records in any random order. One such device is a disc file. Data is recorded magnetically on concentric tracks on a set of discs mounted on the same spindle. Writing and reading are carried out by a recording head mounted on the end of a moveable arm in such a way that it can be positioned quickly over any track on any disc. The actual time take to reposition the arm may be as long as one second; in which case the system cannot process records at a rate faster than a few thousand an hour. Nevertheless, with inactive files, processing can be faster on a disc file than with magnetic tape which requires every record to be read and written, whether it is to be processed or not.

Thus, a random-access file may be faster than a serial file, and it does not require the input to be sorted. Furthermore, it is not even necessary for the input to be punched into cards or paper tape; it can be entered directly into the processor by means of typewriter keyboards, and can then be dealt with as it comes. Typewriters connected to a computer in this way are said to be *on-line*. Since a typewriter is an output device as well as an input device, it can be used for entering queries into a machine and receiving the replies as soon as they are available. Fig. 1.6 shows a system with a disc file and six typewriters connected on-line for file interrogation; there is also an output record on a line printer.

A file may be updated or it may simply be interrogated, information being read from it without its contents being altered, in much the same way as words are looked up in a dictionary. Another way of using a file is to accumulate data in it in the same way as a ledger, with no more processing than is involved in keeping a running balance. These are all examples of file processing. But an important part of commercial data processing may not involve files at all; this is the

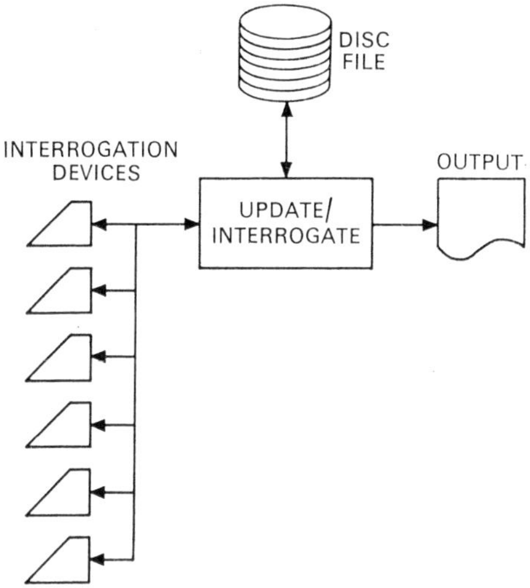

FIG. 1.6. On-line Processing

part concerned with management aids. For instance, one of the duties of management, perhaps its main duty, is to decide how the resources of an organization, whether they be of money, manpower, machinery, or materials, are to be used to the best advantage. To do this accurately might involve trying out thousands of possibilities—a task far beyond the powers of a human being, but not beyond those of a computer. We shall have more to say on this subject in the last chapter.

Data processing is an activity we are engaged in every day of our lives. Most of the time we do it unconsciously, and we are often unaware of the complexity of the processes we are carrying out. In designing and using computer systems, we have to examine closely what we are doing—take our work to bits, so to speak, and find out just how it is made up; then put it together again in the form of logical flow diagrams. There was once a centipede who sat down to work out which order he moved his feet in; and then found that he had forgotten how to walk. Let us try not to be like the centipede.

EXERCISES 1

1. A driver following the flow diagram of Fig. 1.1 runs a risk of being fined for shooting the traffic lights. Amend the diagram to avoid this.
2. Draw a flow diagram for calculating and printing a table of cubes using the method of Babbage's Difference Engine.
3. Use a flow diagram to explain the rules for playing Snakes and Ladders. Remember that every player must throw a six to start, and that the exact number must be thrown to finish. Throwing a six entitles the player to another throw.
4. Six tape transports are available for use with the system in Fig. 1.5. If the main file comprises three reels, suggest how the transports might be used to make the system as fast and efficient as possible. Detail in sequence the tape loading and unloading operations.
5. In Fig. 1.5, the output consists of reports and invoices; the latter have to be separated into batches for sending to regional offices for circulation. Amend the flowchart to show how this could be achieved. What is now the minimum number of tape decks required?
6. Sketch a flowchart for a sequential file-interrogation system. The file is to be on magnetic tape; the queries are punched into cards, and the replies are to be printed on standard forms, batched according to the originators of the queries.

2. *Some Fundamental Ideas*

SCALES OF NUMERATION

THE system of numeration used practically everywhere in the world today is known as the *Hindu-Arabic system*, since it is believed to have had its origin in India, and to have reached Europe via the Middle East. It is based on the number ten; but so are practically all the numeration systems that have ever been invented. The special feature of the Hindu-Arabic system is that it needs no more than ten symbols to express any number, no matter how large. In the ancient Greek system of numeration, the letters alpha to theta were used to represent the numbers one to nine, the next nine letters to represent the multiples of ten up to ninety, and the next nine to represent the hundreds. The Romans improved the system so that they only required symbols for one, five, ten, fifty, and so on; but they still had to have thirteen symbols if they wanted to count up to a million, and more if they wanted to go higher. The contribution made by an unknown genius in seventh-century India was the realization that the significance to be attached to a symbol could be indicated by its position in the series, and that a system could be devised on this basis provided that a symbol was invented to represent zero.

Modern numeration, then, uses a decimal positional system, with the figure on the right-hand end of the series having the least significance, that is, representing the units. Successive positions in the series represent successive powers of ten, so that ten is the *radix* on which the system grows. If our physiology had been different, we might have been using some other radix, twelve for instance, with more factors, and consequently easier to manipulate. Numeration in radix twelve would of course require twelve different symbols.

BINARY SCALE

Any plural number can be used as a radix for numeration. In computer work we use the *binary scale*, or scale of two. We do this because the binary scale requires only two different symbols (written conventionally as 0 and 1) and these can be expressed in an electrical analogue by current and no current in a wire, or by the on and off conditions of a switch. The fact that only two electrical states are recognized means that the circuits that have to discriminate between them can be quite cheap and simple. We shall see later that the adoption of a two-valued arithmetic enables us to make use of the ideas of common logic, which also has two values—true and false. Another advantage of the binary scale is that it is more efficient for storing numbers. With radix eight, for example, we should have to provide four times as many states or discrimination levels as with radix two; but a digit in radix eight is only equivalent to three digits in radix two (8 is 2^3).

Digital computers use a *positional* binary notation. Thus two, the radix, is represented by 10; four, the square of the radix, by 100; and so on. Counting in the binary positional scale proceeds as follows—

one	1
two	10
three	11
four	100
five	101
six	110
seven	111
eight	1000
nine	1001

etc.

Appendix I gives a table of powers of two. We can make use of this in converting numbers from binary into decimal notation. For instance, the binary number—

100110001

is the sum of 2^8, 2^5, 2^4 and 2^0. Its value in decimal notation can then be obtained by addition—

2^8	256
2^5	32
2^4	16
2^0	1
	305

Conversion from decimal to binary can be accomplished in a similar way; but a simpler way is to perform successive additions and multiplications. An example appears in Appendix IV.

The tenth power of two is one thousand and twentyfour, which is therefore represented in the binary scale as 10000000000. Since this number is very nearly the same as 1000 in the decimal scale, we can make the statement that three decimal digits are roughly equivalent to ten binary digits, or that one decimal digit is equivalent to three and a third binary digits. A binary number thirty digits long is equivalent to a decimal number nine digits long, that is, it covers a range of numbers up to about one thousand million. The phrase "binary digit" is usually contracted to the word *bit*.

Most readers will be familiar with a game known as the Towers of Hanoi, in which a number of plates stacked on a peg have to be transferred to another peg one by one, with the restriction that a larger plate must never be placed on top of a smaller. To make this possible, a third peg is provided to act as an intermediate stage in the transfer. The game is shown in Fig. 2.1. The number of

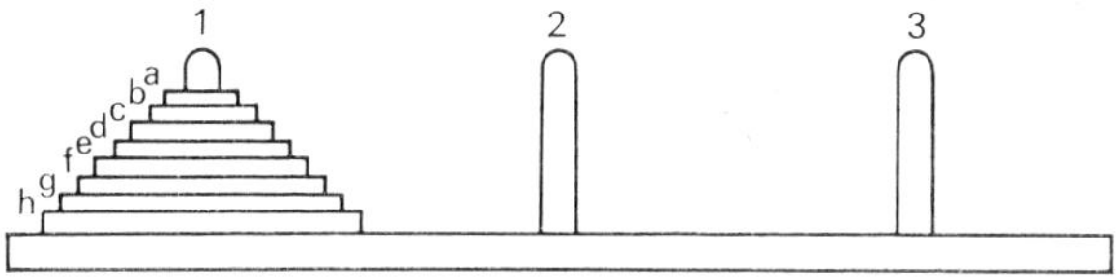

FIG. 2.1. Towers of Hanoi

moves depends on the binary scale of numeration. We can see this if we note first that one plate can be transferred in one move. To transfer two plates, we need three moves, thus (refer to Fig. 2.1)—

a to 2, b to 3, a to 3.

For three plates, the sequence of movements is—

a to 3, b to 2, a to 2, c to 3, a to 1, b to 3, a to 3,

or seven moves in all. Now one, three, and seven in the binary scale are 1, 11, and 111. We can surmise, therefore, that it would take fifteen (1111) moves to transfer four plates, thirty-one (11111) to transfer five plates, and so on. In the original story, the ruler of Hanoi gave the game to a captured foreign monarch, with the promise that he would be released when he had transferred a tower of twenty-five plates. This would have taken (decimal) 33,554,431 moves; at a rate of one move a second, his release would have come in about a hundred years.

Another game whose theory depends on the binary scale is Nim.* Nim is played with matches or counters, which are arranged at the start in three or more rows or piles. It is a game for two players, of whom each may in turn take as many matches as he wishes from

* Said to be from the German *nehmen* = to take.

any one row. The object of the game is to force the other player to take the last match. A player who knows the secret will consider the binary representation of the number of matches in each row. He then takes matches away until the numbers of ones in all the binary positions are even. For example, take the case illustrated in Fig. 2.2, in which there are twelve matches in the first row, eleven in

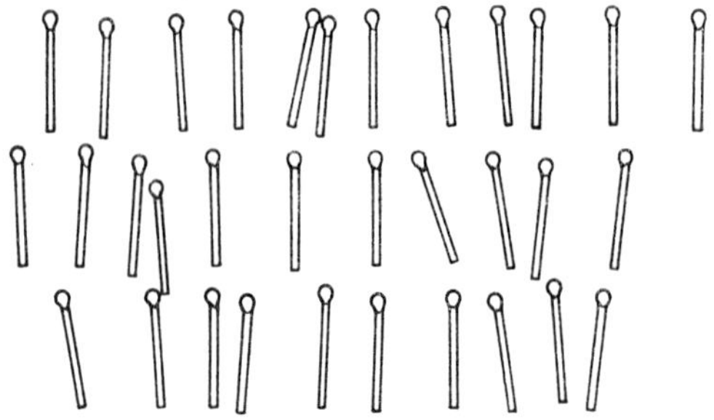

FIG. 2.2. Nim

the second, and ten in the third. If we write these numbers down in the binary scale, we get—

```
1100
1011
1010
```

Here the total of ones in the first, third, and fourth (counting from right to left, in order of significance) positions are odd. They can be made even by taking eleven matches from the first row, five from the second, or three from the third, leaving one or other of the arrangements—

1	1100	1100
1011	110	1011
1010	1010	111

These are winning positions; no matter what the opponent does, the player can always bring the game back to a position in which the numbers of ones in all positions are even, and eventually to a position where he can remove all matches but one.

BINARY-CODED DECIMAL

With four bits (binary digits) we are able to express all the numbers from zero up to fifteen. More usefully, we can express the numbers zero to nine, and use the other six binary combinations to represent plus, minus, point, and other signs. This method of representing decimal numbers by means of binary codes is known as *binary-coded decimal* (*BCD*). It is used in a number of computers as an alternative to, or in addition to, the ordinary binary form of representation.

ALPHABETIC CODES

With six bits, we can represent up to sixty-four symbols; this would enable us to allot codes to the decimal digits 0 to 9, the letters of the alphabet, and a wide range of other characters. Several computers use a six-bit code to represent data in character form and to enable them to store, and even edit, pieces of text. Computers that normally perform their arithmetic in the binary scale may store numbers in character form if they are not to be operated on arithmetically. In the phrase, "16 ACACIA AVENUE", the number 16 is unlikely ever to enter into an arithmetic operation. Data is usually in a six-bit code on six-hole punched-paper tape, and it is often in this form on six-track magnetic tape.

With a seven-bit code we can have both capital letters and lower-case letters represented, and we can add several more special symbols to the repertoire. But seven, being a prime number, is awkward to handle, so it is more usual to find eight bits being used than seven. Eight happens to be a particularly convenient number to use, since it is itself a binary power. In the last chapter we showed an example of a piece of eight-hole paper tape. In fact only seven of the eight tracks were used there to record data, the eighth being used simply to make the number of holes in each code even, as a check against reading errors. Checks of this type are referred to as parity checks. In Appendix II we give a seven-bit code that, with minor variations, is used throughout the world, local variations being required by national alphabets, currency signs, and the like. It will be noticed that the *all-ones* symbol is referred to as *delete*. This means that it is possible to delete any character by punching a hole in every track over it. Codes in the first two columns are used for format instructions to typewriters and fast tabulating printers.

The arrangement of the symbols in the standard seven-bit code calls for some comment. It will be seen that the letters of the alphabet occupy codes with higher numeric values than the numerals, and that the numerals do not have their natural values, but appear with higher-valued codes than most of the special symbols, particularly the space. The reason for this is that if we are using a mechanical sorting procedure based on the numeric values of the codes we shall generally get the sort of sequence we want. Thus Mr. Brown comes before Mr. Browne, since the first gentleman has a space where the second has an *e*. Serial number ABC appears before ABC1, which appears before ABC12, which in turn appears before ABCD. It is worth noting though that the incorrectly spelled Mr. Ffrench will come among the F'S, while the correctly spelled Mr. ffrench may have to wait until after the Zinovievs and Zlotinskys. Anyone intending to use a computer for sorting must make himself thoroughly familiar with the collating sequence of the character codes he is likely to use.

All the facilities of a seven-bit code can be obtained with a six-bit code by using what are known as shifts. These are special character codes that operate in much the same way as the shift key on a typewriter, which is intended to give a choice of up to 84 different characters from only 42 keys. As an example of the use of shifts, we might choose to let our six-bit code normally represent the characters in columns 2, 3, 4, and 5 of Appendix II. We could then decide to use, say, code 1011110 to represent a shift instead of an upward arrow. After the appearance of this code, the normal codes would represent the graphics and special symbols shown in columns 0, 1, 6, and 7 of the table. The special shift would persist until the appearance of a new code transferring back to the normal shift. Various schemes are possible; for instance the shift code might change the interpretation of only half, say, of the codes, or several shift codes might be provided, giving different interpretations to different groups.

BYTES

A group of eight bits, coded to represent a graphic symbol, is known as a *byte*. A set of consecutive bytes, representing a string of symbols, is known as a *field*. In fact we use the term *field* for any sequence of coded symbols that together form a single entity—a sequence of characters on punched tape, for instance, or a set of columns on a card.

Numeric data can be held, as we have said, either in binary form, or in binary-coded decimal form, using at least four bits to each decimal digit. In four-bit BCD, numbers occupy just half as much space as in ordinary byte form, with eight bits to a character. The four-bit BCD form is therefore said to be *packed*, and the byte form *unpacked;* though it must be remembered that a true binary representation is even more economical in space. Earlier we showed that ten bits are equivalent to three decimal digits; but three decimal digits in packed BCD occupy twelve bits—twenty per cent more room than pure binary. Nevertheless, BCD is a popular form of numeric representation, particularly on small machines where the actual amount of arithmetic to be performed is slight, and the effort of converting data from decimal to binary form is not warranted. However, binary remains the natural form of number representation for computers: not only is it more economical in space, but it enables arithmetic units to be built that operate far faster than would be possible with BCD. Computers used for very fast numerical work (*number crunchers*, as they are called in the jargon) all operate in binary. Some computer systems provide both binary and decimal forms of arithmetic, so that the user can choose which type of representation he uses to suit the type of work he is doing.

OCTAL AND HEXADECIMAL SCALES

Two other scales of numeration are of importance in computer practice; these are scales with radices that are powers of two: the *octal scale*, with radix eight, and the *hexadecimal scale*, with radix sixteen. The importance of these two scales is that they are very easy to convert into binary form, and yet give a reasonably compact representation of numbers. They may be thought of as shorthand ways of writing binary numbers. Numeration in the octal scale requires eight symbols, for which purpose the digits 0 to 7 are used. The hexadecimal scale requires sixteen symbols, so, as well as the digits 0 to 9 it is usual to use the first six letters of the alphabet with some distinguishing mark such as a line over the top. Here is the same number in four different scales—

decimal	4 3 8 3 6
binary	1010101100111100
octal	1 2 5 4 7 4
hexadecimal	$\bar{A}$ $\bar{B}$ 3 $\bar{C}$

A computer that performs arithmetic in pure binary operates upon numbers in standard lengths. A binary number of a standardized length is known as a *word*. Different computers use different lengths of word; but by far the commonest word length nowadays is thirty-two bits, which is, of course, precisely the same length as four bytes. With thirty-two bits, it is possible to express numbers from zero up to 4,294,967,295 (decimal); but it is more usual to employ the first bit to indicate the sign of the number, and to restrict the range to 2,147,483,647, positive or negative.

BINARY ADDITION AND SUBTRACTION

Arithmetic in the binary scale is quite analogous to arithmetic in the decimal scale. The process starts at the right-hand (less significant) end. If the sum in any position is equal to or exceeds the radix, in this case two, the excess is divided by the radix, the residue is entered, and the quotient is carried into the next position. In binary addition, of course, only one can be carried, and carry may extend over several positions. Here is an example, with arrows to show where a digit has been carried—

$$\begin{array}{rr} & 1011011001010 \\ + & 111001101001 \\ \hline & 10010100110011 \end{array}$$

⟵ ← ←

The rules for binary addition can be written down formally as follows—

(*a*) Carry is generated only in those places where there is a one in both of the numbers to be added.

(*b*) Carry is propagated up the word until it reaches a position where there is a nought in both numbers.

(*c*) If there is no carry, the sum bit is one when the bits in the two numbers are different, and nought when the bits in the two numbers are the same.

(*d*) If carry has been propagated from the place below, the sum bit is a one if the bits in the two numbers are the same, and a nought if they are different.

Now let us look at subtraction. Again there is a close analogy with the decimal equivalent. If the bit in the bottom line is greater than the bit in the top line (if there is a nought over a one) one radix is borrowed from the next column to make subtraction possible. Borrow may, if necessary, be propagated for several positions up the word. Here again is an example with arrows to show where borrow has been propagated—

$$\begin{array}{rr} & 1000110100101 \\ - & 11000101100 \\ \hline & 101101111001 \end{array}$$

← ⟵

Again we can write the rules down formally—

(*a*) Borrow is generated whenever a nought appears above a one.

(*b*) Borrow is propagated until it finds a one above a nought.

(*c*) If there is no borrow, the difference bit is one when the bits in the two numbers are different, and nought when they are the same.

(*d*) If borrow has been propagated from below, the difference bit is one when the bits in the two numbers are the same, and nought when they are different.

NEGATIVE NUMBERS

At this point we may ask ourselves what happens in a subtraction operation when a larger number is subtracted from a smaller. This is really asking how we shall represent negative numbers. Since sign has only two possible values, plus and minus, we need only one bit to represent it, and conventionally the most significant bit in the word is normally chosen. Now the simplest way, on the face of it, would seem to be to make this bit, say, nought for positive numbers and one for negative numbers, leaving the actual representation of the number unaffected. In this way, we should represent five by 00000101, and minus five by 10000101. But this is not in fact the way that negative numbers turn out when we subtract a greater number from a smaller. Let us take an example, subtracting, say, forty from twenty-five. To fix our ideas, let us suppose that we do this using a standard word length of ten bits, of which the first is intended to represent the sign.

$$\begin{array}{r} 0\ 000011001 \\ -\ 0\ 000101000 \\ \hline 1\ 111110001 \end{array}$$

In this example, borrow has been propagated right up to the top of the word, making a number that, if it were regarded as positive, would be interpreted as one thousand and nine. However the number we expect from this operation is minus fifteen, and it would be natural, therefore, to use a convention in which minus fifteen is actually represented by the positive number one thousand and nine. We notice that fifteen and one thousand and nine together amount to one thousand and twenty-four, or one more than the largest number that can be represented in a ten bit word. The natural convention would be therefore to represent negative numbers by their complements with respect to a number one greater than the largest number that the word will accommodate. Thus, if our word length were thirty-two bits, we should represent the number $-x$ by the quantity $2^{32} - x$. The reader can verify for himself that negative numbers represented in this way can be treated in arithmetic processes in exactly the same way as positive numbers, and that this would not have been so had we decided to represent them in the simple straightforward way. With this form of representation for negative numbers, the computer does not need to determine the sign of a number before performing arithmetic on it.

SET LOGIC—BOOLEAN ALGEBRA

At this point, we shall have to digress a little and talk about the work of George Boole. Boole was that rarest of creatures, a self-taught mathematician. He started his working life as a teacher in a private school in Lincoln, and ended it as a professor of mathematics in Ireland, in 1864. During a comparatively short working life, he laid the foundations of what has come to be known as *Boolean algebra*, or the logic of sets. A set is simply an assembly of objects that, for convenience in some context or other, are to be dealt with together, generally because they have some feature in common. Thus "towns with more than 50,000 inhabitants", "red-headed men", "dachshunds", are all examples of sets; but "the ace of spades and George Washington and the Tower of Pisa" might also be treated as a single set if there were anything to be gained from doing so.

Sets may overlap. For example, the set of all towns with more than 50,000 inhabitants overlaps the set of all coastal towns, and the overlap is of course a set itself—the set of all coastal towns with more than 50,000 inhabitants. There is also a larger set consisting of the combination of the two sets, that is, the set of all towns that are either on the coast or have more than 50,000 inhabitants. Thus we can operate on sets, either by overlapping or by combining, to produce new sets, in much the same way that we operate on numbers by addition and subtraction to produce new numbers. This idea of operations on sets, analogous to arithmetic operations, is the basis of Boolean algebra. We use the symbol & (read *and*) to denote the overlap operator, and the symbol **v** (read *or*) to denote the combination operator. Thus, if A and B represent sets, A & B and A **v** B also represent sets with members drawn from A and B.

The operators & and **v** are used to combine sets in *pairs*; for this reason, they are referred to as binary operators or dyadic operators (no direct connection with scales of numeration). Boolean algebra also includes a unary operator, one that operates on a single class only. This is the *not* operator, which we shall denote by putting a line over the symbol representing the set it is applied to. Applied, say, to the set of all green things, the *not* operator would denote a new set consisting of all those things that are not green.

Strictly, the *not* operator replaces a set by a new set consisting of everything in the universe that was not in the original set. Thus the *not* operator applied to the set *men* denotes a new set consisting not only of women but also of dogs, caterpillars, waterfalls, ideas, and indeed anything else that cannot be described as *men*. Obviously such a set is not a particularly useful entity to deal with, so it is usual to restrict logical operators to a particular *domain*. Within the domain of human beings, the set *not men* implies only *women*, a much more useful concept.

CIRCLE DIAGRAMS

We can express the foregoing ideas diagrammatically by means of what are known as *circle diagrams*, or *Venn diagrams*. We could, if we wished, imagine that all the members of a particular set had been gathered together in one place, and a fence had been thrown around them. The set could then be thought to be represented by the area within the fence. By allowing fences to overlap, we can mark off new areas representing the sets generated by applying the Boolean operators. Figure 2.3 shows several circle diagrams; in every one, the shaded area represents the composite set corresponding to the formula written underneath it.

It is quite easy to show by means of Venn diagrams, or by other means, that Boolean operators & and ∨ are commutative, that is, that—

$$a \mathbin{\&} b = b \mathbin{\&} a$$

and

$$a \vee b = b \vee a$$

They are also associative—

$$a \mathbin{\&} (b \mathbin{\&} c) = (a \mathbin{\&} b) \mathbin{\&} c$$

and

$$a \vee (b \vee c) = (a \vee b) \vee c$$

and distributive over one another—

$$a \mathbin{\&} (b \vee c) = (a \mathbin{\&} b) \vee (a \mathbin{\&} c)$$

and

$$a \vee (b \mathbin{\&} c) = (a \vee b) \mathbin{\&} (a \vee c)$$

However, when the two operators appear in the same formula, we must be very careful to put the brackets in the right places, as the last two diagrams in Fig. 2.3 show.

TRUTH TABLES

Another way of expressing the idea of a Boolean operator is by means of a *truth table*. The operands in Boolean algebra can have either of two values, true or false. We could use the symbols T and F to represent the two values; but it will be more convenient to borrow from the binary numeration scale and use the symbol 1 for true and the symbol 0 for false. Since every variable has two possible values, two variables taken together can provide four possible combinations, namely, 0 and 0, 0 and 1, 1 and 0, and 1 and 1. If the last combination obtains, then an *and* operation applied to the two variables also gives a true result (value 1); but in the other three cases the *and* operation gives a false result. Thus we may write—

a	0 0 1 1
b	0 1 0 1
a & b	0 0 0 1

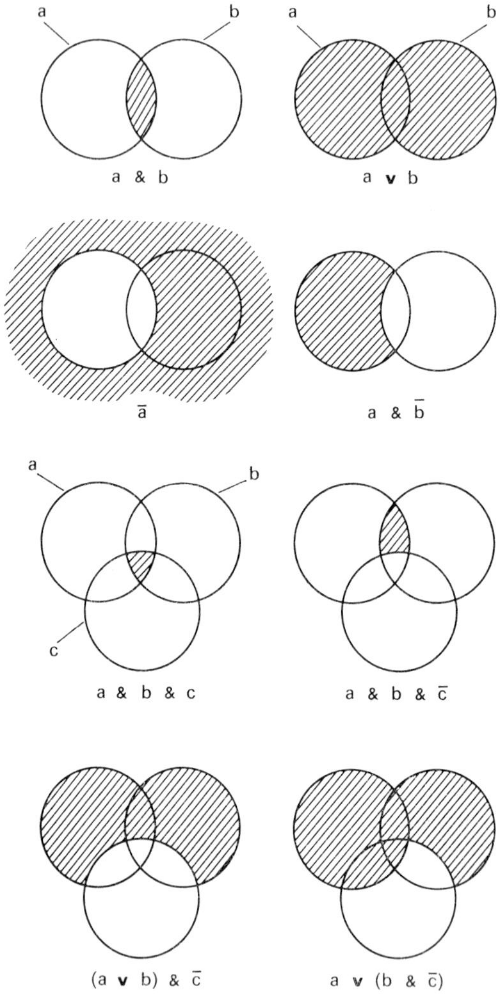

FIG. 2.3. Circle Diagrams

This is a truth table. It gives the values of a & b for the four possible combinatorial values of a and b. Similarly we may write a truth table for the *or* operator—

a	0 0 1 1
b	0 1 0 1
a $\vee$ b	0 1 1 1

EQUIVALENT AND NOT-EQUIVALENT OPERATORS

There are two more operators in set logic that must be mentioned here because of their importance in computers: these are the *equivalent* and *not-equivalent* operators, for which we shall be using the symbols $\equiv$ and $\not\equiv$ respectively. Their effect is shown in the circle

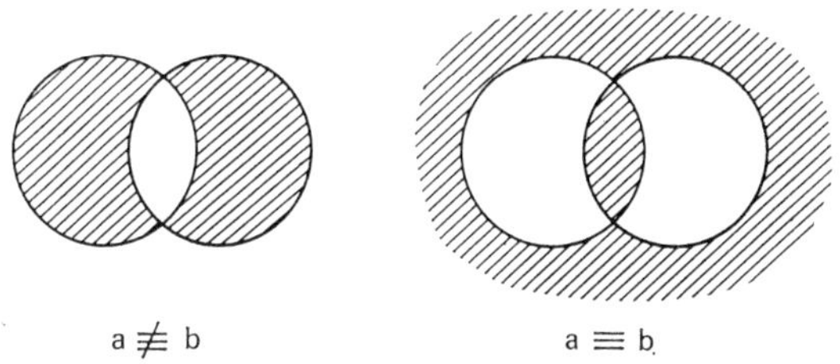

FIG. 2.4.

diagrams of Fig. 2.4. The corresponding truth table is—

a	0 0 1 1
b	0 1 0 1
a $\equiv$ b	1 0 0 1
a $\not\equiv$ b	0 1 1 0

It will be noticed that the two operators are the inverse of one another, that is—

$$a \equiv b = \overline{a \not\equiv b}$$

The *not-equivalent* operator is sometimes called the *exclusive or* operator, for obvious reasons (either, or, but not both). Applied to our example of large towns and coastal towns, it would denote the set of large inland towns and small coastal towns, but would exclude large coastal towns. The *equivalent* and *not-equivalent* operators can be expressed in terms of the *and* and *or* operators thus—

$$a \equiv b = (a \,\&\, b) \vee (\bar{a} \,\&\, \bar{b})$$
$$a \not\equiv b = (a \,\&\, \bar{b}) \vee (\bar{a} \,\&\, b)$$

THE LOGIC OF BINARY ARITHMETIC

Now what is the relevance of all this to binary arithmetic? Well, we can easily find sets among binary numbers: for instance, we can define a set to consist of all those bit positions in which a one appears in a binary number A. Let us call this set a; then the set $\bar{a}$ within the domain of all binary numbers of the same length as A, consists of all those positions where a nought appears in A. We could define a second set b to consist of all those positions where a one appears in a second number B, the same length as A. Then the set a & b would consist of all those bit positions where a one appeared in both A and B; and this in turn would define a new binary number A & B; for example—

A	1010110001
B	1001101011
A & B	1000100001

It is possible thus to apply the Boolean operator & to binary numbers to generate new binary numbers. Similarly we may operate on the same binary numbers A and B to produce—

	$A \vee B$	1011111011
and	$A \equiv B$	1100100101
and	$A \not\equiv B$	0011011010

Now let us look again at the rules we derived for binary addition. We may now rewrite the first rule much more simply, thus—

1. Carry is generated under the condition A & B, where A and B are the numbers to be added.

Similarly, the second rule becomes—

2. Carry is propagated until the condition $\bar{A}$ & $\bar{B}$ holds.

Rules three and four together express the condition for one to appear in the sum. If we use S to represent the sum, and C to represent the carry condition, we get from rule three—

$$S = \bar{C} \ \& \ (A \not\equiv B)$$

and from rule four—

$$S = C \ \& \ (A \equiv B)$$

The two can be combined to give a single rule—

3. The sum is generated under the condition—

$$S = [\bar{C} \ \& \ (A \not\equiv B)] \vee [C \ \& \ (A \equiv B)]$$

The rules for subtraction can be expressed similarly.

1. Borrow is generated under the condition $\bar{A}$ & B, where B is being subtracted from A.

2. Borrow is propagated until the condition A & $\bar{B}$ holds.
3. The difference is generated under precisely the same condition as the sum in addition.

The foregoing rules are used as a basis for the design of adders and subtractors in binary computers. Owing to the close similarity between the rules for addition and subtraction, it is quite usual to find the two operations performed in the same unit. This unit is sometimes referred to as a *mill*, which was the term used by Charles Babbage for the arithmetic part of his engine.

TABULAR ADDITION

The same rules can be used to design adders and subtractors in binary-coded decimal machines, since the basic processes are still binary. However, in some very small machines, addition and subtraction are performed with the aid of tables. In the tables shown below, the sum digit and the carry digit obtained by adding two decimal digits can be found from the junction of the appropriate row and column—

	1	2	3	4	5	6	7	8	9
1	2	3	4	5	6	7	8	9	0
2	3	4	5	6	7	8	9	0	1
3	4	5	6	7	8	9	0	1	2
4	5	6	7	8	9	0	1	2	3
5	6	7	8	9	0	1	2	3	4
6	7	8	9	0	1	2	3	4	5
7	8	9	0	1	2	3	4	5	6
8	9	0	1	2	3	4	5	6	7
9	0	1	2	3	4	5	6	7	8

Sum Table

	1	2	3	4	5	6	7	8	9
1	0	0	0	0	0	0	0	0	1
2	0	0	0	0	0	0	0	1	1
3	0	0	0	0	0	0	1	1	1
4	0	0	0	0	0	1	1	1	1
5	0	0	0	0	1	1	1	1	1
6	0	0	0	1	1	1	1	1	1
7	0	0	1	1	1	1	1	1	1
8	0	1	1	1	1	1	1	1	1
9	1	1	1	1	1	1	1	1	1

Carry Table

REALIZATION IN HARDWARE

We have said that the binary symbol 1 can be represented by the condition *current on*, and the symbol 0 by the condition *current off*, (though there is no logical reason why the opposite convention should not be used if it proves to be more convenient). A binary number several bits long can therefore be represented by a switching on and off of current in the appropriate pattern, causing a train of current pulses and gaps to appear in sequence in a wire, as shown in Fig. 2.5. The rate at which pulses would follow one another to represent a series of ones is called the *pulse rate*, or *bit rate*, of a machine. Most computers nowadays operate at bit rates of one megacycle (one million pulses per second) and higher, and there are computers operating at pulse rates of fifty megacycles and more. Under these circumstances, arithmetic speeds well in excess of one million additions per second are by no means uncommon. Now it is easy enough to determine where the ones come in a number represented electrically; the problem comes in trying to count the number of noughts that the gaps between the pulses are supposed to represent. The way this is done generally is to feed around the computer a train of pulses at the pulse rate of the computer, to be

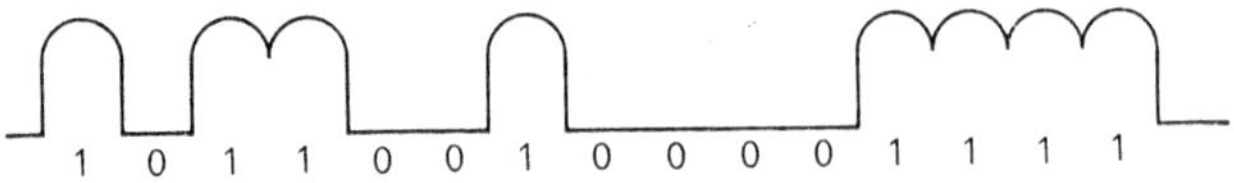

FIG. 2.5.

used for counting the lengths of the gaps, in much the same way as the sprocket holes in paper tape can be used for counting strings of spaces. A train of pulses of this kind is usually referred to as a *clock*, and the pulse rate of a computer is often referred to as its *clock rate*. Simple electronic circuits can be devised to perform Boolean operations upon trains of pulses, giving outputs when the trains of pulses fulfil the appropriate Boolean conditions.*

SERIAL AND PARALLEL MODES

We have been talking up to now of a system in which binary numbers are represented by trains of electrical pulses. Naturally, such trains must be propagated with the less significant end of the number first, since this is the end that enters first into arithmetic operations. A computer that operates in this way is said to be operating in a *serial mode*. An alternative scheme would be to use a separate wire for each bit position in a word, in which case the machine would be operating in a *parallel mode*. Parallel machines using the same electronic devices are generally faster than serial machines, for the same reason that a multi-lane motorway can carry a greater volume of traffic than a single-lane country road; but they are also more expensive. Several machines are built on a compromise

* The reader who is familiar with electronics will realize that an *or* operation on positive pulses can be performed by a simple diode gate with a pull-down to the lower supply level, and an *and* operation by a gate with the diodes the other way round and a pull-up to the higher supply. The *not* operation, of course, is performed by a simple inverting amplifier.

idea, with short sequences of pulses running in parallel along a small number of wires. Such machines are said to be operating in a *serial-parallel mode.*

CORE STORAGE

So much, then, for the dynamic representation of data while it is in the process of being operated upon arithmetically. But a computer also needs to be able to *remember* binary information. Not only does every computer have a stored program, at least part of which must be available the whole time, but it must also be able to store the data it is currently processing. Files of course are held permanently on some medium such as magnetic tape; but there must also be some form of storage within the computer, where each record can be held while it is being worked on.

Practically all computers today use a store (or memory) made up of tiny rings, or *cores*, of magnetic material. Each core is capable of being magnetized in either one direction or the opposite, and is therefore capable of storing one bit. (For practical reasons, it is not possible to make use of the non-magnetized condition.) The core is written into by means of a wire passing through it. When a current pulse passes along this wire, the core is magnetized in a direction depending on the polarity of the pulse. If an attempt is made to write a one when a one is already stored in the core, there will be no permanent effect; but if the current pulse is such as to write a one when a nought has been previously stored, the magnetism is reversed in the core. This fact can be made use of to enable the store to be read, that is, to detect whether a nought or a one is stored in a particular core. A second wire is threaded through the core; whenever the magnetization in the core is reversed, a pulse appears in this second wire, and can be detected by an external amplifier. Thus a one is written by sending a pulse of one polarity down the first wire, and it is detected by using a pulse of the opposite polarity in the first wire to induce a pulse in the second wire. Unfortunately, reading in this fashion destroys the original information, which must be written back again if it is to be preserved. Because of this, the information in a core store is said to be *volatile.*

Magnetic cores are arranged in a rectangular matrix as shown in Fig. 2.6, a typical size being sixty-four by sixty-four. Two wires at right angles pass through each core; these are known as the *select* wires, and they are used to select a particular core for writing or reading. The core is selected by passing through each of the two select wires that thread it a pulse of current just half as great as would be necessary to switch it, that is, to change its direction of magnetization. Only one core in the matrix can be switched at a time, since only one core has the full switching current passing through it. The material of which the cores are made has the property that if insufficient current passes through a core to switch it the magnetization reverts when the pulse has passed to what it was before. This method of selecting a particular core is known as coincident-current selection; it enables the number of selection circuits to be reduced to a number depending not on the number of cores but on the square root of their number.

A second wire that threads all the cores in the matrix is known as the *read* wire. Reading is accomplished by passing pulses of

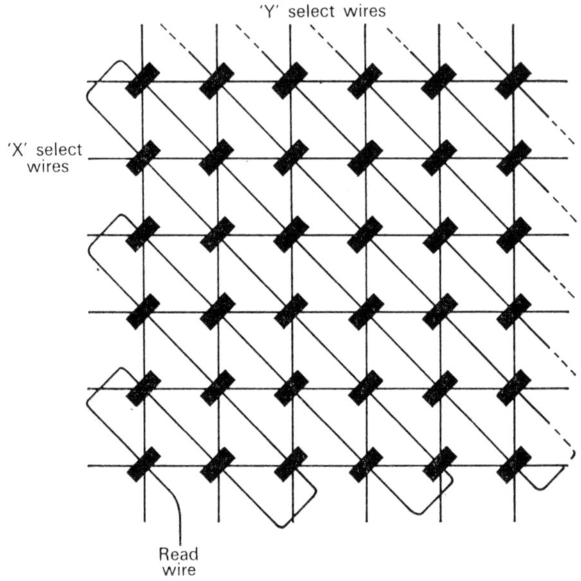

FIG. 2.6. Core Matrix

current in the *nought* sense through the selected core. If the core was storing a one, a pulse is induced in the read wire; if not, no pulse is induced.

A single matrix measuring sixty-four by sixty-four will store 4,096 bits. In a normal store this would represent the bits in the same relative position in 4,096 separate words. To store that number of complete thirty-two-bit words it would be necessary to have a stack of thirty-two matrices. In fact thirty-three would probably be used, the spare matrix being used to store parity-check bits. It is usual to make the parity of words in store odd rather than even; in this way there is a positive check against a word full of noughts, which might happen if the store failed completely to operate.

A section of a store holding just one word is known as a *register*. Every register has a number associated with it, known as its *address*, and this number corresponds in some way with the physical position of that register in the store, so that it can be used to obtain access to it. A store made up of planes measuring sixty-four by sixty-four would be used with an address twelve bits in length. Six bits would be used to indicate the position of the register in one direction across the matrices, and the other six to indicate its position in the perpendicular direction.

INFORMATION THEORY

Finally, to complete this chapter, which we have devoted to fundamentals, we must say something about a branch of science known as information theory. Information is a matter not so much of what you say, but of what you could have said and didn't. The politician who swears that the pound will never be devalued is saying nothing, since he is precluded from saying the opposite for fear of the cataclysm that would inevitably follow. The fashion critic who says that a dress is midnight blue is giving more information than the non-expert who merely says that it is blue, not only because she is using more words (one can use more words and still say less) but because she is selecting a colour from a large range of secondary colours rather than a small range of primary colours. It bears repeating—information is measured not by what we say, but by what we could have said and didn't.

Eight bits can be arranged in any one of 2^8, or 256 ways, each of which, as we have seen, can be used to represent a different one of 256 symbols. Eight bits, then, can "say" 256 different things, and we might represent the information contained in any one eight-bit symbol by the number 256. In fact, it is more convenient to represent the amount of information contained in eight bits by the number 8. If there were sixty-four horses in a race, the information that a particular horse had won would have an information value of 6, since sixty-four is 2^6. (At least this is the opinion of the author, who is naive enough to believe that every horse has the same chance.) If there had been only fifty horses, the same information would have been worth a little less, 5.66* bits to be precise. Information is measured on a logarithmic scale, a feature it shares with sound amplitude, which is measured on the logarithmic decibel scale, and film speed, which can be measured on several scales, arithmetic and logarithmic. Logarithmic measurement has the advantage that

* This value 5.66 is in fact the logarithm to the base 2 of 50, just as 6 is the logarithm to the base 2 of 64, and 8 the logarithm to the base 2 of 256.

separate batches of information can be combined simply by addition instead of multiplication.

The enemy of information is *noise*. We can define noise as any random disturbance that can cause information to be lost. It may be audible noise, electrical interference, smudging of print, defocusing in a picture, or any other type of degradation in information content. Distortion in a communication channel is equivalent to the introduction of noise; but to understand how communication channels can introduce distortion we shall have to examine first the idea of *bandwidth*.

A continuous electric current contains no information. If we wish to use it for communication we must modulate it, that is, switch it on and off in a pre-arranged way such as in a sequence of dots and dashes. Now, it can be shown by analysis that switching a current off and on is equivalent to replacing it by a mixture of continuous tones of different amplitudes and pitches. In fact, an infinite number of these is required if the message is to be reproduced exactly; but a reasonable representation, good enough for all practical purposes, can be obtained by taking only a finite number of tones lying in a band at the low-pitch end. The higher the rate of switching, the more tones must be taken to give adequate reproduction. A communication channel is capable of transmitting only a restricted band of tones. Whether a particular channel is capable of transmitting a particular signal depends upon whether the channel's band is wide enough to contain the band needed to reproduce the message. The greater the bandwidth of a channel, the faster the modulation that can be applied to the signals it carries, and consequently the more information it is able to transmit in a given time.

EXERCISES 2

1. Make a table of the binary equivalents of the numbers from 1 to 9, the tens from 10 to 90, the hundreds from 100 to 900, and the thousands from 1000 to 9000. Use the table to convert to binary radix the decimal numbers 981, 7654, 4096, and the number of the current *Anno Domini*.
2. Write in octal and hexadecimal notation the numbers 981, 7654, 4096, and the number of the current *Anno Domini*.
3. It is possible to find by inspection whether a decimal number is divisible by eleven as follows: add together all the even digits and all the odd digits; subtract the one total from the other; if the difference is zero or a multiple of eleven, the whole number is divisible by eleven. What rule can we make that is the equivalent of this in the binary scale? How can we determine whether a binary number is divisible by five?
4. The numbers on a roulette wheel are divided into the following main sets—

rouge:	1, 3, 5, 7, 9, 12, 14, 16, 18, 19, 21, 23, 25, 27, 30, 32, 34, 36;
noir:	2, 4, 6, 8, 10, 11, 13, 15, 17, 20, 22, 24, 26, 28, 29, 31, 33, 35;
pair:	the even numbers;

impair; the odd numbers;
manque: 1 to 18;
passe: 19 to 36.

Which numbers make up the following compound sets?

(*a*) rouge & pair & manque
(*b*) noir & (pair ∨ passe)
(*c*) rouge ≡ pair
(*d*) manque & (noir ≡ pair)
(*e*) (rouge & passe) ∨ (noir & impair & manque)
(*f*) (rouge ∨ manque) & passe & noir.

5. Two important theorems in Boolean algebra are known as De Morgan's laws. They are—

$$\overline{a \vee b} = \bar{a} \mathbin{\&} \bar{b}$$

and

$$\overline{a \mathbin{\&} b} = \bar{a} \vee \bar{b}$$

Prove them with the aid of Venn diagrams or truth tables.

6. The Boolean operator *nor* can be defined thus—

$$a \mathrm{N} b \mathrm{N} c \mathrm{N} d \mathrm{N} \ldots = \bar{a} \mathbin{\&} \bar{b} \mathbin{\&} \bar{c} \mathbin{\&} \bar{d} \mathbin{\&} \ldots$$

where N is the symbol for *nor*. It has the property that all other Boolean operators can be expressed in terms of it. How?

Draw a truth table for the *nor* operator.

3. Instructions

To help us to understand how a computer is programmed and run, we shall imagine that we have one available to us, that we shall be able to write programs for it, and subsequently run them. It will not be any one of the machines currently on the market, for this is not a book about any particular system; but it will have all the features found in modern computers, and several features that are lacking in some. However, it will be as simple as possible, and it may lack one or two of the subtler refinements, since its only purpose will be to aid our understanding of basic processes. Nevertheless, the features it will exhibit will be in line with current practice.

WORD LENGTH

Since the commonest word length today is thirty-two bits, we shall choose that for our imaginary machine. As we have already seen, this word length will accommodate binary numbers in the approximate range $\pm 2{,}000{,}000$, which is as much as commercial work normally requires. For the present we shall concern ourselves only with integers; though we may notice in passing that binary fractions can be represented by integers just as decimal fractions can be represented as integral numbers per cent. In our case, of course, we should have per 2^{31} instead of per cent.

Thirty-two bits also divide conveniently into four eight-bit bytes. We shall hold textual data in byte form in our imaginary machine, using the code given in Appendix II. Data will appear in this form immediately after input, and it will be prepared in the same form for output. We shall not use the packed decimal representation of numbers, since binary representation alone will be quite adequate for our present purposes. Anyone who has learned to program for binary arithmetic will find little difficulty in adapting his style to a decimal representation.

INSTRUCTION FORMAT

FUNCTIONS

Having decided how we shall represent data, we now have to decide how we shall represent the stored program. It will be recalled that a program consists of a series of *steps*, which are to be performed, jumps permitting, in the sequence in which they are written. Each step is in fact an instruction to the machine to perform a particular *function* (add, subtract, etc.) on one or more pieces of data. A convenient format for an instruction might then be—

X F Y

where F represents the function, and X and Y define two pieces of data that are to be operated upon. We shall refer to X and Y in this connection as *arguments*.* It is most important to realize at the outset that X and Y are not necessarily to be taken as the actual pieces of data to be used, but as definitions of the pieces of data. Thus we make a distinction between arguments and *operands*, which are the actual pieces of data to be used.

In the rest of this chapter, and in the next two chapters, we shall be defining what sorts of functions and arguments can be fitted into this basic instruction format: in short we shall be defining the grammar of a special language that we shall be using to communicate with our computer. Later in the book, we shall discuss some other languages that are used with computers. Computer languages may seem very different from the sort of languages we are used to, for one thing, most statements are in the imperative mood; but they are none the less languages, and they are subject to the same sorts of laws. One thing, though, if you speak English, or French, or even Serbo-Croat, with incorrect grammar, you will probably still be understood. If you make a grammatical error in writing a computer program, the program will probably not be capable of being interpreted.

ARGUMENTS

We shall make the stipulation with regard to the arguments X and Y that under normal circumstances the operation is directed from Y to X; that is, in addition, Y is added to X, not the other way round, and in subtraction it is X that is diminished, not Y. The operand defined by Y, therefore, will be left unchanged at the end of the operation; but the original value defined by X will generally be lost. Thus if we write—

X ADD Y

and if X defines a number 1234 and Y a number 5678, then the sum

* This is the original meaning of the word. The Latin word *argumentum* originally meant subject matter, particularly a subject for disputation, and only later came to refer to the dispute itself.

6912 will replace 1234 as the number defined by X, while the number defined by Y remains unaltered. A subsequent instruction

X	SUB*	Z

would diminish the new value defined by X by an amount defined by Z. Because intermediate operands are lost, the order in which instructions are written is most important. Thus the pair of instructions—

X	ADD	Y
Y	SUB	Z

would generally have a different effect from—

Y	SUB	Z
X	ADD	Y

How do arguments define operands? In the last chapter we introduced the idea of *addresses*, which are simply numbers used to distinguish between the various registers in the store and to gain access to them. Evidently, then, one way in which an argument can define an operand is by giving its address. Thus an instruction of the form—

123	ADD	456

might be interpreted, "Add the number in the register with address 456 into the register with address 123." Similarly, the instruction—

987	SUB	654

might mean, "Subtract the number in address 654 from the number in address 987."

What a commercial computer user really wants to do, though, is to operate on things like balances, credits, prices and discounts. It is going to be most inconvenient if he continually has to remember that the balance is in address 765, the discount rate in 789, and so on. Having to make a mental transposition from name to address every time he writes an instruction is bound to add to the time he takes and, worse still, to the number of mistakes that will eventually have to be found and corrected before the program will run properly. It should be the aim of good computer design to relieve the user as far as possible of any work that is not directly connected with the job in hand, and to eliminate as far as possible any constraints that might be imposed by the physical construction of the

* Functions written in the form ADD, SUB, etc. are known as *mnemonic codes* to distinguish them from functions written in numeric form (01 for add, say, and 02 for subtract) which was the form demanded in the earliest computer languages.

machine. Consequently, most computer systems permit the user to employ alphabetic names instead of addresses, and to write instructions like—

	BALANCE	ADD	CREDIT
or	PRICE	SUB	DISCOUNT

Indeed some systems *oblige* the user to employ symbolic names, and do not permit him to use addresses at all. As we shall see later on, all symbolic names must be converted to addresses before the instructions can actually be obeyed; but this job is carried out by the computer automatically, and without fear of introducing errors, while the program is being loaded into the machine. Because of this, the terms *name* and *address* are practically interchangeable in relation to computer programs. But this idea should not present any difficulty; we are all familiar with the metonymy between names and addresses—"There was no comment from Number Ten", "Best wishes from the Larches."

During a program run, a single name usually takes a number of different values. For example, we might apply the single instruction—

BALANCE ADD PAYMENT

iteratively to credit several different balances on our main file each with a number of different payments. The operand named PAYMENT would then take in turn the values of all the amounts to be added, and the operand named BALANCE would increase in value every time a new payment was added to it, and would take on an entirely different value when attention was transferred from one file record to the next. Similarly we might use—

PRICE SUB DISCOUNT

to subtract discounts calculated at different rates from the prices of all items on an order.

There are some occasions when we know at the outset what value we have to add or subtract. For instance, if we are counting the number of times a loop of instructions is to be obeyed, we must alter the count each time by the constant value one; or, if we have to convert from feet to inches, we know we must multiply by the value twelve. We could perform operations such as these, of course, by putting the constant we wish to use into a register and then either using the address of the register or else giving it a name and using that; but, although it is sometimes convenient to work in this way, it is a clumsy procedure. It would be far better if we could use numeric values directly as arguments in instructions. Numeric arguments in which the argument is actually the operand are known as *literals.* To distinguish them from addresses, which are also numeric, we shall enclose literals in inverted commas, thus—

```
TOTAL          ADD     '12'
```

"Add twelve to the quantity called TOTAL." Naturally, only the second argument can be a literal, since the first must define a location in store, the location where the result of the operation is to be placed.

MOVE FUNCTION

So far we have introduced the two functions ADD and SUB; but there is one function we shall need that is simpler in action than either of these. This is a function to move data from one location to another in the store. In this book we shall be using the mnemonic MOVE for such a function. Following the convention already established, we shall make the movement take place from the second argument to the first, leaving the value of the second argument unaltered. Thus MOVE does not, in the sense in which we are using it, imply taking something away and leaving nothing in its place. We might have used the word *copy* but for the fact that MOVE is more commonly found. Thus we interpret—

```
PRICE          MOVE    COST
```

as, "Make the value of PRICE the same as that of COST." We shall also permit the use of literal arguments with MOVE; in particular, we shall be able to use MOVE to clear registers—

```
CASH           MOVE    '0'
```

"Clear the quantity called CASH to zero."

WORKING SPACE

The type of instruction code we have defined here is known as a two-address or two-argument code. But operations occurring in practice frequently have more than two arguments: for instance, if we subtract cost from selling price to give profit, we are using three arguments. To do this operation, we should need to write two instructions in our language—

```
PROFIT         MOVE    PRICE
PROFIT         SUB     COST
```

Here PROFIT has an intermediate value that is in fact quite different from the profit we are trying to calculate. Sometimes it is necessary to introduce new arguments that are not part of the problem—for instance, if we wish to exchange the positions of two numbers in the store. Suppose that we wish to exchange the values of two arguments, FIRST and SECOND; we do so by first shunting one of them into an extra location, which we might refer to as working space (WS)—

WS	MOVE	FIRST
FIRST	MOVE	SECOND
SECOND	MOVE	WS

These slightly round-about ways of doing things are made necessary by the very elementary nature of the functions that a computer can perform. We shall see later that there are computer languages that do not require operations to be broken down into quite such small detail; but these higher-level languages, as they are called, cannot be used without some reduction in efficiency.

JUMPING

When we were discussing flow diagrams in Chapter 1, we saw that an essential feature of a machine that is to obey a stored program must be the ability to make tests on pieces of data and to take alternative courses of action according to the results. We called this branching, or jumping. In practically all modern computer systems the alternative courses of action provided are either to obey the next instruction in the ordinary way or to jump to another instruction defined in the branch instruction itself and carry on from there. Thus we shall need to be able to write instructions of the form—

X	J	Y

in which we can make X define the test that the machine is to make, and Y define a new instruction to which control is to be transferred if the result of the test is positive. If the test is unsuccessful, control is to pass to the next instruction in the sequence, in the normal way. To start with, we shall consider only literal values of Y, interpreting these as jumps of so many instructions forward or backward in the sequence. Thus—

X	J	'4'

"Jump forward four instructions if the condition defined by X is satisfied, otherwise carry straight on."

X	J	'−7'

"Jump back seven instructions if X is satisfied; if not, carry straight on." Backward jumps, of course, will give rise to loops in the program. Notice, by the way, that the instruction—

X	J	'0'

jumps back to itself if the test X is positive, and that it will continue to jump back to itself until stopped by some *force majeure* such as switching off the machine. A condition such as this is known as a loop stop, since it does effectively bring the machine to a stop. It generally arises as a result of a programming error, though loop stops are occasionally used deliberately, particularly in engineers' test programs.

JUMP TESTS

To give a full specification of a condition for jumping, we should need more arguments than we have available; we should need one to define the thing to be tested, and at least one more to define the test to be made upon it. Since we have only one argument, the X-argument, we shall use it to define the test, and establish by convention what is to be tested. What we shall do is to stipulate that the test is to be performed upon the result of the last operation. The actual tests we shall provide must perforce be very simple; they will consist in determining whether the result was positive, negative, or zero. A few examples should make things clearer—

POS	J	'4'

"Jump forward four instructions if the result of the previous instruction was positive."

NEG	J	'−7'

"Jump back seven instructions if the result of the previous instruction was negative."

ZERO	J	'−23'

"Jump back twenty-three instructions if the result of the previous instruction was zero." For the purpose of the positive and negative tests, we shall treat zero as a positive number. The condition POS should then be read strictly as "positive or zero", or alternatively as "non-negative." It will also be convenient to have a jump condition non-zero as well as zero; we shall use the code NZERO for this. Finally we shall find it convenient to have a method of transferring control unconditionally. We shall do this by simply leaving a space where the first argument would normally be written.

We have said that the test shall be performed on the result of the previous instruction. We shall now amend this, and say that the test shall be on the result of the last instruction that was not a jump instruction. This new definition is more convenient, since it allows us to follow an arithmetic instruction by two or more jump instructions, each testing a different aspect of the result.

Many systems provide the test conditions "positive but not zero" and "negative or zero" as well as the ones we have provided. We shall not do this, since in any case these conditions can be provided in only two instructions. For instance the pair of instructions—

ZERO	J	'6'
NEG	J	'5'

will jump forward six instructions from the first of the pair if the result of the previous instruction was negative or zero.

Now at last we are in a position to illustrate the points we have

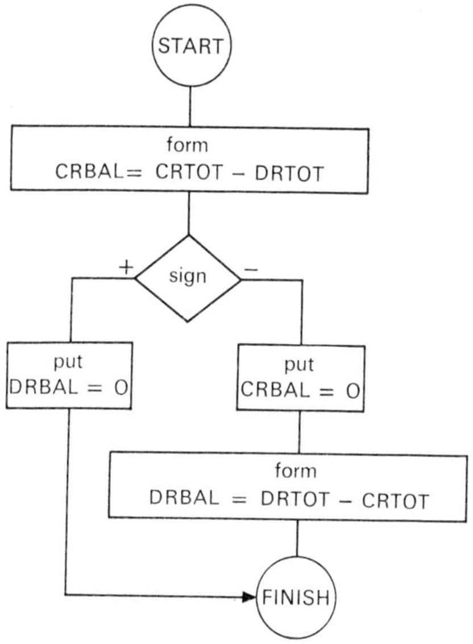

FIG. 3.1.

made by programming some real tasks. Let us take first of all a simple accounting example. When a ledger is balanced, the amounts on the debit side and the credit side are totalled separately; the one total is then subtracted from the other total to yield a balance. If the credit total exceeds the debit total, a credit balance is formed: if the debit total is greater, there is a debit balance. Given a credit total and a debit total, which we shall refer to as CRTOT and

DRTOT, we wish to find the correct values of the credit balance, CRBAL, and the debit balance, DRBAL, one of which must be zero. The procedure we are to follow is shown as a flow diagram in Fig. 3.1. Translated into a sequence of instructions, it becomes—

```
        CRBAL     MOVE    CRTOT
        CRBAL     SUB     DRTOT
    ┌───NEG       J       '3'
    │   DRBAL     MOVE    '0'
 ┌──┼───          J       '3'
 │  └──→DRBAL     MOVE    DRTOT
 │      DRBAL     SUB     CRTOT
 └──→             STOP
```

It is common practice to introduce arrows in written programs to indicate where the jumps are going to; they help to make the picture clearer. Notice that there are more instructions in this piece of program than there are steps in the flow diagram. This is because the flow diagram is entirely conceptual, whereas the program depends on the facilities that the language provides.

We have just introduced a new function, STOP, and we have used it to indicate where the sequence of instructions comes to an end. In practice, of course, a program would not stop at this point, but would proceed with the next part of the computation. Although we shall continue to use STOP in this way, to indicate the end of an instruction sequence, the reader must remember that in a real program its position would probably be occupied by the first instruction of the next sequence, or by a jump to that instruction.

Our next example will be arithmetical: we shall write a sequence of instructions to calculate the highest common factor (HCF) of two numbers. Let us first remind ourselves how we tackle this problem when the numbers are decimal, and let us take as an example the numbers 529 and 1265. We start by writing them down side by side, and subtracting the smaller from the larger as many times as possible, in this case, twice.

```
529     1265
        1058
        ----
         207
```

We then go on to subtract the residue formed in this way from the number in the other column as many times as possible (again twice in this case). We continue in precisely the same way, subtracting the smaller residue as many times as possible from the larger until eventually a zero residue is formed.

529	207
414	115
115	92
92	92
23	0

At this point, when zero appears in one column, the number at the foot of the other column is the desired HCF.

In programming the problem for our computer, we shall use the same algorithm, with one minor exception: there are no facilities in our language for asking the question, "How may times does Y

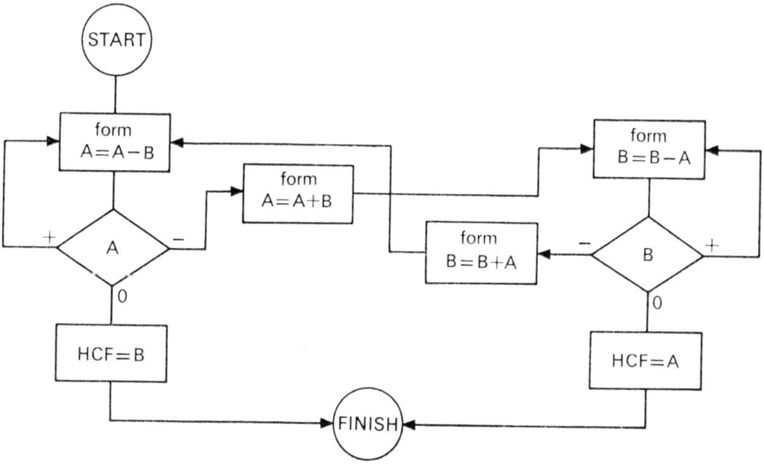

FIG. 3.2.

go into X?" The best we can do is to ask the question, "Does Y go into X at least once?" which is the same as the question, "Is the answer positive when Y is subtracted from X?" The algorithm is shown as a flow diagram in Fig. 3.2. For clarity, it has been arranged in two columns to correspond with operations on the two columns in our worked example. The process is shown starting in the left-hand column; but it could just as easily be started in the other, since the process is symmetrical. Here is the instruction sequence—

```
→A        SUB    B
 ZERO     J      '8'
 POS      J      '−2'
 A        ADD    B
→B        SUB    A
 ZERO     J      '6'
 POS      J      '−2'
 B        ADD    A
          J      '−8'
--------------------------
→ HCF     MOVE   B
          J      '2'
--------------------------
→ HCF     MOVE   A
→         STOP
```

LABELS

Jumps forward or backward a literal number of places are known as relative jumps, because the literal is to be interpreted relative to the address of the current instruction. Relative jumps often prove to be inconvenient, since they have to be altered if the program is modified, or an error is corrected, in such a way that instructions are inserted or deleted within the range of the jump. It is useful, therefore, to have absolute jumps as well, in which the second argument is an address or a name. Names used to designate particular instructions are known as labels. We shall follow the practice of writing a label before the instruction it refers to, and terminating it with a colon, thus—

```
LABEL:   X          SUB    Y
```

We shall be restricting our imaginary machine to at the most, one label per instruction, although there are systems that permit alternative labels to be used on the same instruction.

Our next example concerns pensions. In the Democratic Kingdom of Ostroslovia there is a state pension scheme. A man is entitled to a state pension when he reaches the age of ninety-five. A woman is entitled to a pension at ninety if she is single; but if she is married she does not get her pension until either her husband is ninety-five or she is ninety, whichever is the later. If she is divorced she is not entitled to pension at all. Given the quantities AGE, HAGE (husband's age, where applicable) SEX, and MSTAT (marital status), we shall write a sequence of instructions that will jump to the label PENS if there is an entitlement to a pension, and to the label NEXT if there is not. This implies that there is another sequence of instructions for calculating the actual pension, and a sequence for substituting the details of the next applicant. We shall suppose that we have established conventions in which the quantity SEX is 0 for a female and 1 for a male, and that MSTAT takes the values 0 for divorced, 1 for single, and 2 for married. This time we shall leave the flow diagram for the reader to draw for himself, and go straight on to the instruction sequence.

```
          SEX       MOVE   SEX
        ┌─ZERO      J      FEM
        │ AGE       SUB    '95'
        │ NEG       J      NEXT   Male under 95
        │           J      PENS
        │ ──────────────────────
FEM:    └→AGE       SUB    '90'   Female
          NEG       J      NEXT   under 90
          MSTAT     SUB    '1'
          NEG       J      NEXT   divorced
          ZERO      J      PENS   single
          HAGE      SUB    '95'
          NEG       J      NEXT   husband under 95
                    J      PENS
```

The first instruction in this sequence performs the apparently trivial operation of transferring a word back to the place it was taken from. In fact it is there to provide a result that the jump instruction that follows it can test. We have drawn a horizontal line between the three instructions concerned with males and the eight concerned with females, to show that there is no sequential connection between them. It is not uncommon to find explanatory notes written alongside instructions in manuscript.

OVERFLOW

The reader may have been wondering what happens if addition (or subtraction for that matter) should produce a number too large for a register to hold. This condition is known as *overflow*, or *spill.* To enable the program to take remedial action should it occur, It is usual to make overflow one of the jump conditions. In some systems, overflow is made a more permanent jump condition than the others, the jump being performed if overflow has happened at any time since the last test was made. We shall not do this, but shall make overflow a transient condition just like all the other test conditions.

```
OVR       J       LABEL
```

"Jump to LABEL if the last arithmetic instruction caused overflow."

The sort of remedial action a program might take following overflow is to make the number extend into the next register. For instance, if we were totalling a number of positive items, and we suspected that the sum might overflow we should write—

```
          TOTAL        ADD    ITEM
          OVR          J      REMEDY
```

Then somewhere in the program we should have a label followed by a sequence of instructions for extending the number into the next register. With unsigned numbers the procedure is simple: all that is needed is the single instruction—

```
REMEDY:   TOTAL + 1    ADD    '1'
```

with signed numbers. On the other hand, where the first bit is used to indicate sign, things are complicated somewhat.

Consider the addition with overflow of two signed positive numbers—

```
    0 11.....
  + 0 11.....
  -----------
    1 1......
```

Here there is no spill off the end of the word; but overflow is indicated by the fact that the sum of two positive integers appears to give a negative result. In contrast, with two negative operands greater than half the capacity of the register we get—

```
    1 01.....
  + 1 01.....
  -----------
  1 0 1......
```

In this case a one has spilled off the end, and the result has taken on the appearance of a positive number. Thus correcting overflow involves not only extending the result into another register but also correcting the sign of the result in the original register. But what should be the sign in the original register? Here we have a choice of two conventions: it could be the same as the sign in the extension register, or (and this is more usual) it could simply be zero in all cases. If the second convention is adopted, the correction procedure might be—

```
REMEDY:   TOTAL        MOVE   TOTAL
          POS          J      '4'
          TOTAL        ADD    '— 2, 147, 483, 648'
          TOTAL + 1    ADD    '1'
          return to original sequence
          ------------------------------
          TOTAL + 1    SUB    '1'
          return to original sequence
```

where '−2,147,483,648' is just a sign bit.

DOUBLE-LENGTH WORKING

MULTIPLICATION

Dealing with overflow in the way just suggested amounts to forming a *double-length number*, a number occupying two adjacent registers. Notice also that we have just introduced a new type of argument, one that is a simple arithmetic expression, TOTAL + 1, which means the register with the next address after that of TOTAL. Double length numbers occur in other ways than as a result of overflow. They occur, for instance, after multiplication. When two numbers are multiplied, the number of digits in the product can be as great as those of the multiplier and multiplicand together. The reader can easily verify this for himself using decimal numbers; the same thing applies when the numbers are in binary form. If we multiply two 32-bit numbers together, therefore, we must allow 64-bits for the product.* We shall arrange for the multiplication function in our imaginary machine to expand the double-length product into the next location in store; thus—

```
X           MLT    Y
```

would form the product of X and Y, and place it in X and X + 1, the right-hand, or low-significance, half being in X, and the left-hand, or high significance, half being in X + 1. If we wish to form AREA by multiplying LENGTH by BREADTH, we write—

```
AREA        MOVE   LENGTH
AREA        MLT    BREADTH
```

which would place the product in AREA and AREA + 1. Naturally we should have to make sure first that AREA + 1 contained nothing of any value, since it would be over-written. We shall suppose further that if the product turns out to be only single-length after all, our imaginary machine will fill the upper register with sign bits—zeros for a positive product, ones for a negative product.

DIVISION

Finally we shall look at division. In its most general form, division consists in dividing a double-length number (the dividend) by a single-length number (the divisor) to form a single-length quotient and, unless the dividend was an exact multiple of the divisor,

* Strictly, we need only 63 bits, since we should really be multiplying two signed 31-bit numbers to give a 62-bit product with sign.

a single-length residue or remainder. We must not forget the residue, since it may be this that the programmer is really interested in. We shall organize our division function so that the instruction—

X	DIV	Y

divides a double-length number in X and X + 1 by Y, and places the quotient in X + 1 and the residue in X. This is simply a convention; but we venture to suggest that it will prove to be more convenient in practice than any other that might be devised.

If we wished to divide a *single-length* quantity by another using the function DIV, we should first have to ensure that the next register was filled with sign bits to make the dividend look like a double-length quantity. This would necessitate a sequence of instructions, such as—

X + 1	MOVE	'0'
X	MOVE	X
POS	J	'2'
X + 1	MOVE	'– 1'

To avoid this, which is tedious and time-consuming ,we shall introduce a single-length division function SDIV, with which the dividend must be single-length. However, we shall still use the next register in the store for the quotient.

We have neatly side-stepped a few problems connected with multiplication and division by insisting that the numbers we deal with shall always be integers. The actual position of the bits in a double-length product depends on whether the numbers that formed it were intended to be treated as integers or fractions. For this reason, several systems provide two or more multiplication functions and several division functions as well. The processes of binary multiplication and division are explained in Appendix III for the benefit of any reader who is interested.

The currency system in Ostroslovia is in dols and dims, there being ten dims to a dol. According to the tax laws of that country, no tax is payable on the first 200 dols of annual income; thereafter the next 100 dols are taxed at 3 dims in the dol, the next 200 at 5 dims in the dol, the next 300 at 7 dims in the dol, and the remainder at 9 dims in the dol. Let us write a sequence of instructions for calculating Ostroslovian TAX from a quantity PAY, both being expressed in dims. The method we shall use is not quite the obvious one, so a flow diagram is given in Fig. 3.3. The reader will soon convince himself that the more obvious approach would have taken more instructions. WS is again used to denote working space. It is

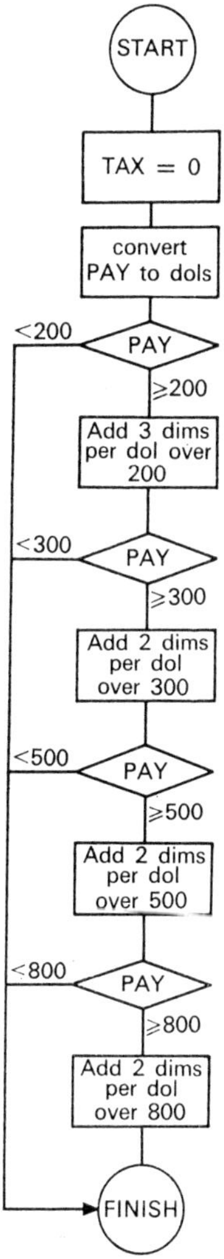
START
TAX = 0
convert PAY to dols
<200
PAY
≥200
Add 3 dims per dol over 200
<300
PAY
≥300
Add 2 dims per dol over 300
<500
PAY
≥500
Add 2 dims per dol over 500
<800
PAY
≥800
Add 2 dims per dol over 800
FINISH

FIG. 3.3.

assumed that location PAY + 1 can be used in this part of the program.

```
          TAX          MOVE   '0'
          PAY          SDIV   '10'
          PAY + 1      SUB    '200'
        ┌─NEG          J      END
        │ WS           MOVE   PAY + 1
        │ WS           MLT    '3'
        │ TAX          ADD    WS
        │ PAY + 1      SUB    '100'
        ├─NEG          J      END
        │ WS           MOVE   PAY + 1
        │ WS           MLT    '2'
        │ TAX          ADD    WS
        │ PAY + 1      SUB    '200'
        ├─NEG          J      END
        │ WS           MOVE   PAY + 1
        │ WS           MLT    '2'
        │ TAX          ADD    WS
        │ PAY + 1      SUB    '300'
        ├─NEG          J      END
        │ WS           MOVE   PAY + 1
        │ WS           MLT    '2'
        │ TAX          ADD    WS
END:    └→             STOP
```

Incidentally, this last example is typical of commercial programs—a great string of instructions with no loops among them. Contrast this with a mathematical program, such as the sequence of instructions developed earlier for evaluating an HCF, which was a mass of interlocking loops. Commercial programs have loops, of course, but they are large loops that may be repeated only once for every item on a file.

RADIX CONVERSION

Data is normally presented to a computer in character form, with numeric quantities in decimal; data to be put out on a printer must obviously be in the same form. On the other hand, for data on files, which are entirely internal to the computer, the user is free to choose the type of numeric representation that is most convenient to his system. If the computer has facilities only for decimal arithmetic, the programmer will be obliged to choose some decimal representation (packed or unpacked); but if the computer has facilities for binary arithmetic, binary representation will normally be chosen, since it is, among other things, more economical on storage space. Naturally, a binary machine must have facilities for converting numbers from decimal into binary and vice versa. It is possible to do this using ordinary multiplication and division functions; but radix conversion is such a common type of operation that it is worth while having special functions for the purpose.

In an instruction for converting from decimal to binary, we must specify three things: the first byte of the string of decimal digits to be converted, the number of digits in the string, and the register in which the converted number is to be placed. Some systems actually provide a three-argument form of instruction: others provide a conversion instruction that converts only one digit, and consequently has to be applied as part of a loop to convert the whole string. We shall do neither of these things in our computer language. We shall provide a two-address instruction in which the second argument is deemed to define not just a single item of data but a whole string of bytes, all of which are to be converted. There are few systems at the present time that permit the user to use names to define whole sets of items; but such a facility is so useful that in the author's opinion it will come to be provided more often in the future, since it is one of those refinements that help the user to concentrate more on the needs of the problem, and less on the constraints of the machine.

Our decimal-to-binary instructions then will be of the form—

X CDB Y

where Y is a name defining a *set* of bytes (or a field) and X defines the register that is to receive the converted number. We shall specify that if the register overflows, or if the field contains any non-numeric codes, overflow is to be set. We shall make an exception to this last rule, however, in that codes 00101011 (plus) and 00101101 (minus) are allowable in the first byte of the field.

The complementary instruction, for converting from binary to decimal, will take the form—

X CBD Y

where Y defines a binary register and X a field. We shall suppose that the function operates so as to align the converted data with the right-hand end of the field defined by X, and that any unused bytes at the left-hand end are filled with spaces (code 00100000). Converted negative numbers will be preceded by the minus code. In the event that the field is too short to accommodate the full number (including the minus sign if it is appropriate) overflow will be set. The method of converting from binary to decimal is given in Appendix III.

INPUT AND OUTPUT

We shall define one more function that operates on a field of bytes, the transfer function TFER. We shall use this for three purposes: to read a field of characters from an input device, to write a field on to an output device, and for copying data from one field to another in the store. The three cases will be distinguished from one another by the different arguments used; and the following names will be used conventionally to designate peripheral devices—

CR	card reader
TR	paper-tape reader
TP	paper-tape punch
LP	line printer
MT	magnetic tape
TP	typewriter

As before, the direction of transfer will be from the second argument to the first. The instruction—

```
DATA          TFER    CR
```

for instance, will cause characters to be read from a card reader into a field in store called DATA. In this connection it should be remembered that a card contains 80 characters, and that it is not possible to stop a card reader in mid-card. Consequently, if DATA is less than 80 bytes long, some characters may be lost. The instruction—

```
DATA          TFER    TR
```

would transfer characters from paper tape into the field DATA. Unlike a card reader, a paper-tape reader can be stopped on any character, so the transfer will normally continue until the field DATA is filled; but we shall make an additional rule that the transfer will terminate if a newline character (00001010) is read. The characters read will then be at the left-hand end of the field, in the same positions as they would have been in if the newline character had not appeared.

Output instructions have the name of the device as the first argument, thus—

```
LP            TFER    LINE
```

Line printers differ in the length of line they are able to print; a typical length is 120 characters. In this case, if LINE were longer than 120 characters, the last few characters would not be printed. If it were shorter, we shall assume that the characters would appear at the left-hand end of the line. Finally, the instruction—

```
TP            TFER    TEXT
```

will cause the characters in TEXT to be sent to a typewriter, which will respond in the appropriate way to newline characters, tabulate characters (00001001) and the rest.

When TFER is used for moving data about the store, both arguments must be field names; the transfer will continue until either one field or the other is exhausted. Notice that the difference between TFER and MOVE is that the former operates on sets, while the latter operates only on single items.

As an example, to illustrate what we have been saying, let us write a sequence of instructions to perform the rather trivial operation of reading two numbers from a length of paper tape, adding them together, and printing the sum on a line printer.

INPUT	TFER	TR
NUMB	CDB	INPUT
INPUT	TFER	TR
SUM	CDB	INPUT
SUM	ADD	NUMB
OUTPUT	CBD	SUM
LP	TFER	OUTPUT

LOGICAL FUNCTIONS

In the last chapter we talked about Boolean operators, and we saw that these could be applied to binary numbers, or, to be absolutely precise, to sets of bit positions in binary numbers. It is usual to find a few Boolean operators provided as functions in a digital computer. We shall provide two in ours: the *not-equivalent* operator (which is also known as the *exclusive or*) and the *and* operator. The effect of—

X	AND	Y

will be to delete from X all the ones in positions where there are noughts in Y. Thus if X is—

00010111010000010100000111010001

and Y is—

10001110101111110011000010101111

the result of the operation is—

00000110000000010000000010000001

The effect of the instruction—

X	NEQ	Y

is to invert (change ones to noughts and noughts to ones) the bits in X in all those places where there are ones in Y. Thus, with the same values as before for X and Y, the result of the operation would be—

10011001111111100111000101111110

It is interesting to note in passing that the sequence of instructions—

A	NEQ	B
B	NEQ	A
A	NEQ	B

exchanges the two numbers in A and B without the need for any extra working space, as the reader can verify for himself.

MASKING

The principal use of the function AND is for masking. A mask is simply a word with a block of ones confined to one part of it. If we wished, for example, to save storage space by packing two short numbers into one word, putting one in the upper 16 bits, and the other in the lower 16 bits, we could separate them by using a mask consisting of sixteen noughts and sixteen ones—

00000000000000001111111111111111

The instruction—

WORD	AND	MASK

would then simply delete the number in the upper half of WORD, leaving the other number unaltered. Similarly, the same instruction obeyed with the inverse of this mask would select the number in the upper half, deleting the number in the lower half. The inverse mask, incidentally, can be generated by the instruction—

MASK	NEQ	'−1'

since −1 in our machine is represented by a word full of ones.

SHIFTING

Having selected a number in the top half of a word by masking, we shall have to bring it down into the lower half so that we can do arithmetic on it in the right significance. To do this, we must have another function—a shifting function. We shall interpret instructions of the form—

X	SH	Y

to mean that a word defined by argument X is to be shifted a number of bit places defined by Y. If Y is positive, the shift is to be from left to right: if negative, the shift is to be from right to left. Thus, having selected a number in the top half of a word, we can write—

```
WORD        SH        '16'
```

to bring it into the right significance.

PACKING

Let us use the example on the Ostroslovian pension scheme, which we discussed earlier, to illustrate the use of the functions we have just introduced. Suppose that the items of data—sex, age, husband's age, and marital status—are packed into a single word DATA as follows—

sex	sign bit (bit 0)
husband's age	bits 1 to 15
marital status	bits 16 and 17
age	bits 18 to 31

Let us suppose also that we have provided ourselves with masks for separating out husband's age and marital status, which we shall refer to as MASK1 and MASK2. A mask for separating out the age is simply the binary number 16, 38³ ($2^{14} - 1$). The sequence of instructions is now as follows—

```
          WS        MOVE    DATA
       ┌─POS        J       FEM
       │ WS         AND     '16,383'
       │ WS         SUB     '95'
       │ NEG        J       NEXT
       │            J       PENS
       │ ─────────────────────────
FEM:   └→WS         AND     '16,383'
         WS         SUB     '90'
         NEG        J       NEXT
         WS         MOVE    DATA
         WS         AND     MASK2
         WS         SH      '14'
         WS         SUB     '1'
         NEG        J       NEXT
         ZERO       J       PENS
         WS         MOVE    DATA
         WS         AND     MASK1
         WS         SH      '16'
         WS         SUB     '95'
         NEG        J       NEXT
                    J       PENS
```

This example illustrates a general result, that the number of instructions in a program may be substantially increased if the data is packed. Nevertheless, the packing of data is often thoroughly justified by the amount of space that is saved on file devices; moreover a packed magnetic-tape file, being shorter, can be run through faster than an unpacked file with the same information, which may reduce the time needed for the job quite considerably, since magnetic-tape jobs are usually file-limited, that is, they depend more on the speed of the file device than on the speed of computation. However, because the program is lengthened, data is not usually packed when store space is at a premium. It is an ability to weigh up such practical considerations that distinguishes a good programmer from an indifferent one. Also, a good programmer will organize the data so that it is as convenient for unpacking as he can make it.

SUMMARY

In this chapter we have been making the first steps towards designing a language for communicating with our imaginary computer. We have introduced a great deal of grammar and vocabulary, and it will be useful at this point to summarize what we have done. First, the language is to consist of statements of the form—

L:	X	F	Y

in which F is a function (or verb), X and Y are arguments, and L an optional label that can be used for referring to the statement. We have defined a number of function mnemonics—

ADD	Y into X
SUBtract	Y from X
MOVE	Y to X (or make X equal to Y)
J	jump to Y if condition X is true
MLT	multiply X by Y, placing the double-length product in X and X + 1
DIVide	X and X + 1 by Y, putting residue in X, and quotient in X + 1
SDIV	divide X by Y, putting residue in X, and quotient in X + 1
CDB	convert decimal field Y to a binary number in X
CBD	convert binary number in Y to decimal, and store in field X, filling unused bytes with spaces
TFER	transfer data from field Y to field X or from field Y to device X or from device Y to field X
AND	Y into X
NEQ	modify X by *not-equivalent* operation with Y
SHift	bits in X by Y places.

Arguments may be—

literals (numerals between ' ')
addresses (numerals without ' ')
symbolic names
names of peripheral devices
set names
jump conditions
simple arithmetic expressions.

The permissible types of argument are generally limited by the range of the function.

Jumps are conditional on a test of the result of the last arithmetic operation. The conditions available are—

POS	result positive or zero
NEG	result negative
ZERO	result zero
NZERO	result non-zero
OVR	result overflowed
(blank)	unconditional.

The reader will find that the grammar and vocabulary of most machines he is likely to come in contact with is similar in principle to what has been given here, though there will be many differences in detail. There is much that we have not said, for fear of over-complicating what is really quite a simple subject. For instance we have not defined the effect on jump conditions of non-arithmetic functions such as TFER. Fortunately ours is only an imaginary machine, so we can avoid such problems as these simply by arranging that they do not arise, at least within the scope of the book.

EXERCISES 3

Note: It will generally be found helpful to sketch a flow diagram before attempting to code an operation.

1. (*a*) Write a pair of instructions that will jump eight instructions down from the first of the pair if the result of the previous instruction was positive but not zero.

(*b*) Write a sequence of instructions to form the positive difference between A and B when it is not known beforehand which is the larger, or even what the signs of the numbers are.

2. The numerical series—

1 1 2 3 5 8 13 21 . . .

is known as a Fibonacci series. Each member is the sum of the previous two. Write a sequence of instructions for generating a Fibonacci series and printing each member on a separate line on a line printer.

3. Write a sequence of instructions for generating and printing the cubes of the natural numbers using the difference method. The flow diagram for this was given as Exercise 2 of Chapter 1.
4. The Ostroslovian Government mint produces coins of denominations 1 dim, 5 dim and 1 dol, and notes of denominations 5 dol and 10 dol. In calculating the payroll, it is necessary to find the numbers of the coins and notes of each denomination that will be needed to make up all the pay packets. Write a sequence of instructions to analyse PAY, given in dims, into the minimum numbers of coins and notes of each denomination, and add the results into running totals in five registers.
5. A word PRICE is made up as follows—

if sign bit = 0
  bits 1 to 15 give price per unit
  bits 16 to 31 give price per dozen
if sign bit = 1
  bits 1 to 15 give price per dozen
  bits 16 to 31 give price per gross.

Calculate the total COST of a quantity of articles given in ORDER. If the price is given per dozen/gross, the quantity should be an exact multiple of 12; if it is not, jump to a label ERROR.
6. A block of data read from magnetic tape contains 32 records. Three words in the block (the first is named STATS) record which of the records have been moved on each of three previous runs of the file. This is done by placing a one in the appropriate word in a position corresponding to the position of each moved record in the block. It is required to determine how many records have been moved once and only once on the last three runs. Write a sequence of instructions to do this.

4. *Modifying and Counting*

MODIFICATION

LET us now consider a problem that might at first sight appear to raise no difficulties at all: the straightforward summation of several binary numbers in a list. Let us suppose that the first number in the list is named LIST, and that the rest are stored in sequentially addressed registers following it. Thus we shall be able to refer to the second number in the list as LIST + 1, the third as LIST + 2, and so on. If we wished to accumulate the sum in a register called SUM, we might write instructions as follows—

```
SUM          MOVE    LIST
SUM          ADD     LIST + 1
SUM          ADD     LIST + 2
SUM          ADD     LIST + 3
and so on . . .
```

Now this sort of procedure is all very well if we have only a few numbers to add; but suppose the list ran into several hundred items! At a rate of one instruction for every number to be added, the program would become rather long—and would be very tedious to write. Moreover, all the instructions would be doing essentially the same thing, adding in the next number in the list. What we really want is some means whereby a single addition instruction can be made to refer to each of the numbers in the list in turn. We could then make this instruction part of a loop, and arrange to go round the loop as many times as there are numbers in the list. Such an arrangement would have the extra advantage that a program written in this way would be more general in its character; it could be made to deal with different lengths of list simply by adjusting the looping arrangement.

One way of making an instruction refer in turn to different addresses is to increase the address by unity every time the instruction is obeyed. A loop such as—

```
INST:    SUM          ADD     LIST
         INST         ADD     '1'
                      J       INST
```

would deal in turn with every member of a list. Of course, some means would have to be incorporated for stopping the loop when the list came to an end. Now there are some inexpensive computers that operate in this way; but they are not always easy to use. For one thing, if a program using this sort of trick goes wrong, it is not easy to see where it has gone wrong, because the program is no longer the same as it was at the beginning.

INDEX REGISTERS

A better mechanism is provided by what are known as *index registers*. These are simply special storage locations with the property that their contents can be used at option to *modify* one or more of the arguments in an instruction just before the instruction is obeyed. The modification is only temporary; the instruction in its location in store remains unaltered. In our imaginary machine we shall suppose that we have eight index registers, and that they actually occupy the first eight locations in the store, so that their addresses are 0, 1, 2, 3, 4, 5, 6, and 7. We shall suppose, too, that we can refer to them by these numbers in ordinary instructions, thus—

```
5          ADD    '3'
```

"Add the number 3 into index register 5." We shall make the grammatical rule in our language that an index register is brought into use for modification by writing its number in brackets after the argument we wish to modify, thus—

```
SUM        ADD    LIST(3)
```

means, "Increase the address LIST by an amount equal to the value of the modifier in index register 3 and add the content of this new address into SUM." If register 3 happened to contain the number 13, the instruction would refer to LIST + 13.

KERNEL

Not all machines have their index registers as part of the main store. In all fast computers, the index registers, of which there may be many more than eight, form a separate small auxiliary store that can be read much more rapidly than the main store. An auxiliary store like this is often used not only for modifiers but also for storing the data that is currently being worked on; for this reason it is sometimes referred to as a *scratchpad*, or a *kernel*. In some systems a kernel store has certain privileges not accorded to the ordinary common or garden registers. The registers in a kernel store are sometimes referred to as *accumulators*.

To come back to our summation problem, we may now write a loop of instructions to sum the items in a list by using the facilities provided by index registers. The loop—

```
SUM          ADD     LIST(1)
1            ADD     '1'
             J       '– 2'
```

will add numbers sequentially from store into SUM. Naturally we shall have to make sure at the outset that the modifier is zero (unless we wish to start the summation at some intermediate point in the list) and we must make sure, too, that SUM is cleared of anything that was in it previously. The loop should therefore be preceded by the two instructions—

```
1            MOVE    '0'
SUM          MOVE    '0'
```

COUNTING

At present, our loop of instructions resembles the Very Great Wheel—there is no means of stopping it. If we should happen to know at the start how many numbers there are in the list, we can use a counting mechanism to terminate the process. Let us suppose that we wish to accumulate the sum of 135 numbers; we establish a new name, COUNT, and proceed as follows—

```
 COUNT       MOVE    '135'
 1           MOVE    '0'
 SUM         MOVE    '0'
┌→SUM        ADD     LIST(1)
│ 1          ADD     '1'
│ COUNT      SUB     '1'
└─NZERO      J       '– 3'
             STOP
```

Every time we go round the loop, the count is reduced by one; the process stops when it has been reduced to zero. Notice that we choose to count down rather than up, since we have a direct means for testing zero, but no simple means of testing for 135.

The processes of modifying and counting are bound so closely together in computing processes that many systems provide index registers capable of holding a modifier and a counter at the same time. Such systems also provide a special function that increases the modifier by one, decreases the count by one, and jumps if the count is still not zero, all in one instruction. We shall provide a similar facility in our imaginary machine. What we shall do, though, is to hold the counter in the next index register above the one holding the modifier. We shall then define a function CTJ (count and jump) thus—

```
X          CTJ     Y
```

"Increase the modifier in X, and at the same time decrease the counter in X + 1 by one. If the count has not yet been reduced to zero, jump to Y." (For the purpose of this function, the congruence $7 + 1 = 0$ will be taken to hold true.)

Now we can rewrite our sequence of instructions for summing the items in a list—

```
   X         CTJ      Y
   1         MOVE     '0'
   2         MOVE     '135'
   SUM       MOVE     '0'
┌→SUM        ADD      LIST(1)
└─1          CTJ      '– 1'
             STOP
```

which is appreciably neater than it was before.

It is often necessary to convert data from one character code to another. For instance, the code of an input or output device may not be the same as the internal code of a computer, or a computer may be dealing with data that has been generated by another machine with a different code. To illustrate the process of code conversion, we shall consider a simple substitution cipher based on the key—

```
A B C D E F G H I J K L M N O P Q R S T U V W X Y Z
Q W E R T Y U I O P A S D F G H J K L Z X C V B N M
```

To encipher a message using this well known sequence as a key, we substitute Q for A, W for B, and so on. The word COMPUTER would become EGDHXZTK.

To use a computer for encipherment, it is necessary first to put the letters of the key (or, to be precise, their equivalents in the computer's numeric code) into store in the desired sequence. Let us use the name KEY to refer to the first item in this set. Now in the code of our imaginary computer the capital letters are represented by the codes 01000001 (decimal 65) to 01011010 (decimal 90). By subtracting 65 from the code of the character we wish to encipher, therefore, we obtain a number giving the position relative to KEY of the code we are to substitute for it. We can then gain access to the desired code by using this number as a modifier to modify KEY. Thus, if we wished to encipher LETTER by substituting for it the appropriate character from the key, we could write—

```
6           MOVE   LETTER
6           SUB    '65'
LETTER      MOVE   KEY(6)
```

In this example we are using the mechanism of modification, not to work sequentially through a set of data, but to give access to the set at intermediate random points. In the next example, we shall use modifiers both randomly and sequentially to encipher a block of text; but, before we do that, a slight digression will be necessary.

In our first example on modification, we considered a list of one-word items; but in code-conversion we are dealing with byte-sized items. Modification in the former case must therefore operate in steps of one word, whereas in the latter case it must operate in quarter words. How is the machine to be able to distinguish the type of modification it is to apply in a given case? Different systems solve this problem in different ways. A common way is to make all modifiers operate in bytes, and provide a special form of count-and-jump function that advances the modifier in steps of four. The way we shall choose, with simplicity in mind, is to make the even-numbered index registers operate byte-wise, and the odd-numbered registers operate word-wise. With this in mind, we can proceed to write a sequence of instructions for enciphering a piece of text starting at TEXT—

```
  4           MOVE   '0'
┌→6           MOVE   TEXT(4)
│ 6           SUB    '65'
│ TEXT(4)     MOVE   KEY(6)
│ 4           ADD    '1'
└─            J      '− 4'
```

Finally we have to incorporate some mechanism for terminating the process. We could use counting; but, to make things a bit more general, so that we shall be able to use the same sequence of instructions to encipher various lengths of text, let us arrange to terminate each block of text with a special character—an asterisk, say, (code 00101010, decimal 42). Our sequence of instructions then becomes—

```
    4           MOVE   '0'
┌──→6           MOVE   TEXT(4)
│   6           SUB    '42'
│ ┌─ZERO        J      '5'
│ │ 6           SUB    '23'
│ │ TEXT(4)     MOVE   KEY(6)
│ │ 4           ADD    '1'
└─│─            J      '− 6'
  └→            STOP
```

Notice that 65 is now subtracted in two stages: first 42, to test for the terminating character, then the remaining 23.

SORTING

The ability to manipulate index registers well is one of the things that distinguishes a good programmer. It will be worth while, therefore, to work through just one more example to illustrate their use further. This time we shall choose another process that occurs time and time again in computing—the process of sorting. Input data arrives at a computer in random, or near random, order, and one of the first things that has to be done with it is to re-arrange it so that its order corresponds with that of the files already held by the computer, when the two sets of data can be scanned in step. Many methods have been devised for sorting data on computers; we shall be dealing with some of them in Chapter 13. The method we shall illustrate here is one of the simplest. It consists in taking the items in turn in pairs. If two items are in the wrong order, we reverse them, if not, we pass on to the next pair.

For example, suppose that we wish to sort the sequence—

3 5 1 8 4 2 9 7 6

into the natural order, with the smallest on the left. On first scanning the sequence, we note that 3 and 5 are in the correct order, but that 5 and 1 must be reversed. 5 now comes before 8, which is its correct position; but 8 and 4 must be reversed, as must 8 (in its new position) and 2. Finally we reverse 9 and 7, and 9 and 6, to yield the slightly more ordered sequence—

3 1 5 4 2 8 7 6 9

A second scan changes this to—

1 3 4 2 5 7 6 8 9

and a third gives—

1 3 2 4 5 6 7 8 9

The fourth scan reverses 3 and 2 to put all the digits in the correct order.

There are many faster sorting procedures than this; but this one has the advantage of being very simple to understand, and so will do quite well for our purpose. We are going to use it to sort the 135 numbers in the list we were dealing with earlier in the chapter into their natural order; but before we do that, there is one further facility that would be useful to have in our imaginary system.

All sorting procedures involve a great many comparisons between the items to be sorted. Obviously it is possible to compare two numbers by means of a normal subtraction instruction; but, if this is used, one of the numbers will be spoiled. We could avoid spoiling it by copying it into another location; but that would take more time. What is more, we are not really interested in what the *result* of the subtraction is, only whether it is positive or negative. To speed up operations in which numbers are compared, most systems provide a special test-subtract (or compare) function, which forms the difference between two numbers but does not put it anywhere in the store. It does, however, record in the normal way whether the result was positive, negative, or zero, so that it can serve as a jump condition. Let us then provide our imaginary system with instructions of the form—

```
X          TSUB    Y
```

which will carry out the operation X − Y, ignoring the actual result but leaving the jump-condition settings in the appropriate state.

We can now write down the sequence of instructions to perform one sorting scan.

```
       1             MOVE    '0'
       2             MOVE    '134'
  ┌──→ LIST(1)       TSUB    LIST + 1(1)
  │ ┌─ NEG           J       '4'
  │ │  WS            MOVE    LIST(1)
  │ │  LIST(1)       MOVE    LIST + 1(1)
  │ │  LIST + 1(1)   MOVE    WS
  └─└→ 1             CTJ     '− 5'
```

Notice that the counter has to be 134, not 135, since the items are taken in pairs. As usual, WS stands for working space.

The last sequence of instructions will scan once through the list, and will improve its ordering; but, as we saw in the original example, several scans have generally to be carried out before the items are finally sorted. How do we know when the process has come to an end? Obviously we cannot use a counting process, since the actual number of scans needed will depend on the amount of disorder in the original sequence. Some other terminating condition must be found. The only thing we can be certain of is that, once the items have been brought into the correct order, further scans will have no effect; in other words, the process is known to have terminated as soon as the machine performs a scan in which there are no reversals. How can this condition be detected? One way would be to raise a flag when we reverse the first two items in a scan. If the flag is up at the end of a scan, we lower it and proceed to the next

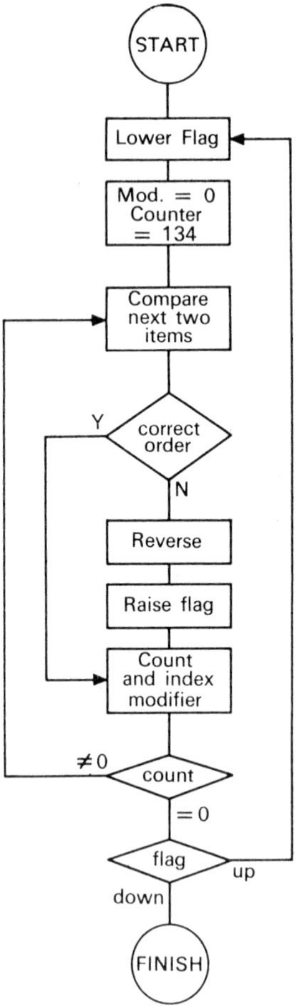

FIG. 4.1.

scan: if the flag is down, however, at the end of a scan, there have been no reversals, and the items must consequently be in the right sequence. A glance at the flow diagram of Fig. 4.1 should make the idea quite clear.

For our flag we shall use a store location, which we shall refer to as FLAG. Raising the flag will consist in making the content of this location one: lowering it will consist in making the content zero, The sorting sequence is then—

```
┌──────→ FLAG          MOVE    '0'
│        1             MOVE    '0'
│        2             MOVE    '134'
│ ┌──→LIST + 1(1)      TSUB    LIST(1)
│ │ ┌─POS              J       '5'
│ │ │  WS              MOVE    LIST(1)
│ │ │  LIST(1)         MOVE    LIST + 1(1)
│ │ │  LIST + 1(1)     MOVE    WS
│ │ │  FLAG            MOVE    '1'
│ └─└→1                CTJ     '– 6'
│        FLAG          MOVE    FLAG
└─────── NZERO         J       '– 11'
                       STOP
```

We see in this sequence of instructions a loop within a loop. In this case, the inner loop is cycled 134 times for every cycle of the outer loop. Computer programs often contain loops nested one within the other, like Russian dolls. Notice that the test subtraction is now performed in the opposite sense. This is to avoid raising the flag when two items have the same value, which would prevent the process from terminating.

ADDRESS BASE AND DISPLACEMENT

In the preceding examples, we obtained access to a particular item in a set by using the name of the first item in the set in an instruction, and putting the increment (position of the desired item in the set) into an index register. But the design of our imaginary machine allows us to work the other way round if it is more convenient, putting the increment in the instruction, and the name in the modifier; this is because modification in our machine is simply a process of addition. Suppose we are updating a file of accounts. We have a block of data called ACCOUNT, consisting of the account currently under scrutiny. Suppose that the fifth word (word 4, since we start at 0) contains the current balance, and that the seventeenth (word 16) contains a negative number giving the permitted limit of credit allowed to this account. The job we are doing may require us to reduce the balance by an amount DEBIT, and then check whether the credit limit has been exceeded, jumping to a label OVER if this has happened. We proceed as follows—

```
3          MOVE    'ACCOUNT'
4(3)       SUB     DEBIT
4(3)       TSUB    16(3)
NEG        J       OVER
```

Notice how the literal marks are used here. In the first instruction we wish to load into index register 3 not the *value* of the account but the actual name ACCOUNT (or, to be precise, the address corresponding to the name). When we write—

```
4(3)        TSUB    16(3)
```

we are then comparing the operands that would normally be referred to as ACCOUNT + 4 and ACCOUNT + 16. ACCOUNT is then referred to as the base of the arguments, and the numbers 4 and 16 as their displacements relative to that base.

DETACHED ADDRESSES

On some occasions it is convenient to write zero in the instruction, and use the index register to supply the whole address. This is an example of what is known as detached addressing, of which we shall have more to say in the next chapter.

ARRAYS

All the sets we have dealt with so far in this chapter (list, key, text) have been one-dimensional; we can picture them as having their items laid end-to-end or side-to-side. But sets of data can have more than one dimension in practice: for instance, tabular data is usually two-dimensional, with the items arranged in rows and columns; college timetables are three-dimensional, since each entry represents a particular class with a particular lecture in a particular room. In computer terminology, structured sets go under the name of *arrays*. The term is often restricted to sets with two or more dimensions; one-dimenisonal sets are also called *vectors*, as also are single rows or columns of multidimensional sets. Arrays occur very frequently in mathematical computation; but they are by no means uncommon in commercial work.

Since a computer store is, at least from the programmer's standpoint, a one-dimensional structure, arrays of two or more dimensions must be stored in a *dismantled* form, for instance with the rows laid end to end, like this—

row 1	row 2	row 3	row 4	. . .

If we wanted to read down a column of an array stored like this, we should have to arrange to leap from the head of the column in row 1 to the corresponding place in row 2, and so on. A modifier used for doing this would have to be stepped by increments equal to the number of items in a row. An array stored in this way is said to be stored *by rows*; sometimes it is more convenient to store arrays by columns instead.

DOUBLE MODIFICATION

Some computers, particularly those designed for fast *number crunching*, provide double modification, a facility whereby an argument can be modified simultaneously from two different index registers, one dealing with the rows, the other with the columns, of an array. Double modification is valuable if speed is the main objective; but it is possible to handle multi-dimensional arrays quite well without it. Suppose that we have an array of 10 rows and 20 columns, and that we wish to find the largest element in, say, the first column. Using index registers 5 and 6, and assuming that the array is stored by rows, we proceed as follows—

```
      LGST      MOVE   '0'
      5         MOVE   'ARRAY'
      6         MOVE   '10'
 ---→ LGST      TSUB   0(5)
|  |--POS       J      '2'
|  |  LGST      MOVE   0(5)
|  |→ 5         ADD    '19'
 ---- 5         CTJ    '– 4'
                STOP
```

Notice, by the way, the distinction between an instruction such as—

```
LGST      TSUB   0(5)
```

which compares the number in LGST with the number whose *address* is given in register 5, and an instruction such as

```
LGST      TSUB   '0'(5)
```

where the comparison is with the actual content of register 5.

Let us look at one last example on arrays. We shall replace the first element in each row of our 10-by-20 matrix by the sum of all the elements in that row. Here we need two modifiers and two counters. The procedure is—

```
      3         MOVE   'ARRAY'
      4         MOVE   '10'
      5         MOVE   3
      6         MOVE   '19'
 ---→ 5         ADD    '1'
|  |→ 0(3)      ADD    0(5)
|  |--5         CTJ    '– 1'
|     3         ADD    '19'
 ---- 3         CTJ    '– 5'
                STOP
```

Here the modifier in 3 moves down the first column, while the modifier in 5 runs along each row in turn. The two modifiers are acting like pointers, and in fact modifiers used in just this way are sometimes called pointers. The counter in 4 controls the outer loop, counting rows, while the counter in 6 counts items in a row, and controls the inner loop.

One other point: the reader will probably have noticed that we have avoided using index register 0. This is because we must have some way of telling the machine that we do not want *any* modification to take place. We do this by writing nothing in the modifier position; but of course the machine cannot simply overlook the piece of an instruction that would normally contain a number referring to an index register, so it puts zero there. Zero, then, means "don't modify"; so index register 0 cannot be used to contain modifiers, though there is no reason why it should not be used for ordinary data, or even for counters.

SUMMARY

In this chapter we have been adding to the grammar and vocabulary of our imaginary computer language. We have introduced the idea of eight index registers occupying the first eight locations in the store, and we have augmented the general form of a statement to—

L:	X(M)	F	Y(N)

where M and N can specify any index register except 0. We have introduced two new functions—

CTJ	count and jump, using modifier in X, and counter in X + 1, and jumping if count is zero,
TSUB	test-subtract Y from X, ignoring the result, but leaving the test conditions appropriately set.

We have introduced a new type of argument—a name in literal marks; and we have made the rule that odd-numbered index registers shall be used for modifying word sets, and even-numbered registers for modifying byte sets.

EXERCISES 4

1. Write a sequence of instructions to scan through the 135 numbers in LIST and place the smallest in a location LEAST.
2. What sequence of characters must be stored in KEY in order to decipher messages enciphered according to the key given in this chapter? What sequence of instructions would be required for deciphering?

3. Write a sequence of instructions for enciphering a piece of text in which spaces (00100000) and fullstops (00101110) appear. Spaces and stops are to appear unchanged in the enciphered message. Assume the text is terminated by an asterisk (00101010).

4. (*a*) Write a sequence of instructions for replacing leading zeros in a string of decimal characters by spaces. Assume that zero is represented by 00000000.

(*b*) Write a sequence of instructions for replacing trailing zeros in a decimal fraction by spaces. Assume that the fraction is terminated by a space code.

5. Write a sequence of instructions that will jump to a label FOUND if a particular value VALUE appears in a sorted list of 135 numbers. (Hint: Look at the middle number of the list; if this is not it, look at the middle number of the half it is likely to be in; then the quarter it is likely to be in; and so on.)

6. Write a sequence of instructions for counting the number of zeros in the major diagonal of a 20-by-20 array.

5. *Subroutines*

It happens not infrequently that a sequence of instructions defines a procedure that can be used in two or more programs, or even in two or more places in the same program. Programming costs are heavy, and anything that can be done to lighten them is to be encouraged; consequently all systems provide facilities whereby a sequence of instructions written for one program can be incorporated, if needed, in another program, or in a different place in the same program. Sequences of instructions that lend themselves to being used in this way are known as subroutines. Indeed there are some subroutines that are of such general usefulness that they are written by the manufacturer, and supplied to purchasers or hirers with the machine in the form of a library on punched cards, punched paper tape, or magnetic tape. Subroutines treated in this way are referred to as utility subroutines; they include such procedures as the evaluation of common mathematical functions (square root, sine, log, etc.), the calculation of standard income tax, or the editing of input and output data in certain standard ways.

OPEN AND CLOSED SUBROUTINES

A subroutine can be incorporated into a program in two ways, as illustrated in Fig. 5.1. It can either be inserted in the appropriate place in the program sequence, or it can be put by itself, at the end of the program, say, with control being transferred to it by means of jumps. Subroutines of the first kind are known as open subroutines; like open tunnels, one passes straight in at one end and out at the other. Subroutines of the second kind are known as closed subroutines. It is obvious that if the same subroutine is going to be used in several places in the same program, it is generally better to write it as a closed subroutine, since, as an open subroutine, space for several copies of it would have to be found in the store. On the other hand, an open subroutine must be faster, at least to the extent of two jump instructions.

The last instruction in a closed subroutine must be a jump transferring control back to the next instruction in the main program. But here we run into a seeming difficulty. If the subroutine is used more than once in the program, what argument can be put as the destination in this terminal jump instruction? Obviously not either of the labels to which it must jump, for then how would it get back to the other? There are several possible solutions to this riddle. The one most commonly adopted is to arrange for the jump to transfer

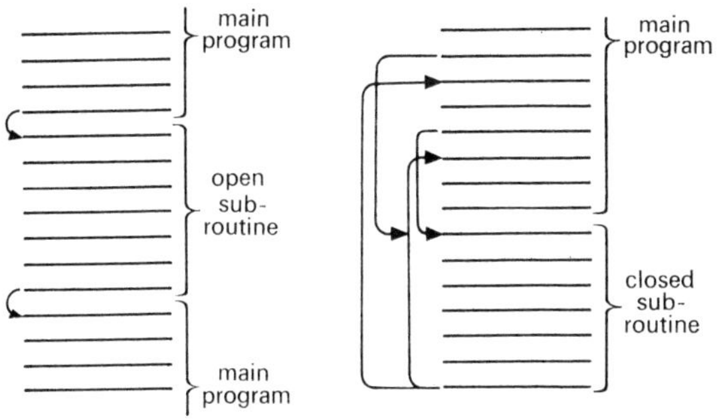

FIG. 5.1.

control not to the address given in the jump instruction but to the address given in a register *named* in the instruction. This is known as *indirect addressing* or *replaced addressing*.

THE LINK

In fact we have already introduced the idea of an indirect address. We encountered it when we were dealing with modifiers. In the instruction—

```
SUM        ADD    0(1)
```

the number to be added is taken not from index register 1 but from the register whose *address* is given in register 1. If, then, using the same convention, we write—

```
           J      0(1)
```

the jump will be made to the instruction whose address is in register 1. This is just what we want for terminating a closed subroutine, always providing that the correct address for the return jump has already been planted in register 1. An address planted in this way, to provide exit from a subroutine, is known as a *link*.

The question we must now ask is, how can the correct link be planted in the first place? If we knew from the outset just where the subroutine jumps were going to be located in the store when the program was obeyed, we could prepare the link addresses beforehand, and arrange for them to be planted in the appropriate place with a

MOVE instruction before the subroutine was entered. But in modern systems it is the exception to know how a program is going to be disposed in store; furthermore, there are many systems in which the program can be moved from place to place in the store during the course of a run. The best solution, then, and the one adopted almost universally in practice, is to arrange for the link to be planted automatically when the subroutine is entered. In our imaginary machine we can arrange this quite easily. The unconditional jump does not need the first argument, so we can write in this space the name of the register where the link is to be placed, thus—

```
1        J        SUBRTN
```

'Jump to label SUBRTN, storing a link in 1.' The link will of course be one more than the address of the instruction that stores it.

SUBROUTINE CALL

We talk of *calling* a subroutine. Calling a subroutine is rather like delegating some of your work to someone else. When work is delegated, it is essential that both the delegator and the delegate have a proper understanding between them, not only about the exact nature of the job that is to be done, but also about the raw material that is to be used for the job. This is best done by establishing a set of rigid conventions, and sticking to them. The same thing applies between a main program and the subroutines it calls. The subroutine must 'know' where to find the data it is to work on, where to put the result or results of its works, and above all where to find the link. These details are established by conventions, which are decided when either the subroutine, or the main program, is written, whichever happens first. Manufacturers who supply a library of subroutines also provide a book setting out the conventions by which each subroutine was written.*

PARAMETERS

Data can be handed over to a subroutine either in the form of actual values or as names (addresses) indicating where the data are to be found. It can be presumed that a subroutine will provide for itself any literals it needs. Numeric data and names handed over from one part of a program to another are known collectively as *parameters*, and they are generally handed over in the form of a *parameter list*, whose address is planted in some pre-arranged location, generally one of the index registers. When the address

* The term interface is sometimes used to describe the set of conventions that must be agreed between the designers of one piece of hardware or software and another that must match with it.

of the parameter list is given in an index register, it can be used as a modifier to give access to the individual parameters themselves.

In the last chapter we wrote a sequence of instructions for summing the items in a list. Let us take that sequence of instructions and turn it into a closed subroutine; but, to make it more generally useful, let us write it so that it will sum any named list consisting of any number of items. The parameters that must be handed over, then, are—

the name of the first item in the list,
the number of items in the list,
the location where the sum is to be put.

These can be handed over in the form of a parameter list. Let us call the first item in this list PLIST, and let us put its address in register 7, the link being planted in register 1. The arrangement is shown diagrammatically in Fig. 5.2. The address in register 7

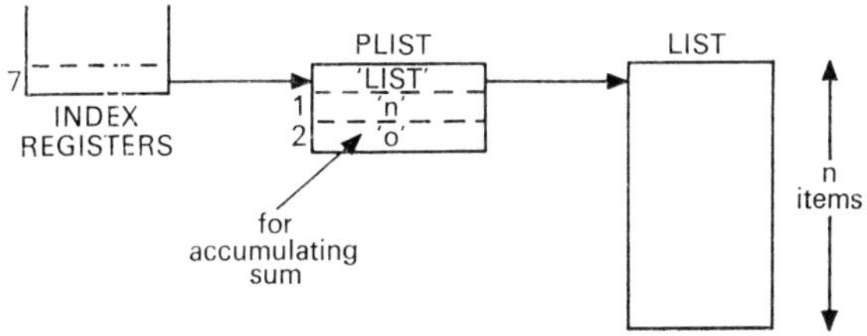

FIG. 5.2.

points to the parameter list, whose first entry points to the list to be summed. The second entry in the parameter list is *n*, the number of items in the list, and the third is an empty register, prepared ready to take the sum.

DUMPING

Before we can write the subroutine, there is a further point to be cleared up. The subroutine is going to need index registers for its own use. In fact, if we look at the original instruction sequence in Chapter 4, we can see that it will need two index registers, one for a modifier, and one for a counter. Since all the registers probably contain valuable material belonging to the main program, the subroutine must put the contents of two of them away safely in the store somewhere until it has finished its work, after which it must replace them. This process is known as *dumping*, and the place where the data is stored temporarily is known as a *dump*.

Now, at last, we are in a position to write the subroutine. Of course it must have a label by which the main program can call it. We shall use registers 3 and 4 for the modifier and counter.

```
ADDLIST:  DUMP          MOVE    3
          DUMP + 1      MOVE    4
          3             MOVE    0(7)        set modifier
          4             MOVE    1(7)        set counter
        ┌→2(7)          ADD     0(3)
        └─3             CTJ     '− 1'
          3             MOVE    DUMP
          4             MOVE    DUMP + 1
                        J       0(1)        link
```

To use this subroutine to add together the 135 items in our list, e must write a *calling sequence* as follows—

```
          7             MOVE    'PLIST'
          0(7)          MOVE    'LIST'
          1(7)          MOVE    '135'
          2(7)          MOVE    '0'
          1             J       ADDLIST→ to subroutine
          SUM           MOVE    2(7)← from subroutine
```

The whole procedure now takes several more instructions than when we treated it as an isolated sequence in chapter 4 (even after allowing for the fact that some dumping might have been necessary in any case.) What we have done, though, is to cut down the amount of programming we have to do, since the new subroutine is applicable quite generally, and might be used in several different contexts. We have traded the running time of the program against the writing time, and development time, of the program, in the hope that the payoff will be in our favour.

The last entry in the parameter list in the previous example was actually an empty location, in which the subroutine was intended to accumulate the sum. (Notice that one of the conventions assumed in writing the subroutine was that the calling sequence will clear this location.) In fact, had we wished to, we could have made the rules so that the *address* of SUM was handed over instead in this location. In this way, we should have avoided the need to move the sum from one place to another after the subroutine had done its work. In this case, the subroutine might have been written—

```
ADDLIST:  DUMP          MOVE    3
          DUMP + 1      MOVE    4
```

```
            3         MOVE   0(7)
            4         MOVE   1(7)
            7         MOVE   2(7)
            0(7)      MOVE   '0'        clear sum
         ┌→0(7)       ADD    0(3)
         └─3          CTJ    '− 1'
            3         MOVE   DUMP
            4         MOVE   DUMP + 1
                      J      0(1)
```

and the calling sequence—

```
            7         MOVE   'PLIST'
            0(7)      MOVE   'LIST'
            1(7)      MOVE   '135'
            2(7)      MOVE   'SUM'
            1         J      ADDLIST
```

In this version of the subroutine we have used register 7 to avoid dumping another register, over-writing the address of the parameter list with the address of the sum.

Let us now attempt to crystallize what has gone before with the aid of another example. Consider the following situation: a firm of merchants keeps all its accounts on magnetic tape. The accounts are of different lengths; but the last word in each account is the balance to date (positive for credit, negative for debit), and the first word in each account is a number one less than the total number of words in the account. As a check, to make sure that the file is being updated correctly, a trial balance is made every time the file is updated; that is, all the credit balances and all the debit balances are totalled separately, and the totals are compared at the end of the run to make sure that they tally. Let us write a subroutine that can be called every time an account is read from the magnetic tape into the store, which will add the balance of that account into a cumulative total. Suppose that each account is read into the same area of the store in its turn, and that the first word in this area has the name ACCOUNT. The parameters that the subroutine will need are—

the name ACCOUNT,
word for accumulating credit balances,
word for accumulating debit balances,

and these will be constant throughout the program.

We shall hand over the parameters in the form of a parameter list, in the order given above, with the address of the first item given in index register 7. The arrangement is illustrated in Fig. 5.3. The link will be in register 1. The subroutine could then be—

```
TRIBAL:     DUMP      MOVE   3
            3         MOVE   0(7)   address of account
```

```
     3              MOVE    0(3)
     3              ADD     0(7)   address of balance
     0(3)           MOVE    0(3)   balance
  ┌—NEG             J       '3'
  │  1(7)           ADD     0(3)   credit
  │                 J       0(1)
  │  ————————————————————————
  └→2(7)            SUB     0(3)   debit
                    J       0(1)
```

INDIRECT ADDRESSING

The reader may have wondered at some point what he would do if he ran short of index registers. Of course, it is possible to get away with very few index registers if one is prepared to do a lot of

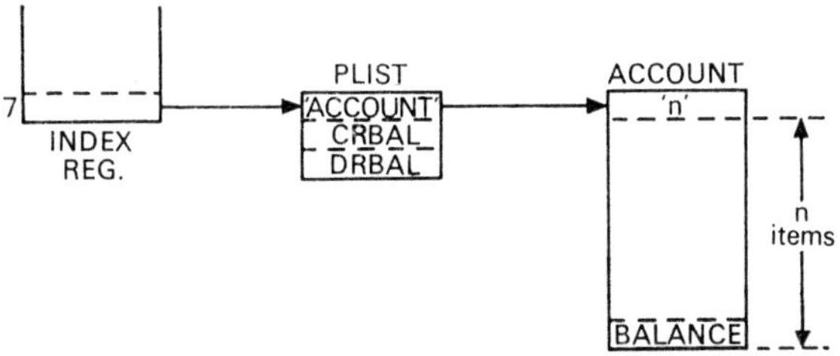

FIG. 5.3.

dumping and restoring; but dumping and restoring can use up a lot of time. The real answer is to have plenty of registers available; but this raises the question, how many is plenty? What is too few for one problem may be too lavish for another; index registers can be expensive. A compromise solution sometimes adopted is to give ordinary registers some of the properties of index registers, particularly the property that they can be used for replacement, or indirect addressing. This, it will be remembered, is the property whereby an argument can be used to give not the name (address) of the *operand*, but the name (address) of the *location* where the operand's name can be found. This is a property already possessed by index registers, so, in extending it to ordinary registers, we shall use again the symbol of round brackets to denote it. Thus—

(X) F (Y)

specifies an operation named not by X and Y but by the operands that X and Y name.

Indirect addressing is particularly useful when calling subroutines; this is chiefly because it confers a greater degree of generality on the system. We can think, if we wish, of a hierarchy of generalities starting with literals, which are completely specific, and running through names to replaced names, and even stretching up to higher and higher levels of replacement. Except in special cases, one, or at most two, levels of replacement are as much as any normal person can handle; though this is not to say that more levels could not profitably be used in an automatic, or semi-automatic manner.

In the last example it took three instructions to form the address of the balance (last word) in the account. With replacement we could easily form this address and hand it over directly as a parameter, thus—

```
            0(7)       MOVE    'ACCOUNT'
            0(7)       ADD     0(7) )
                       J       TRIBAL
```

The subroutine then becomes—

```
TRIBAL:     (0(7) )    MOVE    (0(7) )
         ┌──NEG        J       '3'
         │  1(7)       ADD     (0(7) )
         │             J       0(1)
         │  ──────────────────────────
         └→2(7)        ADD     (0(7) )
                       J       0(1)
```

Notice that an argument such as (0(7)) really involves double replacement: the address in 7 is added on to the displacement (in this case 0) and then replaced in its turn.

In Chapter 4 we wrote a sequence of instructions to find the largest element in the first column of a 10-by-20 matrix. Let us now rewrite this in the form of a subroutine for finding the largest element in an arbitrary column of a matrix of any dimensions. We shall need a parameter list giving the following information—

name of array
number of rows
number of columns
column to be scrutinized
cleared to hold result
link.

In this case we shall hand over the link as the last item in the parameter list instead of in an index register, entering the subroutine with a jump such as—

```
            PLIST + 5      J       LGST
```

We shall hand over the address of the parameter list in register 7. The subroutine might then be—

```
LGST:        2(7)          TSUB    3(7)
             NEG           J       (5(7))
             0(7)          ADD     3(7)
      ┌───→ 4(7)           TSUB    (0(7))
      │  ┌─POS             J       '2'
      │  │ 4(7)            MOVE    (0(7))
      │  └→0(7)            ADD     2(7)
      │    1(7)            SUB     '1'
      └────NZERO           J       '− 5'
                           J       (5(7))
```

Any reader who finds this difficult to follow should remember that 0(7) is equivalent to PLIST, 1(7) to PLIST + 1, and so on. The first two instructions are there to check that the column specified actually appears within the matrix, control being returned to the main program if an error has been made. Apart from this, the subroutine corresponds closely with the sequence of instructions given in Chapter 4, with the exception that, since we are not using index registers for counting, we have lost the use of the CTJ function, and have to use three instructions to do its job.

SWITCH JUMPS

Sometimes a programmer wishes to provide a choice of subroutines at a particular point in a program, calling one or other of them according to circumstances. For example, a merchant may have made several different discounting agreements with different customers according to the value he places on their business, or for some other set of reasons. During an invoicing run, then, he will wish the program to enter different discounting subroutines for different customers. The usual way of organizing this sort of thing is to provide somewhere in the customer's record on the file a code number indicating which discount scheme is to be applied. This number is then used to modify the jump instruction that calls the subroutine. An arrangement of this kind is called a *switch jump*.

In the case just suggested, there might be a choice of four discount schemes, implemented by subroutines referred to as DS1, DS2, DS3, and DS4. Suppose that the last two bits in the fifth word (word 4) of the record are used to specify the discount scheme to be used. The appropriate subroutine could then be called by the sequence—

```
             5             MOVE    RECORD + 4
             5             AND     '3'
                           J       SWITCH(5)
```

Here we are using the literal '3' to mask the two bits we want. SWITCH in this case would be a list of four jump instructions—

SWITCH:	J	DS1
	J	DS2
	J	DS3
	J	DS4

of which the selected one will transfer control to the appropriate subroutine. There are other ways of organizing a switch jump; but this is probably the most common. The arrangement is shown diagrammatically in Fig. 5.4.

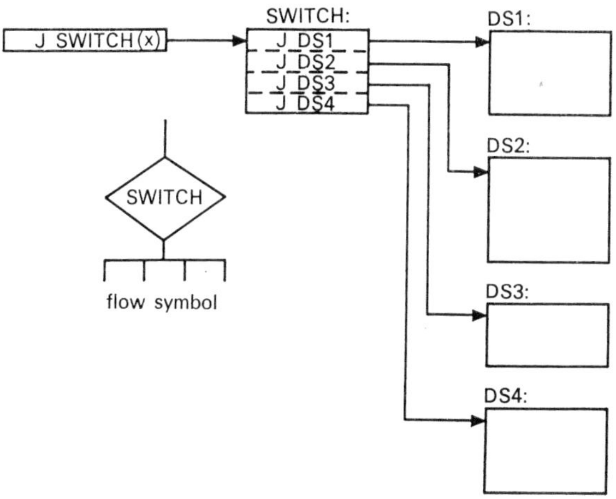

FIG. 5.4.

A word must be said about the method of returning from a switched subroutine. The link must of course refer to the original instruction sequence, not to the switch. If, as in our imaginary system, link setting is optional, the problem is easily solved: the original jump sets the link and the switch does not disturb it. If link setting is obligatory on subroutine jumps, the switch itself will generally have to be written as a subroutine. If the system provides replacement, switching can be achieved by means of a replaced address, thus—

1	J	(SWITCH(5))

when the switch becomes a list of addresses instead of a list of jump instructions, and control is eventually returned to the main program by obeying the link in 1.

NESTED SUBROUTINES

Sometimes it is convenient to make one subroutine call another. This often happens in machines where multiplication and division are performed by subroutines; but there are many other instances. Subroutines called by other subroutines are sometimes described as *nested*, by analogy with nests of occasional tables; and nests may be several levels in depth. Fig. 5.5 shows a typical structural arrange-

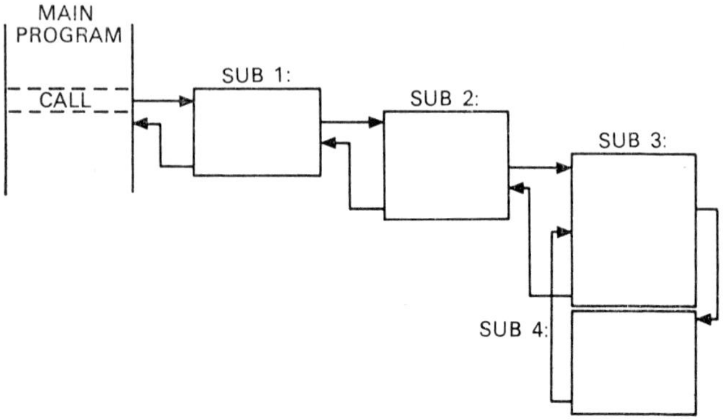

FIG. 5.5.

ment, with a nesting depth of four. The return jumps are shown there as acting through the next level up; this is usually the easiest way to work, but it is not the only way.

PUSHDOWN STACK

In general, when subroutines are nested, it is necessary to preserve the link to the previous level before entering the next level. This can be done simply by dumping; but a more elegant way is to use what is known as a pushdown stack. We can imagine this as a box, open at the top, and with a coiled spring at the bottom. When objects are put into the box, the spring is compressed; and, whenever an object is removed, the spring expands, lifting the next object into the top position. (Anyone who has ever filled a rifle magazine will be familiar with the arrangement.) Only the top object is accessible, and the chief principle of operation is *last in—first out*.

The principle of *last in—first out* is precisely what we need when dealing with links from subroutines nested in the way shown in Fig. 5.5. Only one link at a time is of interest—the last link planted but not yet obeyed. Some systems actually provide a stack in the hardware; but it is not really difficult to simulate a stack in most computers. All that is needed is a modifier (say, in index register 1) giving the address of the last link that was stacked. The calling sequence should then contain the instructions—

```
1        ADD    '1'
(1)      J      SUBRTN
```

which will store a link in what is in effect the next level of a simulated stack. The return jump from the subroutine is—

```
         J      (0(1))
```

and this must lead to an instruction—

```
1        SUB    '1'
```

to move the modifier so that it points to the next link to be obeyed: this is equivalent to making the second level of the stack push up to the top.

Stacks are of value not only for links, of course; any data that has to be preserved through a subroutine call can be stacked for subsequent retrieval. In particular, the contents of index registers may be preserved by stacking. The stacking can be performed by the calling sequence or by the subroutine itself, when it has to make space in the index registers. The second arrangement is more usual except when one of the registers is to be used for passing on a parameter (or the address of a parameter list) when the calling sequence must do the dumping. Stacking facilities can be built into the assembly language of a computer system: if this is not done, a program may allocate one of the index registers to hold a stack pointer throughout the process.

In practice the handling of a simulated stack is a little more complicated than simply incrementing and decrementing a pointer. For one thing, there must be a check against overfilling the area of store allocated to a stack. Then, it may be advisable to provide facilities for returning directly to a low level of the stack without passing through the intermediate stages; this requires the various subroutine levels to be marked in some way. Because of their use with nested subroutines, stacks are sometimes referred to as *nests;* but we shall continue to use the former term.

RECURSIVE PROCESSES

A special case of nested subroutines occurs when a subroutine calls itself. Subroutines that work in this way are said to be *recursive.* A recursive process is, in essence, just a loop; but it is closed not by a simple jump back but by a subroutine call. Moreover, when a recursive process terminates, it may be necessary to work back again one by one through all the earlier subroutine levels in order to get back to the original call. It is sometimes convenient in mathematical programs to write a recursive process as a subroutine rather than a simple loop. In commercial work the problem is more likely to be that of making sure that subroutines do not go recursive through errors.

BACKING STORE

Where the amount of core store is limited, it is common practice to store subroutines, particularly those that are not used very frequently, on what is known as a backing store. This is a device that provides storage much more cheaply (in terms of bits stored per unit of money) than a core store, but is a peripheral device in the sense that instructions cannot be obeyed from it directly. Magnetic drums and magnetic discs are the commonest forms of backing store, though magnetic tape has been used in this way. There is also a cheaper and slower form of core store for use as backing.

OVERLAYS

Subroutines on backing store must be read into the main core store before they can be obeyed, and it is common practice to set aside particular areas of core store to receive them. Whenever a piece of program is read from backing store into the core store, it obliterates whatever was previously written in the area of store it now occupies; for this reason, subroutines handled in this way are sometimes referred to as *overlays*. The sequence of instructions that reads a part of a program from backing store and then enters it, is called a *cue*.

SUMMARY

In this chapter, we have introduced the idea of subroutines, and we have added to our imaginary machine language a form of jump instruction in which the first argument is a register name; the jump then stores a link in the designated register. We have also introduced yet one more type of argument—the replaced address. This is denoted by placing brackets around any name-type argument.

EXERCISES 5

1. Write a general subroutine for raising a given number to a given positive power. State the rules for using it.
2. Show how the sequence of instructions in Exercise 4 of Chapter 3 could be

supplied as a subroutine. Suggest two alternative ways of organizing the parameter list, and show how each would affect the instruction sequence.
3. Rewrite the example given in Chapter 3 for calculating HCF in such a way that it could be called as a subroutine. Specify the layout of the parameter list.
4. The first column of a card carries the identifier A, B, C, D or E according to the type of data punched in it. Read a card, and use the idea of a switch jump to transfer control to the appropriate subroutine for dealing with the data.
5. Write a short subroutine that will examine a byte and—

(*a*) if it is not a zero, obey the link,
(*b*) if it is a zero, replace it with a space and jump to the next instruction after the link.

Now write a subroutine for replacing leading zeros in a string of decimal characters, calling the short subroutine you have just written. Write a suitable calling sequence for the top-level subroutine. (Refer to Exercise 4(*a*) of Chapter 4). Use the concept of a stack for storing indices and links.

6. Write a subroutine for replacing trailing zeros in a decimal fraction by spaces, assuming that the fraction itself is terminated by a space character. Call the same short subroutine that you wrote for the previous exercise. (Refer to Exercise 4(*b*) of Chapter 4.)

6. *How Programs are Assembled*

So far, we have been considering sequences of instructions in the form in which the programmer writes them; but this is not the form in which they are eventually stored in the computer. The programmer writes in an alphabetic language, which is most wasteful of space. If the language has, say, one hundred different functions, there is no need to use any more than seven bits to give each one a different code; but the word MOVE, at eight bits per character byte, occupies no fewer than thirty-two. Also, the names used by the programmer cannot be interpreted by the machine in that form. Each one represents a register, or a set of registers, and must therefore be converted at some time into numbers giving the addresses of the registers referred to. Furthermore, the statements written by the programmer are all of different lengths: the organization of a computer can be greatly simplified, and its speed improved, if instructions can be kept to a few standard lengths bearing simple relationships to the length of a word.

THE ASSEMBLER

Programs in the programmer's symbolic code are converted into the machine's own rigid code by a program usually known as an *assembler*. An assembler is provided by the computer manufacturer—it is regarded nowadays as part of the standard software that every machine must have. In the early days, computers did not have facilities for assembling symbolic languages like the one we have been describing, and users were obliged to write programs in something closely resembling the machine's own internal binary code. With the provision of symbolic assembly languages, incorporating mnemonic function codes and permitting the use of alphabetic names, the task of programming has become a great deal easier; what is more important, the number of opportunities for making errors has been reduced.

The principal functions of an assembler may be set out as follows—

1. to distinguish the different fields of an instruction (label, arguments, function) from one another,
2. to convert mnemonic function codes into numeric codes,

3. to allocate store addresses to argument names, and to substitute addresses for names wherever they occur,
4. to replace labels by the addresses of the instructions they refer to,
5. to accept *preset data* (data included with the program) and, where necessary, convert it from decimal to binary radix,
6. to allocate space for variable data (data that will ultimately be generated by the program, or will be read into the store under the control of the program),
7. to recognize *system names*, and convert them to numeric codes,
8. to detect errors in syntax.

The term *system name* requires explanation. When specifying input and output operations in our language, we used the function TFER in conjunction with names such as CR (card reader) and LP (line printer). CR and LP are called system names, since their significance is pre-determined by the system. They must not be used for any purposes other than those pre-assigned to them. The jump conditions (NEG, ZERO, etc.) are treated as system names when they appear as the first argument in jump instructions, though, depending on how the assembler is written, they may not be so treated when they appear in another context. Function names may or may not be treated as system names (again depending on the way the assembler is written), and the names of certain subroutines provided by the system may also be treated as system names.

SYNTAX

The assembler will treat as a syntactic error any attempt to use a system name in the wrong context for instance, the attempt to use LP as an input device. Syntactic errors arise through applying the rules incorrectly, or through ignoring them: there is nothing that can be done at the assembly stage to correct errors arising from applying the right rules to do the wrong things.

It is a common characteristic of symbolic assembly languages, such as the one we have been postulating, that one symbolic instruction is converted into one binary machine instruction; indeed, the need to do this may often impose constraints and peculiarities upon the syntax of the symbolic language. The reason for a one-to-one correspondence between symbolic instructions and machine instructions is that this makes the assembler itself a good deal simpler; the separate fields of the instruction can be translated into machine code in strict rotation, each giving rise to a predetermined code in a predetermined place in the machine program. This is not to say, though, that the form of the instruction itself does not undergo a complete change; for instance, the positions of the fields relative to one another may change in translation. Again, we have provided a relative form of jump in our symbolic language; but there may not be a relative jump in the machine language. In a case like this, the assembler would have to calculate a label address and insert it in place of the relative literal. In our symbolic language, we have used the same mnemonic functions to denote the same operations, whether the argument is literal or variable. But the machine processes involved in the two cases are rather different, and a machine would probably provide two, or even more, different function codes, from which the assembler would have to select the correct one according to the form of the symbolic instruction. Some literals might be too long to fit into an instruction in machine code. In this case the assembler would have to store the literal in some convenient location and put the address of this location in the instruction instead.

RELOCATABLE PROGRAMS

Some programs, particularly those written for larger machines, are required to be *relocatable*. That is to say, it must be possible for them to be obeyed from any place in the store. The principal reason for this is that larger computers are generally multi-programmed—their stores can contain two or more programs at the same time. We shall see in Chapter 14 why this is desirable; but for the present we shall note simply that a consequence of this is that the programmer cannot know, when he is writing a program, just where that program will eventually repose in the store. If this were not so, the system would be most inflexible, for it would often be necessary to exclude a program from the store because another program was occupying part of its territory. It is perfectly possible in a multi-programming system for a program to be in a different place in the store every time it is obeyed.

Actual addresses, then, cannot normally be inserted into the program until the moment when it is actually being loaded into the store preparatory to being obeyed. In some systems the Assembler assembles programs direct into the store: in others it assembles them on some peripheral device, from which they are subsequently loaded by another program (often appropriately called the *Loader*). The only exception to the ban on the programmer's use of absolute addresses is the set of index registers, which, at least from his point of view, always occupy the same region of store. In more sophisticated systems, programs are *dynamically relocatable*. This means that they can be moved from place to place in the store while they are being obeyed. We can see how useful such a feature might be by looking at Fig. 6.1. In the first diagram, the store contains three programs, A, B, and C, leaving a small unused region at the end.

In the second diagram, program B has finished, and has been deleted. At this point it is desired to load a new program, D. This is too big to occupy the space left by B; but, by relocating C, it is possible to make a space big enough to accommodate it (third diagram). We shall explain in Chapter 14 how dynamic relocation can be achieved. At this stage it must suffice to point out that, where dynamic relocation exists, absolute addresses cannot be finally formed until just before an instruction is actually obeyed.

DIRECTIVES

Now, if an assembler is to do its job properly, the programmer must provide it with certain fundamental pieces of information: he must tell it when he wishes it to assemble instructions and when

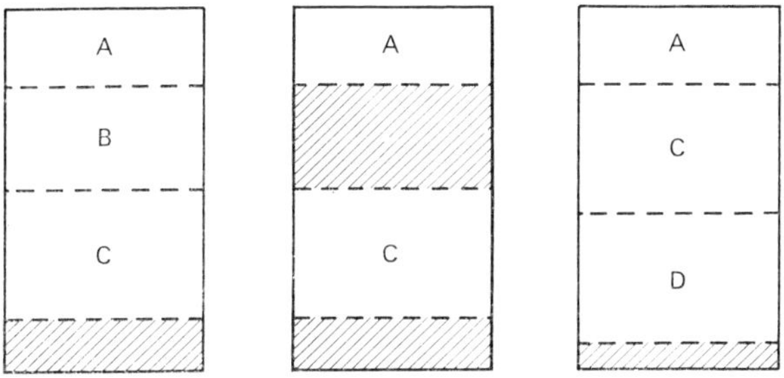

FIG. 6.1. Dynamic Relocation

to accept data, since there is nothing inherent in the form of an instruction that distinguishes it from any other arbitrary string of characters. The assembler must be told, too, when numeric data has to be converted into binary radix and when it should be treated simply as a string of characters; and it must be told how much space to leave for variable data.

For clarity we have been writing each one of our instructions on a separate line. When preparing programs on paper tape, which is done on a typewriter with a tape-punching attachment, it would be natural to terminate every instruction with a newline code (00001010), which returns the carriage and feeds to the next line. The assembler could then use the newline character as an indication that an instruction was complete. We shall also suppose that the newline character is used to separate pieces of preset data, though many assemblers permit the use of an alternative terminating symbol, such as a comma. When programs are prepared initially on punched cards, it is usual to move to a new card for each new instruction or piece of data.

To indicate to our assembler that a sequence of lines are to be assembled as instructions, we shall use the word PROGRAM;

and we shall use the words DATA and NUMERIC to preface pieces of preset data, NUMERIC being used when the data is to be converted from decimal to binary. The words PROGRAM, DATA, and NUMERIC used in this way are known as *directives;* in effect they are instructions to the assembler to carry out particular processes. To make it easier for the assembler to distinguish between directives and ordinary names, we shall preface every directive with the symbol @. This means that it will be possible to use the names DATA, NUMERIC, and PROGRAM without the symbol @ as ordinary names, but that @DATA, @NUMERIC and @PROGRAM are reserved for use as directives. Indeed, to make the assembler's work a little easier still, we shall make the rule that @ must not be used in any sense other than to introduce a directive. (This is unlikely to cause much pain.) All directives will be terminated by a newline, or will be punched on a separate card. Pieces of preset data will be enclosed in literal marks and preceded by the name by which they will be referred to, thus—

```
@NUMERIC
COUNT '135'
@DATA
DATE '14/JUL/1789'
TEXT 'THE QUEEN WAS IN THE PARLOUR'
```

We shall also use @NUMERIC to introduce sets of preset numbers. In this case, the individual items will be separated by commas, and the set itself will be terminated with a newline, thus—

```
@NUMERIC
PRIMES '3, 5, 7, 11, 13, 17, 19'
```

In cases where there are too many items to fit on to a single card, it is usual to punch a *continuation* symbol and continue on the next card.

VARIABLE DATA

Data introduced by @DATA and @NUMERIC are preset data, that is, their value is already known when the program is written. The assembler must also be able to allocate space for data that will be generated or read in subsequently. We shall suppose that the assembler does this automatically for single items whenever it encounters their names; but for *sets* of items, to which access is normally made by modification through a name attached to the first item, we must have a special directive. For this, we shall use the directive @SPACE, which will be followed, by a number of names, each on a separate line, with the number of items in the set in brackets. To distinguish between word sets and byte sets, we shall distinguish the latter by a solidus /.

```
@SPACE
ACCOUNT (43)
KEY (26/)
PRODUCT (2)
```

We shall also suppose that our assembler is written in such a way that the directive @SPACE clears the areas of store it allocates, making all word items zero and all byte items, space characters.

Directives can be defined to provide the user with quite powerful facilities: for instance, he can be given the power to define one piece of preset data from another, or he can make two or more names refer to the same set—as might be necessary if two or more programmers had collaborated, with insufficient liaison between them, to write one program, and had used different names for the same thing. Directives can also be provided to define sub-sets from larger sets. It is important to appreciate, however, that the influence of assembly directives only extends over the period when a program is actually being assembled. If two items are defined initially so that they have the same value, this does not mean that they will necessarily remain equal during the whole time the program is being obeyed. Notice too, that there is a clear difference between making two names refer to items with the same initial values, and making two names equivalent, that is, making them both refer to the same item throughout.

PROGRAM NAME

For our present purposes, we shall recognize only three more directives. The first is intended to allow the user to attach a name to his program, so that he can refer to it on future occasions. For this purpose we shall use the directive @NAME.

```
@NAME
FILEUPDATE
```

will attach the name FILEUPDATE to the program that follows it. By convention, we shall always make @NAME the first directive; it will then have the additional purpose of calling the assembler into operation. In subsequent references to a program, the name must appear exactly as it appeared under the directive @NAME. The same name spelt wrongly, or with an extra space inserted (e.g, FILE UPDATE) will be treated as an entirely different name. Computers only deal in identities; they cannot recognize similarities, however close.

COMMENTS

Several assemblers permit the user to insert comments of his own into the program to help him and others to follow what is going on. The assembler does not store comments with the program: their purpose is simply to clarify the program in its printed form. They are introduced by a special directive, for example—

```
@COMMENT
THE SUBROUTINE THAT FOLLOWS IS INTENDED
TO CONVERT DATA INTO A FORM SUITABLE
FOR OUTPUT ON A LINE PRINTER.
```

Finally, we must have some way of telling the assembler when to stop assembling. We shall do this with the directive @END. It is important to be clear about the difference between this and the instruction STOP, which is an instruction to the machine to cease obeying a program. @END is a directive to the assembler to cease assembly, and it may in fact be implemented by a jump to a STOP instruction by the assembler. The directive @END may also be used to give a temporary pause in assembly, in order, for example, to allow more data to be loaded. In this case, the program would have to be restarted by the operator. Restarting is dealt with in the next chapter.

To illustrate the foregoing points, let us have an example—

```
@NAME
CARDSELECT
@COMMENT
THIS PROGRAM READS 100 CARDS AND PRINTS
THE CONTENTS OF ALL THOSE WHOSE FIRST
COLUMN IS A £ SIGN. PRINTOUT IS PRECEDED
BY A HEADING.
@DATA
HEADING 'CARDS STARTING WITH A £'
@NUMERIC
COUNT '100'
@SPACE
CARD (80/)
@PROGRAM
LP           TFER    HEADING
2            MOVE    COUNT
CARD         TFER    CR
CARD         TSUB    '36'
@COMMENT
£ CODE IS DECIMAL 36.
@PROGRAM
NZERO        J       '2'
LP           TFER    CARD
1            CTJ     '– 4'
             STOP
@END
```

The perceptive reader will have noticed that this program forces the card reader to delay its next transfer until the printer has completed its last transfer. This is not the most efficient way to operate these devices, and we shall take up this point again in Chapter 13; meanwhile, since our present concern is with the form of the program rather than its content, we shall let it stand. The order in which the directives appear is important: those defining data must precede the directive @PROGRAM so that the assembler can interpret the instructions containing set names (HEADING, CARD) correctly, and not treat them as single items. Directives introduced in the wrong order would be treated as errors by the assembler.

SEGMENTATION

Commercial programs usually run to several thousand instructions, and are often the result of collaboration between several programmers, who are each made responsible for one or more *segments*. The program is split into segments in such a way that each segment can be written, and as far as possible tested, independently of the others. The same segment may be incorporated in two or more different programs if it carries out a common procedure. Some assembly systems preserve the structural features of a segmented program: others consolidate all segments to produce a working program that might appear to have been written all in one piece.

One advantage of preserving a segmented structure is that a segment can the more easily be corrected or amended without disturbing the rest of the program; another is that segments not in constant use can be transferred to backing store to leave more room in the working store for the rest of the program. A third advantage of segmentation is that names can be made local to the segment in which they appear; this means that programmers do not continually have to be looking over one another's shoulders to make sure that they are not using the same names to denote different things. The localization of names also means that common names such as COUNT can be used without the fear that their values might be changed by instructions written by another programmer.

LOCAL AND GLOBAL NAMES

It should go without saying, that the various segments of a program must be able to communicate with one another; that is, they must be able to call one another, and refer to common data. Consequently it follows that there must be some names in the program that are regarded as *global*, rather than local to one segment. For a fully consolidated system this imposes no problem; ultimately there is only one segment, and *local* and *global* become the same thing. Systems that retain a segmented structure solve the problem of *globalization* in several different ways. To illustrate one way it can be done, we shall rewrite our program CARDSELECT in three segments, one for input, one for output, and one to do the actual processing. Although the example we are giving is rather trivial, the reader will probably be able to imagine a practical program with the same basic structure as this, but in which input involves a good deal of data conversion and checking, output some complicated editing procedures, and processing a lot more than merely testing for the appearance of a £ sign.

We shall continue to use the directive @PROGRAM to introduce sequences of instructions; but we shall introduce a new directive, @SEGMENT, to introduce each segment in turn. Segments include, of course, not only instructions but also local data. A new directive, @GLOBAL, introduces global names. Since the names in a segment are normally lost as soon as the segment has been assembled, the directive @GLOBAL must appear before the first segment in which a global name appears. The global names in this example are mostly labels; but there is one data set. Notice that @GLOBAL merely introduces names; it does not define in any way what they

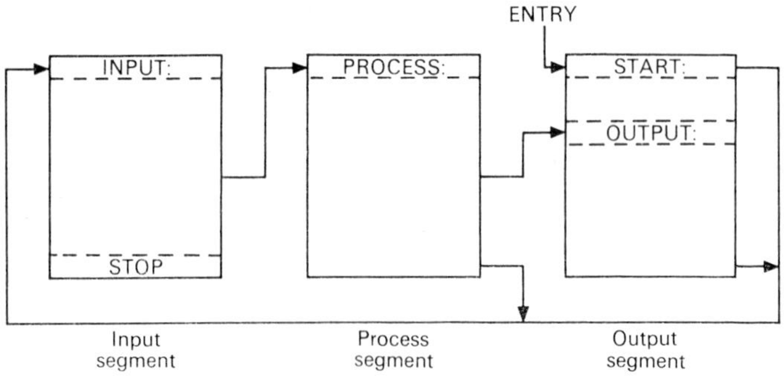

FIG. 6.2. Structure of SEGCARDSELECT

mean. The structure of the program is shown in Fig. 6.2; in full it is—

```
@NAME
SEGCARDSELECT
@GLOBAL
INPUT1, INPUT2, START, OUTPUT, PROCESS,
CARD
@SEGMENT
```

```
            @COMMENT
            READS 100 CARDS
            @NUMERIC
            COUNT '100'
            @SPACE
            CARD (80/)
            @PROGRAM
INPUT 2:    COUNT            SUB      '1'
            POS              J        '2'
                             STOP
INPUT 1:    CARD             TFER     CR
                             J        PROCESS
            @SEGMENT
            @COMMENT
            PRINTS HEADING AND SELECTED CARDS
            @DATA
            HEADING 'CARDS STARTING WITH £'
            @PROGRAM
START:      LP               TFER     HEADING
                             J        INPUT1
OUTPUT:     LP               TFER     CARD
                             J        INPUT2
            @SEGMENT
            @COMMENT
            SELECTS CARDS STARTING WITH £
            @PROGRAM
PROCESS:    CARD             TSUB     '36'
            ZERO             J        OUTPUT
                             J        INPUT2
            @END
```

Segmentation has made the program a great deal more involved; but the same thing might be said of any job that has been reorganized so that it can be shared between three people. We have had to introduce five labels with global significance, to provide entries at the right points to the three segments, and we have introduced several unconditional jumps for transferring control from one segment to another. The global area CARD is defined in the input segment because this comes first; but it could have been defined in any segment if they had been put in a different order. To simplify the procedure, we have not used an index register for counting, since it would have had to have been dumped for safety on entering a new segment, as no programmer can know how the writers of the other segments are going to use the index registers. In fact it is usual practice to use index registers only for transitory data, and not to carry them across from one entry of a segment to the next.

It is important to appreciate the distinction between *segments* and *subroutines*. The most important difference lies in the local significance of names; names in a subroutine are not necessarily hidden from the rest of the program, though this will happen if a subroutine occupies a complete segment. Subroutines, as their name implies, occupy a subordinate position to a master program. When a subroutine has finished its work, it usually hands control straight back to the part of the program that called it (either the master program or a subroutine standing above it in the hierarchy). Segments can have equal status, and in general they can hand control from one to the other in any order, as in our example. However, some segmentation schemes do require one segment to be designated as the master segment, and require control always to be transferred through it; such an arrangement can lead to faster programs and a simpler assembler, since some of the mechanism devised for subroutines can be made use of for handling segments.

One further point: the existence of global names would appear to vitiate the principle of independence of the segments, for altering the address of a global name in one segment would seem to involve searching through all the other segments for references to the same address and altering those too. Now it is not always possible to do this, since addresses often do not exist until after an instruction has been modified. The simplest solution to the problem is to re-assemble the whole program after a modification has been made to any one of its segments; but there is another solution, and that is to keep somewhere an index of global addresses. Instructions referring to global addresses can then be made to operate by replacement through the appropriate entry in this list. Such a scheme might mean that there were some functions that could not operate on global addresses, since some functions might not be able to operate on replaced arguments. However, if such an arrangement can be adopted, it enables a segment to be altered without affecting anything outside it other than, possibly, the index of global addresses. Moreover, it is not necessary for the programmer even to know of the existence of such an index, since it can be handled entirely by the assembler.

As well as assembling written instructions, assemblers usually permit the user to incorporate within his program utility subroutines written and supplied by the manufacturer. These can be of three types, which we shall refer to here as *macros*, *system codes*, and *library subroutines*. Unfortunately, these terms are used rather loosely in fact, so the reader must not be surprised to find the same terms used in senses different from those given here, or to find different terms used to denote the same concepts. The science of computers is very new, and its terminology still in a state of flux.

MACRO-FUNCTIONS

Macros (in full, *macro-codes* or *macro-functions*) are open subroutines, often as short as two or three instructions. The programmer calls them simply by writing a single instruction, which is subsequently converted by the assembler into as many instructions as are necessary to perform the operation. An example should make this clear; the pair of instructions—

X	MOVE	X
ZERO	J	LABEL

together cause a jump to LABEL if X is zero. There is no single function in our imaginary machine that does this; but we might decide to represent an operation as common and useful as this by a macro of the form—

X	JZERO	LABEL

If the Assembler had been written to accept the macro-function JZERO, it would replace this single instruction by the pair of ordinary instructions we have written above, which together perform the operation desired. Since the assembler would be replacing one written instruction by two, it would also have to adjust any relative jumps that jumped over it.

Since macros do not get converted directly into machine instructions, they are not necessarily obliged to follow the normal instruction format exactly; in particular, they need not be confined to only two arguments. The two instructions—

X	TSUB	Y
ZERO	J	SUBR

would jump to a subroutine label SUBR if X and Y were equal. They might therefore be represented by a three-argument macro of the form—

X	JEQ	Y, SUBR

where a comma is being used to separate the second and third arguments.

Most systems provide a set of standard macros, of which the examples given here may be regarded as typical. It is usual also for the user to be given the opportunity to write his own macros, usually with the aid of a special directive. The directive is followed by the name of the macro, a list of its arguments, and the instructions that compose it. For instance, a macro MAX might be defined as follows—

```
@MACRO
(MAX, X, A, N, B)
X          MOVE   '0'
X + 1      MOVE   'N'
B          MOVE   '0'
B          TSUB   A(X)
POS        J      '2'
B          MOVE   A(X)
X          CTJ    '– 3'
```

This macro places the largest member of a list A of N items into location B, and uses index registers X (for modification) and X + 1 (for counting). It is called by writing a statement of the usual form, whit parameters written in the same order as they appear in the macro definition. For instance, if we wished to use this macro to find the largest member, LGST, of a set LIST consisting of 135 items, using index registers 3 and 4, we should write—

```
3          MAX    LIST, 135, LGST
```

The arguments in the macro-instruction then replace the corresponding symbols in the definition, which have only local significance. Of course, the same end could have been achieved by writing and calling a subroutine in the normal way; but macros are easier to use because the parameter hand-over is carried out automatically by the assembler. This is possible because a macro is an *open* subroutine: it is repeated once for every time it is used, and the actual arguments can be different on each occasion.

SYSTEM CODES

System codes, in contrast to macros, are *closed* subroutines. They are held permanently in store (working store or backing store), and they are not incorporated into the program but are called in much the same way as any other closed subroutine. However, as with a macro, the calling process is that of writing what is to all appearances an ordinary instruction. The commonest system codes are those used for controlling peripheral equipment; the function TFER would be rendered in practice as a system code. This is because the control of peripheral devices is, as we shall see later, a fairly complex procedure. As well as sending control signals to the device to operate switches and actuate solenoids, the system centre must carry out a whole series of checks and must make entries in tables in store. System codes are provided so that the user does not have to burden himself with a lot of additional, and largely repetitive, work, and so that he has less opportunity to make errors, which, in this case, might seriously damage the program.

Subroutines representing system codes are called in either of two ways. In some systems an instruction such as—

```
DATA            TFER    CR
```

containing a system code, is actually obeyed as if it were a special sort of subroutine jump. The addresses DATA and CR are stored in pre-arranged locations, and a link is set that will eventually be used for returning control to the main program. The procedure is carried out entirely automatically when the program is running, the assembler having treated the system code in the same way as an ordinary instruction, replacing the mnemonic by a numeric code, and the arguments by the corresponding addresses. System codes dealt with in this way are sometimes called *extracodes.*

The other way of dealing with system codes is for the assembler to convert them into a standard calling sequence, such as—

```
1               MOVE    'PLIST'
PLIST           MOVE    'DATA'
PLIST + 1       MOVE    'CR'
PLIST + 2       J       TFER
```

Naturally in this case anything of value in register 1 must first be dumped. (The programmer who has read his manual properly will know which registers are likely to be over-written when a system code is called.) In some machines, dumping and restoring are avoided by providing a special set of index registers specially for the use of system codes.

An interesting application of macros and system codes arises when a manufacturer offers a series of compatible machines—a set of machines of different sizes capable of accepting the same programs. Some of the functions built into the more expensive machines of the range can be provided in the cheaper machines at very little cost by means of macros or system codes. Naturally they will operate much more slowly than if they had been built in; but that is only what is to be expected of a cheaper machine. Functions often handled in this way are multiplication, division, and radix conversion.

LIBRARY SUBROUTINES

Library subroutines are subroutines of quite general usefulness, which are supplied by the computer manufacturer. They include procedures for evaluating common mathematical functions, for editing input and output data, and for doing common commercial jobs such as calculating tax. They are normally held on some file device while the program is being assembled, and those that are required are added on at the end of the assembly process. Since they are actually incorporated into the program (sometimes as an additional segment) the library medium can be detached from the computer when assembly is complete.

In some systems, library subroutines are called in a similar way to system codes—by writing special functions, which the assembler converts into subroutine calls: in other systems, the programmer is obliged to write his own calling sequence, as he would have had to do had he written the subroutine himself. There is no difference in principle between library subroutines and the user's own. Some systems even allow the user to add subroutines of his own to the library.

MINIMUM MACHINE CONFIGURATION

One final point on assemblers: an assembler is a fundamental part of a computer system, as necessary as the hardware itself, and it sets a minimum limit to the size of a computer configuration. In general, a computer used for assembly must have—

- enough store to hold the assembler and its working space,
- an input device for the symbolic program,
- an output device for the assembled program (the medium must also be suitable for re-input),
- an input device for the subroutine library,
- an output device for recording errors.

A typical minimum configuration might therefore be, a card reader (program and data input), two magnetic-tape units (assembled output and re-input, and library), and a line printer (error printing).

An assembler such as we have been describing would probably require between 4,000 and 8,000 instructions, occupying more store possibly than the assembled programs themselves might require. The size of an assembler can naturally be reduced by reducing the number of facilities offered; but it is doubtful whether a lower cost of storage really offsets the increased costs incurred by programmers working with curtailed facilities. Nevertheless, manufacturers often offer a choice of two or more assemblers. The alternative solution, that of offering small users assembly facilities on a larger bureau machine, does not seem to have found much favour.

SUMMARY

In this chapter we have been devising a language for communicating not directly with a computer but with an assembly program controlling it. This new language consists of a number of directives, each occupying a line of its own and followed by a definition or by a set of data. The directives we have introduced are—

@COMMENT	introduces a comment.
@DATA	introduces a list of names, each one followed by a string of text in quotes.
@END	terminates assembly.
@GLOBAL	introduces a list of global names.
@MACRO	introduces a list of parameters in brackets, then a sequence of instructions.
@NAME	calls the assembler into operation and defines the program name.
@NUMERIC	introduces names and values of data for radix conversion.
@PROGRAM	introduces instructions for assembly.
@SEGMENT	introduces a new segment.
@SPACE	requests space for sets whose names and sizes follow. A solidus indicates a byte set.

EXERCISES 6

1. Rewrite CARDSELECT to deal with any number of cards, the number to appear in the first four columns of a special card placed at the top of the stack.
2. Rewrite SEGCARDSELECT on the basis of one master and two subsidiary segments. Make the processing segment the master by writing it first, and assume that control is initially passed to the first instruction written. Control must always be passed to or from the master segment.
3. Write a one-segment program for counting the numbers of A's, B's, C's, etc. in a stack of 100 cards, and printing the results on 26 separate lines. Assume all columns contain alphabetical punching.
4. The encoding example given in Chapter 4 can be regarded as a segment of a complete program. What directives would you expect to find associated with it? Which names would be most likely to be global?
5. Design a macro that will jump on the first appearance of a designated symbol in a string of text, and will not jump if the symbol does not appear.
6. Use the macro designed in Exercise 5 above in a sequence of instructions intended to replace all the spaces in a text of 120 characters by hyphens (space = 32, hyphen = 45).

7. *How Programs are Run and Checked*

HAVING assembled our program, we shall want to bring it into operation. Some assemblers assemble programs direct into store; but this is possible only when there is enough store to hold both the assembler and the whole of the program that is being assembled. Consequently it is more usual for the program to be assembled on to some file device, and subsequently loaded into the store in place of the assembler when this has completed its work. Naturally there must be a program to control the loading process, and this must be a permanent program, since it has to be in the store at the same time as the program it is loading.

THE CONTROL PROGRAM

The Loader could, if we wished, be a separate program; but loading is so intimately bound up with a lot of other processes that go on both before and during a program run that it is more convenient to make the loader a segment of a much more extensive permanent program. Every system has a different name for this permanent program.* We shall call it simply the *Control Program.* It will include, as well as the Loader, all the subroutines that deal with peripheral devices—not only the system subroutines that call them into operation but also the subroutines that perform the operations that are necessary after a transfer has been completed. The Control Program will also include sequences of instructions that will make it possible for a human operator to communicate with the machine and influence the work it does, and sequences of instructions that will enable the operator to monitor the course of a program and find out what stage it has reached.

The Control Program is held permanently in the working store—at least the kernel of it is held there; many systems permit segments of the Control Program to be packed away on backing store temporarily when they are not required. Because of its permanence, the Control Program can almost be regarded as if it were part of the

* Executive, Supervisor, Monitor, etc.

hardware; indeed some of the things it does were done on the earliest machines by specially designed hardware.

The reader may have been prompted to ask the chicken-egg question, how does the Control Program get into the store in the first place, before there is a loader to load it? Three techniques have been used. The first is to put the store temporarily into another computer, copy the program into it from the other computer's own store, and then transfer it bodily into the new machine. The second, and commonest, is to provide a special piece of hardware to control the reading of the program from a selected peripheral device. The program must be on the selected device in binary form, that is, as an exact image of the way it will appear in the store eventually, since any translation or interpretation of the input medium would unnecessarily complicate the hardware unit. A variant on this technique is to read a special loader into the machine in this way, and use that to load the Control Program proper. A third technique is known as *bootstrapping* (from the idea of lifting oneself by one's own bootstraps). It consists in using a set of key switches (such a set is usually provided for use by maintenance engineers) to feed into the store enough instructions to enable a few more instructions in binary image to be read from a selected peripheral device. These in turn are used to read more instructions, this time in a form a little closer to the normal assembly language. This step-by-step process continues until enough instructions have been assembled to read the rest of the Control Program punched in the normal way. Bootstrapping avoids the need to translate large pieces of program into binary image; but nowadays it is more likely to be used in connection with small special-purpose, or experimental, machines.

PANEL CONSOLES

The normal sequence of events with a program is assemble—load—run; or, to be more precise, load assembler—run assembler—load object program—run object program. It would be quite possible to build this sequence into the system so that it was carried out automatically at the touch of a button. In fact this is just what was done in the earliest computers. The assembler was loaded on to a specified peripheral device, or kept permanently on backing store, and a key marked *start*, or some such legend, was operated. The program to be assembled was then loaded on to a peripheral unit and, sometimes with, sometimes without a second operation of the key, the program was assembled, loaded, and obeyed. The *run* operation was normally initiated by a special directive at the end of the program. A similar system obtains on many of the smallest computing systems today. The operator controls the operation through the medium of an operating panel carrying a number of switches, most of which are for the use of the maintenance engineers. To make the system a little more flexible, the programmer is permitted to terminate his program with special codes that specify how it is to be run.

Systems controlled from an operating-panel type of console must be used according to a small number of rigid conventions. But, in practice, a number of variations on the simple basic sequence of operations is desirable. The assembler may be held permanently on backing store, or it may have to be read from one of several peripheral devices; the object program may initially be on one of several media, too. Besides, there are many other pieces of information that may have to be fed into the machine along with the program. Therefore there should in general be some means whereby a human operator can communicate directly with the Loader and with the rest of the Control Program.

TYPEWRITER CONSOLES

The most convenient device for communication between a human being and a digital system is an electric typewriter. It is a two-way device, permitting messages to be passed in either direction, and it produces a printed log of everything that has occurred. This last feature is of great help in tracing what has happened if a run has been faulty, and also in giving exact times so that charges for using the computer and its peripheral equipment can be made equitably. It is common practice to fit the typewriter with a two-colour ribbon, and to arrange for messages passing in and out to be typed in different colours.

COMMAND DIRECTIVES

Messages issued by the operator to the Control Program are called *commands*, or *command directives*. In our imaginary system, we shall preface commands with @, like ordinary directives; though it is important to bear in mind that ordinary directives are addressed to the *Assembler*, whereas commands are addressed to the *Control Program*. Before any others, we shall require a command that causes a program to be loaded, and another that causes control to be transferred to it; for these two purposes we shall use the commands @LOAD and @GO, each of which must be followed by the name of the program concerned. It will also be necessary to give with @LOAD the name of the device from which it is to be loaded, though, as we shall see, it will be possible to provide this same information in other ways.

The control Program should be organized in such a way that it will reply to the operator when it has completed the task of loading a program, and it must also reply when a program run has been completed.* We shall also arrange for the Control Program in our imaginary machine to print out the letters OK on the typewriter in confirmation that it has accepted a command and is able to carry it out. To assist the operator in logging the system's activities, it is common practice to arrange for the Control Program to print the time to the nearest second whenever it puts out a message. A typical typewriter record might then look something like this—

```
@LOAD ASSEMCRMT MT2
OK 10.54.16
ASSEMCRMT LOADED 10.55.08
@GO ASSEMCRMT
OK 10.59.22
ASSEMCRMT FINISHED 11.09.36
@LOAD UPDATE
OK 11.12.14
UPDATE LOADED 11.12.56
@GO UPDATE
OK 11.15.09
UPDATE FINISHED 11.38.17
```

Here we are loading an assembler ASSEMCRMT (which, as its name indicates, takes a program on cards and assembles it on to magnetic tape) and then using it to assemble a program UPDATE. The lines preceded by @ are commands; in practice, they might be in red, while the rest of the printing was in black (though naturally only the top copy would show colour differences). Notice that there is no need to specify where the program UPDATE is to be found; the Control Program will already have this information.

After the program UPDATE has been tested, and when all the errors in it are believed to have been corrected, it will probably be stored in assembled form with all the other working programs on a single magnetic tape. If it happened to be some way up this tape, the command—

```
@LOAD UPDATE
```

might take some time to complete. To save time, therefore, it might be worth while to anticipate the need for this program by typing the command—

```
@FIND UPDATE
```

* That is, when a STOP instruction is obeyed. This means, of course, that the STOP function must cause entry to the Control Program, in other words, it must be a system code.

some time before the program was actually required. The Control Program would then immediately reply OK, with the time, and proceed to search for it. Later it might type—

UPDATE CANTFIND

meaning that it had searched through all the likely tapes without finding it (probably because the operator had forgotten to mount the program tape on to a mechanism).

OPERATING INSTRUCTIONS

The operator who actually runs a program is most unlikely to be the same person who wrote it; consequently, since he will be quite ignorant of what it is that the program is supposed to do, he must be supplied with a detailed set of instructions on how to proceed. There is usually a *pro-forma* for this. The instructions for the assembly and running of UPDATE written out in full might conceivably be—

Use assembler ASSEMCRMT.
Load program cards UPDATE on CR.
While assembling, load magnetic tape MAINFILE and a scratch tape.
Load cards UPDATETEST.
Load program UPDATE and go.
If program fails, dump store on LP.
At end, label scratch tape MAINFILE and date it.

A scratch tape is a tape whose contents are no longer wanted, and which can therefore be used for recording new data. Notice that we have not specified which magnetic tape is to be mounted on which mechanism; most systems nowadays permit magnetic tapes to be mounted on any convenient mechanism. We shall show how this is possible when we discuss file devices in detail in Chapter 13.

OPERATOR ERRORS

The Control Program must not only be able to deal with the normal sequence of events; it must also be able to take appropriate action if the operator makes a mistake—if he forgets to load the cards into a card reader, for instance, or, having loaded them, forgets to switch the device on. The Control Program must also be able to report to the operator if it finds that a certain peripheral device is not operating as it should. The operator will then rectify the fault if he is able; if not, he will call for the assistance of an engineer. There is no need, by the way, for the Control Program to report the exact nature of a fault on a peripheral device, since the operator is perfectly cable of finding this out for himself by inspection. All peripheral devices have warning lamps to assist in locating faults.

To illustrate what might happen if things went wrong, here is the sort of record that might appear on the typewriter under less happy circumstances than before—

```
@LOAD ASSCRMT MT2
OK 10.53.16
ASSCRMT CANTFIND 10.55.08              1.
@LOAD ASSEMCRMT MT2
OK 10.58.22
ASSEMCRMT LOADED 10.58.54
@GO ASSEMCRMT
OK 11.00.01
CR FIX 11.00.04                        2.
ASSEMCRMT FINISHED 11.12.25
@LOD UPDATE
WHAT 11.14.41                          3.
@LOAD UPDATE
OK 11.16.27
UPDATE LOADED 11.17.04
@GO UPDATE
OK 11.18.44
MAINFILE CANTFIND                      4.
SCRATCH CANTFIND                       5.
@LOAD SORT
UPDATE BUSY 11.36.17                   6.
@FIND SORT
OK 11.37.23
CR FIX 11.55.52                        7.
UPDATE FINISHED 12.04.11
```

Here is a list of the mishaps as they occurred—

1. The operator typed ASSCRMT instead of ASSEMCRMT. Since there is no such program, the Control Program could not find it.
2. The operator failed to load the program cards.
3. The operator typed @LOD instead of @LOAD.
4. The operator forgot to load tape MAINFILE.
5. The operator failed to load a scratch tape.
6. The operator tried to load a new program, SORT, which the system could not accept. He therefore changed the command to @FIND.
7. A temporary jam developed on the card reader, which the operator was able to free.

In the examples we have given so far, the end of a command is signalled by a newline. A better arrangement is to have an *accept* button and a *cancel* button on the typewriter. When the operator is sure that he has not made a typing error, he presses the *accept* button, which causes the machine to act on the command. If he finds that he has made an error, he presses the *cancel* button and types again, thus—

@LOD UPDATE *cancel*
@LOAD UPDATE *accept.*

MULTIPLE ENTRY POINTS

The command @GO causes the object program to be entered. It would normally be entered at some place fixed by convention, such as the first instruction written. But it is often desirable to have a choice of starting points, so that the initial procedures can be adjusted to fit particular circumstances. For instance, it is sometimes necessary to re-start a program after a machine failure or after it has been temporarily supplanted by a more urgent program. It is possible to give a choice of starting points by adding a label on to the end of the @GO command: the format might be—

@GO UPDATE @AT RESTART

where RESTART is the label of the first instruction to be obeyed. If this were the whole story, though, the system would have to retain every label in alphabetic form after assembly had been completed, since any one might be used as a re-entry point. This would be impracticable on a small or medium-sized machine. To avoid this, a special assembly directive can be provided for nominating starting points; thus—

@ENTRY
START, RESTART, INPUT, TESTOUT

The @GO command could then take the form given above, or it could simply be made to refer to the position of the desired label in the list, thus—

@GO UPDATE @AT 2

in which case the system would not even have to retain the names of the entry labels.

Restart procedures are dealt with more fully in Chapter 13 .Another reason why it is advantageous to have a choice of starting points is that a program may sometimes be written in such a way that it can perform several different but closely similar jobs, such as processing data, from one of several different types of peripheral device. The starting point can then be chosen to determine the precise mode of operation.

When the system creates new data, for instance when it writes a new main file, it must have some way of indicating to the operator where he can find it. Sometimes this is obvious: in the last example, for instance, only one scratch tape was loaded, so this must have been used for writing the new main file. If the system has a choice, however, it must be able to type a message such as—

UPDATE MAINFILE ON MT3

where MT3 is the number allocated to the particular transport mechanism. This is its designation by the system, what is sometimes called its *geographical name;* it does not necessarily bear any relationship to the name by which the mechanism has been referred to in the program. In some simple operating systems, the converse requirement applies: the operator must have some direct way of informing the system where he has loaded a particular file. In most modern systems this is not necessary. The first block of information on every tape carries what is known as a *header*, which gives all the leading details about it. When the program calls for a particular file, the system searches through the headers on all the idle reels until it finds the one required. Headers are considered in more detail in Chapter 13.

PROGRAMMED MESSAGES

Several systems permit the programmer to have messages typed out at intervals during the run of the program. This can be achieved with the aid of an instruction of the form—

TYPE TEXT

which would cause the characters of the set TEXT to be displayed on the typewriter. The whole message might be—

UPDATE TYPE 04.15.23
LOAD NEXT CARD DECK NOW

The facility can be used to give the operator instructions, to report progress, and in many other ways.

JOB CONTROL

A computer can respond to a message almost instantaneously; but the same cannot be said of a human operator. When a message is typed for him to act upon, he may be busy with another job, or simply wool-gathering. When this happens, an expensive machine may be kept idle quite unnecessarily for several minutes, waiting, for example, for another command to be typed. It helps a little if the machine is fitted with an audible warning device to attract the operator's attention, and it helps still more if enough operators are available for one to be kept permanently at the console; but a better solution still is to make more of the machine's operation automatic. This can be done by supplying all the necessary commands in advance, right at the start; they could be punched on a short length of paper tape, or on a small stack of cards. Information supplied in this way is sometimes called *steering information.*

To go back to our original example, we might prepare a set of steering cards as follows—

```
@LOAD ASSEMCRMT
@GO ASSEMCRMT
@LOAD UPDATE
@GO UPDATE
@FINISH
```

These cards would be put in the card reader on top of the set of cards carrying the program, and they might be brought into control by means of a single type-writer command such as—

```
@STEER CR
```

The system would then respond with OK followed by a time check, and, if the Control Program had been written to do so, it would report each stage of the process as it was carried out, thus—

```
OK 10.53.16
ASSEMCRMT LOADED 10.53.48
ASSEMCRMT FINISHED 11.03.01
UPDATE LOADED 11.03.38
UPDATE FINISHED 11.28.22
```

with no unnecessary delays, provided that all the peripheral units required were loaded in time.

Obeying a program once, from entry to completion, is known as a *run.* A sequence of runs making up a single complete process is known as a *job.* For instance, in the last example we had a job consisting of two runs, assembly and updating. The information given on steering cards or tape is therefore a description of the whole job, and the cards that carry it, or the length of paper tape, are sometimes referred to as *job cards* or a *job tape.* In some operating systems the form taken by the job description may not be at all like a sequence of commands. For instance, in a job consisting of a card-input run, a sorting run, an updating run, and a printing run, all programs having already been assembled and stored on a program tape, the job description might be—

```
@JOB DAILYJOB
1 CARDIN
2 SORT3DECK
3 UPDATE
4 INVOICEPRINT
```

This might be brought into operation by a simple command such as—

```
@GO DAILYJOB
```

The system would then take over, issuing periodic instructions to the operators to load various peripheral units with the data it needs.

So far, in this chapter, we have been discussing what is known as the *operating system* of a computer. An operating system can be defined as the set of rules that has to be followed to make a system carry out a job. The same term is also used to denote the part of the Control Program concerned with getting programs running and controlling them when they are running. We have described here one particular type of operating system; but there are many others equally possible. In fact, in Chapter 14 we shall be discussing several more. Moreover, numerous variations are possible on the system we have described in this chapter. One acceptable reason for the differences between operating systems (there are many unacceptable ones) is that small cheap machines with small stores have not got the space to spare for elaborate control programs, whereas large expensive machines must have sophisticated operating systems so that the periods when expensive equipment is left idle are kept to a minimum. Thus we find that a series of computers, compatible in every other respect, may have very different operating systems.

PROGRAM DEVELOPMENT

It seldom happens—one might almost say, never—that a newly assembled program, or segment of a program, is free from error. Newly written programs, therefore, must first go through a period of development. (In programmers' jargon, they must be *debugged*, or in America, *checked out*.) The sort of mistakes that are made when a flow diagram is being translated into a sequence of instructions seldom cause a machine to give wrong answers; they are much more likely to cause the program to be suspended altogether because it is being asked to do impossible things. A common sort of error is one that makes the machine 'run out of program', that is, jump to a piece of data and try to obey it as if it were a sequence of instructions.

Even if the first word or two have some meaning as instructions, sooner or later the control will encounter an illegal function code, that is, one to which no meaning has been allocated, or an address that lies outside the range of the store. Conditions such as these are detected by the hardware, which then passes control to the Control Program for appropriate action to be taken. This might be to type a message such as—

UPDATE FAILED 03.45.17

leaving the operator to decide what further action to take.

LOOP STOPS

If an arbitrary error does not cause a program to be suspended, it is quite likely to cause a *loop stop*, that is, a loop closed by a jump depending on a condition that is always true, and which consequently cannot be escaped from. Similar in its effect to a loop stop is a counting loop that is trying to count down from such a high number that it would take hours, or even days, to finish. For instance, this sequence—

```
6       MOVE   '0'
SUM     MOVE   LIST(5)
5       CTJ    '– 1'
```

contains a loop that must be cycled 2^{32} times. Even at a loop time of one millionth of a second it would take more than an hour to complete.

It is not easy to detect loop stops directly. If the program is fairly short, a time limit can be set within which it should have finished its work, and the Control Program can be made to suspend it if it exceeds this time. If it is a long program, it can be made to report progress at intervals; otherwise the programmer has to rely on the experience of the operator, who can often tell from the appearance of indicator lights, and other signs, whether a program is running as it should. Sometimes a loop stop is indicated when a peripheral device unaccountably stops running, the instruction that operates it being outside the loop. Some machines incorporate an audible device that can be used to listen to the 'heart-beat' of some functional unit; a continuous tone on such a device often indicates a loop stop.

POST-MORTEM DUMP

It is comparatively easy to detect the *presence* of an error in a program. What is much more difficult is to discover precisely where it lies. In the early days of computers, a programmer was able to sit at the console of the machine and run through the suspect parts of his program instruction by instruction, stopping after each to observe, on whatever monitoring device was available, exactly what effect it had produced. Nowadays there just is not enough machine time available in relation to the number of programmers for single-shot operation to be practicable. The programmer must do all his fault-finding at his own desk, with whatever information he can obtain after the faulty run. One useful source of information is a *post-mortem dump*, that is, a print-out of the whole content of the relevant part of the store. To be really useful, a dump of the store should show the parts of the store that contain instructions (or that should contain instructions) in instruction format, and the rest in numeric (decimal) or character form as appropriate. By comparing the dump with his original program, the programmer can get a good idea of what has gone wrong; though why it has gone wrong is more difficult to discover.

TRACING

By far the most useful aid to program development is a *trace*. This is a record of certain events as they happen during a program run, the particular events to be traced being selected in advance by the user, who can select various modes of tracing. For instance, a programmer might decide to trace all satisfied jumps; these would then be printed as they occurred, showing the addresses to which they actually jumped. With the aid of a trace, a programmer can follow more or less exactly the course of a program and determine when it went off the rails. Systems differ widely in the trace facilities they allow: some permit modes of tracing that record peripheral instructions; others provide special instructions that are inserted into the program simply to provide tracing points. A trace is usually brought into operation either by a special command or by a special entry in the job description. Some systems also permit tracing to be specified by a directive on assembly.

The program that controls the trace is not usually part of the Control Program, but a program introduced into the store specially. This means that the maximum size of program that can be traced is a little smaller than the maximum size that can be run. Another and more important disadvantage of tracing is that a program in a tracing mode runs more slowly, sometimes at only a fraction of its natural speed. In the worst case, the program controlling a trace has to scrutinize every instruction in turn as it is obeyed, though in more up-to-date systems it is the hardware control that causes entry to the trace program whenever control is passed to an instruction that may have to be traced. In some systems the assembler inserts special tracing instructions into the program to provide entry to the trace program at appropriate points. In such systems, the program may have to be assembled again without the tracing instructions when it has passed the final test.

In the days when programmers could trace their own programs manually from the console of the machine, facilities were provided for modifying the program in store. Nowadays the program is generally altered in its original form, by repunching cards or paper tape, and re-assembling it for its next run. Of late, however, the wheel seems to have come a full circle, and systems are being developed in which the programmer is once more in direct communication with the computer. This means that once more it will be possible to make corrections to programs *in situ*.

If a program gives a wrong answer instead of just stopping, it usually means that there was an error in the original conception, in the fundamental logical flow on which the thing was based. It may have overlooked some special circumstance, or made some invalid assumption. When programs are tested, therefore, the data used should if possible be such that the results of the run are already known. If this is not possible, a routine can sometimes be written to check the results, for example by substituting solutions in original equations and testing for equality. Before testing a commercial program, it is often possible to process some data by hand to serve as a check; also, a computer system can be made to run for a while in parallel with the manual system it will eventually replace, the outputs of the two systems being checked against one another. Naturally, test data must be chosen very carefully, so that every routine in the program is tested in as many different circumstances as possible; nevertheless, in spite of the most careful precautions, it often happens that some unforeseen circumstance crops up, often after the program has been running correctly for some time, to cause it to give an incorrect result. There is no point at which a program can definitely be said to be correct; programs must be thought of as organic things that go on developing throughout their lifetime. Computing is more a matter of subjective confidence than objective scientific certainty.

VERIFICATION OF DATA

Not only programs, but also the data they operate on, must be made as nearly accurate as human frailty and economic conditions will allow. It is common practice, in spite of the expense, to prepare punched cards and punched paper tape twice, comparing the results to eliminate errors. The comparison process is known as *verification*. Punched cards are produced on a key punch and are afterwards fed into a *verifier*. This is identical to a key punch, except that instead of punching holes in new cards the operator is checking the holes in cards that have already been punched. A wrongly punched card is rejected, and a new card is produced in its place, either on the verifier (which can generally be turned into a normal key punch by the operation of a lever) or elsewhere. A similar system is available for punched paper tape.

VALIDITY CHECKS

Verification is a good check against errors made by a punch operator; but it cannot check the accuracy of the original data that was presented to her. There are, however, certain safeguards that can be put into an input program to check the accuracy of the data; these are generally known as *validity checks*. The exact nature of validity checks must depend on exact details of the data to be used; but there are certain types of check that can be applied fairly generally. Numeric data, for instance, can be checked to make sure that it comes within a permitted range of likely values. When a series of numeric values is involved, they can be totalled, and their sum used as a check on their accuracy (even if, as a sum, it has no logical meaning). Another common type of check is to make sure that every field of the data contains the right type of information; some fields should be wholly numeric, others alphabetic, and others alpha-numeric, containing both numbers and letters. More sophisticated forms of checking can be used on data that has arisen as output of a mechanical system. For instance a hash sum can be made; this is a sum of all the pieces of data, regardless of their significance, treating them all as numbers. Such a sum has no meaning in itself other than as a unique check on the data it has been formed from. Hash sums are sometimes formed with end-around-carry; the sum is held to a standard length, and any digits that overflow from the more significant end are added in again at the other end. Validity checking is also referred to as *data vetting*.

SUMMARY

In this chapter we have been devising an operating system and, by way of illustration, we have proposed a two-way language for communication between the operator and a program, which we have referred to as the Control Program. It consists of a number of operator commands and a number of responses: the commands we have mentioned are—

@LOAD	load the program specified
@GO	enter the program specified
@FIND	locate the specified program preparatory to subsequent loading
@AT	used optionally after @GO to specify an entry point
@STEER	obey steering tape on specified device.

The responses we have mentioned are—

OK	command can be accepted and carried out
LOADED	program has been loaded
FINISHED	program has terminated
WHAT	command meaningless
CANTFIND	program or file cannot be located
BUSY	command cannot be accepted because system is occupied with another program
FIX	a peripheral device requires attention
TYPE	prefaces a message from an object program
FAILED	the program has failed.

Each of these replies is followed by a time check, and each is preceded by a program name, with the exception of FIX, which is preceded by a device name, and OK and WHAT, which stand alone.

We have suggested a form of steering input, with commands in their normal form, and terminated by @FINISH. We have also suggested a form of job description, preceded by the identifier @JOB, and carrying steering data in a more condensed form.

We have introduced into our assembly language one more function—

TYPE	type the text specified by the second argument,

and we have added one more assembly directive—

@ENTRY	introduces a list of entry labels.

EXERCISES 7

1. A data-processing job consists of a sorting run, in which a stack of punched cards is sorted on to a magnetic tape, followed by an updating run, in which the input data is used to update a single-reel file, producing at the same time a set of printed invoices. The programs are available, ready assembled, on a program tape. What record should you expect to find on the typewriter at the end of the job? (Assume that sorting takes 4 minutes and updating 27 minutes and 14 seconds.)

2. How would you prepare a set of steering cards to control the job in question 1?
3. Write down a set of instructions such as might be given to an operator when the job described in question 1 is to be run—

(*a*) with the operator controlling it direct,
(*b*) with the aid of steering information.

Assume that four tape transports are available.
4. A *report program* is a program used for extracting summary information from a file. Since a large variety of report programs may be needed, it is usual not to write them direct but to *generate* them as needed by a *report-program generator* in accordance with parameters supplied on, say, punched cards. What sort of record should you expect to find on the typewriter after a program REPGEN has been called from a library tape to generate a program REPORT, which in turn has been used to write summary information from a 2-reel file on a line printer?
5. How might the record in question 4 be affected if—

the operator forgot to load the parameter cards,
the operator forgot to load paper in the line printer,
the report program contained an instruction to type a message warning the operator in advance to load the next reel of the file?
6. A stack of cards is being read one by one into an area of store referred to as CARD. Write a sequence of instructions to check that—

(*a*) the first 5 columns contain a decimal integer below 50,000,
(*b*) the next 20 columns contain either alphabetic characters or spaces,
(*c*) the next 10 columns contain either alphabetic characters or numbers but no spaces.

8. *The System Centre*

THE process known as assembly involves translating instructions from the symbolic assembly code used by the programmer into a purely numeric code that the machine is able to interpret. In this chapter we shall be looking more closely at the method by which a computer obeys instructions, and we shall see some of the influences that engineering considerations have upon the aspect that the machine presents to the user.

MACHINE CODES

By way of illustrating some of the problems involved, let us first look at the form that a binary machine-code instruction must take. An instruction in our imaginary system comprises a function and two names, either or both of which may be modified. Since we have postulated eight index registers, we must allow three bits for specifying each modifier. For the function, we shall need at least six bits, giving up to sixty-four different functions (though by modern standards this is a bit meagre, especially if some system codes are to be accommodated as well). If we were intending to fit an instruction into a word, we should be left with only ten bits for each address. Since the addresses are intended to range over the whole store, and since our system allows us to address individual bytes, we should be limited to a store of only 1,024 bytes (256 words). On the other hand, if we decided to take two words for each instruction, we could increase the function to, say, eight bits and the addresses to twenty-five, giving a maximum store size of 33,354,432 bytes, which is more than lavish. Since arguments are often short literals or index registers, such long addresses would be wasteful of space.

We have chosen for our imaginary machine a *two-address*, or *two-argument*, language; that is to say, instructions in the language of our machine perform operations of the form—

$$A = A + B$$

in which there are two operands. A two-address language is quite convenient for expressing commercial procedures; though a *three-*

address language would be even more convenient, since it would enable more general operations such as—

$$A = B + C$$

to be expressed in single instructions. However, a three-address language would require even longer machine instructions, or else shorter addresses to fit into the same length of instruction. Moreover it would be even more wasteful of space, since the full three-address facilities are often not needed—the reader will probably have noticed that by far the most frequently used function is MOVE, which is two-address by nature. Here we see what is probably the fundamental problem of the computer designer: how to design an instruction format that will at one and the same time accommodate enough information for the longest instructions and avoid wasting space with the shortest instructions.

Several machines have been designed with *one-address* languages. In fact there is a second address (there must be, since most operations need two arguments) but this is supplied by convention, and is that of a special register usually referred to as an *accumulator*. This name arises because, following the grammar of the language, it is usually the most convenient location in which to accumulate totals. Most one-address functions are directed towards the accumulator, that is, addition is into the accumulator, and in subtraction it is the accumulator content that is diminished. Naturally, such a language must have at least one function directed in the opposite sense—to unload the accumulator. To perform a three-argument operation such as—

$$A = B + C$$

with a one-address language, it is necessary to write three instructions—

MOVE	B	B *to accumulator*
ADD	C	
STORE	A	*result to* A

One address languages are usually quite adequate for mathematical work—in fact they can improve the speed of computation, since intermediate results are not returned to store unless it is necessary; but a one-address language is more primitive, and therefore more tedious to use. It is particularly inconvenient for processing strings of bytes.

MULTIPLE ACCUMULATORS

It is possible to achieve a compromise between the one-address and two-address forms of organization by restricting one of the two addresses to a small range of registers while permitting the other to range over the whole store. A language that does this is sometimes referred to as a *one-and-a-half-address language*. It retains most of the advantages of a two-address language, while an instruction is nearly as compact as in a one-address language. It is the usual practice in languages of the one-and-a-half-address type to restrict the shorter address either to the index registers alone or to the index registers and a small group of other registers in the same region of the store. Registers in this restricted group are used in rather the same way as a one-address accumulator, and for this reason they are sometimes referred to as *multiple accumulators*.

It should be an aim in designing an instruction code to do so in such a way that programs occupy as little space as possible. This is not only because of the cost of storage; it is also because an instruction occupying two words generally takes twice as long to extract from the store as an instruction occupying only one word; furthermore, if an instruction can be reduced to only half a word, two can be extracted from the store in the same time. Now all instructions do not have the same information in them. An instruction such as—

```
3            MOVE    '0'
```

could be coded in many fewer bits than one like—

```
COST(3)      ADD     MARKUP(5)
```

Several systems recognize this fact by providing a choice of different instruction formats of two or three different lengths, for use in different circumstances. Thus no space is wasted by writing low-information instructions in long formats, and there is no necessity for high-information instructions to be mutilated to fit into a format too small for them.

Another way of providing different lengths of instruction is to use modifiers to extend the lengths of addresses. The instruction itself contains quite a short address: if the user wants access to a part of the store beyond the range of this address, he uses a modifier, which can be much longer. It is interesting to notice that an organizational feature such as this must have a profound effect on programming strategy, since, from the point of view of the user, the store is divided into two parts: a lower store that can be addressed directly, and an upper store that cannot be addressed except by modification, and for which a modifier must have previously been loaded into an index register.

DETACHED ADDRESSES

Some computers use a *detached-address* form of instruction. We have already seen that an instruction of the form—

0(3)	ADD	0(5)

takes its addresses in effect from index registers 3 and 5 and not from the instruction. A detached address code is one in which this is the normal form of the instruction. We might, in such a case, dispense with the zeros and write simply—

(3)	ADD	(5)

which must not be confused with—

3	ADD	5

in which the operands are the actual contents of the registers, and which is also permissible in a detached-address format, as are the variants—

	3	ADD	(5)
and	(3)	ADD	5

Brackets indicate that the register gives the operand's address, while the absence of brackets indicates that the register contains the operand itself.

Detached-address instructions like these can be fitted conveniently into sixteen bits (half a word); but a detached-address language must also have some means of specifying literals. This can be done by putting the literal in the location in store following the instruction that uses it (or, what comes to much the same thing, by providing the option of a 32-bit format for a limited number of functions). Such an arrangement would provide literals up to 16 bits long. Longer literals can be provided as preset data, with long-format instructions giving their addresses.

It is not generally realized that a detached-address form of code can be made to give equivalent facilities to an attached-address code. In particular, the two-address assembly language we have been discussing in this book could be implemented quite well by a detached-address machine code. Each attached-address statement would of course have to be translated into several detached-address instructions; for example, the statement—

COST(4)	ADD	MARKUP(6)

might become—

```
     3        MOVE   'COST'      2
     3        ADD    4           1
     5        MOVE   'MARKUP'    2
     5        ADD    6           1
     (3)      ADD    (5)         1
```

Where the figures 1 and 2 in the margin indicate short-format and long-format instructions respectively.

From the foregoing, it might appear that a detached-address code is rather inefficient; but this is not being quite fair to detached-addresses. Naturally a code will look inefficient if it is used to implement sequences of instructions written with an entirely different type of code in mind. But, if a programmer knows that his work is going to be assembled into a detached-address code, he naturally approaches the problem in a suitable frame of mind. For instance, the simple add-listing example given at the beginning of Chapter 4 might, with a detached-address code, take the form—

```
     1        MOVE   'LIST'      2
     2        MOVE   '135'       2
     3        MOVE   'SUM'       2
     (3)      MOVE   '0'         1
  ┌→(3)       ADD    (1)         1
  └─1         CTJ    '− 1'       1
              STOP               1
```

Four short and three long instructions instead of six long instructions, and two short instructions in the loop instead of two long ones.

THE CONTROL SYSTEM

Whatever the format of an instruction, the means by which the computer obeys it are fairly standard. Instructions are extracted from the store in sequence, and placed in a special register known as the *instruction register*, from which they are able in turn to control the active units of the machine. The instruction sequence is controlled by another register, called the *instruction-counter register* (instruction-number register, control-address register, control-number register, or what you will). This register holds the address of the instruction currently being extracted from the store. While the instruction is being obeyed, the instruction counter (control number, control address, etc.) is increased by unity, ready for extracting the next instruction in the sequence. Thus the basic cycle of operations is—

┌→extract next instruction
│ obey instruction
└─increase counter by one

The sequence is a little different in the case of satisfied jumps, when the number in the instruction counter has to be replaced by the new jump address, thus—

→extract next instruction
test whether condition is satisfied
—if not, increase counter by one; if so, replace counter by new address

Fig. 8.1 shows a typical layout for the instruction control in a computer. The store is assumed to be of the core type, which means

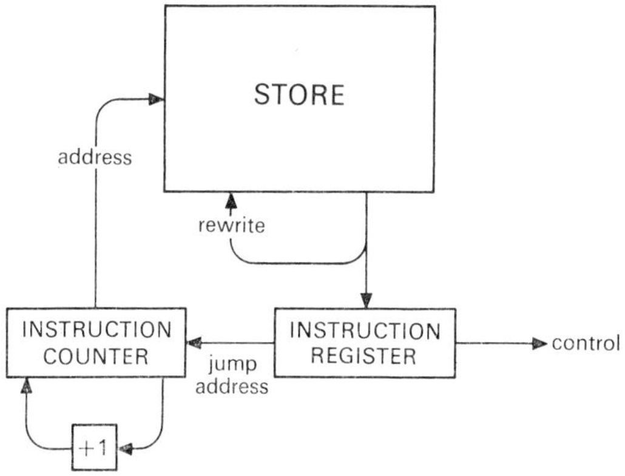

FIG. 8.1. Instruction Control

that the instruction must be written back to the store after it has been read. Fig. 8.2 is a flow diagram showing the operation of the unit. A new jump address can come from any one of three places: in absolute (label) jumps it comes from the jump instruction itself; in relative jumps it is the number in the instruction counter, increased or decreased by a literal given in the instruction; in jumps obeying a link it generally comes from one of the index registers.

A typical function, addition for instance, requires two operands, and therefore—since a normal core store can be read in only one place at a time—two cycles of the store. It also requires at least one register outside the store in which to hold the first operand while the second is being fetched. The two operands can then be passed together through an arithmetic unit, or *Mill** as it has been called.

* The term *Mill* was originally used by Babbage to describe the arithmetic unit of his Analytical Engine.

The Mill performs addition, subtraction, logical operations, and shifts; multiplication is achieved by successive additions, and division by successive additions and subtractions. (The algorithms for

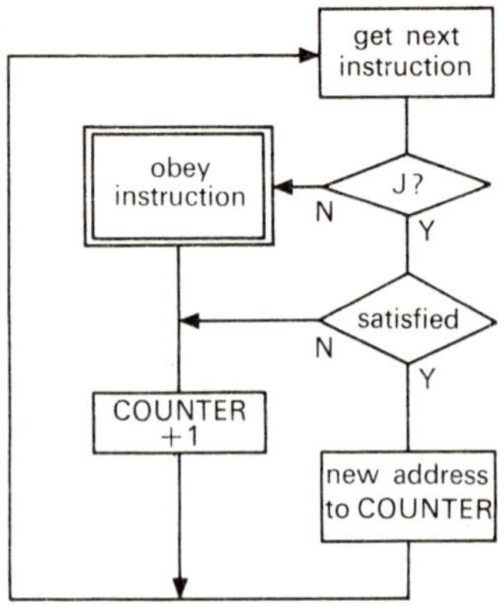

FIG. 8.2.

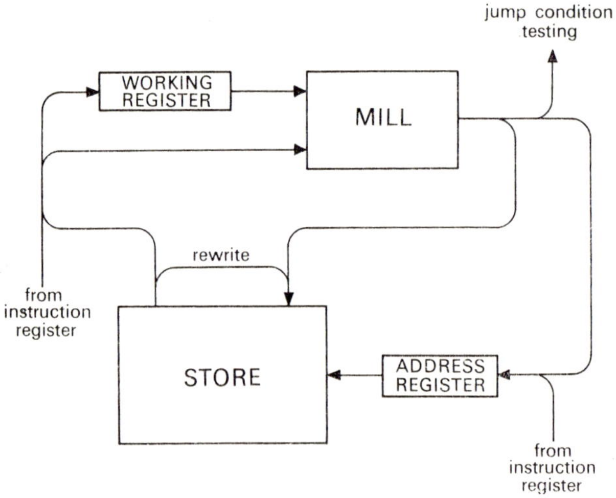

FIG. 8.3. Simple Dataflow

multiplication and division are discussed in Appendix III). Multiplication and division are usually performed in the Mill; but in larger systems a separate unit is sometimes provided. Fig. 8.3 shows a typical layout of the basic units of a computer performing simple arithmetic operations. The sequence of events when an instruction such as—

A ADD B

is performed are—

read operand into working register from store at address B
write back to store at B
read operand from store at address A
feed both operands through Mill
write output of Mill back to store at A, at the same time setting jump conditions.

The sort of diagram shown in Fig. 8.3 is known as a *dataflow*. This particular dataflow is very much simplified; it takes no account of multiplication and division, for which at least two more full-length registers are necessary. Another term used for the same thing is *slice*. The name derives from the structure of a parallel machine, where several bits are processed together, each one travelling along its own set of channels sandwiched between identical sets of channels on either side of it like slices in a cut loaf. As in a cut loaf, so in a computer, the slices at the ends have a rather different structure from those in the middle.

Figure 8.3 also hints at something called *jump-condition testing*. This is simply an arrangement for testing whether the output of the Mill is zero or non-zero, positive or negative, and whether overflow has occurred. The results of the tests are recorded on one-bit stores, or *staticisers*, which can be tested in their turn by the next instruction if it is a jump.

THE MICROPROGRAM

We have seen that a simple instruction like—

A ADD B

which from the programmer's standpoint is a single elementary operation, is really made up of a sequence of operations even more elementary. Even the instruction—

A MOVE B

involves a sequence of operations—

read store at B into working register
rewrite back to B
read store at A, allowing content to be lost
feed data from working register through Mill
write back to A.

A sequence such as this, and the one we gave earlier, is known as a *micro-sequence* or *micro-routine*, the operations specified in it *micro-operations* or *micro-instructions*, and the total of all micro-sequences a *microprogram*.

OVERLAP

The principal difference between microprogram and ordinary program, apart from the elementary nature of the operations involved in microprogram, is that ordinary instructions must be carried out in strict sequence, whereas it is often possible to carry out several micro-instructions concurrently. This is because every ordinary instruction uses the whole central unit of the machine, whereas micro-instructions are performed in separate sub-assemblies of the central unit. For example, the full micro-sequence for—

A MOVE B(X)

might be—

1. read instruction into instruction register
2. rewrite store
3. index instruction counter
4. read index register X into working register
5. rewrite store
6. pass modifier through Mill, adding to B, and route result to address register
7. read store at address B(X) into working register
8. rewrite store
9. read store at A, losing content
10. feed content of working register through Mill
11. write back to store at A.

In this particular case, it would probably be possible to overlap operations 2 and 3, operations 5 and 6, and operations 9 and 10. This sequence, with overlap, is shown diagrammatically in Fig. 8.4.

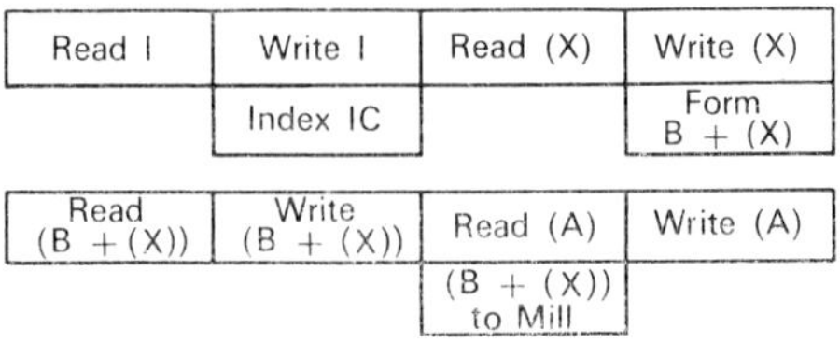

FIG. 8.4. MOVE Microsequence

The amount of overlap that is possible depends on the number of different sub-units provided in the central control of the machine and on the complexity of the interconnections between them.

Since overlap confers greater speed, it is used widely in the fastest machines; indeed it is not uncommon in very fast systems to find overlapping at the level of the ordinary program, a new instruction being started while the previous instruction is still being carried out. In fact it is sometimes possible to find several instructions overlapping in time. Such a system has been referred to as *look-ahead*, because the control looks through several instructions to determine whether there are any bits of them that can be carried out in sub-units that happen to be idle at the time.

FIXED STORES

In modern computers, the microprogram is often treated in a similar way to an ordinary program. It has a language of its own, the micro-code, designed for expressing elementary micro-operations; consequently the microprogram can be written down formally, converted into a binary numeric code, and held in a store of its own. The type of store generally used for this purpose is known as a *fixed store*. It is so called because, unlike an ordinary core store, the information it holds is not destroyed by reading: in fact its contents cannot be erased at all, except by taking the store to pieces; but this is a positive advantage, since the microprogram is permanent. Fixed stores have another characteristic: they are very much faster to read than volatile stores. Whereas a core store may take typically one microsecond (one millionth of a second) to read, a typical fixed store can be read in perhaps one tenth of this time, one hundred nanoseconds. In a fixed store, speed has been traded against the power to change the contents.

There are two main types of fixed store: the *transformer* type, and the *air-coupled* type. The transformer type consists of a row of cores of magnetic material, as many cores as there are bits in the micro-instruction. Each core has a pick-up wire wound a few times round it. The bit-patterns in the micro-instructions are represented by wires, one wire to each micro-instruction, which thread the cores in positions where the corresponding micro-instruction has ones, and by-pass the cores in positions where the corresponding micro-instruction has noughts. When a current is sent through a selected word-wire, currents are induced in the pick-up wires corresponding to bit positions where there are ones in the micro-instruction. The arrangement is shown in the first diagram of Fig. 8.5, where three word wires are illustrated, giving bit patterns 101, 110 and 100 respectively.

In the air-coupled type of fixed store, which is shown in the second diagram in Fig. 8.5, the word-wires and pick-up wires are laid at right-angles to one another in the form of grids on the two sides of a thin sheet of copper. Holes are punched in the copper sheet in positions corresponding to ones in the microprogram, and these allow local electromagnetic coupling between the wires on the two sides. When a current is passed through a word wire, currents are induced in those pick-up wires that can 'see' it through holes in the copper sheet. The air-coupled type of store is more expensive than the transformer type, partly because of its form of construction, and partly because the induced currents are weaker and need more

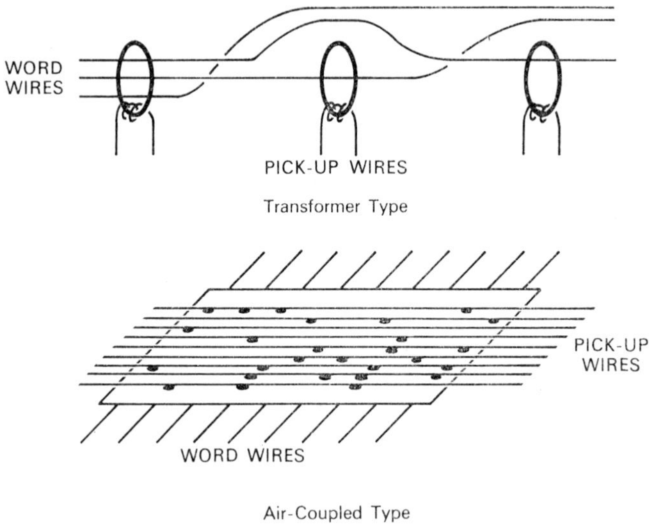

FIG. 8.5. Fixed Stores

elaborate amplification; but the air-coupled type is faster, and is preferred for that reason in more expansive machines. Another advantage of the air-coupled type is that it is comparatively easy to modify the contents, all that is necessary being the replacement of one copper sheet by another. Incidentally, the wiring in fixed stores usually consists of copper film deposited in the desired pattern on a substrata of insulating material.

GATES

The microprogram controls the dataflow. It does so by opening *gates* in the correct sequence, so that operands are routed in the desired manner. A gate is simply a circuit that performs the analogue of an *and* operation between a digit signal and a control signal derived from the microprogram, just as a *gate* in the ordinary sense might be said to perform an *and* operation between a flock of sheep and a farmer. If the farmer is not there (and there have been no careless hikers passing through lately) the gate stays shut, and the sheep remain in the field.

The simplest form of micro-instruction is one in which each bit controls a separate gate or, in a parallel machine, a set of parallel gates, the gate being open when the bit is a one, and closed when it is a nought. Such an arrangement allows any arbitrary set of gates to be opened at the same time; but so much flexibility is not at all necessary. Certain gates are mutually exclusive, that is to say, it is pointless for them to be open at the same time. It is possible, therefore, to save bits in the micro-instruction, and reduce the cost of the fixed store, by causing gates that are mutually exclusive to be opened not by individual bits but by different patterns of the same groups of bits. A group of three bits in a micro-instruction can be arranged in any one of eight patterns, each of which can, if so desired, be made to control a different gate.

DECODING

The process whereby control signals are generated from different patterns of bits is known as *decoding;* it is no more than performing certain logical operations on the control bits. The simplest decoding of three bits gives eight exclusive combinations, which we may write as—

$$abc \quad ab\bar{c} \quad a\bar{b}c \quad \bar{a}bc \quad a\bar{b}\bar{c} \quad \bar{a}b\bar{c} \quad \bar{a}\bar{b}c \quad \bar{a}\bar{b}\bar{c}$$

where the juxtaposition of two symbols is intended to represent an *and* operation, and a bar over the top represents inversion. Sometimes the gating signals are not required to be entirely exclusive. For instance, it is possible to decode three bits in such a way that six gating signals are produced, of which either the first two or the second two can occur together. The decoding arrangement that does this can be expressed symbolically as—

$$ab \quad ac \quad \bar{a}b \quad \bar{a}c \quad a\bar{b}\bar{c} \quad \bar{a}\bar{b}\bar{c}$$

In this case, the combination of bits 111 would cause the gates controlled by the first two signals to open together, whereas the combination 011 would open the gates controlled by the second two signals. All other combinations of bits would activate only one of the gating signals. It is because much of his time is spent on solving logical problems of this kind that the engineer concerned with the detailed design of computer systems is called a *logical designer*.

EMULATION

The operations that a computer can actually perform are determined by the structure of the dataflow; but the repertoire of machine functions available for use by the programmer is *further* limited by what has been put into the microgram. Because of this, it is possible to change the aspect of a computer simply by changing the contents of its fixed store. In particular, one computer can be made to resemble another quite closely by this means—closely enough for the first computer to be able to accept programs originally written for the second computer. However, there is a limit to what can be done in this way. If two machines are to be made to resemble one another, they must have the same facilities available not only in the microprogram but also in the dataflow, since obviously no amount of microprogram can control features that do not exist. Nevertheless, with a minimal addition to the dataflow, and a new or extended fixed store, a computer of a new design can be made to obey programs originally written for an older system. Such a facility is called *emulation*. It is a very valuable feature to have, since it may save the purchaser of a new machine a great deal of re-programming, which he would otherwise have to do to convert the programs originally written for his old machine. However, it is unwise to expect too much from emulation. It is simply not practicable to make one system resemble another in every smallest detail. Even if the instruction code can be made compatible, the two systems are sure to have different peripheral units and a different operating system. Consequently, even with emulation, some modification to programs is generally unavoidable if they are to run on an alien machine.

AD-HOC MICROPROGRAMS

Fixed stores are not used for microprogram in either the very largest or the very smallest machines. In small computers, the repertoire of built-in functions is small. But fixed stores have a minimum basic cost apart from their size; consequently it has been found that fixed stores confer no cost advantage on small systems. In large systems, even the fastest fixed stores are too slow at the microprogram level. In both small and large systems, therefore, the microprogram is made up from the same circuits as the dataflow and other parts of the machine. A microprogram made in an *ad hoc* manner from ordinary logical elements is not only faster than a fixed store, its informal structure allows the designer to use his ingenuity to cut a few corners and reduce the amount of electronics involved. What is more, a computer with an *ad hoc* microprogram can be designed asynchronously. By this we mean that, whereas a fixed store has a fixed cycle time, micro-operations in *ad hoc* logic can be allowed to take as little or as much time as they actually need. Thus, by speeding up the shortest operations, the whole system can be speeded up.

COMMUNICATION WITH PERIPHERALS

To complete this chapter, we must consider how a system centre communicates with peripheral devices. For simplicity, we shall confine our attention to those devices in which the basic unit of information transfer is the byte; these include eight-hole paper tape, punched cards, line printers, nine track magnetic tape, and several other devices. Devices operating in other modes are handled in the same way; but the process tends to become a little more complicated. A single transfer of data (that is, the operation that is set going by a single TFER instruction) involves a string of bytes, for which we shall use the term *block*. In some devices the block is of a fixed length—card machines operate on blocks of 80 bytes—but in other devices the block length can be varied.

AUTONOMOUS TRANSFERS

In the earliest computers, peripheral devices used to transfer data to or from an intermediate store, or buffer, data being transferred subsequently between the buffer and the main store in complete blocks. In most modern computers, however, transfers take place direct between the store and the peripheral devices. In some small, cheap systems, the program has to be suspended while a peripheral transfer is in progress: in most systems, however, transfers can be concurrent with the computation. In this case, peripheral transfers are said to be *autonomous.*

HESITATION AND INTERRUPTION

Core stores, by the way they are constructed, cannot be read or written in two places simultaneously; consequently, whenever a peripheral device wants access to the store, to extract or deposit data, the program must be temporarily suspended. We shall refer to such temporary suspension of normal operation as a *hesitation.* (The term *data break-in*, among others, has been used for the same thing.) Hesitations generally occur between instructions, though faster machines usually provide several hesitation points within the micro-routines of the longer functions. Of course a hesitation only occurs if, when the control reaches a hesitation point, one of the peripheral devices is ready to transfer data.

It is common practice to allot addresses to the terminations of the data lines from the peripheral devices. Such addresses may appear as extensions to the main store, or they may be in a separate notional store. In either case, data transfers then become ordinary *move* operations at the microprogram level, and can be handled by the normal mechanism, special micro-routines being provided for dealing with hesitations.

During a hesitation, the control needs two pieces of information; it must have the main-store address of the byte to be transferred, and it must be able to count how many bytes yet remain to be transferred. In short, the control requires the equivalent of a counter-modifier pair. We shall refer to this as a *peripheral control word* (though in fact it may occupy more space than one word). At each hesitation, the system must perform the equivalent of a CTJ operation on the control word, advancing the address, and reducing the count, by unity. The actual sequence of operations involved in a hesitation (to fix our ideas, let us assume an outward transfer) is—

read word containing required byte
rewrite store
send selected byte to peripheral
increase address by one
decrease count by one
return to main microprogram.

Of course some of these operations may be overlapped.

When the counter in the control word has been reduced to zero, that is, when the transfer is complete, the Control Program is entered. This is, among other things, so that the operating program, which may have been suspended pending the end of the transfer, can be brought back into operation. Entries to the Control Program we shall refer to as *interrupts*, and we shall have more to say about them in Chapter 14. The terms *program break-in* and *device break-in* have also been used. Of course, if the last hesitation in a transfer occurs at a hesitation point in the middle of an instruction, the instruction must be allowed to finish before current program is interrupted and the Control Program is entered.

FAST PERIPHERALS

In some small and medium-sized computers, the control word is held somewhere in the store. This means that every hesitation involves two cycles of the store, one to extract the control word, the other to extract or deposit the data. Since there are other operations to perform as well, a machine with a two-microsecond store is unlikely to be able to hesitate for less than, say, six microseconds. Now a magnetic tape recorded at 800 bytes per inch, and running at 150 inches per second, is transferring data at a rate of 120,000 bytes per second. With a hesitation time of 6 microseconds per byte, 72 per cent of the time of the machine would, on a first analysis, be taken up with hesitations, and only 28 per cent would be left for computation.

In fact, what would happen in a case such as this is that the magnetic tape would stop for short whiles between blocks, to allow the computation to catch up. This would be bound to happen, since the tape could not proceed to the next block until the program had advanced to the next TFER instruction. Under such conditions, the system as a whole would be working inefficiently, since fast, expensive magnetic-tape equipment would be forced to work at the speed of slower, cheaper processing equipment. If more than one magnetic tape channel were attached to the machine, the situation would be even worse.

To enable users to operate their fast peripheral equipment efficiently, manufacturers provide, sometimes as an option, sometimes not, an alternative faster hesitation system. The extra speed is achieved in either or both of two ways. The first is to hold the control word not in the store but in a special immediately accessible register. By saving one store cycle in this way, the hesitation time can be reduced from, say, six microseconds to four, which would reduce the loading of the magnetic tape in our example from 72 per cent to 48 per cent—still a substantial proportion. The other way of reducing the total hesitation time is to assemble bytes into groups in a small buffer register before allowing the system to hesitate. The simplest size of group to use is four bytes, or one word, which can usually be extracted from, or deposited in, store in one cycle. If the magnetic tape in our example required a hesitation only after every fourth character, the loading on the system, even with a hesitation time of six microseconds, would be reduced to 18 per cent. With the control word in a fast register as well, it would be reduced to 12 per cent.

Computers differ widely in the way their hesitation systems are arranged, and a host of names have been coined wherewith to refer to the different units involved; but the only real differences between systems depend on whether the control word is held within or outside the main store, and how many bytes are transferred to or from the store at one time.

CRISIS TIME

Different peripheral devices can afford to wait different lengths of time before it becomes too late for a character to be accepted. With paper-tape readers, which are able to halt for an indefinite time on a single character, it is never too late; punched-card readers, on the other hand, pass from one column to another in typically half a millisecond; the magnetic-tape system we have just been discussing has only eight microseconds between one byte and the next. We shall refer to the time within which a device must be serviced as its *crisis time*. If a device is not serviced within its crisis time, a character is generally lost, and the Control Program must be called in to take remedial action.

There is a certain maximum time that can elapse between a device's request for service and the earliest moment when it can be dealt with; this is the longest period between hesitation points in the program; it is either the length of the longest instruction or, if hesitation points are provided within instructions, the maximum period between them. Typically, in a machine with a two-micro-second store, this period might be twelve microseconds or so, which is longer, of course, than the crisis time of fast magnetic tape. However, we have already said for other reasons that fast magnetic tapes should be allowed to hesitate only after every fourth byte, which means that the effective crisis time of the medium is multiplied by 4.

When two or more devices are waiting for service at the same time, the ones with the shortest crisis time must be allowed to take priority, for, if the queue were served in strict rotation, the crisis times on the fastest devices might be exceeded. Priority arrangements are usually built into the hardware of hesitation systems. Suppose that we have a machine with a maximum period between hesitation points of 12 micro-seconds, and a hesitation time of 6 microseconds and suppose we attach to it a card reader, a printer, and several magnetic-tape channels. If the crisis time of the magnetic tape is 32 microseconds, let us determine how many channels can be attached.

Without a priority system, the card reader and printer might be serviced first. The first magnetic-tape channel would not then be serviced until after 24 microseconds, a second channel could then be serviced after 30 microseconds, but a third channel might miss out, since it could have to wait as long as 35 micro-seconds—more than the crisis time. With a priority system, four magnetic-tape channels could be handled, however, even if they were all waiting for attention at the same time, for they could all get attention within a period of 30 microseconds—less than their crisis time.

Strictly speaking, it is always necessary to carry out a crisis-time calculation before it can be definitely established that a particular peripheral configuration is feasible on a particular computer. However, the simpler determination of percentage loading on the store time gives a rough rule-of-thumb to which a system analyst can work. If all the peripheral units operating together occupy less than half the time of the store, it can generally be said that the system is feasible as regards crisis time.

EXERCISES 8

1. Make a comparison of one-address, one-and-a-half-address, two-address and three-address codes by showing how the following operations might be performed with equivalent functional facilities in each—

(*a*)	Move A to B
(*b*)	A + B to register 4
(*c*)	Exchange A and B
(*d*)	Jump to B if A = O

2. Write down the sequences of micro-operations involved in performing the instructions—

(*a*)	A	ADD	'27'
(*b*)	B(X)	SUB	A
(*c*)	(A)	ADD	(B)

What additions would have to be made to the dataflow of Fig. 8.3 to make these three operations possible?

3. Show by writing down the logical functions how three bits can be decoded to give six gating signals of which the first three can occur either all together or one at a time, and the last three can occur either all together or one at a time. What bit configurations activate—

(*a*) the first three together,
(*b*) the last one alone?

4. Write down the sequence of micro-operations involved in transferring one byte to store during a hesitation.

5. Given a computer configuration with the following peripheral units—
paper tape at 1,000 characters per sec.
card reader at 1,000 cards per min.
printer at 1,000 cycles of 120 characters per min.
two channels of magnetic tape at 500 bytes per inch and 120 inches per second, calculate, with all devices operating at full speed, what proportion of time is used in hesitations—

(*a*) with 6-microsecond hesitations per byte for all devices,
(*b*) with 4 microseconds per byte for magnetic tape only,
(*c*) with 6 microseconds for each group of four bytes on magnetic tape only.

6. Calculate how many magnetic-tape channels operating at 200 bits per inch and 120 inches per second can be attached to a system with a hesitation time of 20 microseconds and a time between hesitation points of 30 microseconds—
(*a*) with one hesitation per byte,
(*b*) with one hesitation every fourth byte.

9. *Faster! Faster!*

It probably seems at times to people on the outside, that those who are concerned with the design and application of computers are worshipping speed for its own sake. Surely a machine that can perform a million additions in a second is able to accomplish any task entrusted to it! Why try to go any faster? Why design machines with high processing speeds, when the speeds of most commercial jobs are limited anyway by the mechanical limitations of peripheral devices? In this chapter we shall look into some of the reasons why still higher speeds are being sought, and we shall consider some of the ways in which they are being attained.

Most commercial jobs are time-dependent in some way—in the sense that they must be completed within an eight-hour shift, for example, or between the delivery of a morning post and an afternoon collection. Several mathematical jobs are time-dependent too. For instance, a great deal of work has been done towards devising methods of weather forecasting with the aid of a computer. The methods involve mathematical calculations, and a deal of searching in past records. Obviously, the sooner a weather forecast can be made available, the more valuable it is, and equally obviously, a forecast of weather is no use at all unless it arrives before the weather itself. There is, too, a class of computer job that simply would not be practicable at all without a very fast machine; this is the sort of job that involves an enormous number of trials to find a solution to a problem. The recent availability of very fast computers has made it possible to employ cruder numerical methods than heretofore, and by doing so to obtain exact, or nearly optimal, solutions to problems that previously had been susceptible only to approximate analysis. The trend towards brute-force computation has led to very fast computers being referred to as *number crunchers.*

Another point in favour of fast machines is that they can be used less efficiently. By this we mean that on a faster machine we need take less trouble to write a program that will do a job in as little time as possible, and that we can compile programs using methods that have been devised for simplicity rather than for producing efficient object programs in the end. What all this means is that we can employ less highly skilled programming labour, which, even if it is not all that much less expensive, is at least easier to recruit.

But by far the most telling argument for faster machines comes from the economic nature of computers. It actually costs less money to do a job on a fast machine than on a slower machine. This effect is most clearly seen when hiring time on a bureau machine; but it applies with just as much force when a machine is rented or bought outright. If we took a selection of current systems and plotted their speeds against their prices, we should find that the points lay on or near a curve like that shown in Fig. 9.1. Over most of its length,

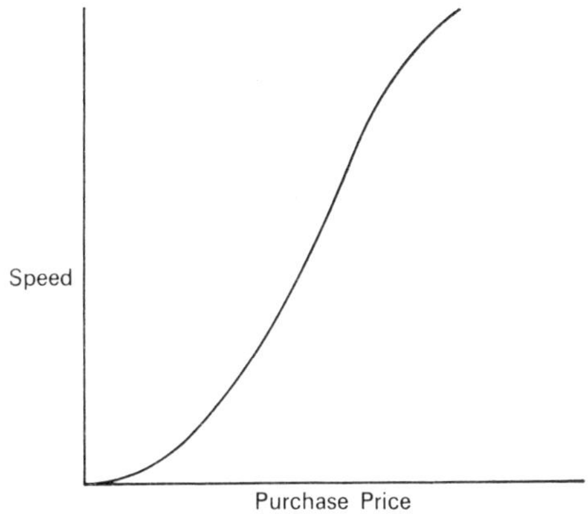

FIG. 9.1.

this curve represents a square law; that is to say, if we are prepared to pay twice as much, we can get a machine four times as fast, and if we spend ten times as much, we get a machine a hundred times as fast. However, the curve reaches a limit beyond which the square law ceases to apply—the point at which technology is stretched to its utmost.

The information in Fig. 9.1 can be shown in another way. What the user is primarily interested in is how cheaply a machine will do his job, and we can represent this in terms of the number of instructions obeyed per £ spent. (Again the concept is easier if we think of the money as a hire charge.) Fig. 9.2 shows number of instructions per £ plotted against system cost. The curve rises to a peak and then falls again, showing that there is a maximum size (and speed) of machine beyond which it is not worth anyone's while to go, since machines larger than this are actually more expensive to use.*

* Economists will recognize this as an example of falling marginal efficiency.

No scales are shown on the graphs of Fig. 9.1 and 9.2 because actual scales change from year to year as technological advances are made. It has been estimated that the actual amount of computing that the user of a new computer gets for his money goes up by an average of about eighty per cent per year. The position of the

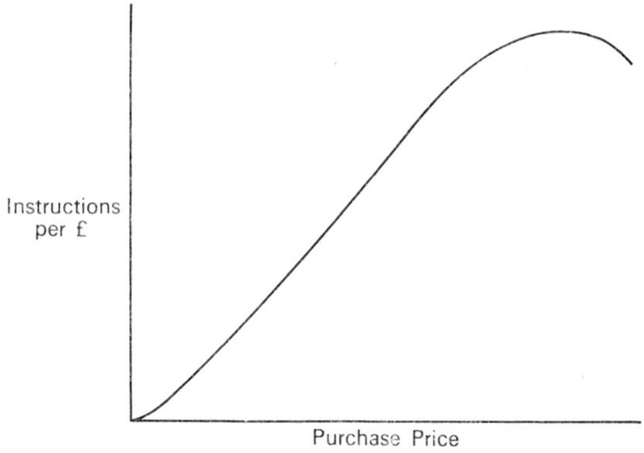

FIG. 9.2.

peak in the second graph has in the past moved to the left at a rate of about twenty per cent per year, which means, by corollary, that the speed of the largest machine that is worth building nearly doubles every year. These estimates are based, of course, on past experience: there is no certainty that things will remain the same in the future, though it is a reasonable hypothesis to assume that they will. Technological improvement is the prime cause of change but its magnitude is governed too by commercial considerations.

MEASURING COMPUTER SPEED

In the graphs, we have expressed the speed and power of machines in terms of the number of instructions that they can obey per second. It is not difficult to derive a mean instruction time for a machine if the times for the various sorts of instruction are known, and their relative frequencies. Naturally it is the frequencies of instructions *as obeyed* that are wanted here, not the frequencies with which they occur in written programs, since some instructions are encountered in loops more frequently than others. The list of frequencies with which individual instruction times are to be weighted is referred to as a *mix*. Mixes have been derived for most machines, and they do provide a rough index of computing power; but of course what is to be regarded as a mean instruction time for one machine does not necessarily correspond in any way with the mean time for another machine. A machine with a three-argument code will probably have a longer mean instruction time than one at the same price with a two-argument code, though the two machines may be equivalent in computing power. It cannot be too strongly emphasized that a mix derived for one machine should not be used in estimating the mean instruction time for another machine, unless of course the two have the same instruction code. Another pitfall with mixes is that they are not always derived from the same types of program; instruction frequencies differ between mathematical and commercial programs, and between hand-coded programs and programs compiled by other means.

A simple way of obtaining mix frequencies, which can be used on some, but not all, machines, is to arrange for the machine to be interrupted at regular intervals while it is engaged on its ordinary work. At every interruption, control is passed to a special analysing program (this can be done in the same way as an entry to a trace program) which examines the instruction about to be obeyed and records certain details about it. At the end of the day, or at some other convenient time, the results of the analysis are printed out. Ideally an experiment like this should occupy several days and be carried out on several installations engaged on different types of work. Even if it has only been carried out on the manufacturer's own premises, where the work cannot be regarded as truly representative, it can provide some valuable information.

To make a proper comparison between two or more systems, though it is necessary to apply the same objective test to them all. Naturally, what ultimately concerns every prospective user, is how fast each machine will do his particular job; but, since he cannot find this out without going to the expense of programming it completely for each machine he is interested in, he must rely on some more general method of comparison. Some prospective purchasers insist upon having a few well chosen routines programmed and run on machines identical with those they are being offered, or, if the machines are still under development, they may agree to accept calculated running times, with certain guarantees written into any subsequent contract. Most of the routines used in this way are chosen to test the effectiveness of the machines in particular situations; but a few are of more general applicability.

THE GAMM UNIT

A German firm of consultants, called GAMM (Gesellschaft für Allgemeine Mathematik und Mechanik) has proposed a simple test of a machine's mathematical computing power. It consists of five very short loop-type subroutines that occur very frequently in mathematical work. These are to be programmed, and then timed for the machine under test. Their times are then combined in a weighted mix, which is supposed to represent the relative frequencies of the types of loop in practice, to give a final figure that, like mean instruction time, is actually a figure of demerit, that is, the larger it is, the slower the machine. Since the speed of most mathematical programs is dominated by the speeds of their inner loops, the GAMM estimate gives a pretty good index of mathematical performance. It gives little help, however, in determining the probable performance of a machine on commerical work.

THE POST OFFICE METHOD

A good method for assessing the performance of computers on commerical programs has been devised by a group working in the

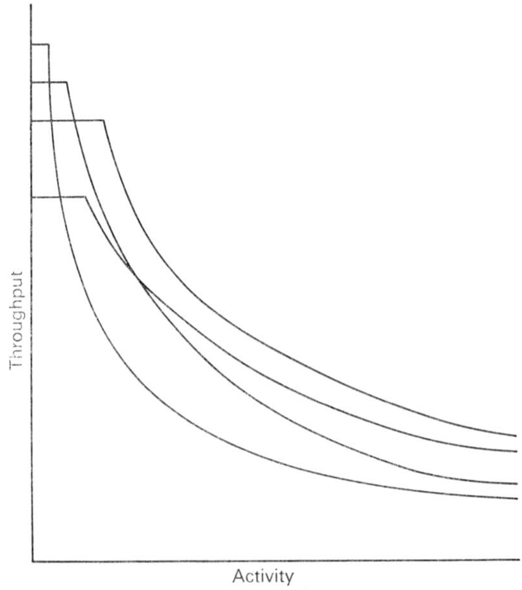

FIG. 9.3. Post Office Curves

British Post Office. The Post Office method involves first of all writing several short sequences of instructions performing operations that frequently occur in commercial programs, timing them, and calculating a weighted mean of the times. This mean, which is again a demerit figure, is called the *Post Office unit*, and in itself it is a good index of the internal speed of a computer. But the Post Office method goes further than this, and considers the performance of a complete magnetic-tape system. The throughput of a system, that is, the rate at which data can be processed, depends on two factors: the power of the processor (which is measured by the work unit, or rather, by its reciprocal) and the amount of work that has to be done on each piece of data, which we can refer to as the activity of the process. Once a work unit has been calculated for each of several systems to be compared, curves of throughput against activity are plotted, like those in Fig. 9.3.* The horizontal cut-off at the top of each curve represents a limit set by the maximum speed at which the system's magnetic tape units can be operated. In general, the best system is the one whose curve lies farthest to the right, since this gives more throughput for a given activity or, conversely, allows more computation per unit of data for a given throughput.

THE AUERBACH METHOD

The Auerbach Corporation of America publishes test reports on all machines of American manufacture. Their method of comparative testing is to program a standard commercial job for every system they report on, and calculate its running time for various amounts of file activity. The results are shown graphically. Although the Auerbach standard job is much simplified in comparison with a real commerical job, the assessment still takes a long while to complete. Whether it is in the end more accurate than other, quicker methods is a matter of opinion; it can be argued that the Auerbach assessment is too often dominated by the speed of one or other of the peripheral units, usually a line printer. Auerbach also include an assessment of performance on a standard mathematical job and a standard statistical job in their test reports.

It has to be mentioned at this point that of course the cost of running programs is only part of the cost a user incurs. The costs of programming and of developing and correcting programs are just as important, and a system that achieves high processing speeds at the expense of programming convenience may be an expensive system to use in the long run. However, the same argument does not necessarily hold for computers used for process control, or in certain military applications, which may only ever have to obey one program in the whole of their working life.

* For the benefit of the mathematically minded, these curves are rectangular hyperbolas. They are not asymptotic to the Y-axis, but displaced slightly to the left, because some allowance has to be made for the time-consuming hesitation process.

UNITS OF TIME

Time intervals in computers are measured in milliseconds (thousandths of a second) and microseconds (millionths of a second). In most computers, a simple linear operation such as addition takes between one and one hundred microseconds, depending on the price of the machine. Multiplication and division can be as fast as a microsecond or two; but in machines where they are performed by subroutines, they may take as long as a hundred milliseconds. For measuring the duration of events at the level of microprogram, we use nanoseconds (thousand-millionths of a second), and for the future we have picoseconds (million-millionths) available.

STORES

The principal factor that controls the speed of a computer is the speed of its store. This is because arithmetic processes generally take less time than accesses to store, and because every instruction involves at least one store access, to extract the instruction itself. (Most instructions involve at least one access for data as well.) The store can conveniently be considered in two parts: there is the storage medium itself, which, in practically all systems, is a matrix of magnetic cores, and there are the electronic circuits that select the desired word and amplify it. Core stores in modern computers have cycle times (for reading followed by rewriting) down to a quarter of a microsecond, and even less. Average store cycle times are in the region of one or two microseconds.

The cycle time of a core store depends on the time it takes to switch a core from one state of magnetization to the other. The smaller the core, the faster it can be switched; but the minimum size of core is obviously limited by practical considerations, such as the number of wires that have to thread it, and by problems of manufacture. (Most modern cores measure thirty-thousandths of an inch across.) It would be possible to make a core switch more rapidly by using a larger pulse of current to switch it; but in most core stores the pulse amplitude is fixed, since they operate on the principle of coincident selection, by which current pulses slightly greater than half the minimum needed to switch a core are fed into two sets of wires at right-angles to one another; only the cores threaded by both wires are then switched. Another limitation on the size of current pulses is heat: although the amount of heat dissipated in a single core cycle is minute, the amount dissipated in a core store that is being operated a million or so times a second can be quite appreciable. Since a core matrix occupies only a few cubic inches, the removal of surplus heat may pose quite a problem.

The coincident-selection idea has been abandoned in a few very fast core stores. In these, each drive wire selects a *group* of words, which are consequently all read at the same time, even though only one of them may actually be wanted. Such an arrangement increases the amount of electronics associated with the store, though it does allow the store to operate faster. In cases where several words of the group are wanted in sequence, as for instance when they represent a sequence of instructions, it can be arranged for them to be held outside the store until they are actually required, to save the time of further access to store. A store of this type is said to have a *width* of several words.

MAGNETIC FILMS

A great deal of work has been done with a view to finding a faster or cheaper substitute for the core type of store configuration, and one of the most promising lines of research has been the thin magnetic film. A film of magnetic material is deposited on a substrate of glass or non-ferrous metal, and the selection and read wires are laid over the top. Individual bits are stored by local magnetization over small areas of the film, magnetization in two different directions (usually at right angles) representing respectively one and nought. A thin film needs a much smaller switching current than a core store, and it can be made to switch faster; but signal levels are low, and electrical noise is a serious problem. Thin-film stores have been used in a few machines; but so far they have not provided any serious competition to the ubiquitous core store.

KERNEL STORE

It is true of stores, as it is true of other things, that the larger they are, the slower they are. This happens with stores partly because large stores consume more power, which brings problems that cannot easily be resolved except by degrading performance, and partly because larger stores contain longer wires, which slow down the propagation of signals. Even if a larger store is made by combining several smaller stores, their full potential speed cannot be realized, since something is always lost in the linking mechanism. It is common practice, therefore, when a computer has to have a large store, to combine this with a much smaller fast store, which can be used to hold items in current use that are continually being fetched and returned to store. This is one of the ideas behind the so-called *scratch-pad*, or *kernel* store, which was mentioned in Chapter 4, and which may or may not include the index registers. The same idea underlies the one-and-a-half-address form of instruction code, in which the *half* address is intended to refer to a kernel store. The kernel structure underlies the detached-address form of code too, since this is most efficient when the detached addresses are held in a small, fast kernel. A machine's speed is improved by having a kernel, not only because the kernel is fast in itself but also because two pieces of data can be fetched simultaneously, one from the kernel, the other from the main store. Thus the kernel form of construction confers speed, as well as leading to a compact instruction format.

SLAVE STORE

Another way in which an auxiliary small fast store can be used is as a temporary store for instructions. A great deal of time can be saved in this way when a short sequence of instructions is obeyed over and over again, as happens when the instructions are in the form of a loop. One way of organizing an auxiliary store to hold instructions is to establish some sort of correspondence between each location in it and a set of locations in the main store (a many-to-one mapping, in mathematical terms). Then, whenever an instruction is extracted from the main store, it is copied into the corresponding location in the auxiliary, from which it can be extracted much more rapidly on subsequent occasions. An example should make the idea clearer. Suppose that we have an auxiliary store of 128 words, and that our main store has a capacity of 131,072 words, then there are seven bits in an auxiliary-store address and seventeen in a main-store address. Whenever an instruction is extracted from the main store, it is copied into the auxiliary store at an address corresponding to the last seven bits of the main-store address, and the other ten bits of the main-store address are put into the auxiliary store as well. As each instruction in turn is called for, the system tries first to find it in the auxiliary store, and goes on to the main store only if it does not succeed. An auxiliary store used in this way is called a *slave store*, since it plays an entirely subordinate role in the process. Obviously, the greatest advantage is to be gained with loops no longer than the slave store, though there is still some gain in speed with longer loops.

DELAY LINES

In a serial machine, an auxiliary store can be constructed out of delay lines. A train of pulses, a word, say, fed into one end of a delaying device is in fact stored therein for a short period; if it can be arranged for the length of delay to be such that the first pulse emerges from one end just after the last has been fed in at the other, the pulses can be fed in once more, and they can be kept circulating in this fashion until they are required. Delay lines are of two types, electrical and sonic, according to whether the pulses circulating in them are pulses of electric current or mechanical strain. The two types are limited in storage capacity by the distortion that they inflict on signals passing down them. Sonic lines are able to store many more bits than electrical lines; but they are not capable of working at such high bit frequencies, and are consequently suitable only for quite slow machines.

FLIP-FLOPS

In parallel machines, and in some serial machines too, auxiliary stores are built from an array of one-bit stores. The commonest type of one-bit store is an electronic circuit known as a *flip-flop*. This is a circuit with two stable states, between which it can be *flipped* (or *flopped*) by means of an electrical pulse. After gates, flip-flops are the commonest circuits in computers. The two states are designated *one* and *nought* and, since they are both stable, they can be used to store a single bit indefinitely. A flip-flop store has the advantage that its contents are not destroyed by reading.

TUNNEL DIODES

There are several other types of one-bit store. One of them uses a device known as a *tunnel diode*, or *Esaki diode*. This has the property that for a given current flowing in it there are two possible stable voltages; this is again a two-state property, and confers upon the device the power to store a single bit.

CRYOGENICS

Another form of one-bit storage uses the phenomenon of *superconductivity*. When certain metals, particularly tin and lead and their alloys, are cooled to a very low temperature they lose all electrical

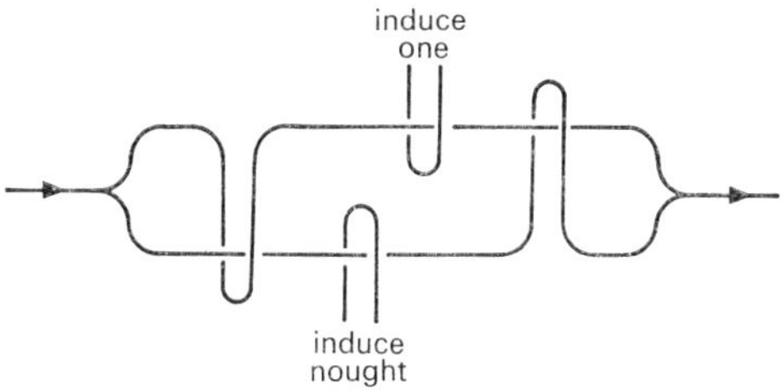

FIG. 9.4. Superconductive One-Bit Store

resistance. Once an electric current has been induced in a loop of material in this condition, it continues to flow indefinitely. Superconductivity is destroyed if the temperature is raised; but it can also be destroyed by inducing a magnetic field in the material, and this last fact is used to make a superconductive one-bit store in the manner shown in Fig. 9.4. A current flows in a piece of superconductive material divided into two branches. Because of the arrangement of the circuit with each branch looping around the other so as to be able to induce a magnetic field in it, a superconductive current flowing down one branch increases the electrical resistance of the other. Thus, current is able to flow in only one of the two branches at a time, so that the device has the necessary two-state property. It is made to change from one state to the other by means of an external pulse, which destroys the superconductivity of the conducting branch. Superconductivity offers a means of making the fastest store yet devised; furthermore, not only storage elements but also gates and amplifying devices can be made using superconductivity. The devices are very cheap to manufacture, since they and their interconnecting wiring can be laid down by processes of etching and vapour deposition. Unfortunately, the practical problems connected with refrigeration down to the low temperatures required have so far proved to be almost insurmountable when it comes to exploiting the ideas commercially. The science of very low temperatures is known as *cryogenics*.

TRANSISTORS

The greatest single advance in computer technology came with the invention of the transistor. Their small size (transistors measure about a twentieth of an inch across and are usually mounted in cans measuring a quarter of an inch or so) makes it possible to build very fast circuits. Firstly, the actual time of transit of electrical signals through a transistor is small; secondly, transistors can be packed closely together so that the propagation time for signals passing between them is kept small. Close packing, incidentally, is possible not only because of their small size but also because they will operate with much smaller signals, and consequently with less dissipation of heat.

Transistors are solid-state devices, that is to say, they are made from a solid piece of material, in contrast to thermionic valves, in which the current is carried by electrons moving *in vacuo*. Transistors are made from a class of substances known as *semi-conductors*, among which the metals germanium and silicon are the most important in this application. Semi-conductors are so called because the conduction of electricity within them takes place by the migration of electrical charges or *carriers* predominantly of one sign, in contrast to ordinary conductors, in which both positive and negative carriers are involved. In a semi-conductor the carriers can be of either sign. depending on the type of impurity that the specimen contains. Semi-conductors of either *p*-type (positive carriers) or *n*-type are made by *doping* the pure material with suitable impurities during manufacture. The negative carriers, of course, are electrons, which are negatively charged. Positive carriers are known as *holes*. Holes, as their name implies, are in fact electron deficiencies, which are capable of migration like electrons, but in the opposite direction.

A junction between a piece of semi-conductor of one type and a piece of the other type will pass current easily in one direction but not the other. Such a device is known as a *diode*. Diodes are used for the construction of gates, the unidirectional property making it possible to close a diode gate simply by establishing a potential across it in the 'wrong' direction.

Modern transistors are made in the form of a sandwich, in which a filling of one type of semi-conductor is held between two slices of the other type; thus we can describe transistors as being either *n-p-n* or *p-n-p*. The filling is known as the *base* of the transistor (a name that is derived from an early design of the device) and the two slices as the *emitter* and the *collector*. Because the base is very thin, the device does not operate (as one might be led to expect) like two diodes back-to-back, but like a single piece of semi-conductor in which it is possible to control the current. By pushing current into, or drawing it out of the base, it is possible to modulate the current flowing between the emitter and the collector; moreover, the changes in emitter-collector current can be made much greater than the changes in base current that caused them; thus the transistor can be used as an amplifier. In computers, transistors are usually used as switches; the base current is varied between extremes, so that the transistor is either fully conducting (*bottomed*, as it is called) or else switched right off, these two conditions corresponding to bit values one and nought. *p-n-p* and *n-p-n* transistors operate on exactly the same principle, the only difference being that voltages and currents are in opposite senses in the two.

MANUFACTURE

Several hundred transistors can be made at the same time from a single slice of silicon or germanium by a process of etching and diffusion. A typical method is illustrated in Fig. 9.5. The slice is printed with a grid of acid-resistant material, and the spaces that are not covered are etched away under carefully controlled conditions. Next, semi-conductor material of the other type is diffused in, to fill up the etched holes, and the slice is printed again with a resistant grid, this time with smaller spaces. After etching again, semi-conductor material of the first type is diffused into the holes, the acid resist is removed, and the slice is diced into individual transistors. Sometimes a mask is used instead of printing with an acid resist. Modern computer transistors are mostly made of silicon; this is because silicon will withstand a higher working temperature than germanium.

Transistors have not only brought higher potential speeds, they have also reduced costs and improved the reliability of computers. Costs have fallen because the devices themselves are cheap to manufacture; because they can be used in simpler circuit configurations

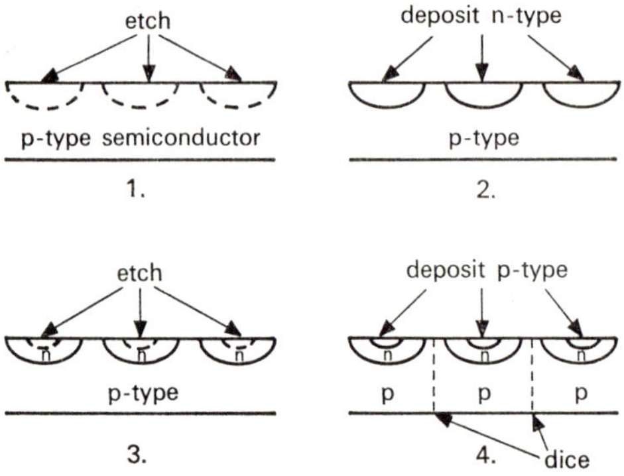

FIG. 9.5. Manufacture of *p-n-p* Transistors

than valves; because they are smaller and lighter and can be assembled by automatic and semi-automatic processes; and because they operate at much smaller voltages—as little as two or three volts, compared with the two or three hundred needed for valve circuits.

RELIABILITY

Transistors are reliable because they do not age in the same way as valves. Thermionic valves rely on a phenomenon known as *thermionic emission*, the emission of electrons from a heated surface. With time, the emissive power of the surface deteriorates, and the valve becomes unable to fulfil its role in the circuit. The mean lifetime of the sort of valve that used to be used in computers was generally less than ten thousand hours. This meant that in a machine with ten thousand valves faults would be developing at a rate of one an hour. Even allowing for the fact that incipient faults could be detected and corrected during regular daily maintenance, a fault rate as high as this was inconvenient, to say the least. It is not easy to obtain accurate figures on the reliability of transistors, since, by the time enough data has been gathered, a particular device has probably become obsolete anyway. But one thing is fairly certain:

the size of computer that can be built today is not limited by considerations of reliability.

PACKAGED CONSTRUCTION

Most computers use a packaged form of construction. Several circuits are built together on a rectangular sheet of reinforced plastic known as a card, and the machine is made up from cards mounted side by side in rows. The cards are plugged into a common panel, which carries interconnection wires between them. The advantage of this form of construction is that a repair can be carried out simply by removing a faulty card and replacing it with a sound card. The computer can then be used again immediately, while the faulty card is taken away to be mended at leisure. The wiring on the cards themselves, and sometimes also on the larger panel, is of the kind miscalled *printed.* In fact what is actually printed is a pattern of acid resist, which is laid over a thin sheet of copper bonded to the card. The uncovered part of the copper laminate is then etched away leaving the desired pattern of wiring. A single card may carry several identical or closely similar circuits, or it may carry several different circuits connected together as a functional unit. The number of circuits that a card can accommodate in the non-functional case is limited by the number of pins on the connector, which must carry all the signal inputs and outputs of the circuits as well as the power supplies. However, the number of functional package types that can be used is limited by manufacturing considerations and by the cost of carrying spares; in general, at least one spare should be carried for every package type in the machine.

REFLECTIONS

The chief disadvantage of the packaged form of construction is the length of the interconnecting wires. Something can be done towards reducing wire lengths by careful layout or placement of the cards, and programs have been written to determine optimal, or nearly optimal, solutions to placement problems in specific cases. Ultimately, however, there are some signals that have to travel several yards. The wires that connect the store to the arithmetic circuits are particularly critical. Signals actually travel along wires at speeds of the order of the speed of light; but the trouble is that not all the signal is absorbed when it gets to the other end. Some is reflected back to the transmitting end, where some again is absorbed and some reflected. It is not until the signal has been reflected and re-reflected a great number of times that the system has settled down well enough for the conditions *one* and *nought* to be distinguished unambiguously. All this takes time, and the amount of time it takes is proportional to the length of the wire. What this means in effect is that wires impose a delay of several nanoseconds per foot on signals travelling along them. Now although a few nanoseconds are neither here nor there in a small, cheap machine, the effect of wiring delays can vitiate any advantage gained from the fast transistors used in the most expensive machines.

MATCHING

Before discussing how reflections can be avoided, we must introduce the concept of impedance. Impedance is simply the ratio between voltage and current; the word does not imply any hindrance to the passage of a signal. The higher the impedance, the smaller the current that a given voltage will drive. Every piece of wire has its own characteristic impedance, which depends on its thickness and its proximity to earth or to a nearby conductor that is earthed. If the impedance of the circuit at the end of a wire is not the same as that of the wire itself, there is an imbalance between voltage and current; there would appear to be either a surplus of current with no voltage to drive it, or else a surplus voltage with no current arising from it. Of course, such a situation cannot possibly exist, and Nature resolves it by reflecting part of the signal. It is obvious, then, what must be done to prevent reflections: the characteristic impedance of the wires must be matched by the impedance of the circuits. Strictly, it is necessary to match only one end of the wire, since it is continued to-and-fro reflections that cause the trouble. Naturally the wires must have a constant impedance throughout their length; but this can be assured by keeping them a constant distance from an earthed conductor, for instance by printing them on one side of a sheet of plastic material that has a continuous sheet of copper bonded to the other side and earthed.

INTEGRATED CIRCUITS

In recent years computer manufacturers have been introducing *integrated circuits*, or *IC's*. These are of two types: in the earlier type the circuit wiring and the passive components (resistors, capacitors, inductors) are laid down on a small rectangle of ceramic material by printing or by diffusion through a mask. The active components (transistors and diodes) are then soldered into position on top of the wiring. A number of ceramic units, each of which carries several circuits, can be attached by solder pins to a larger board carrying the interconnections between them. This form of construction has two advantages: a great number of circuits can be packed into a small space, reducing the lengths of their interconnections, and the arrangement lends itself well to automatic, and consequently cheaper, methods of manufacture and assembly.

But the process of micro-miniaturization has been carried further than the ceramic module: complete circuits have been forged from a single chip of the semiconductor material itself by a method that is similar to the process by which transistors themselves are made. It takes many more stages of etching and diffusion to make an integrated circuit, of course; but all the components, active and passive alike, can be fabricated in the same way. Resistors are made of semiconductor with an appropriate amount of doping; diodes can be made to act as capacitors by making use of a phenomenon known as *hole storage*. Insulation between one layer of semiconductor and another can be assured by organizing that the voltage between them shall be in the wrong direction for conduction to take place. The manufacture of single-chip IC's can be made quite automatic, and it can be carried out with relatively inexpensive equipment. Further development depends principally upon the ability of circuit designers to devise circuits suitable for this method of manufacture, and in a wide enough range to satisfy the needs of the system designer. It must be said, however, that integrated circuits, at the present time, are generally slower than the same circuits would be if they were made from conventional components.

OVERLAP

Having selected the fastest store available, increased its effectiveness by using auxiliary stores, and chosen the fastest circuits available for the dataflow and microprogram, there is one more thing we can do to increase the speed of a system: we can introduce overlap. We have said something about overlap, or look-ahead, in earlier chapters, and there is not much more that can be said in general terms. As we use the term here, we mean the ability of two or more sub-units of the central machine to operate simultaneously, so that two or more instructions can be in progress at the same time. The commonest form of overlap is for one instruction to be in course of preparation (extraction from store, and modification or replacement) while a previous instruction is still being evaluated. But in fact any instruction can be made to overlap an earlier instruction if it does not depend on it in any direct way, and if there is a sub-unit available for it to be obeyed in. Even jumps can be overlapped; though this means either that both branches are prepared together, or else that the most likely branch is chosen, with the possibility of having to back-track if the choice proves to be wrong. The whole subject of overlap and look-ahead gives scope for most ingenious design; but there is a limit to what is practicable. There comes a point, in other words, when additional complexity degrades performance by more than the advantage it confers.

EXERCISES 9

1. Analysis of programs yields the following instruction frequencies in a computer language—

MOVE	literal	20
	name	30
CTJ		16
TSUB	literal	8
	name	6
ADD	literal	2
	name	8
J		4
TFER		4
SUB	name	1
MLT	name	1

Also, fifty per cent of all instructions are modified. Other frequencies are negligible.

A range of three computers using this language has the following instruction times (in microseconds)—

		1	2	3
MOVE	literal	16	4	2·5
	name	24	6	3
ADD, SUB, TSUB	literal	20	6	3
	name	28	8	3·5
CTJ		24	8	2
J		10	4	1
MLT	name	3200	68	10
TFER	(mean)	400	50	25
modification		8	2	0·5

Calculate mean instruction times for the three systems.

2. The Post Office unit on a particular computer is calculated to be 10 milliseconds. Hesitation takes 4 microseconds for every group of four bytes. The magnetic-tape system fitted runs at 120 inches per second and is recorded at 555 bytes per inch. By sketching a graph of throughput (thousands of bytes in and out per second) against activity (number of P.O. units per thousand bytes), or by any other method, find—

(*a*) maximum activity possible at maximum throughput,
(*b*) speed of throughput for an activity of 2 units,
(*c*) level of activity that will cut the throughput down to half the maximum.

Calculate figures for a two-channel and a one-channel tape system. (Neglect the effect of blocking on tape.)

10. *Floating Point**

SCALED NUMBERS

WHEN we were postulating an imaginary machine in Chapter 3, we said that we would restrict ourselves in the first place to considering only integral numbers. But, at the same time, we added a rider to the effect that fractions can be expressed as integers by imagining that there is a scaling factor attached to each number. For instance, the decimal fraction 0·009876 is equivalent to the integer 9876 multiplied by the scaling factor 10^{-6}. In this chapter we shall be talking about the various ways that are available for handling fractional numbers, the problems involved, and the consequences that flow from them.

As long as all the scaling factors involved in a calculation are the same, the calculation can be performed just as though no scaling factors were present at all. Thus adding 9876 to 2469 to give 12345 is just as valid whether these numbers represent the quantities they appear to or whether they represent 0·009876, 0·002469, and 0·012345, or 9876000, 2469000, and 12345000, or for that matter any other set of three numbers with the same digits and a consistent scaling factor. Unfortunately, scaling factors do not always remain the same. One of the things that leads to rescaling is overflow. When a number exceeds the capacity of a register, it may be quite legitimate to lop off the least significant digit and then rescale. For example, let us suppose that the capacity of a register is equivalent to ten decimal digits, and let us suppose that we wish to add the two numbers 123·456789 and 998·8776654, which we are representing by the integers 1234567890 and 9988776654, both with scaling factors of 10^{-7}. The sum is 1122·3344544, which is eleven digits long, and therefore too long to fit into a register. The last digit must be dropped, to give the sum as 1122·334454, represented in scaled form as 1122334454 with a scaling factor of 10^{-6}. Naturally some precision was lost when one digit was cut off; but this might be considered a small price to pay for the convenience of getting the whole number into a single register.

* This chapter may be omitted by readers interested solely in commercial applications of computers.

Multiplication is another process that might necessitate rescaling. Not only does it generate as many digits as there are in the multiplier and the multiplicand put together, but the product is on an entirely new scale. The product of 123 and 456 is 56088; but the product of the fractions 0·000123 and 0·000456 is 0·000000056088. In this second case, the two scaling factors of 10^{-6} have combined to give a new scaling factor of 10^{-12}.

Another reason why it is not possible in general to work with constant scaling factors is that it is not always possible to know what factor to choose. Even if all the original data and the final results can be fitted into the same numeric range, there is no guarantee that results formed at intermediate stages in the computation will also fit into the same range. If we cannot rescale we risk a serious loss of precision.

RANGE AND PRECISION

It is most important to get a clear idea of what is meant by *range* and *precision* when these terms are applied to numeric quantities. A screw micrometer is generally regarded as a very accurate device. It will measure distances down to a thousandth of an inch or less. But a micrometer is not capable of dealing with distances any greater than an inch or two. Consequently, anything a screw micrometer can tell us can be said in four or five decimal digits. Land surveyors use methods that enable them to measure distances of several miles, and their measurements are accurate to within a few yards; consequently a surveyor's measurements can be expressed in four of five digits as well. The surveyor and the fitter are working to much the same degree of *precision*, though the *ranges* over which they make their measurements differ by a factor of something like one million.

We must make a distinction too between those numbers that are by their nature exact, like accountants' balances, and those that are derived from physical measurements, and are consequently known only to a limited degree of precision. It is with numbers of the latter class that we are concerned in this chapter. Exact numbers are nearly always integers; if not, they can be handled with a constant scaling factor. They must on no account be truncated.

For most practical purposes, five or six decimal digits (twenty bits, say) are all that are needed to express the numerical observations that we are capable of making, provided that we can attach the right scaling factor to them. However, as we shall see, it is advisable to start with a great deal more precision than this to avoid the inaccuracies introduced by successive truncating and rescaling.

Suppose that we start with the two numbers—

0·034567 and 0·00054321

which we represent as—

34567 and 54321

with scaling factors of—

10^{-6} and 10^{-8}

If we wish to add these two numbers, we must make the scaling factors the same, which we can do either by scaling down the larger or by scaling up the smaller. In practice it is not always possible to scale the larger number down, since the resulting number (in this particular case, 3456700) might no longer fit into a register. Thus we are obliged to scale the smaller number up, expressing it as 00543 with a scaling factor of 10^{-6}. Our numbers are now to the same scale and so we can add them to give the result 35110 with a scaling factor of 10^{-6}. If we wish, we can now take the process one step further and, without any loss of precision, express the answer as 3511 with a scaling factor of 10^{-5}, which of course is equivalent to 0·03511.

NORMALIZATION

The number 0·03511 is identical to the integer 3511 multiplied by the fifth power of -1. The quantity 3511 is known as the *mantissa** of the number, and the quantity -5 as the *exponent*, ten being the *base* of the exponent in this case. Since we are writing the number in decimal form, it is reasonable to presume a decimal exponent base, and write simply—

3511E-5

as a convenient way of expressing the number.

Equally well we could write—

0·3511E-1

or even, if we so wished—

3511000E-8

It is usual to choose one of the many possible representations of a number to be the *normal* form, always converting new data and newly generated numbers to this same form. One possible choice for normal

* It is also sometimes known as the *argument;* but we have already made use of this word in an entirely different sense.

form is the one in which the mantissa is the smallest possible integer, in this case—

3511E-5

Another is the one in which the mantissa is the largest possible fraction—

0·3511E-1

This is a better form to use because, with a fractional mantissa, any non-significant zeros are held at the lower end of the number, and it is these that will be dropped first if there is any rescaling to be done. Thus, had we been performing the addition in the last example on a machine with a register length of eight decimal digits, we could have expressed our two numbers in normal form as—

0·34567000E-1 and 0·5432100E-3

Rescaling the second number gives—

0·00543210E-1

and adding gives—

0·35103210E-1

which does not need normalizing.

It might be objected that the sixth and seventh digits of this last sum are meaningless, since the original data was known only to a precision of five digits, and consequently nothing was lost when the last two were dropped in the earlier example. There is something in this; but, on the other hand, there is nothing inherent in the number 0·34567000E-1 that says that the accuracy is only five figures—the sixth figure might have been accurately zero. Besides, even if the last two digits of the sum are meaningless, at least they are doing no harm.

To recapitulate, let us consider one more example, a subtraction this time. Let us subtract—

0·76543000E3 from 0·76531000E3

This time the two exponents are the same, so there is no rescaling to do. The difference is—

−0·00012000E3

which in normal form becomes—

−0·12000000E0

FLOATING POINT

Many computer systems, particularly those used for scientific work, provide special facilities for handling numbers in mantissa-and-exponent form. In such machines, rescaling and normalization are wholly automatic, and the process of combining scaled numbers is often carried out in a unit quite separate from the ordinary Mill used for combining integers. The facility is usually referred to as *floating point*, though this is really a misnomer—it is the string of digits that floats, not the point, which remains fixed in position, usually at the more significant end of the word. Unscaled arithmetic is usually referred to as *fixed-point.*

FORMAT

In a binary computer, naturally, the mantissa of a floating-point number is in binary form. The simplest base to use for the exponent is obviously two, and the exponent itself is necessarily expressed in binary form. Mantissa and exponent are usually packed together in one word, or one pair of words, the unpacking being carried out automatically by means of appropriate routes in the dataflow. A typical floating-point format for a thirty-two-bit word allows eight bits (one byte) for the exponent, and the remaining twenty-four bits for the mantissa. If the most significant bits of mantissa and exponent were used to indicate sign, this format would give a precision of one part in 8,388,608, and a range between 2^{127} and 2^{-128}.

EXPONENT BASE

Some machines use exponent bases that are powers of two rather than two itself; exponent bases of eight and sixteen are common. The effect of course is to extend the range far beyond what would be obtainable with an exponent of the same length to the base two. However, the precision is reduced slightly. This is because the mantissa in its normal form may have several zeros immediately after the point. With an exponent base of sixteen, the mantissa in normal form must lie in the range plus one to plus one sixteenth or minus one sixteenth to minus one. In these circumstances there may be as many as three zeros (or, in the case of negative numbers, ones) immediately after the point, with a corresponding reduction in the number of significant digits.

An advantage of larger exponent bases that is probably more valuable than merely increasing the exponent range (which could be achieved as well by increasing the length of the exponent at the expense of the mantissa) is an increase in speed. Time is saved in rescaling, since the larger the exponent base the greater the chance that two numbers will already have the same exponent. Time is also saved in renormalizing, since the greater the exponent base, the smaller the chance that an arithmetic operation will generate an unnormalized result.

OVERFLOW

A floating-point mantissa cannot overflow, since overflow is taken care of by re-normalizing after the operation. However the *exponent* will overflow if a result is generated that lies beyond the end of the exponent range. Exponent overflow can be handled in much the same way as fixed-point overflow, by providing a jump test and allowing the programmer to specify what remedial action he wishes. Numbers smaller than the minimum of the floating-point range are generally treated as zero; and computers do not necessarily make any distinction between very small floating-point numbers and true zero.

TRUNCATION

When a number is rescaled preparatory to addition or subtraction, one or more bits are lost from the less significant end of the mantissa. The same can be true when a product is cut down to normal mantissa size. In some systems no allowance is made for bits lost in this way, and the truncated results enter into subsequent operations just as if no bits had been lost. As a result, all subsequent results are biased; since the numbers are a little smaller than they should be, the results are under-valued. In involved processes, in which the number of arithmetic operations, and consequently the number of truncations, is large, quite serious errors may be introduced.

ROUNDING

A way of avoiding truncation* errors is to round truncated results. Rounding in binary machines is the same in principle as the way we learned in school for rounding decimal numbers; if the digits lost amount to half the radix or more, unity is added to the digits remaining; otherwise no action is taken. In binary processes this means that, if the most significant bit of those lost is a one, one is added to the bits remaining in the mantissa. Fig. 10.1 shows how truncation gives a downward bias while rounding does not.

* The word truncation is also used to denote another type of error—that introduced when an infinite series is represented by a finite number of its terms. This is confusing, since the context does not always indicate which sense is meant.

A disadvantage of rounding is that it takes time, since it may involve an extra addition, with the need to propagate carry an indefinite distance up the mantissa. An alternative process, not involving addition, is to force the least significant bit remaining in the mantissa to be always one. As can be seen from Fig. 10.1, this is, in fact, a rounding process. It is also completely free of bias, since just as many numbers are increased as are decreased.

Whatever precautions are taken to avoid truncation bias, they cannot avoid introducing some error of one sign or the other. Errors are cumulative, and the more involved the calculation the more they

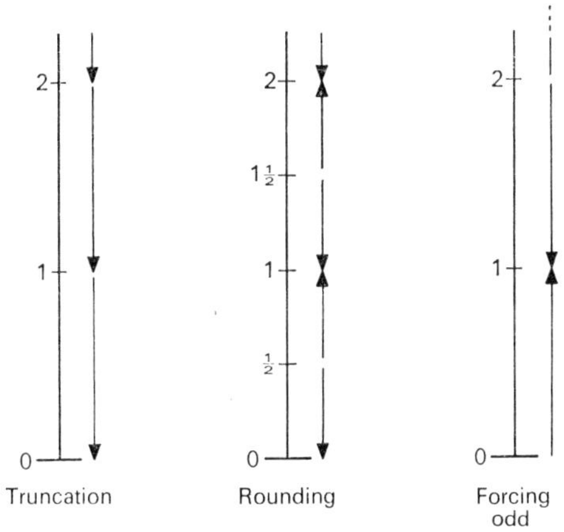

FIG. 10.1.

can accumulate. Although an unbiased system will produce a zero *mean* error, the actual *spread* of errors in several calculations can be quite large, and individual results may be seriously wrong. One way of reducing such errors is to provide a mantissa of much greater precision than is absolutely necessary. Some systems provide a choice of two degrees of precision, thus a system might have a single-word format with an eight-bit exponent and a twenty-four-bit mantissa as well as an alternative format using a double word and providing a fifty-six-bit mantissa. Naturally, operations at high precision are slower than operations at low precision: the user must choose one or the other according to the size of error he expects and the error he regards as tolerable. If there is any doubt, he can perform the same calculation once in each degree of precision, using test data; if the results do not differ significantly, the lower precision is adequate to the task.

STANDARD-SIGNIFICANCE WORKING

Short of a lengthy analysis, there is often no direct way of determining the amount of error involved in a floating-point calculation. Some idea can be obtained, as we have just suggested, by doing the thing in two different ways, either by using different degrees of precision or by using a different programming approach. Some systems provide an optional *standard-significance* mode of operation, in which the numbers are not normalized after every operation; this too can be used to give another set of results for comparison. Many of the commonest types of calculation have been analysed to find the approach that is least subject to rounding error. Beyond this, accurate mathematical programming is largely a matter of experience; the expert avoids those lines of approach that in the past have led to serious errors.

We have just mentioned *standard-significance* working, in which the result is not normalized. Every bit then has the same numerical significance as the corresponding bit in the original operands. Of course there is no *logical* need for normalization; it adds nothing to the information in the result or to its accuracy. All it does in fact is move non-significant zeros from one end of the mantissa to the other. And it takes time. Consider for instance the two unstandardized numbers—

0·00004321E7 and 0·09876543E5

Under the normal rule for rescaling, we shift the number with the smaller exponent, converting it to—

0·00098765E7

The sum of the two numbers is then—

0·00103086E7

But if the numbers had been standardized in the first place—

0·43210000E3 and 0·98765430E4

we should have had to rescale the first number to—

0·04321000E4

and add, giving—

1·03086430

which then must be normalized to—

0·10308643E5

Now it might be argued that the normalized result is more accurate than the unnormalized result, since the first contains two digits that were lost in generating the second. But these two digits have no real significance: they represent a quantity that is less than the error inherent in the first of the two original numbers, and consequently inherent in the sum of the two. At the worst, all the loss of the two digits can do is reinforce the original error; but it is just as likely to reduce it.

The chief argument against standard-significance working is that it is unfamiliar. This is a valid argument. Over the years, programmers have developed a number of short cuts to speed up floating-point calculations, and these have been devised on the basis of normalized results. Until a new set of short cuts has been devised, the preference will probably remain in favour of normalization rather than standard significance. However radical a programmer is politically, he knows in his professional life that conservatism saves effort, and therefore money.

IMPLEMENTATION

Several computers provide separate units for floating-point and fixed-point work. This means that floating-point and fixed-point operations can go on concurrently, overlapping in time, the floating-point unit carrying out a subtraction, say, while the fixed-point unit is busy modifying the address of the next instruction. In very large systems, floating-point addition and subtraction may be carried out in a different unit from multiplication.

In systems where all floating-point operations are performed in the same unit, it is common practice to provide a single-argument type of instruction for floating-point work. This is because mathematical algorithms often require the result of one operation to be held for use in the next, and not returned to the store. Consequently, floating-point instructions are best directed toward an accumulator situated within the floating-point unit, subsequent storage of results being entirely within the control of the programmer.

In our imaginary machine we might postulate floating-point instructions as follows—

```
FADD    Y
FSUB    Y
FMLT    Y
FDIV    Y
```

In the first of these, the operand named by Y is added into the floating-point accumulator; in the second it is subtracted from the content of the accumulator. In the third, the product is left in the accumulator, and in the last the operand Y is divided into the content of the accumulator, which is left holding the quotient. Notice that the concept of a residue is meaningless in floating-point work, where operands are in any case only approximate.

Our imaginary machine will also need instructions for storing the content of the floating-point accumulator, and for loading it with new data; consequently we shall need instructions of the form—

```
FSTO    Y
FLOD    Y
```

We might consider improving the system still further by providing facilities for subtraction and division to operate in the opposite sense, subtrahend and divisor being taken from the accumulator instead of Y; but the facilities we have already mentioned will suffice for the present.

Let us illustrate the use of a set of floating-point instructions, such as those just postulated, to form the sum of the terms of a polynomial. A polynomial is an expression of the form—

$$A_0 + A_1x + A_2x^2 + A_3x^3 + \ldots A_nx^n$$

In fact we can obtain a much neater sequence of instructions if we rewrite the polynomial in the form—

$$((\ldots((A_nx + A_{n-1})x + A_{n-2})x + \ldots)x + A_1)x + A_0$$

Let us suppose that there are twenty terms ($n = 19$) and that the twenty coefficients are stored in reverse order in a set A. We proceed as follows—

```
  1            MOVE   '1'
  2            MOVE   '19'
               FLOD   'A'
 ┌→            FMLT   X
 │             FADD   A(1)
 └─1           CTJ    '− 2'
               FSTO   POLY
               STOP
```

EXERCISES 10

1. Express the following in scaled form, using E as a separator between the mantissa and the exponent. Use a decimal base for the exponent, and express the mantissa as the largest possible fraction.

0·00056789	24680000	3·14159
876·543	20000003	23400E249

2. Perform the following operations, scaling up the smaller number and expressing the answers with the mantissa as the smallest possible integer. Round where necessary to keep the same word length.

123E19 + 456E20
87654E107 − 87654E100
87654E107 + 87654E104
87654E107 − 87645E107
12418E–56 + 53219E–54
987654E21 + 432144E20

(In the last case assume that the capacity of the mantissa cannot exceed six digits.)

3. Evaluate by rescaling and rounding—

0·1234E3 + 0·5216E–1
0·998E–7 + 0·261E–9
0·4206E4 + 0·7781E6
0·8181E0 − 0·4453E–2
0·829E–16 − 0·804E–16
0·829E–16 − 0·804E–16
0·4096E8 + 0·2011E10

Assume that the mantissa capacity cannot exceed four digits, and give answers in normal form.

4. Perform the following operations, giving the answers in normal form with the mantissa as the largest fraction. Assume that the mantissa capacity is twelve bits. The exponent bases to be used are given in brackets after each example. Round where necessary after shifting.

0·100100010010E001 + 0·100111010100E011 (2)
0·100010110010E101 − 0·100101001111E010 (2)
0·011010100101E110 + 0·100110010100E100 (8)
0·111110001010E101 + 0·100111010010E100 (16)

5. Two positive numbers are held as integers in X and Y with scaling factors in the form of exponents to the base 2 in X + 1 and Y + 1. In the absence of floating-point facilities, write a sequence of instructions to add the two numbers. The sum is to be left in X and X + 1 in normal form, and Y and Y + 1 are to be left unaltered.

6. Given three vectors A, B and C and a scalar quantity P, all single-length floating-point quantities, use the floating-point instructions proposed in this chapter to write sequences for calculating—

(*a*) vector sum according to $A_n + B_n = C_n$
(*b*) scalar product $P = \Sigma A_n B_n$

The dimension of the vectors is given as SIZE.

11. Programming at a Higher Level

In the earlier chapters of this book we were developing a programming language for our imaginary machine. It was a machine-oriented language; that is to say, statements were similar in form and content to instructions as they would eventually appear in the machine's store. Because of this, several constraints had to be imposed on the language because of features in the hardware that had nothing to do with the algorithms the language was intended to express. Nevertheless, the language we developed was a great deal closer to the needs of the user than the languages that had to be used with the earliest computers. For one thing, we permitted the use of alphabetic names instead of machine addresses; we replaced numeric function codes by alphabetic mnemonic codes; and we provided simple means for incorporating subroutines of various kinds. All these things in fact are features of modern computer assembly languages.

Another thing we provided in our imaginary machine was the ability to handle sets as well as individual data items. This is something that is only just beginning to become available in assembly languages. Nevertheless our language is still far from ideal; anyone who wants to use it to express algorithms is obliged to split what he may think of as a single operation into components corresponding to the elementary operations that the machine can perform. The mathematical programmer is particularly ill-served. What he would like to write are arithmetic statements like—

$$A = B + C^2D/E$$

and—

$$X = Y_n + 24Z_n$$

In order to make programming easier for the ordinary user, and consequently reduce the incidence of errors, a number of higher-level languages have been devised with characteristics oriented towards the job rather than the machine. Some of these are available for only one or two machines, but there are several that are available for most of the computers currently on the market. The languages that have been widely adopted serve another purpose too: they make it possible to interchange programs between different computers. It is not our intention to give an exhaustive description of any of these job-oriented languages here, or to make a detailed comparison between them; these are subjects that are already well covered in the literature. Our purpose is simply to give the reader some understanding of what these languages are trying to do. Programs written in higher-level languages are eventually converted into machine code so that they can be interpreted by the machine. The process of conversion is known as *compilation.* There must be a *compiler* for every language for every machine that will accept it, and compilers form a substantial part of the software that is supplied with machines. Programming with the aid of compilers is sometimes called *automatic programming.*

AUTOCODES

The earliest attempts at job-oriented languages were known as *autocodes.* Some of these have been particularly successful, and are still widely used. The principal advantage of autocodes over machine-oriented languages is that they permit the writing of arithmetic statements, such as the two quoted above, in something very close to normal algebraic notation. Usually the only data symbols permitted are single letters, and some convention must be established to differentiate between variables and subscripts. The only form of arithmetic statement commonly permitted is an equality with an arithmetic expression on the right-hand side and a single symbol on the left. This type of statement corresponds to a normal computational process, in which an expression is evaluated and a single result is placed in a named register.

STANDARD FUNCTIONS

The bulk of an autocode program consists of sequences of arithmetic statements. Facilities are also provided for iteration, that is, for performing a sequence of operations a stated number of times. Autocodes also supply several standard functions—roots, circular and hyperbolic functions, logarithms, etc.—and some have input and output facilities as well.

FORTRAN

The first really successful attempt at a true high-level programming language is known as FORTRAN (FORmula TRANslation). FORTRAN, in spite of its limitations, is probably the most widely used programming language today. It is available on all commercial computers, and programs written in FORTRAN for one machine can be run with little, sometimes without any, modification on another machine. Because it is familiar to so many people, FORTRAN is sometimes used for describing algorithms, even when there is no intention of carrying out a computer evaluation.

Like the autocodes, FORTRAN permits the writing of arithmetic statements; but names are not confined to single letters. FORTRAN distinguishes between two types of variable, *integer* and *real.* Real quantities are any quantities, integral or fractional, that do not have an imaginary part, that is, a quantity derivable from the square root of a negative number. The distinction between integer and real in FORTRAN generally corresponds to the distinction between fixed point and floating point in a computer. In the absence of a statement to the contrary, all names starting with I, J, K, L, M, or N are taken to refer to integers, and all other names are taken to refer to real quantities.

FORTRAN can handle sets. These are known as *arrays* in the language, and they may be either one-dimensional (as lists or vectors) or two-dimensional (tables, matrices, etc.). Arrays can be handled whole in certain types of statement, notably input and output statements; but in arithmetic statements they are handled item by item with the aid of subscripts. Subscripts are written in brackets after the array name, thus—

MATRIX (4, 7)

which indicates the seventh element in the fourth row of an array MATRIX. (Notice that the first row and column are labelled 1, not 0.) The *dimension* or *dimensions* of an array (the number of items in a one-dimensional array, or the number of rows and columns in a two-dimensional array) must be declared early in the program, so that the compiler can allocate the correct amount of space for it. It is not possible in FORTRAN to vary the dimensions of an array while the program is running.

Because of the conventions for writing names, multiplication cannot be indicated, as in ordinary algebra, simply by proximity. The symbol used for multiplication is an asterisk, and it must not be omitted. A pair of asterisks is used to denote exponentiation (raising to a power).

FORTRAN also includes a number of statements written in ordinary English. Among these are statements corresponding to the various kinds of jump instruction. For instance, the words GO TO, followed by a statement number, denote an unconditional jump. Statement numbers are used in much the same way as labels: not every statement need be numbered, and numbers need not even be consecutive. FORTRAN does not normally permit the use of alphabetic labels.

Another form of the GO TO statement is—

```
GO TO (45, 178, 16, 24), I
```

This corresponds to what we referred to in Chapter 5 as a switch jump. The jump destination depends on the value of I at the time; if the value is 1, the jump goes to statement 45, if its value is 2, the jump goes to statement 178, and so on. It is known as a computed GO TO statement.

The counting type of jump is achieved by means of statements starting with the word DO. A typical example might be—

```
DO 85 J = 8,28,1
```

This would give rise to a loop terminating in the statement labelled 85. An integer variable J would be set initially to the value 8, and it would be increased by unity at the end of each cycle of the loop until it exceeded 28, when the loop would terminate. This particular statement might preface a sequence of operations intended to perform some repetitive series of operations on all the elements in the second, third, and fourth rows of a seven-column array. Because DO statements give rise to loops, they must be used in accordance with the rules of loops. Thus one DO loop may be nested within another; but loops must not interlock. The compiler program should be able to detect violations of the rules for writing DO statements.

The ordinary conditional jump corresponds to FORTRAN statements starting with IF. A typical statement might be—

```
IF (QTY) 57, 84, 56
```

This would cause a jump according to the value of the expression QTY. In this case, if QTY were negative, the jump would go to statement 57, if zero to statement 84, and if positive to statement 56. Some versions of FORTRAN also provide a form of IF statement that can be used for testing overflow.

An interesting form of the IF statement is that referring to sense switches; an example might be—

```
IF (SENSE SWITCH 5) 69, 43
```

This causes a jump to 69 if sense switch 5 is on, and to 43 if it is off. Sense switches on some machines are actual physical switches: on others they are simulated by messages on a console typewriter. The purpose of the sense-switch facility is to enable an operator to influence a FORTRAN program while it is running.

INPUT AND OUTPUT

FORTRAN also provides quite extensive facilities for input and output. The principal purpose of input and output statements is to associate fields on the medium of a particular input or output device with names in the program. Input and output operations in FORTRAN are initiated by statements starting with READ or WRITE. A typical READ statement might be—

```
READ (CR1, 72) ((MATRIX (I, J,), I = 1, 20), VECTOR (J), J = 1, 10),
X, Y, TEXT
```

This statement would cause five pieces of data referred to as MATRIX, VECTOR, X, Y, and TEXT to be read from a device CR1. It would already have been declared whether these were real or integer quantities. The number 72 in this statement is the statement number of a FORMAT statement giving the precise form the data takes on the input medium.

FORMAT DEFINITION

The minimum information a FORMAT statement must supply is—

the number of characters in each field,
whether the data is alphabetic or numeric,
if numeric, where the point (if not explicit) lies.

A FORMAT statement consists of the word FORMAT followed by a list of field definitions corresponding to the list of names in the READ or WRITE statement. Thus, corresponding to the READ statement given above we might have a FORMAT statement—

```
72 FORMAT (200E10·5, 10I8, E12·0, E12·0, A24)
```

This would cause the first 200 ten-digit fields to be read and converted as if there were five figures after the decimal point. These would be entered (referring to the READ statement) as the elements of MATRIX. Ten 8-digit integers would then be read and entered as the elements of VECTOR. Then would follow the two 12-digit quantities X and Y, and a 24-character piece of text.

As well as the standard functions available with FORTRAN, which are quite extensive, the user is able to define functions of his own and to write subroutines. These facilities are similar to those we have provided in our imaginary assembly language, though the arrangements differ in detail. Most versions of FORTRAN also permit the user to incorporate segments and subroutines written in other languages. Another feature in some, but not all, versions of

FORTRAN is the existence of logical variables, variables with only two possible values, true or false. Logical variables can be used in logical statements and as expressions defining jump conditions.

To give the reader some idea of the look of a FORTRAN program, we shall rewrite the sorting procedure we gave in Chapter 4, in FORTRAN. The flow diagram will be found in Fig. 4.1. What we are about to write is neither a complete FORTRAN program nor a complete segment of a program; it is simply a sequence of statements defining a particular procedure, like the original sequence in Chapter 4.

```
      REAL LIST(135)
      .
      .
      REAL WS
      INTEGER FLAG
10    FLAG = 0
      DO 20 I = 1,134,1
      IF (LIST(I) - LIST(I + 1) ) 20,20,
      WS = LIST(I)
      LIST(I) = LIST(I + 1)
      LIST(I + 1) = WS
      FLAG = 1
20    CONTINUE
      IF (FLAG) ,,10
      .
      .
      .
```

Where statement numbers are omitted in IF statements, the inference is that control passes to the next statement in sequence. Notice the use here of the dummy statement CONTINUE to complete the loop; this is because the statement—

```
      FLAG = 1
```

must be jumped over by the IF statement that precedes it.

As an example of a complete FORTRAN segment let us take again the procedure for evaluating a highest common factor, which we described in Chapter 3. The flow diagram is in Fig. 3.2. In FORTRAN, the segment might be—

```
      FUNCTION HCF (A, B)
      GO TO 510
509   B = A + B
510   A = A - B
      IF (A) 515, ,510
      HCF = B
      GO TO 520
      A = A + B
```

```
515    B = B − A
       IF (B) 509, ,515
       HCF = A
520    RETURN
       END
```

To make use of this function, it is necessary only to write HCF followed by suitable arguments in any arithmetic statement. For instance, the statement—

```
BOUND = HCF (529, 1265)
```

would replace the quantity BOUND by the calculated value 23. The statement RETURN, of course, obeys the link.

It may be objected at this stage that the formulation of a procedure in FORTRAN is no neater than a formulation in an assembly code, and it is quite true that modern assembly languages are becoming so powerful that FORTRAN can hardly any longer be regarded as a shorthand form, except perhaps in the evaluation of complex arithmetic expressions. Moreover, a compiled FORTRAN program generally runs to many more machine instructions than the problem would have required had it been programmed in the machine's own assembly language. However, FORTRAN is still a universal language, and programs and routines in FORTRAN can have quite wide application. Unfortunately, there are many different versions (or dialects) of FORTRAN. The commonest is known as FORTRAN IV, and there is an older dialect still in wide use, known as FORTRAN II. On top of this, the implementations of FORTRAN on various machines may differ from the standard dialects by having various extensions or restrictions. Just because a program is written in FORTRAN it does not follow that it will run on any machine that claims to implement FORTRAN.

ALGOL

A more powerful language than FORTRAN for mathematical programming is ALGOL (ALGOrithmic Language). Like FORTRAN, ALGOL divides variables into the classes of real and integer, and, like FORTRAN, it permits the direct evaluation of arithmetic expressions, though the conventions for writing them are rather different. ALGOL will handle arrays, and permits individual array elements to be addressed by subcripts; also ALGOL arrays are permitted to vary in size during a computation.

BOOLEAN VARIABLES

Conditional statements in ALGOL are conditional not only upon arithmetic expressions but also upon relations between arithmetic expressions, a much more flexible arrangement than that provided in most dialects of FORTRAN. Loops are introduced by the word *for*, and the variable used for counting may be advanced in fractional steps if desired. Another feature of ALGOL is the use of *boolean* variables and expressions, which can have only the values *true* and *false*. They are used to set conditions for testing in conditional statements.

BLOCK STRUCTURE

Probably the most significant feature of ALGOL is its block structure. A block is a sequence of statements prefaced by the word *begin* and terminated by the word *end*. Names and labels introduced within a block are entirely local; moreover their values are lost outside the block, and they cannot be presumed to have the same values the next time the block is entered, unless special steps are taken to ensure this. Blocks can be nested within one another; in such cases, names introduced in an outer block are presumed to apply within the inner block unless they are actually redefined therein. The nested-block structure of an ALGOL program is usually indicated by indentation of the written statements.

Here, as an illustration, is the sorting procedure again, this time written in ALGOL—

```
begin array LIST (1: 135);
        real WS; integer I;
        boolean FLAG;
        for FLAG:= true while FLAG do
        begin FLAG:= false;
                for I:= 1 step 1 until 134 do
                if LIST (I) > LIST (I + 1) then
                begin WS:= LIST(I);
                        LIST(I):= LIST(I + 1);
                        LIST(I + 1): = WS;
                        FLAG:= true;
                end
        end
end
```

ALGOL has no input or output facilities; it is a purely procedural language. Input and output facilities must be provided by manufacturers implementing the language. Although what is provided follows the general structural plan of ALGOL, the methods used differ in detail between systems, which means that ALGOL programs cannot be carried over as a whole from one machine to another, although the purely procedural blocks of a program are generally transferable. The current form of the language is known as ALGOL 60; it is fully defined in a report issued by the International Federation for Information Processing.

COBOL

ALGOL and to a lesser extent FORTRAN, were designed primarily with the needs of the mathematical programmer in mind. On the other hand, several languages have been designed for use by commercial programmers; of these the most widely used is COBOL (COmputer Business-Oriented Language). COBOL was sponsored by the U.S. Department of Defence, which decided that there was an urgent need for a common programming language that could be used on all its different computers.

The needs of a commercial programmer differ from those of a mathematical programmer in that, while the latter is concerned mainly with the evaluation of complex algebraic expressions, the former seldom has to evaluate anything more complicated than a single addition or multiplication; on the other hand, the mathematical programmer seldom has to handle more than one input channel and one output channel, whereas the commercial programmer is quite likely to have to deal with half a dozen or more separate channels. In a commercial language, therefore, the emphasis must be on a clear method of describing data files, and on providing simple means of access to any item on a record.

FOUR DIVISIONS

A COBOL program is divided into four parts. First comes the *identification division*, which carries the name of the program, and other information, such as its author and the date when it was written. After this comes the *environment division*, which describes the machine configuration on which the program is to be run—the computer, size of store, and peripheral devices. This section assigns names by which channels will be referred to, and also allocates input and output areas in the store.

The next division is the *data division*, which is concerned with detailed descriptions of the files. We have already discussed several ways of describing input and output data: by directives, as in assembly languages, and by FORMAT statements, as in FORTRAN. There is also an implied data description in the procedure that manipulates the data in most languages. In COBOL an attempt has been made to effect a complete separation between the description of the data and the procedure that operates on it. This means that a COBOL procedure should be independent of the form of the data either inside or outside the machine; it should work on both decimal and binary machines, though it is unlikely to be as efficient on both. Although the data division simply *defines* data formats, every description implies a *procedure*, and in fact the data division may generate more instructions than the formal procedural statements. A procedural statement such as—

MULTIPLY RATE BY HOURS GIVING WAGE

seems deceptively simple, until one realizes that the real work is implied by the fact that HOURS is a decimal quantity on an input clock card, RATE a binary quantity on an employee file, and WAGE a sterling quantity on a printed payslip.

The format of a data description is quite complicated, and we shall not attempt to go into it in any detail here. The essential information given for every file is—

file name
size of block
names of all data records.

There is also a full description of every item in every record; this gives—

level
data name
size (words, characters)
class (numeric, alphabetic, etc.)
picture.

The *level* is a numerical quantity that enables the programmer to give the data a hierarchical structure consisting of items, sub-items, and (if necessary) sub-sub-items. The *picture* is a means of indicating such things as the position of a decimal point, and whether non-significant zeros are to be suppressed (converted into spaces).

The data division also contains a section for describing working storage and for defining tables of constants.

The last division of a COBOL program is the *procedure division.* This consists of a sequence of procedural statements similar in principle to the procedural statements in FORTRAN, except that they tend to be rather more wordy. We have given one example above; here are some others—

```
MOVE INVENTORY PRICE TO INVOICE PRICE
ADD MARKUP TO COST GIVING PRICE
READ OLD-EMPLOYEE-RECORD
IF ACCOUNT CREDIT IS GREATER THAN CREDIT-
  LIMIT GO TO REPORT-PRINT OTHERWISE SUB-
  TRACT DEBIT FROM ACCOUNT CREDIT
```

A feature found in COBOL and other commercial languages is the facility for opening and closing files. We shall have more to say on this subject in Chapter 13; for the present it must suffice to say that this involves a checking procedure designed to guard against errors on the part of the operator, some of which might be catastrophic, and to make the operation of the system easier. Files are opened and closed in COBOL simply by writing suitable statements in the procedure division, for example—

OPEN INPUT OLD-CUSTOMER-FILE, PAYMENTS, OUTPUT NEW-CUSTOMER-FILE

which would open two input files and one output file.

TABULAR LANGUAGES

We have been talking up to now about what might be termed procedural languages, that is, languages containing series of statements describing computational procedures. But procedural statements are not the only possible means of describing algorithms. Let us look back to Chapter 3, where we described a pension scheme, and the conditions under which a pension was payable. The rules given there could be set out in tabular form in the manner shown in Fig. 11.1.

	rule 1	rule 2	rule 3	rule 4	rule 5	rule 6	rule 7
sex	M	M	F	F	F	F	F
age	≥95	<95	≥90	≥90	<90	any	≥90
married state	any	any	S	M	any	D	M
husband's age	—	—	any	≥95	any	any	≤95
pension	Y	N	Y	Y	N	N	N

FIG. 11.1. Decision Table

In fact the table of Fig. 11.1 is a description of the algorithm for determining whether or not a pension is payable, and it is a perfectly legitimate alternative to a procedural description. In fact the whole procedural section of a program can be replaced with a set of such tables. Several tabular languages have been devised, though none has been at all widely adopted. Although tables may often be more convenient for describing a problem than procedural statements, the tabular form of language is one step further removed from the natural language of a computer, which is of course procedural, and it must therefore be just that much more difficult to implement and compile.

LIST PROCESSING

Before finishing this brief review of computer languages, we must mention list processing. Everyone is familiar with lists; they are found everywhere. The human mind likes to classify the information presented to it, and a list is a convenient way of expressing a form of classification. Here, for instance, is a section from the International Library Classification—

510 Mathematics
- .78 Computation
- .782 Analogue instruments
  - .7823 Slide rules
  - .7824 Differential analysers
- .783 Digital machines
  - .7832 Adding and calculating machines
  - .7834 Computers

511 Arithmetic
- .1 Numeration systems
- .2 Fundamental operations
- .3 Prime numbers and factorizing

.
.

512 Algebra

.
.

513 Synthetic geometry

.

and so on

Here we see the principal feature of lists, in the sense in which we are using the term here, ramification into sublists and sub-sublists. In this example, the sublist Mathematics is divided into sub-sublists on computation, arithmetic, algebra, and so on; and any item in any sub-sublist may head a new list at a lower level. Ramification goes on right down to the level of individual books—and even they may consist of two or more volumes.

Quite a lot of data processing can be regarded as the processing of lists. For example, an inventory file is obviously a form of list—

```
File
  Heading block
  Record 1
    Part number
    Description
    Price
      Pounds
      Shillings
      Pence
    Quantity held
    Supplier
      Name
      Address
  Record 2
    Part number
    etc. . . .
```

It is possible to go even further than this. Any piece of text has a list structure: it is made up of individual words, which in themselves are lists of letters. Moreover the words may group themselves into phrases according to the sense. A particular form of textual list is a statement in a higher-level computer language, and in fact compilers use list-processing techniques for handling procedural statements, taking them to pieces and converting them into instruction sequences. For instance, the last COBOL statement given above—

```
OPEN INPUT OLD-CUSTOMER-FILE, PAYMENTS, OUT-
  PUT NEW-CUSTOMER-FILE
```

can be regarded as a list structure—

```
OPEN
  INPUT
    OLD-CUSTOMER-FILE
    PAYMENTS
  OUTPUT
    NEW-CUSTOMER-FILE
```

The things we want to do with lists are add and delete items, not only at the ends but also at intermediate points, rearrange items and sublists, combine sublists and split them. For this we need a new set of statement formats not found in any of the standard programming languages. A few special list-programming languages have been devised, several of them as annexes to the standard programming languages—annexed in rather the same way as input-output facilities have to be annexed to ALGOL.

Now any list can be stored simply as a sequence of the items that comprise it; but such a simple arrangement would not be of much

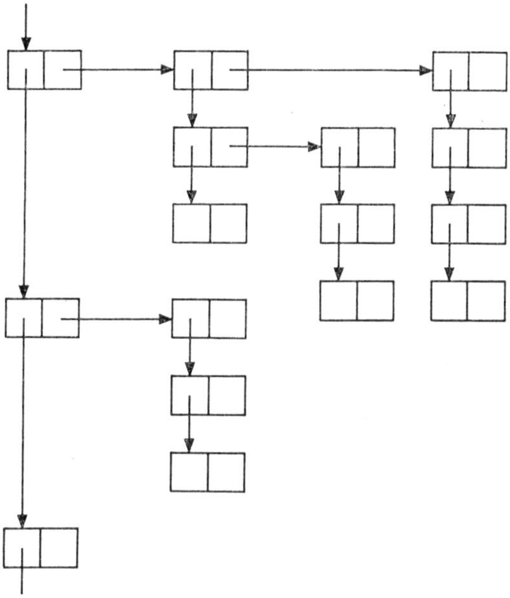

FIG. 11.2. Simple List Structure

value. In the first place, it would not show how the list was structured, and in the second place, if an item had to be added to, or deleted from an intermediate point in the list, all the items below it would have to be shifted.

Each item in a list can be thought of as having in general two links: one to the next item at the same level, the other to the first item of the sublist below it. Thus a list structure can be shown diagrammatically in the manner of Fig. 11.2. In a computer, each element of such a structure could be represented by a pair of addresses, the first pointing to the next address-pair at the same level, the second pointing to the first address-pair at the level below. However, Fig. 11.2 represents only the structure of a list; it does not include the actual values of the list items. We could include these by adding a third address to each item to point to the register holding the value; but a more general method is to add more address pairs, in the manner shown in Fig. 11.3 for example. In this figure, values are shaded to distinguish them from address pairs.

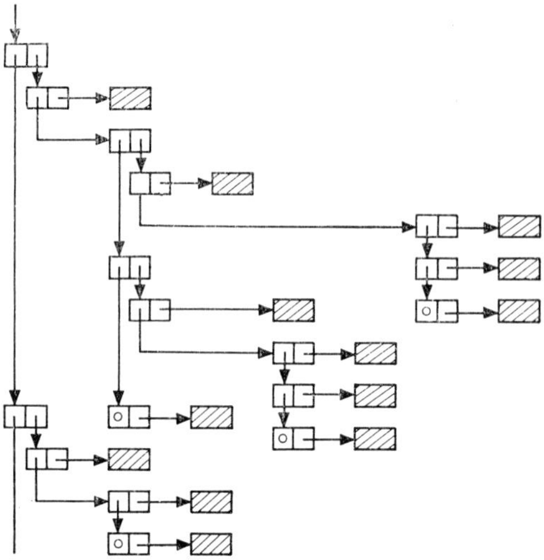

FIG. 11.3. List Structure With Values

Figure 11.4 shows a section of a computer store as it might appear when holding the list structure shown in Fig. 11.3. Adding and deleting items under this arrangement simply involves adjusting addresses. For instance, to add another item between the two items whose values are in 2348 and 2349, we must first find a register to hold the new value—2358, say. Then we find a register to hold its address pair—say 1251. Into this register we put the pair—

1240 2358

and we change the first address in 1239 to 1251. Similar procedures apply when exchanging items, or when manipulating sublists. There is no need for any data to be moved; all operations are performed by manipulating addresses.

COMPILATION

Programs in higher-level languages have to be translated into machine code before they can be obeyed. This is usually done direct;

1234	1247	1235
5	1236	2345
6	1241	1237
7	1238	2346
8	1239	2347
9	1240	2348
1240	0	2349
1	1246	1242
2	1243	2350
3	1244	2351
4	1245	2352
5	0	2353
6	0	2354
7	etc.	1248
8	1249	2355
9	1250	2356
1250	0	2357
1		
2		
⋮	⋮	⋮
2345 6 7 8 9 2350 1 2 3 4 5 6 7	VALUES	

Fig. 11.4. Stored List

but sometimes it is done through the medium of an assembly language. The program that performs this task is called a *compiler*. Each statement in the language is equivalent to a short sequence of machine instructions. What the compiler has to do is to compile a series of short instruction sequences into a complete program, inserting addresses as appropriate. For instance, the FORTRAN statement—

IF (I) 10, 20, 30

corresponds to the sequence of instructions—

I	MOVE	I
NEG	J	P
ZERO	J	Q
	J	R

where P, Q, and R are addresses corresponding to the statement numbers 10, 20, and 30. On encountering this particular FORTRAN statement, a compiler would plant the corresponding sequence of instructions in the appropriate place in the program, and insert the appropriate addresses. But here we come up against a slight problem: it is easy enough to insert addresses for *backward* jumps; but what about *forward* jumps? The statement numbers referred to in forward jumps will not yet have been encountered, so no addresses will be associated with them. There are several possible solutions to this problem. One is to leave the insertion of addresses as something to be done on a second run through the whole program, by which time all addresses will be known. Another solution is to jump not to the statement specified, but to another jump instruction, which in turn will jump to the desired statement. This second jump can be compiled at the end, when all addresses will be known; but its own address can be allocated when the IF statement is compiled, and inserted in the appropriate place in the instruction sequence immediately. A third solution to the problem, similar in principle to the last, is to use replacement addressing (if the target machine incorporates such a feature). The jump is compiled as—

NEG	J	(P)

say, where location P (probably somewhere at the end of the program) will eventually contain the address corresponding to statement number 10.

The FORTRAN statement—

IF (M − N) ,75, 75

corresponds to the pair of instructions—

M	TSUB	N
POS	J	P

where P is the address corresponding to statement 75. But a simple-minded compiler might express it as—

```
M       TSUB   N
NEG     J      Q
ZERO    J      P
        J      P
```

just like the earlier example, using four instructions instead of two. Moreover P and Q might themselves be addresses of jump instructions. Compiled programs are consequently much less efficient in terms of the number of instructions than hand-coded programs, in which a programmer is able to use his ingenuity. Compiled programs run a good deal slower than hand-coded programs, the actual running speed being dependent upon the complexity of the compiler and the trouble it takes to optimize particular instruction sequences. We have already seen that a better object program is produced if the compiler can go through it a second time to insert addresses. In fact some compilers are organized to operate over several passes, each pass adding a little more to the final program, or eliminating a few unnecessary instructions. Multi-pass compilers have the further advantage that they can be larger than the store of the computer, since at any one time the store need only contain the part of the compiler that is performing the current pass. Sometimes a program is optimized by hand after it has been compiled. This technique is particularly rewarding with mathematical programs whose running time depends on the speed of inner loops. Hand optimization of inner loops can often improve the speed of a program by a factor of two or more.

English-language statements such as IF, DO, and GO TO statements can generally be made to correspond to a fixed sequence of instructions: not so arithmetic statements. The FORTRAN statement—

```
X = A - (B + C) * (D + E)/F
```

obviously compiles into more instructions than—

```
X = P + Q ** 3
```

and the sequences will be quite different in appearance. Compiling arithmetic statements then is not simply a question of inserting addresses into a fixed pattern; the pattern itself must be determined first of all. To see how this can be done, let us consider how we should go about evaluating the first of the two expressions just given. The rule is that multiplication and division must precede addition and subtraction, but that bracketed expressions must be evaluated first of all. Thus the sequence of operations is—

Take B and C and add.
Take D and E and add.
Multiply the two results obtained so far.
Divide by F.
Subtract from A.

POLISH NOTATION

The problem is, how can this sequence of operations be derived mechanically from the original expression. We can see how, if we write the same expression down in what is known as *Polish*† *notation*, thus—

$$A\ B\ C + D\ E + *\ F\ /\ -$$

The rules for evaluating expressions written in this form are—

work from left to right,

apply each operator in turn to the pair of operands immediately preceding it,

when two operands have been combined, the combination is to be treated thereafter as a single operand.

These rules of course lead immediately to the sequence of operations normally followed.

STACK

All that we have to do now is to find a means of converting expressions in conventional algebraic notation into Polish notation. This can be done with the aid of a pushdown stack. We introduced the idea of a stack in Chapter 5, where it was used to hold subroutine links. The idea is that of a box in which only the last object put in is accessible at any time, and objects can be removed only in the opposite order to that in which they were inserted.

Figure 11.5 shows how a stack can be used to convert the algebraic expression—

$$A + (B * C - D) * E$$

into Polish notation. The algorithm is shown in the form of a flow diagram in Fig. 11.6.

† It was named Polish notation in honour of its inventor—Lukasiewicz. To be precise, what we have written here should be referred to as *reversed* Polish notation, since Lukasiewicz's original convention would have put the symbols in the opposite order.

It is perhaps worth noting at this point that a stack can be used in the *evaluation* of arithmetic expressions as well as in their translation; indeed there have been computers designed on just this principle. The idea is that an arithmetic unit should be attached to the top of a stack in such a way that arithmetic instructions apply

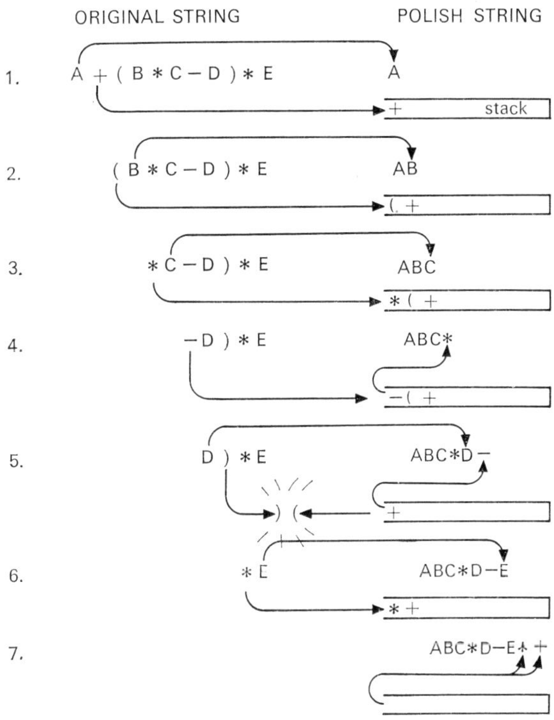

FIG. 11.5. Stack Compilation

to the top two layers of the stack. Whenever an item is lost from the stack, either by the arithmetic combination of two items or by unloading, the lower levels move up to fill the space. With a stack-type arithmetic unit, the arithmetic statement—

$$X = A * (B + C) - D$$

which in Polish notation is—

$$X\,A\,B\,C + * D - =$$

is evaluated as follows—

load A into stack
load B into stack
load C into stack
add top two layers
multiply top two layers
load D into stack
subtract top two layers
unload stack to X

which follows the Polish notation exactly.

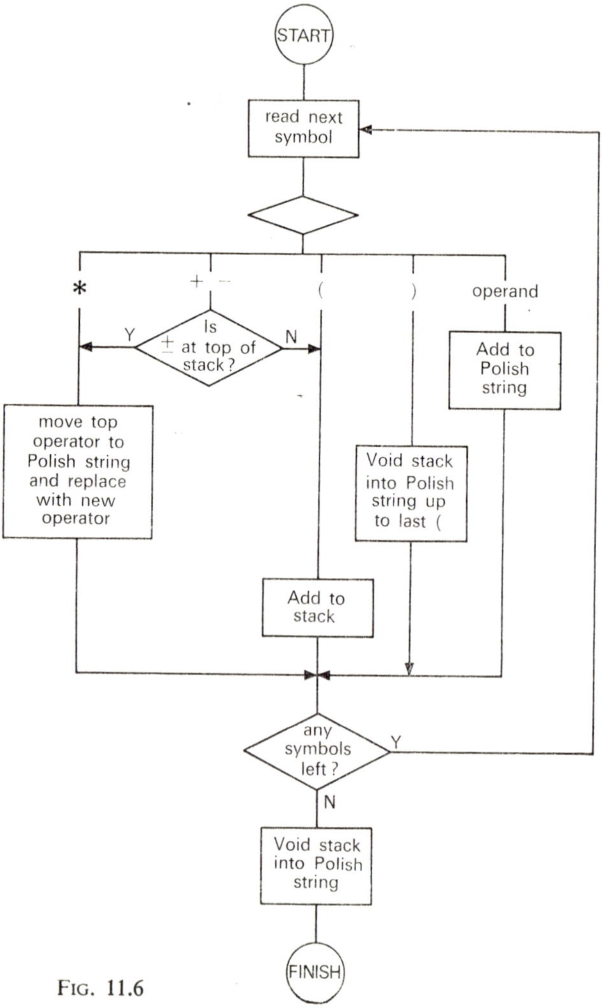

FIG. 11.6

COMPILER-COMPILER

A large part of the cost of putting a new computer system on the market goes on providing it with an adequate set of compilers for all the common programming languages and dialects. In fact a manufacturer will spend a comparable amount on developing software to that which he spends on designing the hardware. In these circumstances, anything that can be done to lessen the labour of writing compilers is welcome. One approach that has been used has been to provide a *compiler-compiler* for writing compilers automatically.

SYNTACTIC DEFINITION

A programming language is simply a set of symbols combined with a set of rules for manipulating them. This being so, it should be possible to devise a language for describing programming languages themselves as a series of formal statements, and hence to write a program that will convert such a sequence of statements into a program that applies them. In fact several such languages do exist. They are known as languages of *syntactic definition*. Here, for instance, are some syntactic definitions from the ALGOL report*—

⟨digit⟩ : : = 0|1|2|3|4|5|6|7|8|9
⟨unsigned integer⟩ : : = ⟨digit⟩|⟨unsigned integer⟩⟨digit⟩
⟨integer⟩ : : = ⟨unsigned integer⟩| + ⟨unsigned integer⟩| − ⟨unsigned integer⟩
⟨decimal fraction⟩ : : = · ⟨unsigned integer⟩

The first of these statements defines a digit as any of the ten symbols shown. The second says that an unsigned integer is a string of one or more digits; the third that an integer is a string of digits optionally preceded by + or −; and the last that a decimal fraction is an unsigned integer preceded by a point. Notice that it is necessary to define integer through the intermediary unsigned integer because this is the simplest way of expressing the idea of only one plus or minus sign.

A compiler-compiler, once constructed, can accept the syntactic definition of any language and convert it into a compiler. Moreover, it should be possible to keep a compiler-compiler permanently on backing store together with the definitions of the commonest languages, so that the computer is always in a position to accept and compile programs. The compiler-compiler approach should be

* These are written in what is known as Backus-Naur form.

particularly useful in connection with less common languages and dialects, for which it is not really worth while writing separate compilers.

BOOTSTRAPPING

Another way of saving effort on compiler writing is to use what is known as bootstrapping.* Suppose, for instance that we need a COBOL compiler for our new ZEUS computer. It will be very much easier and quicker to write this in some higher-level language, say COBOL itself. Now it so happens that we already have a COBOL compiler on our old WOTAN computer, which we might consider using to compile our new COBOL compiler. Unfortunately though,

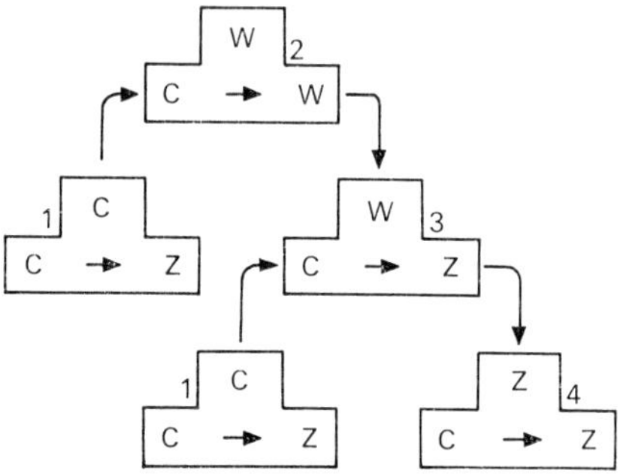

FIG. 11.7. Bootstrapping Compilers

the result will be in the language of WOTAN not ZEUS. Never mind! We now have a COBOL-ZEUS compiler, which can be used to translate the original compiler we wrote into the language of ZEUS. If this seems a bit complicated, look at Fig. 11.7. We start by writing a COBOL-ZEUS compiler in COBOL (symbol 1) and we use our old COBOL-WOTAN compiler (symbol 2) to translate this into WOTAN (symbol 3). We now use this new compiler to translate the original (symbol 1 again) into the language of ZEUS (symbol 4).

INTERPRETATION

It is not strictly necessary for a program in a high-level language to be compiled before a computer can obey it; it can be interpreted instead. A program obeyed in an interpretive mode is held in the store in the original form in which it was written (or something close to it). A program in machine language then scrutinizes the statements

* From the idea of lifting oneself by one's own bootstraps.

of the object program in turn, performing the sequence of operations prescribed by each one in its turn. The common high-level languages do not lend themselves easily to being obeyed in an interpretive mode; but it is quite common for special-purpose languages, for instance languages designed to perform operations in some special branch of mathematics such as tensor calculus, to be interpreted. Interpretation is also commonly used to enable programs in the language of one machine to be run on another machine; the second machine is then said to be *simulating* the first. A machine may even obey interpretively programs written in its own language; this sometimes happens when a program is being traced.

PROGRAM GENERATION

A process that is similar in some ways to compilation is *program generation*. What a program generator does is to take what amounts to a complete skeleton program and fill in the blank spaces in accordance with parameters supplied by the user. Program generation is used when the object program is one of a class of many closely similar programs—sorting programs for example. Instead of writing a separate program for sorting each type of data item, and for every possible configuration of file devices, it is better to write a program generator. This can be supplied with parameters giving the record size, the location of the sorting key, and the number of sorting devices available, to suit any particular occasion.

Another type of program that is often produced by generation is a report writer. This is a program used for extracting data from a file in accordance with rules laid down by the user. It may only be summary data that is wanted, or the requirement may be to copy parts of certain selected records. Whatever the requirement, it is generally better to generate a report-writer program to fulfil the needs of the moment than to try to use a general-purpose report writer that tries to be all things to all men. The scope of the generative technique is widening, and generators are now being written to produce updating programs suitable for simple commercial systems.

In this chapter we have mentioned several ways in which the immense amount of labour involved in programming can be reduced. High-level languages reduce programming effort in several ways: firstly, they are usually closer to the way that the programmer thinks about the job; secondly, they reduce the possibility of making silly mistakes in writing the program; thirdly, they are easier to correct than assembly languages when they go wrong, partly because they involve fewer statements, and partly because the statements themselves are more nearly self-explanatory; and fourthly, they can take over a great deal of the tedious manipulation associated with input and output. However, assembly languages are improving; they are being provided with new features to make them more natural to use. This trend will naturally weaken the future demand for high-level languages—at least at levels no higher than FORTRAN.

Another modern trend is the movement towards on-line programming, that is, the building and development of programs by users who can be put in direct touch with the machine through an extension console. This may possibly lead to a shift in emphasis away from compilation and toward interpretation. In any case, what it must certainly lead to is the development of new languages more conversational in character, languages that do not simply consist of a string of imperatives, but permit the user to ask questions of the system, and the system to reply. Finally, we should see in the future some improvements in the field of error diagnosis—possibly with the aid of so-called *learning* programs, that is, programs that are able to modify their operations in the light of experience.

EXERCISES 11

1. Write a sequence of instructions in the language of the imaginary machine to correspond with the FORTRAN statement pair—

```
DO 85 J = 8,28,1
85 SUM = SUM + ARRAY(J)
```

Treat all variables as integers.

2. Write a sequence of instructions to correspond with the FORTRAN statement—

```
A = ( (B + C) * D - E * F ** 2)/G
```

Use floating-point operands.

3. In the list structure of Fig. 11.3 and 11.4 show how you would—

(*a*) add another item after the item whose value is in location 2353,
(*b*) reverse the order of the two main lists, which start in 1234 and 1247,
(*c*) eliminate the item whose value is in 2346 and raise the sublist depending on it to the next level up,
(*d*) move the value in 2354 to the end of the sublist starting in 2351.

4. Convert to reversed Polish notation—

(*a*) (A + B * C) * (D − E * F)
(*b*) A − B − C * D + E * (F + G)
(*c*) A − (B − C) * D + E * F + G

5. Show with the aid of a flow diagram how a compiler might compile instructions corresponding to FORTRAN statements of the form—

IF (arithmetic expression) p, q, r

6. Write the following statements in the language of syntactic definition—

(*a*) An operator is any one of the symbols +, −, *, /.
(*b*) An identifier is any string of letters and digits starting with a letter.
(*c*) Arguments are identifiers or integers with or without quote marks.

12. *Input and Output*

PUNCHED CARDS

PROBABLY the commonest type of computer input device at the present time is the punched-card reader. Practically all the cards used today conform to the same specification, measuring $7\frac{3}{8}$ inches by $3\frac{1}{4}$ inches, and carrying data punched with rectangular holes in any of twelve row positions in eighty columns.* Fig. 12.1 shows a

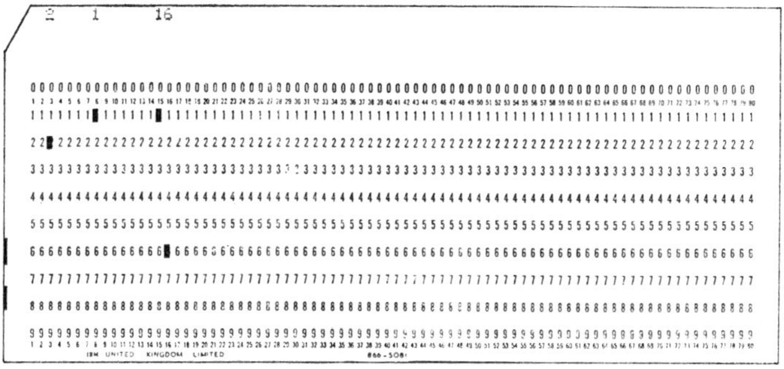

FIG. 12.1.

typical card. Card codes generally permit up to three holes to be punched in any one column; more holes would make the card too flimsy and might cause difficulties with the reading mechanism. One of the top corners of the standard card is cut off. This is to make sure that the cards cannot be inserted into the reader the wrong way up (when the reader would encounter impermissible codes, and stop) or the wrong way round (when the characters would probably be read correctly, but in the reverse order).

In the normal mode of use, each card holds a separate item of input, that is, one set of data, or one language statement. If the item is more than eighty characters long, continuation cards may be used, a continuation symbol being punched either at the end of one card or at the beginning of the next. Sometimes the first column

* There are also in existence 65-column cards and 40-column cards; but these are to be found mostly on older equipment.

is used conventionally for an identifier indicating the type of information in the card. It is common practice to overprint cards with some indication of the use to which each field is put. Some systems use a colour coding of the cards to assist operators.

CODES

In Appendix III we give a card code recommended by the European Computer Manufacturers' Association. When two holes are punched in a single column, one appears in one of the lower nine rows (numbered 1 to 9), and the other in one of the top three rows (two unnumbered rows and 0). These two sets of rows are known respectively as the lower and upper *curtates*. With one hole alone, or with one hole in each curtate, it is possible to represent thirty-nine different symbols; that is, it is possible to represent the numerals 0 to 9, the letters of the English alphabet, and three additional symbols, usually &, – and /. When a third hole is punched, it is generally in row 8. The number 8 in conjunction with the numbers 2 to 7 could be used to represent identically the hexadecimal numbers ten to fifteen, and hence the symbols corresponding to these numbers in the byte code of the machine. However, there is not in general a simple relationship between card codes and byte codes, since the former have generally had their origin in codes designed for punched-card systems.

The conversion from the card code to the machine's internal code is usually performed electrically with the aid of normal logic circuits. In most systems, this is done in the card machine, and data is transmitted between the card machine and the system centre in the internal code of the computer. However, in some smaller systems an exact image of the card is transmitted to the system centre, and the conversion is carried out by program. This is done because in a small system the cost, in time, of conversion by program is less than the cost in hardware of conversion electronics. The facility of being able to read a card image is often provided in addition to the normal hardware conversion. This is so that cards punched in a non-standard code can be accepted—a particularly useful feature when a job has to be transferred from a punched-card installation to a computer, or even from an old computer to a newer one.

In punched-card installations, in contrast to computers, there is usually a desire to record as much data as possible on a single card. Keeping the number of cards small not only simplifies problems of storage and handling, it also speeds up the processing itself. Consequently many tricks have been devised for packing punched-card data; for instance, it is often possible to record two symbols on the same column, one in the upper curtate and one in the lower curtate. This is known as *overpunching*. Such tricks are not generally used in cards for computer input; but in small computers where cards are used as the file medium, it is not uncommon to find fairly tight packing.

READERS

Card readers are available operating at speeds from a few hundred cards a minute to well over a thousand. Card magazines are generally large enough to carry enough cards for a run of several minutes at full speed. Cards are fed one at a time from an *input magazine*, or *hopper*, along a length of track to a *receiver*, or *stacker*. There is sometimes a second receiver to which cards can be diverted by a command from the system centre. In some readers, two or more cards can be in transit at the same time; this makes for faster reading, but it poses a number of problems of program control. In modern readers, cards are read column-by-column photo-electrically, and the accuracy is checked by reading each column twice. This is done either by having two separate sets of photocells or, less satisfactorily, by 'looking' twice with the same set of photocells.

PUNCHES

Cards are seldom used as an output medium on computers. When they are, it is because they will be required for subsequent re-input, either to the same system or to another computer or a punched-card installation. This happens when the computer is the centre of a data-processing complex spread over several locations, or when cards are being used in a small system as a file medium. Card punching is a slower operation than reading; this is because punching involves the physical movement of metal punch knives through a card, which must be brought to rest for the punching to be done, and then accelerated afterwards. Reading, on the other hand, is performed by a light beam, and the card can be in motion the whole time. The fastest card punches operate at only a few hundred cards a minute.

Card punches may operate column-by-column, or row-by-row, or they may punch the whole card in a single block. Row-by-row punching is probably the most common, since it avoids the cumbrousness of block punching; it is faster than column punching, since it involves only twelve punching movements instead of eighty. A punch operating in a row mode must be capable of scanning all eighty characters of data twelve times, once for each row, to determine when to set the punch knives. What this means in practice is that either the eighty characters must be sent from the computer to the punch twelve separate times, or the punch must contain a buffer store large enough to contain twelve characters. Card punches are checked either by reading after punching, or by sensing that the punch knives have been operated in the correct sequence.

READER-PUNCH

Card punches are often found combined with readers in a single unit. A reader-punch unit may be designed with the reader and punch entirely separate, sharing only the power source and some of the electronics, or it may be designed with the two operating on the same track, cards passing first through the reader and then through the punch, which would then normally operate column-by-column. In this latter case, cards can be read and then punched with extra data either calculated by the computer or else derived from another source. Such a feature is particularly useful if the cards are being used as a file medium.

KEY PUNCH

Data for input to a computer is punched into cards on a *key punch.* This is simply a device with a keyboard giving all the symbols in the repertoire of the card code, a hopper for supplying cards, and a stacker for cards when they have been punched. There is also a reject stacker into which the cards can be directed in case of mis-punching. Cards are usually verified after punching, using a *verifier,* which is identical to a key punch, except that instead of punching holes it compares holes already punched with those corresponding to the keys pressed by the operator. What happens in the case of error depends on particular circumstances: some verifiers stack suspect cards the wrong way round, so that they can be inspected afterwards to determine whether the punch operator or the verifier operator made an error. Punched cards can also be checked with an *interpreter.* This is a device that reads a card and types along its top edge graphic symbols corresponding to the punched codes. There is a popular type of reader-punch that also incorporates an interpreter.

HAND PUNCH

Portable hand punches are also available. These are used by programmers to re-punch cards that have been found to be in error during program development, thus saving the delay inherent in any central punching service. Hand punches are very simple in principle. They generally require the user to depress at the same time as many keys as there are holes to be punched in a column.

PAPER TAPE

After punched cards, the most important input medium is punched paper tape. Paper tape had been used in connection with telegraph systems for many years before the advent of the digital computer; consequently techniques for converting paper-tape information into electrical signals were well advanced, and equipment suitable for computer input and output was already available. The principal advantage of paper tape lies in the cheapness of the equipment for handling it; and it tends to be used when the amount of input data is small, as happens with small machines that are being used principally for scientific calculations. Paper tape is also used in preference to cards if it can be prepared as a by-product of some other activity; some typewriters and some cash registers incorporate a tape-punching device. Paper tape can also act as an interchange medium between computers. Indeed it is not uncommon to find an auxiliary paper-tape channel on a system whose main input is on punched cards.

Each character is recorded in the form of a row of holes across the tape, with a pitch of one tenth of an inch. The most common widths of tape allow five, seven or eight holes to be punched, giving, in principle, repertoires of 32, 128, and 256 symbols. Nowadays, five-hole tape is seldom used, except in connection with telegraphic communication. It is the usual practice with seven-hole and eight-hole systems to use one track as a parity check to guard against faults in the reading mechanism. Even parity is chosen on eight-hole tape, as this makes both blank tape and the *all-ones* character acceptable. The latter is used for erasure, since it can be punched over any code to obliterate it. A row of small holes runs along, or close to, the centre line of the tape. These are known as *sprocket holes*, though no paper-tape reader in fact uses sprocket drive today. They are punched when the data is punched into the tape, and they serve to locate the position of each code unambiguously; in other words, the sprocket holes *clock* the information.

READERS

Paper tape is read at similar speeds to punched cards; readers are available operating at speeds of from a few hundred characters a second to some two thousand. With slower readers, the tape, after it has been read, is allowed to fall loosely into a bin, whence it can be spooled later if it has to be retained. Faster readers incorporate a spooling device. The holes, both the data holes and the sprocket holes, are read photo-electrically. Data is read once only; there is no check-reading as with cards, since the parity check is adequate for the detection of errors.

There are two principal modes of reading paper tape, the transfer instruction generally making the selection according to the programmer's wish. The system can either read a stated number of characters, stopping when the designated store area has been filled, or it can read up to the next newline character, stopping if the designated store area becomes filled before this is reached. Other reading modes permit some code conversion, according to the requirements of the system; or a binary image of the tape may be read, parity checking being suppressed.

PUNCHES

Paper-tape punches, like card punches, are slower than the corresponding readers, owing to the need to bring the medium to rest while the punch knives operate. As with cards, slow punching is no serious drawback, since the volume of output is generally a great deal less than the volume of input, output in the form of paper tape generally being intended for subsequent re-input.

EDITING EQUIPMENT

The chief disadvantage of paper tape as an input medium is that it is difficult to edit or modify. While cards can be re-ordered at will, and individual cards can be removed from, or inserted into, a pack, similar operations with tape can be achieved only by tedious cutting and splicing, with the expectation of more difficulties when a much-spliced tape is fed into a reader. Instead of cutting and splicing, it is better to copy the whole tape, putting in amendments wherever they are necessary. This can be done on a computer, of course; but it is generally better to do it off-line on special editing equipment.

A *tape-editing set* generally consists of one or two tape readers (usually quite slow), a typewriter, a tape punch (often integral with the typewriter) and a control box for switching the units on and off. The equipment is set up to copy from one of the readers on to the punch, at the same time producing a typed copy of the data. When the set reaches a part of the tape that an operator knows to be in error, he stops the reader and types in the correct information. An inching device is usually provided to make it easier for him to stop the reader at the correct point. The equipment can also be used for other purposes: to merge two tapes into a single tape, to verify a tape already punched, or to compare two tapes punched from the same set of data for purposes of verification.

PRINTERS

The output from a computer is generally required in the form of print. For a scientific machine, the output from a typewriter is very often enough; but a commercial installation produces a great bulk of print, and requires a fast printing device. Computer printers print a whole line at a time, and they are capable of working at speeds of from a few hundred to a few thousand lines a minute.

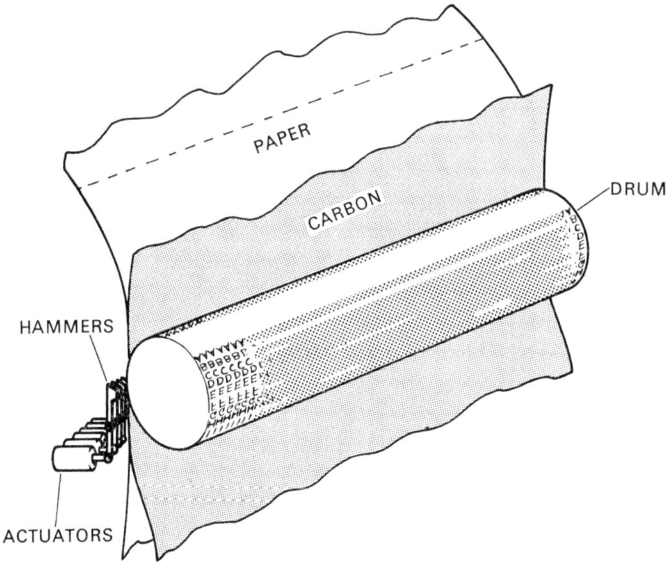

FIG. 12.2. Drum Printer (Diagrammatic)

The stationery used is generally pre-printed forms, and these are supplied in a continuous strip, folded fanwise. Many different principles have been used in the past for designing fast printers; but by far the commonest today are *drum* or *barrel printers* and *chain printers*. We shall describe the drum type first.

The characters are carried embossed on the surface of a continually rotating drum, as shown in Fig. 12.2. There are as many complete sets of characters as there are printing positions along a line (typically 120) and the characters appear in the binary order of their codes (which are not necessarily the same as their codes within the computer). The paper is driven by sprockets engaging holes along its edges, and runs between the drum and a set of hammers, one for each printing position. A hammer is operated when the character to be printed in that position appears opposite to it, and forces the paper up against the carbon ribbon and the drum, causing an imprint. The paper is stationary while printing is taking place, and there is usually a blank sector on the drum to allow time for the paper to be advanced at least one line. In an alternative design, the drum makes two cycles to every line of print, one for printing, the other for advancing the paper; with this second arrangement it is often possible to print at twice the speed if a restricted character set is used, the paper being advanced while the unused characters are opposite the hammers. Some printers operate in an asynchronous mode, that is, the printing cycle starts not with the first set of characters on the drum, but with the set of characters that happened

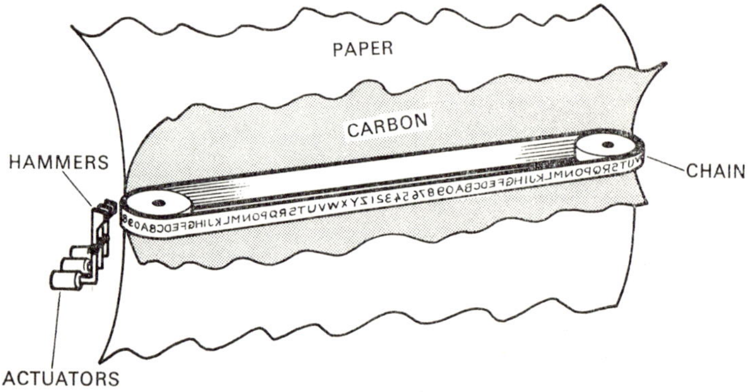

FIG. 12.3. Chain Printer (Diagrammatic)

to be in position opposite the hammers at the end of the previous movement of paper.

A disadvantage of the drum-type printer is that a slight maladjustment of the hammers causes some to operate a little too early, and others too late; this shows up as a misalignment of the print, some characters appearing above, and others below, the line, giving it an untidy appearance. There may also be some vertical smudging, since the drum, if not the paper, is moving during printing. In fact, alignment cannot be kept absolutely perfect, and printing from a drum printer is easily recognized by the form of degradation it suffers.

In a chain printer, the characters are embossed on a chain or band, which moves at right angles to the direction of paper feed, as shown in Fig. 12.3. The chain carries four or five complete sets of characters, depending on its length. As with the drum printer, the printing is done by hammers, which strike the paper from behind when the desired character is in the right position; but the principle is a bit more complicated, since one hammer may be printing an A at the same time as another hammer twenty-five positions away is printing a Z. Printing from a chain printer does not suffer from vertical misalignment, since any displacement is along the line. Unless it is particularly bad, horizontal misalignment is not noticeable. Since the surface speed of a chain is greater than that of a drum for the same printing speed, smudging tends to be a little worse however.

The usual way of ensuring that the hammers are activated at the right moment is to scan the data once for every character in the repertoire just before that character comes opposite to the hammers. This means either that the whole line of information must be transmitted to the printer as many times as there are characters in the repertoire (typically sixty), or else the printer must incorporate a buffer store one line wide, which can then be scanned as many times as necessary.

PAPER FEED

In most commercial jobs, printing is spaced out on the form for easy reading; so most of the data actually supplied for a single line of print consists of spaces. It is unusual to find more than ten or twenty characters actually printed on a line, and more than ten per cent or so of the lines actually printed. Most printers allow a paper feed of several lines in a single print cycle. If a longer feed is required, one or more extra cycles are necessary, the paper drive being accelerated much faster than normally; this is known as *paper-throwing*, or *skip-feeding*. It is controlled in one of three ways: the simplest way is by special *start feed* and *stop feed* commands from the system centre, which actually times the paper movement; another way is by sending to the printer a count of the number of lines to be skipped. The last way is by means of a loop of paper tape or plastic tape the same length as the form to be printed. Holes are punched in this tape in positions corresponding to the positions at which paper-throw is required to finish, and the loop is mounted in a special sensing device attached to the paper drive. A command from the system centre then causes the paper to be thrown up to the next hole in the tape loop. If there is to be a choice of layouts on the form, the tape loop is provided with several channels of holes, and the computer command must specify the channel that is to control a particular throw. Some printers even provide two webs of paper, which can be fed at different rates. Paper feeding can be controlled, as has been said, by special commands from the system centre. An alternative method is to attach special paper-feed codes to the stream of data for each line.

XEROGRAPHY

Another form of fast printer uses the principle of xerography.* The letters to be printed are copied on to a rotating drum in the form of patterns of electric charge; the copying is done by an optical process. The charge on the drum picks up the ink (a dry powder), which is charged in the opposite sense, and transfers it to the paper, where it is fixed by heat treatment. The xerographic printer is very fast indeed. It also enables the form itself to be printed on blank paper at the same time as the variable data. But the equipment is expensive, and it suffers from the added disadvantage that carbon copies cannot be produced.

There is at present no positive way of checking the accuracy of printing (beyond employing clerks to read it). But there are a few partial checks that can be applied, such as checking that every hammer that was required to operate has in fact operated. An error in alphabetical data is usually acceptable, since normal text contains quite a lot of redundancy of information; but a printing error in numerical information can have serious consequences. One way of reducing the risk is to print all numeric quantities twice or more.

ANCILLARY EQUIPMENT

A large range of off-line devices is available for dealing with the output from a computer printer. These include *form bursters*, for separating the forms and for removing the margins carrying the sprocket holes, *form folders*, and *envelopers*.

OPERATION

In Chapter 7 we gave an example of a trivial program transferring selected data from a card reader to a printer, and we noted then that the program we had written might prove to be inefficient in practice, since it obliged each device to wait while the other completed its transfer. Now there are some simple computer systems in which only one transfer can be in progress at a time, and where computation has to be suspended during a peripheral transfer; but on nearly all modern systems it is possible for several peripheral devices to be operating at the same time, and programs should take advantage of such a feature to reduce the running times of jobs. The trouble with our example in Chapter 7 was that there was only one data area in the store, which could not be refilled until it had been emptied to the printer. The arrangement is shown in the first diagram in Fig. 12.4.

* Greek *ξερος* = dry, *γραφω* = I write.

MULTIPLE BUFFERS

By providing separate input and output areas, as in the second diagram of Fig. 12.4, we can ensure that the card reader and printer

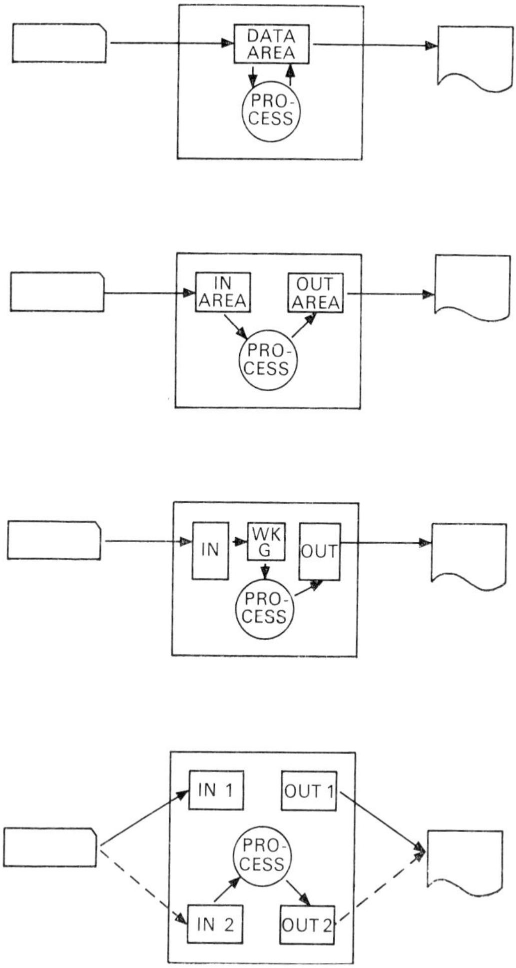

FIG. 12.4.

are able to operate at the same time; but each must still wait upon the processing phase, which uses both the input area and the output area. A solution to this problem is shown in the third diagram. Here the input data is transferred to a working area, where it is processed preparatory to being transferred to a third output area. The disadvantage of this arrangement is that every piece of data is transferred across the store at least once, while those that are to be printed are transferred twice. The amount of data movement within the store is reduced by the arrangement shown in the fourth diagram, in which two areas are allocated to input and two to output. The process is operating on two of the areas while the other two are in communication with the peripheral devices. When all operations

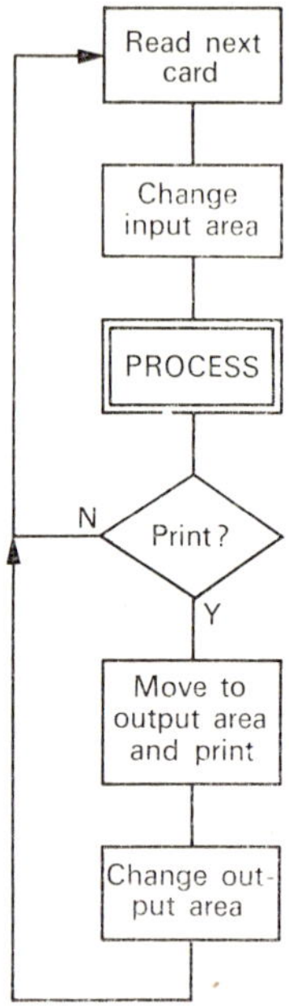

FIG. 12.5.

have been completed, the process changes to the other two areas, and the peripheral devices are put into communication with the two areas just relinquished. The flow diagram for the last arrangement is shown in Fig. 12.5. Notice that the words *read* and *print* should be interpreted *start reading* and *start printing*. In this case, since once started, the transfers proceed autonomously. The system is very simple to implement by program if all references to data areas are made with the aid of modifiers; changing from one area to another is then simply a matter of changing the modifier that points to it.

LOCKOUTS

It will usually happen that the computing processes involved in a loop take less time than the peripheral transfers. In this case, the next *read* or *write* instruction is reached while the device is still busy with the previous instruction. Since peripheral devices normally permit only one transfer at a time, the second instruction must not be allowed to take effect immediately—it must be *locked out*. The easiest way of doing this is to suspend the program until the previous transfer has been completed. This is done by the Control Program, which is entered on all peripheral transfer instructions.

It is easy enough to lock out instructions that refer to active peripheral devices—all that is necessary is for the Control Program to test the status of the device before issuing the command.* However, there is another type of instruction that may have to be locked out: that is an instruction referring to an area of store that is still in communication with a peripheral device. If it is an input device, the data cannot all be trusted to be correct until the transfer has finished: if it is an output device, the instruction may alter the data before it has been transmitted. Now there is no easy way of determining whether a particular address comes within a forbidden area of store. One solution to the problem is to preface critical routines in the program with an instruction that causes the program to be suspended if a particular peripheral device is still busy. The chief disadvantage of doing things this way is that it puts an added burden upon the programmer, giving him one more opportunity to make errors, and consequently increasing the time that it might take him to get the program running.

It is better, though more expensive, if store lockouts can be imposed automatically without the need for the programmer to take special precautions. What is needed is some means of defining store areas and of imposing some sort of condition that makes an area inaccessible to the program. One way is to divide the store into blocks of a fixed length. If each block is then associated with a group of bits in an auxiliary store, a special code configuration of the bits can be interpreted as locking the block out, the content of the appropriate bit group in the auxiliary store being tested by special hardware every time a reference is made to the main store. When a peripheral transfer has finished, the Control Program changes the code in the auxiliary store to make the block accessible again.

This system is strictly applicable only to blocks of a fixed length, though there is nothing to prevent a fixed-length block, or a set of

* Some devices are arranged to make a *refusal* response if issued with a command that they cannot carry out immediately. This simplifies the Control Program somewhat.

fixed-length blocks, from containing variable amounts of information, with some words remaining unused. However, methods have been devised for locking out variable areas of store. One of these is to associate with every peripheral device a pair of addresses defining the bounds of the store region it is using. Every time there is a reference to the store, the instruction address is checked against every one of these bounds to make sure that it does not refer to an area that is locked out.

Another, rather neater, way of locking out variable areas is to lock out the modifier that is to be used to give access to them. (We have already noted that the easiest way to organize switching between store areas is to make access with the aid of modifiers.) A modifier can be locked out either by associating a special lockout bit pattern with it, and testing with special hardware for the appearance of this, or by replacing the modifier with a special code that can be recognized automatically. With such an arrangement, all references to data must be made with the aid of modifiers. This is not difficult to arrange: the programmer normally uses symbolic names for data items; whether the reference is then made direct or through a modifier is a matter for the assembler to determine.

Some systems make a distinction between *strong lockouts* and *weak lockouts*, that is, between lockouts that prevent an area of store from being either read or written to, and those that merely prevent writing. The distinction is generally the same as that between input and output areas, the data in input buffers being in process of changing, while output areas can be read from without harm. Some systems also provide *progressive lockouts*, in which the area locked out shrinks progressively as the transfer proceeds. It is questionable whether any of these tricks really improve performance in proportion to their cost on any but the very largest systems. It is not uncommon to find different lockout arrangements for slow and fast peripheral devices.

If peripheral transfers are to be autonomous, the Control Program must be informed when a transfer terminates. This is done by a signal from the device, which is known as an *interrupt*, and which causes the Control Program to be entered at the earliest possible moment to release all lockouts associated with that device. Interrupts are dealt with in greater detail in Chapter 14.

INPUT-OUTPUT SYSTEMS

When we were devising an assembly language for our imaginary machine, we proposed a single portmanteau function TFER to deal with all peripheral transfers. In fact this was an oversimplification of what is wanted. There are many different modes of input and output transfer, and specifying them involves a number of parameters. With early computers, the user was expected to write his own input and output routines, providing data editing and conversion to suit his own requirements. Nowadays, systems provide a wide selection of macros and library subroutines to aid the user in specifying input and output operations. These are known collectively as the *input-output package*, or some such name.

Input-output systems differ widely between computers, and it is not our intention here to go into any of them in detail. All of them enable the user to express in a formal manner the various parameters that are needed to specify fully an input or output transfer. In the last chapter we gave a brief résumé of the method used in FORTRAN to specify input and output operations; similar remarks apply in principle, if not in detail, to all input-output systems. The essential information that must be supplied to the assembler is—

name of device,
format on input or output medium,
instructions for numeric conversion,
editing details,
internal format,
buffering arrangements,
location of error routine.

Most systems check against formulation errors in input data, and some also check its validity. In the event of an error, control is transferred to a routine specified by the programmer, a code defining the type of error being passed over as a parameter. Some systems treat peripheral incidents (card stacker full, printer paper exhausted, etc.) in a similar way. The facility for specifying buffering arrangements enables the user to select between several plans such as those shown in Fig. 12.4.

INTERROGATION DEVICES

So far we have dealt with only two types of input medium, cards and paper tape, and with the principal output medium, printed forms; together these account for the bulk of input and output equipment. In the majority of systems input data arrives by post, is punched into cards or paper tape and presented to the computer; the printed output is inserted into envelopes and sent to its destinations. But there are systems in which the output is required immediately, or almost immediately, after the input has been presented. Such systems are referred to as *real-time systems*. Seat reservation systems are cases in point. The computer is first of all interrogated to find if there is a seat available on the route at the time requested. If there is a vacancy, and if the client accepts it, a ticket is made out, and the vacancy is removed from the system. An enquirer would expect a clerk to deal with all this within the space of a few minutes.

TYPEWRITERS

For real-time applications like seat reservations, when a rapid response is demanded, the user must be put in direct communication with the computer: some sort of peripheral device is needed that can transmit a query and subsequently display the system's response. Devices of this kind are known as interrogation units. At one time, teleprinters were used almost exclusively for the purpose; nowadays electric typewriters, modified for computer input, are more common. We have already mentioned (Chapter 6) one application of an electric typewriter—for transmitting operator commands and displaying computer responses and messages. Typewriters are used in large numbers in some installations to give simultaneous access to a number of users.

CATHODE-RAY DISPLAYS

Another type of interrogating unit is a cathode-ray-tube display, with which is incorporated a keyboard for entering messages. The computer's response is displayed on the screen in alpha-numeric form, the shapes of the letters and numerals being generated by circuits within the device. The advantage of a cathode-ray display over a typewriter, particularly when there is a lot of material to be displayed, is that the response is instantaneous; the user does not have to wait upon the operation of a comparatively slow typewriter mechanism (typically 10 characters a second).

LIGHT PENS

Cathode-ray units can also be used to display information in graphical or diagrammatic form. Such displays are often fitted with what is known as a *light pen.* This is a misnomer, since the device, though resembling a pen in appearance, is actually not a *source* of light but a light *detector.* It is used basically to define for the computer a particular point on the screen, the point that it is being made to touch; it does this by emitting an electrical pulse at the moment when the scanning beam strikes it. (The screen of course is being scanned all the time by the cathode-ray beam, either in lines, like a television system, or in some other mode).

Displays with light pens have potentially a great number of applications. A diagram can be projected on to the screen, and the pen used to amend it or add to it; or the diagram can be 'drawn' in the first place by the pen, the computer being used to improve the sketch, straightening the lines, and smoothing the circles; after this, the pen can be used to adjust the diagram, the operator trying out various arrangements until he finds one that satisfies him. The main drawback seems to be that each separate application needs its own complex program, and the cost of writing the program is comparable with the cost of doing the job in a conventional way. Cathode-ray displays are sometimes provided with a camera for making a permanent record (or *hard copy* in the jargon).

MULTIPLEXING

Interrogating devices usually transfer data at a very low rate, and it would be wasteful of equipment to allocate to each one a separate computer channel, which would normally be able to handle data at a rate a hundred times faster than such devices require. Consequently, several such devices are normally attached to the same channel through what is known as a *multiplexer*. This is a device that scans the units attached to it in turn to determine whether any of them require attention. Each active device is connected in turn to the computer channel for a period long enough to transfer one item of data (usually one character together with a code identifying the unit that supplied it). In some systems, multiplexing is used only when there are a number of devices of the same type, as for instance when a computer has several interrogating consoles: other systems use multiplexing for all input and output devices. A multiplexer for typewriters is quite a simple device; but a multiplexer for cathode-ray displays must normally include a core store, since the information must be displayed anew on every scan of the screen.

DOCUMENT READERS

Transferring input data to cards or paper tape is costly and time-consuming; consequently a great deal of effort has gone into devising means whereby a computer can be made to read original documents. Document readers can be divided into three classes: mark sensers, magnetic-ink character readers, and optical character readers.

MARK SENSERS

Mark sensers accept pre-printed forms on which variable data has been entered in the form of pencil lines in appropriate positions. The marks can be sensed optically or electrically (pencil lead, especially of a soft pencil, is a fairly good conductor of electricity). Fig. 12.6 shows a typical mark-senser form.

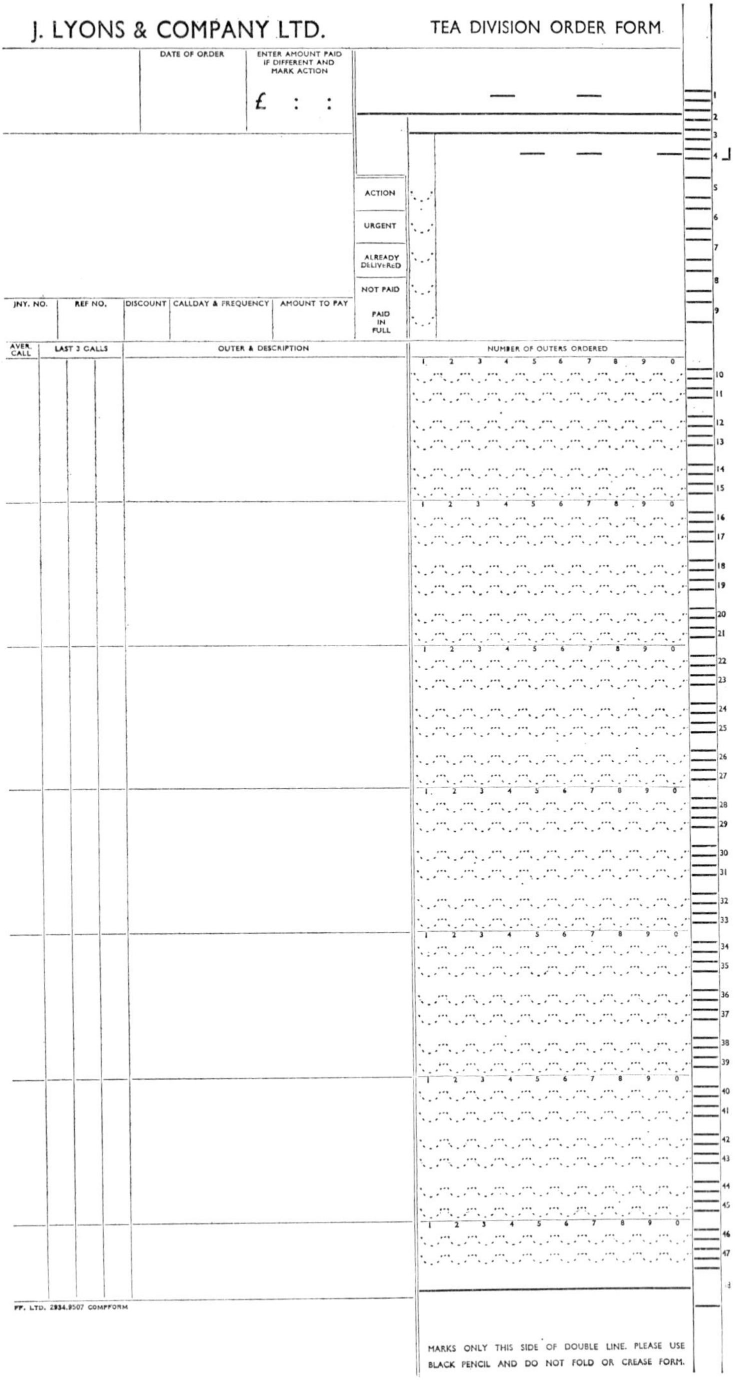

J. LYONS & COMPANY LTD.

TEA DIVISION ORDER FORM

DATE OF ORDER

ENTER AMOUNT PAID IF DIFFERENT AND MARK ACTION

£ : :

ACTION

URGENT

ALREADY DELIVERED

NOT PAID

PAID IN FULL

JNY. NO.

REF NO.

DISCOUNT

CALLDAY & FREQUENCY

AMOUNT TO PAY

AVER. CALL

LAST 3 CALLS

OUTER & DESCRIPTION

NUMBER OF OUTERS ORDERED

1 2 3 4 5 6 7 8 9 0

FF. LTD. 2934.9507 COMPFORM

MARKS ONLY THIS SIDE OF DOUBLE LINE. PLEASE USE BLACK PENCIL AND DO NOT FOLD OR CREASE FORM.

FIG. 12.6. Mark-senser Form

MAGNETIC INK

Anyone with a cheque book will be familiar with the type face used in one kind of *magnetic-ink character reader*. This particular type face is known as E13B. The characters are printed in ink containing a substance with strong magnetic properties, and can therefore be read by a device sensitive to changes in magnetic flux. The ink itself is not magnetized; it merely influences the magnetic field in the vicinity of the detector. The peculiar shapes of the characters are intended to effect a compromise between familiarity to the eye and legibility to the reading device (the result being distinctly in favour of the latter). On the continent of Europe, another magnetic-ink type face has found favour; this is known as CMC7. The characters are made up of series of bars of different widths, coded in such a way that the pulse patterns induced by the different characters are as widely separated as possible. An example of the type face E13B is shown in Fig. 12.7.

FIG. 12.7. Example of E13B

OPTICAL CHARACTER RECOGNITION

Ever since the early days of computers there has been a desire for an input device that will read 'ordinary print.' Today, that desire has at last been realized. The principle of *optical character recognition* can be stated very simply: the character is scanned by a spot of light, and the variations in brightness are converted into an electrical signal that is peculiar to the character and should serve to identify it. Fig. 12.8 shows the scanning of the letter A and the electrical waveform that arises from it.

The difficulty in optical character recognition arises from the fact that printing is never perfect. Individual characters may be displaced on the line, or they may be slightly rotated. The ink may be smudged, or it may lie unevenly, so that some of the lines are narrow or broken. For some reason not fully understood, a moderate degradation in print quality does not cause the human reader with normal eyesight much concern; though it can cause a mechanical reader to substitute one character for another, or to fail to recognize the character altogether. Because of the imperfections of print, each character must be made to correspond not to a single invariable pulse pattern but to a family of patterns, any of which should be identifiable. There is the additional problem that there are certain pairs of characters that are particularly easy to confuse: O and Q, for example, or E and F. Nevertheless, the problems are being overcome one by one. A special computer type face has been designed

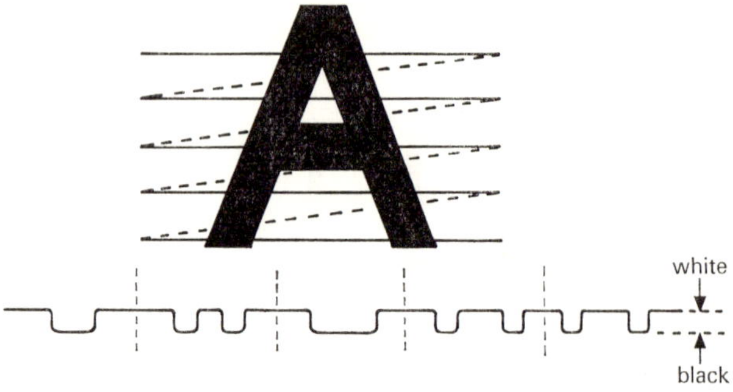

FIG. 12.8. Scanning the Letter A

which, unlike E13B, is almost indistinguishable from standard type faces, but eliminates close similarities between characters.

OTHER DEVICES

VOICE INPUT

An even wilder dream than the mechanical reading of print is the mechanical interpretation of speech. In spite of a few more or less convincing demonstrations, this ideal is very far from being realized. The only attempt made so far has been to design a device that will recognize not words but characters spelled out one by one. A voice-input device on these lines, however, would probably be no faster than a keyboard in skilled hands.

KIMBALL TAGS

A multitude of devices has been used to supply computer input for special purposes, and a few of them deserve mention. There are, for instance, *Kimball-tag* readers. Kimball tags are, in effect, small punched cards. They are supplied in strips of half a dozen or so, all punched with the same information. They have found particular favour in the clothing trade. A strip, punched according to style, colour, size and price, is attached to each garment. At the warehouse one tag is torn off and retained, and at the retail shop two more might be removed, one being kept, and the other being returned to head office. What is left passes to the purchaser, who usually destroys it. Special machines have been designed for handling Kimball tags; but some might eventually find their way to a computer installation, where they could be used as an input to an accounting program, a stock-control program, or a sales-analysis program. Kimball readers are available for direct computer input.

EDGE-PUNCHED CARDS

Another special-purpose medium is the *edge-punched card.* This is a card that is normally used for holding written information, but on which a small amount of mechanically and optically readable information can be held in the form of nicks along the edge. In one application the card is actually read by sensing pencil marks made by the operator, the edge punching being used only to record output from the system.

BADGE READERS

We might also mention *badge readers.* A *badge*, as the term is used here, is a small piece of metal or plastic punched or embossed with identifying codes. One application might be in a machine shop where job-scheduling is being done by computer. Data on the progress of each job must be fed back periodically to the computer, together with information on the machines and operators. This could all be done by means of keyboards; but there is less likelihood of error if each operator and each machine, and even each separate job, has a distinguishing badge that can be presented to the special reading device whenever the job passes from one stage to the next.

ANALOGUE-DIGITAL CONVERSION

Sometimes it is necessary to supply a digital computer with *analogue* signals. An analogue is simply a representation of a numerical quantity by a physical entity of equivalent magnitude. The analogue may be electrical, as for instance a voltage or current, or it may be mechanical, as the angular position of a shaft or the linear position of a scale. Analogue signals form part of the input whenever a computer is being used to control or monitor a piece of machinery. Electrical analogues can be converted into digital form by standard circuits, which we shall not discuss here; but the conversion of mechanical analogues involves an interesting technique, which it will be instructive to consider.

Let us take a mechanical analogue in the form of a shaft position.

Its value can be determined digitally by attaching to the shaft a disc divided into zones, with each zone coded by transparent and opaque areas, as shown in Fig. 12.9. The disc is read optically to give a unique binary code for every angular position. But there is a further consideration. If the codes are arranged in the normal numeric sequence, an ambiguity arises. Imagine what would happen as the disc moved from zone 15 (01111) to zone 16 (10000). Unless all the optical sensors were perfectly aligned, and there was no additional delay in the amplifying circuits (all of which is virtually

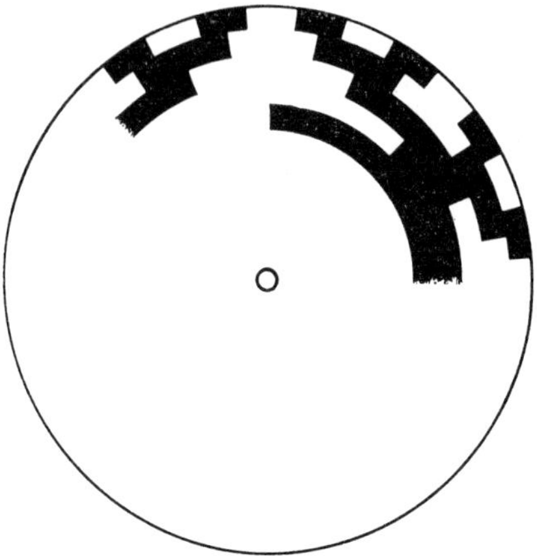

FIG. 12.9. 5-Zone Analogue Converter Disc

impossible), the digits would change their values at different instants, giving the impression that the disc was moving wildly from one zone to another. Worse than this, which could be overcome, it would be possible for the disc to position itself between two zones in such a way that only a few of the digits had changed, giving the impression that it was in an entirely different position. The codes must therefore not be arranged in numeric sequence, but in some sequence in which only one bit changes from one code to the next. A sequence with this property is said to be *cyclic-progressive*.

A cyclic-progressive sequence can be derived from a numeric sequence by the following algorithm—

The first bit of the c-p code is the same as the first bit of the corresponding numeric code.

To determine the other bits, scan the numeric code, putting a one in the c-p code whenever there is a change in value from one bit to the next, and putting a nought whenever two adjacent bits are the same.

For example—

Numeric Code	*Cyclic-progressive Code*
01100	01010
01101	01011
01110	01001
01111	01000
10000	11000
10001	11001
10010	11011
10011	11010

GRAPH PLOTTER

Finally, one more output device: a *graph plotter*. Like a cathode-ray display, a graph plotter can be used in a variety of ways, not only to present numeric data in graphical form, but also to draw diagrams or write special symbols. The simplest form of graph plotter carries the paper on a drum, with the pen moving axially on a bar above it. Since the information supplied to the device is digital, the plot is drawn in a series of steps, vertical movement being achieved by rotating the drum, and horizontal movement by shifting the pen. The step size is determined by the design of the plotter, the smaller the steps, the smoother the plot. Some plotting systems permit letters and numerals to be shown.

DATA LINKS

Input and output devices, particularly interrogating devices, are sometimes located at a distance from the computer. Over short distances—between rooms in the same building, for instance—the normal method of connection is usually adequate. Over slightly longer distances it may be necessary to boost signals; but over distances of several miles the system must have recourse to a data link using telegraph or telephone lines.

MULTIPLEXERS

Telegraph lines are suitable for low data rates. The data must be reduced to serial form, with pulses of standard lengths and amplitudes, and must be reconstituted at the remote end. The line may be operated in a *simplex* or a *duplex* mode, that is, data may pass in one direction only, or messages may be sent alternately in the two directions.

Telephone lines will handle fairly fast peripheral devices, or they may be used with multiplexers to handle several slow devices at once. The multiplexer may use the sampling technique we have already described, or it may use the technique of modulation, whereby pulses are used to switch a continuous tone off and on. Several tones at different pitches may be sent simultaneously along the same line, and then separated at the receiving end, where the original pulse forms are reconstituted.

Long lines, whether telephone or telegraph, are liable to pick up noise, that is, they are liable to interference that can cause additional pulses to appear, or transmitted pulses to be lost. Noise is always dealt with in the same general way—by introducing redundancy. The simplest case of redundancy is the parity check: an extra bit is transmitted with each group, carrying no information in itself but serving to indicate whether a bit in the group has been altered by noise. At the other extreme, one hundred per cent redundancy can be introduced by transmitting every message twice and comparing the received messages. In fact, this is not the best way of using one hundred per cent redundancy, since there is no way of knowing, in the case of disagreement, which received message is correct.

ERROR-CORRECTING CODES

With twelve bits, it is possible to transmit more than four thousand different codes. If we decide to use only, say, 256 out of all the possible codes, four bits become redundant, and can be used to carry check information. Morevoer, if we choose the 256 codes that are used carefully enough, we can arrange matters so that an inversion of a single bit cannot cause one code to change into any of the others that have been chosen. Under these circumstances a code remains unique even after it has been distorted, and no information is lost, provided always that the noise level is low enough to cause only an occasional inversion of a bit. Codes chosen in this way are known as *error-correcting codes* or *Hamming codes.*

ERROR-DETECTING CODES

With four redundant bits in twelve, it is possible to *correct* only one error, but it is possible to *detect* more. The actual sets of codes chosen for error *detection* are different, naturally, from those chosen for error *correction;* but it must always be true that it is possible to detect more errors than it is possible to correct. Error-detecting codes are generally more useful than error-correcting codes, except in very special circumstances, since it is usually possible to obtain a correction by calling for a retransmission provided that the error was detected in the first place. Besides, errors on data links tend to occur in heavy bursts with long periods of error-free transmission in between.

PERIPHERAL INTERFACE

The set of signals passing between any two units in a system is known as an *interface*. (The term has been used to refer not only to mechanical systems but also to software systems and even to human organizations.) The most clearly defined interfaces in a computer system are those between the peripherals and the system centre. It is very advantageous for all the peripheral devices to have the same interface, for then the units in the system centre that deal with the peripheral cabling can be made to the same design, and the devices can be plugged into any outlet. In fact, a completely standard interface has not yet been devised, and is probably not realizable at a reasonable cost; but most general-purpose computer systems today have reduced the number of different peripheral interfaces to a few variants on a general theme.

COMMANDS AND STATUS

Signals passing between the system centre and the peripherals can be grouped under four headings—

(*a*) data from computer to peripheral,
(*b*) data from peripheral to computer,
(*c*) commands from computer to peripheral,
(*d*) status information from peripheral to computer.

By the term *status* we mean the conditions obtaining within the device—whether or not it is switched on; whether it is busy with a transfer; whether, if a transfer has terminated, it was performed correctly; and so on. Commands include not only instructions to the device to start or stop, read or write, but also instructions to change its mode of working.

STANDARD INTERFACES

Standard interfaces differ so widely from manufacturer to manufacturer that there is little that can be said in general about them. Even the number of wires crossing the interface can vary from two or three up to a hundred or more, the four groups of signals occupying separate sets of wires on some interfaces and being duplexed on one or two sets of wires on others. Codes may be transferred in parallel, or they may be serialized in a single wire. In fact the bandwidth of ordinary cables is usually great enough for data from even quite fast devices to be transmitted serially.

RING AND STAR SYSTEMS

The separate peripheral devices can be connected to the system centre by separate cables, or a single cable can be provided visiting each device in turn. The former arrangement is known as a *star system*, the latter as a *ring system* (though the ring need not necessarily be closed). The ring system is generally cheaper, but it requires every message to carry an identification code to indicate which device it is meant for. Some ring systems establish priorities by the positions of the devices on the ring.

Peripheral devices differ widely in their modes of working, as we have seen from the brief review of equipment given above. They differ in their data rates, in the amount of data that can be transferred at one time, in the sorts of commands they can act upon, and in the status they can take. With a standard interface, all these differences must be reduced to codes and code sequences, and for this to be possible, every peripheral unit must contain a substantial amount of electronic equipment, for decoding commands and generating signals, to operate the various actuators, and for converting the outputs of various sensing devices into status codes. For this reason, a device used as peripheral equipment on a computer can cost several times as much as the same device used alone or as part of a simpler installation.

One final point: reducing the individual peculiarities of the various types of device to one standard specification of interface has meant that software controlling the different types can contain more common routines than was possible before the advent of standard interfaces. This has had an appreciable effect upon the sizes of control programs, and has made it possible to provide more sophisticated features and improve the efficiency of the whole system.

EXERCISES 12

1. What is the speed in characters per second of—

   (*a*) a reader operating at 1,200 cards per minute,
   (*b*) a punch operating at 300 cards per minute,
   (*c*) a line printer operating at 1,000 lines per minute and printing 24 alphabetic characters on a line of 120 print positions?

2. A form is laid out as follows—

   5 lines of print
   4-line space
   1 line of print
   3-line space
   2 lines of print
   1-line space
   1 line of print
   8-line space.

Calculate the printing speed on—

(*a*) a 1,000 line-per-minute printer with no skip facility, (assume that normal line spacing can be achieved within the print cycle)
(*b*) a 400-line-per-minute printer that can skip up to six lines within the print cycle.

3. A computer run involves the following sequence of operations—

read a card,
process,
print a form.

The peripheral devices used have the following specifications—

printer speed—100 forms per minute,
printer loading time—3 minutes,
capacity—2000 forms,
card-reader speed—500 cards per minute,
card loading time—1 minute,
magazine capacity—2500 cards.

Assuming that the processing time can be overlapped, but that only one peripheral device can be operating at a time, calculate the time needed to process 10,000 cards. Devices must be stopped by loading.

4. If, in question 3, the two peripheral devices were capable of running concurrently, how would the job time be affected?

What would be the speed of the slowest card reader, which, running concurrently with the printer, could complete the job in the same time? (Assume the same magazine capacity and reload time as before.)

5. Rewrite the procedural part of the program CARDSELECT (see Chapter 6) to correspond with each of the systems illustrated in the second, third and fourth diagrams of Fig. 12.4.

6. Generate ten successive codes in an 8-bit cyclic-progressive sequence.

13. Files and File Devices

PRACTICALLY all the devices used for holding computer files have some form of magnetic film as the recording medium. The film, which is usually based upon an oxide of iron, may be deposited on rigid drums or discs, or it may be in the form of plastic sheeting, either in the form of rectangular *cards* or else as lengths of tape wound upon reels. In every case the principle of recording is the same: data is recorded digitally in small areas of local magnetization, induced when the medium moves under a recording *head.* When a magnetized film passes under another similar head, current pulses are induced corresponding to the pattern of magnetization. Data is not destroyed when it is read in this way, as it is when it is read from a stationary medium such as a core store.

A magnetic recording head is shown diagrammatically in Fig. 13.1. It consists of a *magnetic former* on which a coil is wound

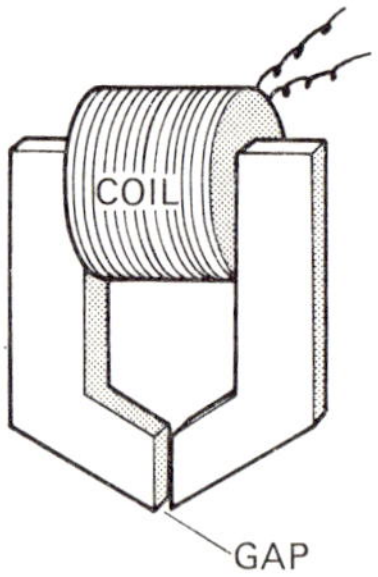

FIG. 13.1 Magnetic Recording Head

which is to carry the signal to be recorded. There is a narrow gap in the *former*, through which magnetic flux can escape and induce magnetic patterns in the film. Heads for reading and writing are identical in structure. Some file devices have separate sets of heads for the two purposes; others use the same heads for reading as for writing.

The simplest way to record digital data is to magnetize the medium in one direction for a one and in the opposite direction for a nought.

This mode of recording is known as *return to zero*, or *RTZ*. A better mode is known as *non-return*, or *NRZ;* in this mode, a one is recorded by reversing the direction of magnetization, and a nought is recorded by leaving the direction unaffected. Fig. 13.2 compares the

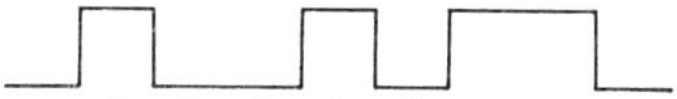

Return to zero

Non-Return

FIG. 13.2

two modes of recording. The number of reversals is greater in RTZ than in NRZ mode. We interpret this by saying that the bandwidth is less in the second case, and that consequently it is possible to record more data on a given length of tape.

MAGNETIC TAPE

The commonest file medium is magnetic tape. Magnetic-tape mechanisms are comparatively cheap, and the size of file that can be accommodated is virtually unlimited; though of course the number of reels that can be *on-line* at one time is limited to the number of mechanisms available. Information is recorded on several parallel tracks in the way just described. Separate sets of heads are used for writing and reading, and the writing process is checked by reading back immediately afterwards: to make this possible, the writing heads are mounted a little in advance of the reading heads. The tape usually runs in contact with the heads. Although friction in this case does reduce the life of tapes somewhat, modern tapes have in fact a very long life, and in-contact operation does give good strong signals with a low incidence of error.

BLOCKING AND UTILIZATION

The tape drives used on computers operate at speeds of the order of 100 inches per second. Since data cannot be written or read properly unless the tape is running at full speed, a gap must be left in the record whenever the tape drive is stopped, to avoid recording during deceleration and subsequent acceleration. Consequently recorded data always appears in the form of discrete *blocks* with gaps between them. The size of block is under the control of the programmer, who fixes it according to the amount of data that his program can handle at one time, that is, according to the amount of space that he can allocate for the purpose in the store, Consequently, on a system with a small store, there may be no more than one file record per block; whereas on a larger system several records can be *blocked* together, giving better *utilization* of the tape. Blocks can vary in length, if that is the form the data naturally takes; though an upper

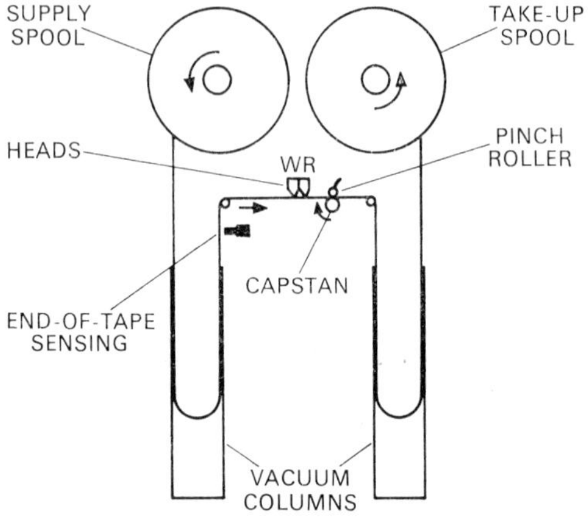

FIG. 13.3. Magnetic-Tape Transport (Diagrammatic)

limit must be put upon block length—the size of the store area that is set aside to receive it.

To keep the inter-block gap as short as possible, the tape must be capable of being accelerated and brought to rest in a short space of time. This imposes a severe constraint on the design of the transport mechanism. It is impracticable to accelerate and decelerate heavy tape reels at the rate demanded, so it is usual to keep reservoir loops of tape between the reels and the heads. The loops are kept in tension either mechanically or, more usually, by being held in vacuum columns. The reels need then only change their rate of rotation comparatively slowly, the only stipulation being that they must move fast enough to prevent the loops from becoming either too long or too short. Figure 13.3 shows a sketch of a typical magnetic-tape mechanism. The tape is actually driven across the heads by a rotating capstan, against which it is pressed by an idling pinch-roller. When the pinch-roller is released, the tape stops moving.

REWINDING

It is normal practice to rewind a tape back on to its supply spool after the last block has been read or written. This avoids having to

by Anna Ragon

Mes arrière-neveux me devront cet ombrage.
        Hé bien! défendrez-vous au sage
De se donner des soins pour le plaisir d'autrui?
Cela même est un fruit que je goûte aujourd'hui;
J'en puis jouir demain, et quelques jours encore;
        Je puis enfin compter l'aurore
        Plus d'une fois sur vos tombeaux.

Mais il y a beaucoup de pièces où les différents mètres abondent, comme nous l'avons montré en parlant du vers libre, que nous retrouverons dans le chapitre *les Strophes*.

relabel the spools, and makes sure that all tapes are stored the same way round. Most transports rewind tapes faster than they can read them or write them. The tape is lowered so that it is out of contact with the heads while it is being rewound, and the reservoir loops are eliminated. Since no data is transmitted during rewinding, a tape transport can be switched out of communication with the computer, releasing a channel for use, if need be, by another transport.

STANDARD FORMATS

There is a standard magnetic-tape format that has now gained wide acceptance throughout the industry. The tape is half an inch wide, and it carries seven recording tracks. Data is recorded in groups of six bits in *stripes* across the tape, and the seventh track is used for a parity check. Odd parity is chosen, since the stripes are then clocked automatically, that is to say, each stripe has at least one reversal of magnetization to define its position. Recording is in the non-return mode; and at the end of every block, before the gap, an extra stripe is added in such a way as to return the magnetization on every track to the zero condition. In effect, this last stripe represents the longitudinal parity of the tracks, and provides an extra check upon the accuracy of the information.

The inter-block gap in the standard format measures 0·7 inch. A transport designed to accept tapes written in the standard format must then be capable of stopping and restarting not just in 0·7 inch, but in 0·7 inch less whatever is the spacing between the reading and writing heads. To keep the spacing small, the two sets of heads are normally made as a single unit. There is a choice of three standard recording densities: 200, 555, and 800 bits per inch on each track; mechanisms are sometimes made so that they are capable of operating at two, or even all three, densities, the selection being made by a command from the system centre. The speed of the tape is not included in the specification, since it cannot affect the interchangeability of tapes provided that the transports conform to the specification in all other respects. In addition to their normal use as files, magnetic tapes in the standard format can be used for interchanging information between different machines. In recent years, a variant on the standard specification has appeared; this is identical in every way except that nine tracks are used instead of seven—eight information tracks and one parity track. As well as storing more information in a given length, nine-track tapes are particularly convenient to use with a byte machine.

A tape transport moving at 120 inches per second, and recorded at 800 bits per inch, is transferring data at the rate of 96,000 stripes per second, that is, at 576,000 bits per second for six data tracks, or

768,000 bits per second for eight. Contrast this with the data rates below 10,000 bits per second that are all that can be achieved with cards or paper tape.

LEADERS

The beginning and end of the recordable portion of standard tapes are marked by strips of reflecting material that are sensed by a photo-electric device close to the heads, a signal being passed back to the system centre when they are detected. The portions of tape outside these marks are known as leaders. In some systems, the leader on the take-up spool is permanently attached, and it terminates in a *buckle* that can be clipped on to the end of the tape from the supply spool for easy loading. After loading a tape, the operator normally presses a button, which causes the tape to advance to the first silvered marker, known as the *load point*. When a reel is rewound, it normally stops at the load point.

REEL STORAGE

Magnetic tapes must be stored in a controlled environment. This is because ambient temperature and humidity affect the base material (usually a form of nylon), altering its length and consequently the density of recording. It is important, too, for tapes to be protected from dust, not only in storage but also when they are near, or mounted on, the mechanisms. A speck of dust adhering to a tape while it is being read can lift it away from the head, so that the signal is weakened and information lost. Tapes are normally kept in boxes, and when they are stored outside the computer room they should be kept in an air-conditioned cabinet. The computer room should be kept as far as possible dust free, with filters in the air-conditioning supply, and dust-absorbing mats at the door. The operators should also wear clean lint-free overalls. Sometimes the additional precaution is taken of installing tape transports in a room of their own.

FAULTS

We have mentioned that tapes are checked by the reading head while they are being written. It is normally only the parities that are checked, since a complete comparison would require more computer time than the frequency of error warrants. In the event of a writing fault it is common practice for the Control Program to step the tape back and make an attempt to write the information again. Usually, after a few tries, the dust particle, or whatever is causing the fault, is dislodged, and the operation is successful. If this does not happen, if there is a blemish in the magnetic coating, or if the tape has suffered damage, that portion of the tape is abandoned, and another attempt made to write the information further along. Automatic repetition is used too when a read instruction fails. If, however, the information cannot be recovered after several tries have been made, it must be regarded as lost, and must then be reconstituted from an earlier generation of the file, which should have been retained for just such a contingency. It is sometimes possible to recover information from a damaged tape by altering the level at which the reading circuits discriminate between ones and noughts. Incidentally, on some systems the check after writing is always performed at a higher discrimination level, that is, under more stringent conditions than normal reading.

Tapes do have blemishes, usually in the form of pinholes in the magnetic film, which reduce the length of the usable portion. The number of blemishes tends to increase with use; but, provided that a tape has been supplied by a reputable manufacturer, and provided that it has not been used beyond its recommended lifetime, the number of faults and failures should be quite small.

One other way in which information can be lost from a tape is by being over-written in error. In an attempt to prevent catastrophic damage, most systems require a positive manual act to be performed before a transport can be put into a writing condition. This usually means fitting a detachable ring to the hub of the reel. When the reel is mounted on a transport, the ring operates a switch, which permits current to flow in the writing heads. With the ring absent, any attempt to write is treated as an error, and may result in suspension of the program, and some indication (such as a typed message) for the operator.

HEADERS

Unfortunately a *write-permit ring* is not in itself enough, since it is still possible for an operator to fit a ring to the wrong reel, or more likely to leave a ring fitted after writing has finished. What is really needed is some means whereby the system can check for itself whether a particular tape may or may not be written on. In fact, the writing status of a tape is one of the pieces of information among others written in a special block known as the *tape header*.

The header usually occupies the first block on a magnetic tape. It contains two sorts of information: information for use by running programs, and information for engineering or statistical use. It is generally prefaced by some distinguishing string of characters, for instance, the string @HEADER. The program information includes some or all of the following items—

name of tape
reel sequence number (for multi-reel files)
generation number
writing status
date written
retention period
number of blocks and/or records written
maximum block length.

The *retention period* of a tape is the period over which the information on the tape is to be regarded as inviolable. At the end of this period the information may be deemed to be obsolete, and the tape can be over-written without harm. Throughout the retention period the tape must be used with the writing status that appears on the header: after that period, the tape becomes a *scratch tape*, and can be used for general purposes. Even with the protection afforded by a header, though, a write-permit ring should still be used, to guard against possible loss of information from machine faults.

The engineering information on a tape includes the serial number of the tape, which it retains throughout its lifetime, and which serves to distinguish it from all the other tapes in the system no matter what is written on it. There is also sometimes a count of the number of times a tape has been run, in order to determine when it should be scrapped, and possibly also a count of the number of fault repeats that occurred when it was last written and last read, as an indication of its condition.

TRAILERS

The number of blocks on a tape may be written on the header after rewinding; but it is more usually written on a *trailer block* at the end of the tape. The main purpose of a block count is a check to ensure that no information has been missed out in reading. There may also be a count of the number of records as well. The trailer is usually prefaced by an identifier (e.g. the characters @TRAILER). It may also include a *hash sum*. This is a sum formed by adding together the items of information on the tape, treating all strings of bits as numeric information whether they are or not; it serves as a further check on reading accuracy.

TAPE MARKS

The header and trailer labels are usually preceded by *tape marks*. These are records that are recognizably not normal records (for example, they may be shorter than the minimum record length), and they serve to call into operation a special section of the Control Program. As well as announcing headers and trailers, tape marks may be used to divide tapes into sections, for instance, to mark off separate programs on a library tape. They may also be used to announce checkpoint dumps (see below).

OPENING AND CLOSING FILES

Since all programs deal with headers in the same way, the instruction sequences that do the work are best treated as standard subroutines. Not only does this approach save programming effort, but it also avoids the danger of writing erroneous or even meaningless headers. The process of reading and checking a header is known as *opening* a tape file. There are various ways in which this can be done; the commonest is to provide an OPEN function in the repertoire. Thus an instruction such as—

```
OPEN        'CUSTOMERFILE'
```

would cause the system to search the tape transports until it found a tape with the name CUSTOMERFILE in its header. It would check this for write status and would then allocate it to the program. If the OPEN instruction is written with an address instead of a literal as the argument, it becomes even more useful; the name of the tape can then be made variable. Thus an instruction of the form—

```
OPEN        FILENAME
```

would search for a tape whose name is to be found in the location FILENAME. This sort of facility is essential when using multi-reel files, since the sequence number, which must be checked with the name, changes from reel to reel.

We have talked of the system searching for a tape with a particular header, and in fact some systems do just this, reading the headers on all the tapes that have not yet been allocated to a program. An alternative arrangement is for the header to be read as soon as a new tape has been loaded and the operator has re-engaged the mechanism; the header information is then retained in the store until it is needed. Re-engaging a mechanism consists in pressing a button that advances the tape to the load point and causes an interrupt in the computer, leading to entry to the Control Program. Alternatively the device can be engaged from the console, either by a typewriter message or, better, by using a special *engage* panel. One common system requires the operator to operate a common *engage* switch and then dial a number identifying the device he wishes to engage. A similar arrangement can be used with input and output devices as well as file devices. It is the practice in some systems to preface a stack of cards with a header or *sentinel* card (often of a different colour from the rest of the pack) and then engage the card reader in the standard manner. Similarly a length of paper tape can be preceded by a header block.

When the transport signals that it has detected the end-of-tape marker, no more data blocks may be read or written, and the tape must be *closed*. With output tapes, closure involves writing the trailer label and rewinding the tape. There must also be some indication to the operator when a tape has been closed. Closure of an output tape may also involve altering the write status in the header, to protect the tape on its next run. Tapes are seldom closed automatically; there are too many possible modes of closure. It is more usual to provide the user with a special CLOSE function (or more than one function) that he can apply as appropriate.

Most systems permit a file to be referred to in a program by a different name from the one that appears in the header. Not only does this permit the programmer to use a conveniently short name in the program, with long unambiguous names in the tapes themselves, but it also gives programs more generality—the same program can be used to perform similar processes on two or more entirely different files, and two or more programs can refer to the same file by different names. There are various ways in which a program name and a header name can be associated; one is to use the OPEN function, thus—

```
MT1     OPEN     FILENAME
```

would associate the tape whose header is in FILENAME with the program name MT1.

The foregoing remarks apply of course only to input tapes, that is, to tapes that already have a meaningful header label. Tapes that are to be used for output are scratch tapes, and their headers have no relevance to the current job. The programmer must supply most of the data for the new header. One convention that might be used is to extend the OPEN function still further; an instruction of the form—

```
MT2     OPEN     FILDATA
```

referring to an area of store, FILDATA, containing—

(*a*) an indication that the tape is for output,
(*b*) the tape name, reel number and generation number,
(*c*) the writing status,
(*d*) the retention period.

The system would then search for a scratch tape, and write the header, supplying the day's date itself, and allocate it to the program under the name MT2.

Every system should supply some means of handling non-standard tapes, that is, tapes without headers, or with headers written on another machine and according to an entirely different set of rules. Naturally, the ordinary OPEN and CLOSE functions cannot be used in this case; but it must still be possible to allocate a tape to a program and to associate it with a name in the program. A common way of doing this is by means of a console message, which must quote the number of the mechanism on which the tape is mounted—its *geographical name.*

HOUSEKEEPING

The OPEN and CLOSE functions are only two out of a number of special functions provided (generally as macros or library subroutines) to aid the user. Together they are usually referred to as a *file-control package*, or a *housekeeping package.* The package is

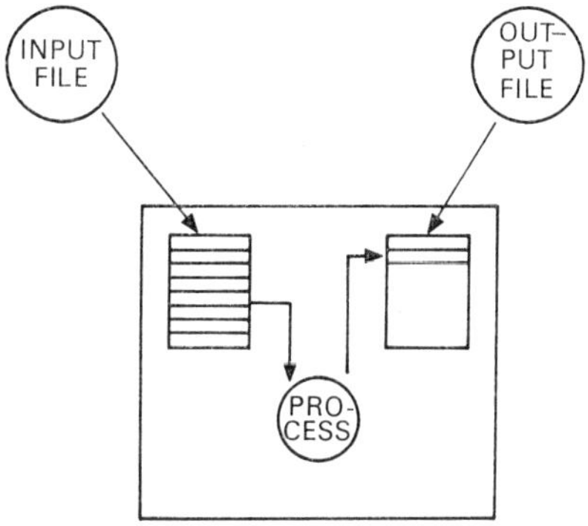

FIG. 13.4.

usually made up in the form of several functions, since this is a convenient way of achieving modularity, that is, of providing the user with a simple means of selecting those features he needs and ignoring those he does not need. The package provides the user with a simple method of specifying the number of buffer areas to be allocated to each file, and for specifying a routine to which control is to be passed should an error or exception condition (such as an end-of-tape mark) arise. Unlike input-output packages, file-control packages do not normally provide facilities for data conversion and editing. Since data written on a file is accessible only to a computer, it can take the same form as in the computer's own store,

Figures 13.4 and 13.5 illustrate the process of updating a magnetic-tape file. Only one buffer area each has been allocated to the input and output tapes in the diagram; but the general principle is the same if more areas are allocated. Each buffer holds a complete block, which comprises several records; and at any one time the process is operating on only one record in each buffer. When all

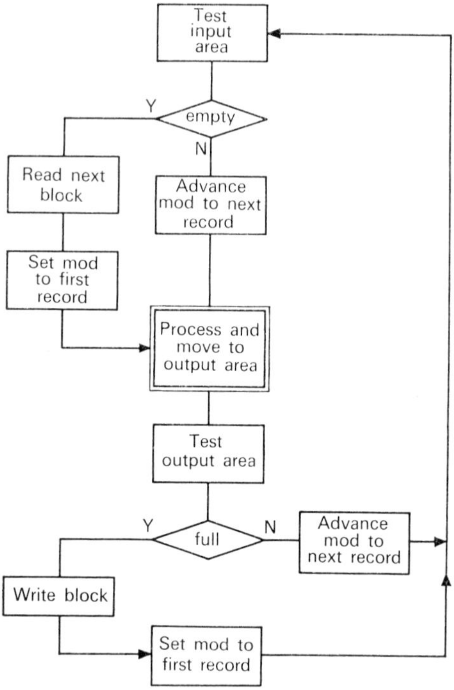

FIG. 13.5.

the records in the input buffer have been processed, it must be replenished, and when the output buffer is full it must be written away; in general, if records are being created or deleted, replenishment and output will occur in different processing cycles. The normal practice is to use modifiers to point to the actual records that are being processed, advancing these at the end of each cycle, and resetting them to the beginning of the buffer area after an operation of input or output.

A housekeeping package will usually permit the *logical processing* of records, that is, it will permit the program to be written at the *record* level, with the blocking and unblocking of records being taken care of by standard subroutines included with the package. Having defined the block format, the programmer need then only write instructions of the form—

	RECORD	TFER	MT1
or—	MT2	TFER	RECORD

Depending on the system, these instructions may actually give rise to the transfer of data across the store, or they may work simply by manipulating modifiers. Tape marks and end-of-tape markers will be signalled to the program in their *logical* position, not when they are actually sensed. Signalling is usually accomplished by transferring control to an error-exception routine defined by the user, a code defining the type of error or exception being passed over as a parameter.

Magnetic-tape operating systems differ widely in their organizational details, some of these reflecting hardware differences, others arising from arbitrary differences in conception. All, however, have the same fundamental features—

(*a*) file identification and protection by means of header labels,
(*b*) some means of defining files and indicating how they are organized,
(*c*) a set of instructions representing general macro-operations for reading, writing and checking data and scheduling operations.

It is unfortunate that there should be so many different ways of organizing magnetic-tape housekeeping. Those who are constantly bewailing the fact that there is no universal machine language would do well to reflect that a universal language would only affect the procedural parts of programs and would accomplish little so long as operating systems remained unstandardized.

CHANNELS AND CLUSTERS

Any two peripheral devices that can operate simultaneously are said to have separate *channels* to the system centre. It is not necessary for the channels to be physically separate; as we saw in the last chapter, several devices can transfer data along the same set of wires at the same time by multiplexing. However, with fast devices like magnetic tape, separate channels normally do imply separate sets of cables. It is not necessary for every tape transport on an installation to have a separate channel; indeed it would be wasteful if they did, for at any one time there are likely to be several transports rewinding, or being loaded or unloaded, or simply standing idle. Consequently it is common practice for two or more mechanisms to be arranged in a group or *cluster* sharing the same data channel and therewith an appreciable quantity of electronic equipment.

It is important to appreciate clearly the difference between *clustering* and *multiplexing*. The two arrangements are both intended to save equipment, and in both cases several devices may be allocated to the same program at the same time. But it is possible for two multiplexed devices to be running simultaneously and at full speed, whereas two devices on the same cluster must take it in turns to transfer blocks of data. Thus the data-transfer rate of a cluster is only that of a single mechanism; and if several devices are active on the same cluster their effective transfer rates are reduced in proportion. The cheapest computer installations have only one magnetic-tape cluster, which must carry all the files—old main file, new main file, and all the detail files. Jobs on a one-channel installation are commonly tape-limited, when running time becomes the same as the sum of the running times of the separate files.

To improve throughput, two or more clusters can be used at the same time; but this could make the system difficult to use. With several clusters, the operator must try to keep the loading on all channels as nearly balanced as possible; for, if he fails to do so, channels are either under-used or over-used, and throughput suffers. A reasonable balance can usually be achieved on a single-program machine; but with a multiprogrammed system it is practically impossible to maintain a proper balance all the time. This problem would not arise of course if every file device had its own channel; but neither would it arise, even with fewer channels than devices, if any device could have access to any free channel.

CHANNEL SWITCHING

Several magnetic-tape systems provide switching, either within the cluster or as an optional addition, for connecting any one of several devices to any one of several channels. A typical arrangement is shown in Fig. 13.6. An instruction (other than REWIND) can be accepted only if there is a spare channel available to transfer the data; otherwise it must wait until a channel becomes free. As soon as a mechanism accepts a command it pre-empts a channel, relinquishing it only after a complete block has been transferred or a transfer has been found impossible to carry out.

SORTING

It is necessary with jobs using a main file on magnetic tape for input details to be sorted into the same sequence as the records on the file. Sorting is performed on a serial number, or *key*, which will serve during the updating to associate input items with records. We considered in Chapter 4 a simple sorting procedure for one-word items (see Fig. 4.1); and there is nothing to prevent a similar idea from being used to sort longer items on magnetic tape—nothing, that is, except time. Each sorting pass could consist in copying all the items from one tape to another, taking the items in pairs and reversing their order if necessary. After being copied from one tape

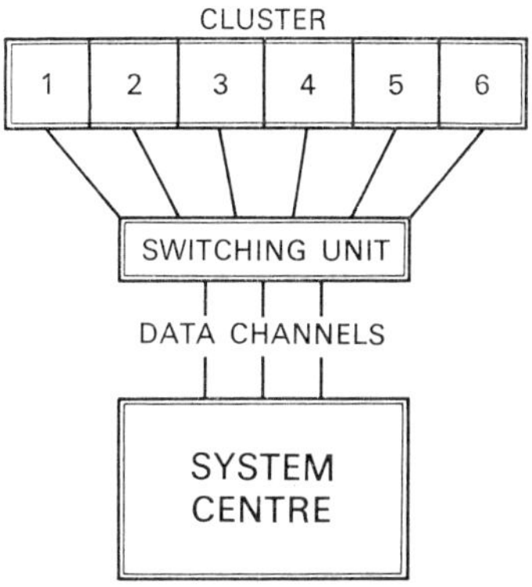

FIG. 13.6. Multi-Channel Cluster

to the other and back again enough times, the data would eventually come into the correct order; but it would take a long time. In the worst case, a single item might have to be transferred right from one end of the tape to the other. At a rate of one reversal for each pass of the tapes, this would take one pass fewer than there were items. With, say, 600 feet of tape running at, say, 120 inches per second, it would take one minute for every pass. If there were 40,000 items, the total time might be as long as 40,000 minutes—or nearly a month (and even that does not include rewind time).

MERGING SORT

A very much faster process is known as a *merging sort*. It can best be understood by imagining first of all four tapes—call them A, B, C, and D. The data to be sorted is divided into two equal parts and written initially on to tapes A and B. An item is then read from each tape, and the two keys are compared. The item with the lower key is written on to one of the other tapes, say C, and replaced by another item from the tape it originally came from. If the key of the new item is higher than that of the last item that was written, then the two remaining items are compared and the one with the lower key is written out to tape C and replaced as before. This continues until the keys in both items in store are lower than the key of the last item that was written. Tape D then becomes the output tape, and the whole process is repeated. The run finishes when tapes A and B are exhausted; then tapes C and D become the input tapes and A and B the output tapes. The process terminates eventually when all the data has been assembled on one tape.

This all sounds rather complicated; but reference to the flow diagram in Fig. 13.7 should help. What is actually happening is that

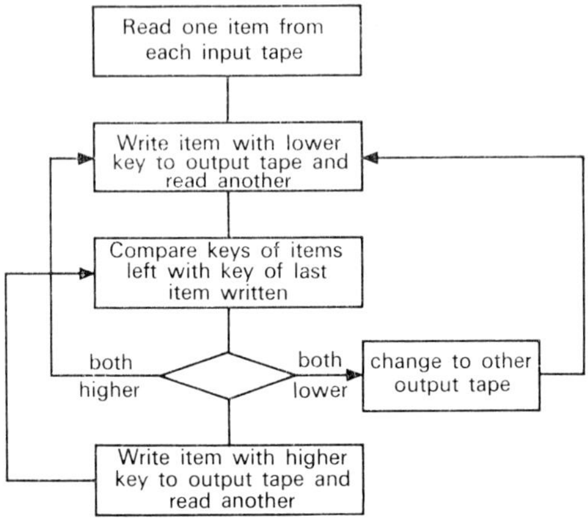

FIG. 13.7 Four-tape Merging Sort

strings of items in sequence are being built up. When a string cannot be built any further, that is, when the last two items read have lower keys than the last item written, the process turns to the other output tape and starts building a new string. Subsequent passes merge strings in pairs until eventually only one string is left. Suppose that the items started off on the two input tapes thus—

I, E, A C M O P, F K
G H, J R, Q, B D L N

Commas have been put in here to show the length of the strings that happened to be present originally. After one pass the strings have been merged in pairs, and the data is sorted to—

G H I, A C M O P Q
E J R, B D F K L N

After a second pass, only one string remains on each tape—

E G H I J R
A B C D F K L M N O P Q

and one further pass merges these into a single string.

Since the number of strings is halved by this method on each pass, it is possible with n passes to sort at least 2^n items (more if there are some strings in the original data, as there are almost certain to be). Conversely, it is possible to sort N items in at most $\log_2 N$ passes. Since tables of logarithms to the base 2 are not easy to come by, it is more convenient to express this formula as—

$$3{\cdot}3 \log_{10} N \text{ passes to sort } N \text{ items.}$$

To sort 40,000 items in this way, therefore, needs at most 16 passes. Since the process only writes to one tape at a time, the time taken for a pass is the time taken to copy every item. If two channels are available, this is simply the throughput time for the data, which, for 600 feet of tape running at 120 inches per second is one minute. Thus the sorting time for 40,000 items on 600 feet of tape, even after doubling the time to allow for rewinding, is at most 32 minutes on a two-channel installation, or 64 minutes on a one-channel system.

THREE-TAPE SORT

It is actually possible to sort at this same speed using only three tapes. The way it is done is as follows. Two thirds of the data is written on one tape (call this tape A), and the remainder on a second tape (tape B). Items are then merged on to the third tape (tape C) until tape B is empty, when C will have two thirds of the data. Tapes B and C are then rewound, and tapes A and C are merged on to B until A is empty in its turn. With this arrangement there are always two tapes to be merged, and one to receive the merged strings. A new string is started on the same tape as the previous string. Thus, starting with—

H P, I, C F Q, D L, B G N O
A E, K, J M R

the first pass would give—

A E H P, I K, C F J M Q R
D L, B G N O

and so on. Each pass halves the number of strings in two thirds of the data; but, since the pass time is only two thirds of the copying time for the whole data, we can still use the same formula, namely—

$$\text{sorting time} = 3{\cdot}3\, T \log N$$

where T is the copying time for the whole data, and N the number of items.

With four tapes available a better procedure is to split the data between three tapes in the proportions 3:2:1, and carry out a three-way merge on to the fourth tape until one of the original supply tapes is empty. Two tapes are then rewound and the next merge is started. Each pass reduces the number of strings on half the data by a factor of three, and takes half the copying time for the whole data. Thus a four-tape sort like this is fifty per cent faster than the three-tape arrangement. The more tapes, the faster the sorting; and there are procedures, more complex than those we have described, yielding even faster sorting. However, in estimating sorting times in the remainder of this book, we shall always use the three-tape formula given above.

UPDATING FILES

Having sorted the data into the desired order, we can now turn to the procedure for updating a magnetic-tape file. The basic flow diagram is shown in Fig. 13.8. It is a simplified flow, each block representing a fairly long routine derived either from an input-output package or a housekeeping package, or else specially written. A record is updated if its key corresponds to that of the next input item. If there is no correspondence, the record is moved direct to the output area. If the two keys do match, the record is updated either before or after it is moved, and a test is made to see if there is to be any printing.

The time taken to update a file depends on the autonomy of the peripherals and the amount of buffer storage provided. Fig. 13.9 shows two extreme cases: the first might apply in a simple system with only one magnetic-tape channel and a restricted store; the other provides alternate buffers for the two files, and would be applicable only if they could be run on separate channels. In Fig. 13.10 we show typical timing diagrams for the two systems, assuming that on average three records are processed in each block, and that one gives rise to a printed form (four lines). There is no need for alternate buffers for input or output as the timing appears here, since the speed is entirely limited by the magnetic tape, and even with single buffers the processing and printing are finished long before the next block is available from the tape.

Now at this stage we are in a position to consider a practical example of a tape-processing job. Let us suppose that it consists of three separate tasks, or runs—

transcription of cards to tape,

sorting detail tape,
updating main file and printing output.

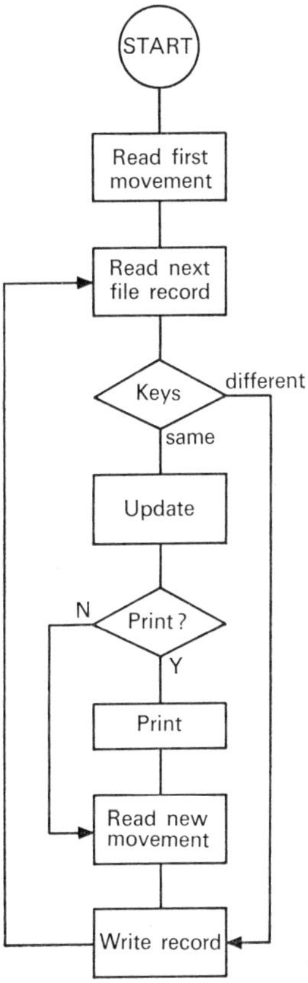

FIG. 13.8. Updating

Let us suppose also that the sizes of data items are—

input item	80 bytes (one card)
main-file record	400 bytes
output form	10 print cycles,

and that the quantities are—

daily input	5,000 cards
main file	130,000 records
daily output	5,000 forms

We shall use nine-track magnetic tape recorded at 555 bits per inch with 0·7 inch gaps, and we shall assume that there are two channels.

STORE ORGANIZATION

The first thing to be decided is how many records to be packed to a block on the main file; this will depend principally on the amount of store available. Suppose that we decide that we can spare space for, say, 16,000 bytes; then we might organize the main file in

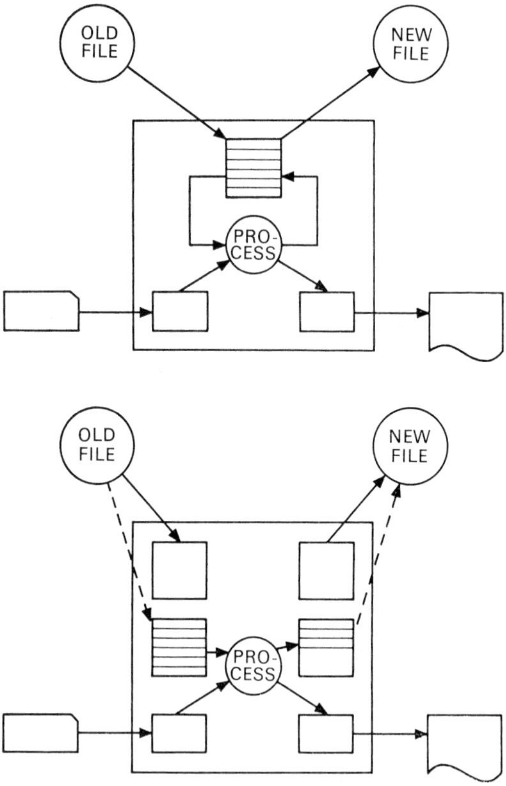

FIG. 13.9.

blocks of ten records (4,000 bytes) allowing a total of four buffers. Let us assume that we do not block the input details. This is an inefficient way to use the tape, in fact; but the volume of input data is small enough for efficiency not to matter particularly.

We can now calculate the lengths of our files, thus—

detail item

$$0{\cdot}14 \text{ in.} + 0{\cdot}7 \text{ in. gap} = 0{\cdot}84 \text{ in.}$$

detail file

5,000 items at 0·84 in. = 350 feet

main-file record

0·72 in.

main-file block

10 records at 0·72 in. + 0·7 in. gap = 7·9 in.

main file

13,000 blocks at 7·9 in. = 8,600 feet,
say, three 3,000-foot reels.

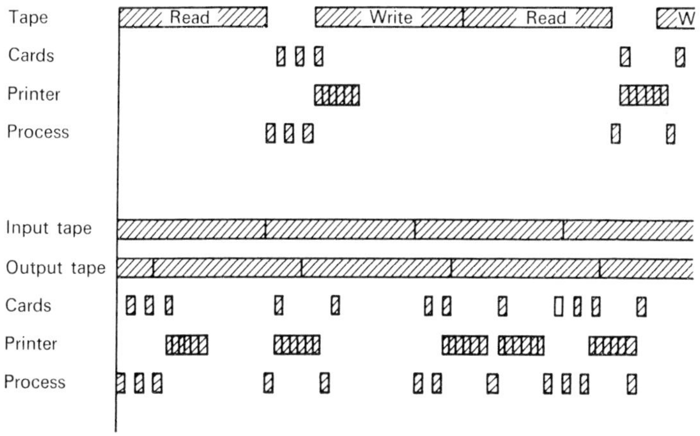

FIG. 13.10.

Let us suppose that the peripheral devices run at the following speeds—

card reader	500 cards per min.
magnetic tape	120 inches per sec.
printer	1,000 cycles per min.

then running times can be calculated as follows—

card transcription

5,000 cards at 500 per min. = 10 min.

sorting

for 5,000 items the number of passes is

$$3{\cdot}3 \log (5{,}000) = 12$$

pass time for 350 feet at 120 in. per sec. = 35 sec.
plus another 35 sec. for rewinding

12 passes at 70 seconds each = 14 min.

updating

file-running time

3 reels at 5 minutes per reel = 15 min.
(assuming rewinding concurrent)

printing time

5,000 forms at 100 forms per min. = 50 min.

therefore the updating run is printer-limited, and takes 50 minutes.

Total job time = 74 minutes.

With a job that was printer-limited to this extent, there would really be no need to use two tape channels. On a single channel, the old and new main files and the detail file can all be run through in 30 minutes and 35 seconds, which is well below the printing time. The only run to be affected by changing to a single channel would be the sorting run. The pass time would be increased to 105 seconds (rewinding is not channel-dependent, so all units can rewind together), and the run time to 21 minutes.

File processing jobs are often constrained to be completed within a certain time. For instance, it might be thought desirable to update a certain main file daily. The input comes with the morning post, and takes some time to transcribe on to cards. When this has been done, the computer processing can start; but it may also be necessary to get the output posted during the day, so the run must be finished in time for the forms to be separated and inserted in envelopes to catch the last post. The upshot may be that no more than three hours or so of an eight-hour day are available for the main-file run. More computer time can be made available by treating the input in batches, taking the first batch as soon as the cards are punched, and processing it immediately. In this case the first batch is ready for enveloping much earlier as well.

SPLIT FILES

The time taken for a run can be reduced by using faster equipment or, if the fastest units are already being used, by using more of them. With a printer-limited run like the updating run in the last example, the natural solution would be to fit two or more printers, modifying the program to suit. With a tape-limited run it is not always easy to make use of extra channels. In fact a single sequential file cannot use more than two channels, one for input, the other for output. One solution is to use a split file, putting the records with odd-numbered keys on one set of tapes and those with even-numbered keys on another set. Two input and two output files can then be run concurrently using four channels.

TRANSIT FILES

Another way of reducing the run time for a file is to update only part of it at a time. The file is split into, say, four parts, and read on as many channels as can be made available; but only one quarter of the file is actually rewritten on each run, the amended records for the other three quarters being put out on to a *transit file* for subsequent merging with unmoved records when their turn comes

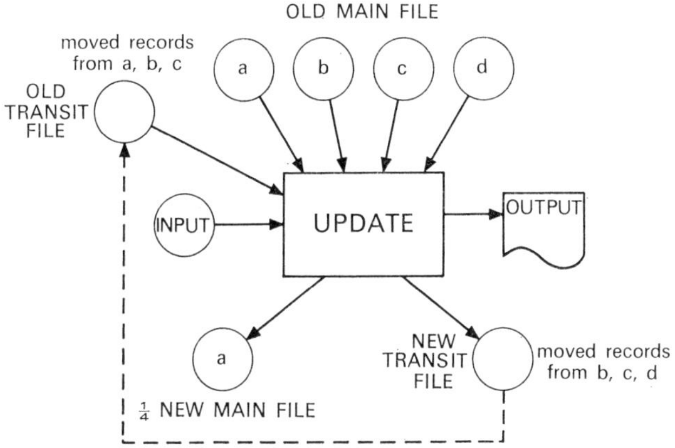

FIG. 13.11. Use of Transit File

to be updated. The arrangement is shown as a system flowchart in Fig. 13.11. This type of processing is satisfactory only when the file activity is low, that is, when only a small proportion of the records are moved.

SKELETON FILES

Another scheme is to use a *skeleton file*. This is a file of shortened records condensed from the main file and containing enough data on each item to enable the most urgent transactions to be carried out immediately. The skeleton file can then be run daily, and movements that cannot be carried out without the full file are either merged into the skeleton file or else put out on a transit file for treatment later (perhaps at weekly intervals). A complete file may sometimes be treated as if it were a skeleton file, with some of the movements being reserved till later. This may be done speed up a run that is actually limited by the speed of computation; but it is more likely to be because there is not enough space in the store of the machine to accommodate enough program to perform all the movements that the input data might demand.

RESTARTING

In Chapter 7 we mentioned the need for restarting a run after it had been interrupted through a breakdown or because it had been supplanted by a more urgent program. To save having to go right back to the beginning of a program, it is usual practice to preserve the whole content of the store at a number of *checkpoints* during the course of the run; then after interruption it is necessary to go back only to the last checkpoint. The store is preserved by dumping it, either on the main file or on some other file device, and checkpoints are established at the most convenient places for this to be done, for instance at the beginning of each new reel of the main file. The system must also preserve a set of parameters specifying the states of the peripheral devices allocated to the program, so that the exact conditions can be reproduced when the run is re-started. These may be added to the dump or put out on another device. To aid the user, functions are provided in the control package to set up a checkpoint; and a *restart* program or routine is provided to set up the system as it was at a chosen checkpoint. To restart the operator has to reload all relevant peripheral units, destroy any output produced after the checkpoint, and enter the restart program or object program at the restart label.

HYPERTAPE

The rate at which data can be transferred to or from magnetic tape depends on two factors: the rate at which the tape moves, and the density of recording. These two factors are both limited by what is known as *skew*. Skew denotes the extent to which recordings made on parallel tracks deviate from perfect synchronism. It arises from small variations in the heads occurring during manufacture, from variations in the delay introduced by the reading and writing circuits, but most of all from the fact that the tape, being a flexible medium, is liable to twist and flutter as it passes under the heads. Skew is more serious with high recording densities than with low, and in the limit there can be ambiguity about which stripe a particular reversal of magnetization should be included in.

To achieve faster rates of transfer, the uncertainties caused by skew must be eliminated. This can be done by reading the tracks individually, delaying or advancing the bits to bring them into synchronism. This last function is performed by a device known as a *de-skewing buffer*. But there is another problem as well. With the standard modes of recording, ones can be detected but not noughts, since only ones induce reversals of magnetization. How, then, are we to determine how many noughts lie between each pair of ones? In short, how are the tracks to be clocked individually?

SELF-CLOCKING

Two methods have been used. The simplest is to generate clocks electronically within the transport mechanism, one clock signal for each track. A very stable oscillator is used, and it is pulled into synchronism by every one that is read from the corresponding track. This method is suitable up to recording densities of two thousand bits per inch or so. The other method is to use a self-clocking mode of recording, that is, a mode in which there is a reversal of magnetization not only for the ones but also for the noughts. Fig. 13.12

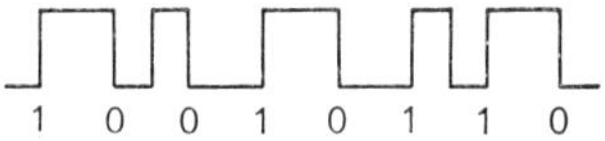

FIG. 13.12. Phase Modulation

shows one self-clocking mode, known as phase modulation. A one is represented by a reversal of magnetization in one sense, a nought by a reversal in the opposite sense, with extra reversals in between whenever necessary. By such methods it is possible to achieve recording densities of three thousand bits per inch and more. Magnetic-tape systems that are not limited by skew are known as *hypertape systems.*

BACKING STORES

MAGNETIC TAPES

So far we have been treating all magnetic-tape processing as if it consisted of reading and writing data in a forward direction only, copying from one tape to another *mutatis mutandis*, and dealing with blocks strictly in the order in which they are on the tape. Several systems permit reading in reverse however, and a few permit writing in reverse as well. There are also some systems that allow *selective over-writing* of tapes, that is, they allow a block to be altered without affecting other blocks above or below it. The chief thing to guard against when a block is over-written is leaving any of the old information behind. This means first of all that only complete blocks may be over-written, and it helps if all blocks are the same length. It also means that the tape must be erased for a short distance before writing actually starts, and it must be erased again for a short distance at the end of the block, to make sure that the whole of the old block was deleted. When there is selective over-writing, therefore, inter-block gaps are generally a little longer than when processing is strictly serial.

SEARCHING

If blocks are to be over-written in a random fashion, there must be some unambiguous means of identifying them; in short, every block must have a unique *address*. The address may be written on a separate track, or it may simply consist of a few characters at the beginning of the data. Reading and writing instructions must then quote the address of the block that is to be operated on. The repertoire of instructions may also include a *search* function whose purpose is to move the tape into a position where the designated block is adjacent to the head assembly.

CASSETTE TAPES

Magnetic tapes that can be over-written selectively are used for backing storage, that is, as temporary storage for data and routines not in current use. Because of the long access time to arbitrary blocks, magnetic tapes can only be used in this way over short lengths; but there is in existence at least one type of magnetic-tape transport intended expressly for random access. The tape is in the form of a loop, which is not wound on reels but held in a cassette. It is possible to get access to any block on such a tape within a few seconds; but even so, the device is best used serially if it can be arranged to do so.

DRUMS

Magnetic drums are the commonest devices *specifically* designed for use as backing stores. Data is recorded in parallel tracks on a magnetic film deposited on the curved surface of a rotating cylinder. The recording head is similar in construction to the head used for magnetic tapes; but there are differences in the way it is used. Firstly, the same head is used for writing and reading; secondly, since most drums employ a separate head for each recording track, there may be several hundred heads on a single drum. In fact the greater part of the cost of a drum lies in the heads. Thirdly, the heads do not run in contact with the magnetic film, since it is not possible to make the drum lie too close because damage results if the heads are allowed to touch the surface. However, the heads do lie very close to the surface. They are usually not mounted rigidly, but float upon the thin film of air that, thanks to the laws of aerodynamics, the drum carries round with it.

The capacity of a drum is much less than that of a magnetic tape. Drums are available with capacities ranging from a few thousand bytes to several million. Data can be recorded serially on a single track, or several tracks can be written simultaneously, depending on the system employed. Some drums can be used completely randomly, that is, giving access to individual words. However, it is more usual, and more efficient, for transfers to be made in blocks to the core store, where items can then be treated individually if desired. The blocks transferred may be blocks of data, or they may be segments of program. We mentioned at the end of Chapter 5 the use of a backing store for overlays.

The time taken to transfer a block of data to or from a drum is made up in two parts. First there is a wait until the part of the surface carrying the desired block comes under the heads; this is known as the *latency* time. After this comes the reading or writing time itself. With a drum rotating at 4,000 r.p.m., the average latency, which is of course half the rotation time, is nearly 8 milliseconds. Even if a whole track were to be transferred at a time, the latency would still account for an appreciable part of the transfer time, unless the transfer of a whole track were permitted, as in some systems, to start at any point.

FIXED BLOCKS

Drum transfers are much easier to organize if all blocks are of a standard length, which should be a simple fraction of the amount of information that a track will hold. If the rest of the system permits blocks to vary in length, the drum is still arranged with fixed block lengths, and the system's natural blocks are fitted into them as convenient, with some space wasted where no information is stored. The wasted space is a small price to pay for the convenience of having a fixed-length organization on the drum.

PAGE ADDRESSING

In more sophisticated systems the user may not even need to be aware of the existence of a drum at all. He simply addresses data as if the core store were extended indefinitely. If the particular block of data addressed is not in the store but on a drum, a transfer is automatically initiated by the Control Program. With such a system, of course, the addresses in the program cannot be the same as the store locations they correspond to. We may draw a distinction then between *pages*, which are the blocks the program is based on, and store blocks, and there must be some fast means of converting from the one to the other. One way is to use what is known as a *content-addressed store;* this is an auxiliary store that responds to an address by giving a word that matches the address in part. In this application the store is addressed with the page address, and responds by giving a word containing the page address and the corresponding block address, which may refer either to the core store or the drum. Another method is possible if all addressing is done through modifiers: loading a modifier into an index register involves converting from a page address to a block address and then, if necessary, reading the designated block from the drum.

In general, when a block is read from a backing store, a block already in the core store is over-written. If there is not already an exact copy of this second block on the drum, that is, if it has been amended since it was last read from the drum, it must first be written back in order to preserve it. Several algorithms have been devised for determining which block or blocks can be overwritten with the least disturbance; most of these require some record to be kept of how frequently a block is being used.

BULK CORE STORES

As an alternative to a drum, some systems provide bulk core storage. Most of the cost of a normal core store lies in the access system, and the cost of a store can be reduced considerably by substituting a cheaper, slower access system. Bulk core stores have access times in excess of ten microseconds, compared with one microsecond for normal stores. They have capacities of up to several hundred thousand bytes. Bulk core stores have the advantage over drums of greater speed, and of course there is no latency to be taken into account; but their cost per bit is very much higher. Drums and bulk core stores can be treated as peripheral devices, when transfers are generally made through a standard peripheral interface: on the other hand, they may be integrated into the system, in which case transfers are very much faster, and may not even need to proceed autonomously.

RANDOM FILE DEVICES

It is unusual to find a drum being used to hold a main file, the capacity is generally too small. On the other hand, drums and even core stores are sometimes used for short auxiliary files, particularly if the records have to be referred to in a random order. For instance, it might be necessary to process a file of customer records, stored according to customer number, at the same time as a file of accounts relating to area sub-offices. The customer file, being large, would be processed serially, but unless the customer numbers happened to relate to area offices (which is unlikely for, even if things had started off that way, the customers would probably have moved about a bit since) the area-office file would have to be referred to at random. This would be quite easy if the customer file were held on magnetic tape and the area-office file on a drum. Drums are commonly used, too, in sorting short detail files; in fact the number of passes in a sorting run can be reduced considerably if a drum is used to build up initial strings as long as space will allow.

DISC FILES

Where it is necessary to have access at random to a large main file, a disc recording device may be the answer. On a disc file the magnetic film is deposited on both surfaces of a set of rotating discs mounted concentrically on the same spindle. The recording heads

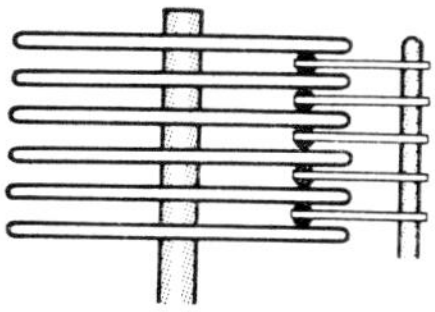

FIG. 13.13. Disc File (Diagrammatic)

are mounted on arms, which are able to move in the spaces between the discs. The number of heads varies. In most designs, there is one head per surface, and one arm to every space between two discs, as shown diagrammatically in Fig. 13.13; though in some systems, to reduce the amount of arm movement, several pairs of heads are mounted on each arm, and in others there is only one arm altogether, which must be able to move up and down the stack of discs. When there are several arms, it is usual for them all to move together. The same head is used for both reading and writing.

Data is recorded on concentric tracks, usually serially, though sometimes two or more tracks are taken in parallel. In the simplest systems the same amount of data is stored on every track. But this arrangement limits the use of the outer track by the density of recording that can be achieved in the innermost track. Consequently some systems divide the discs into two or more concentric zones, recording on the inner zone or zones a simple fraction of the amount of data that can be accommodated in the outer zone.

Disc files are of two main types: those in which the discs are fixed, which typically have capacities of 50,000,000 bytes, and those

9—(B.822)—36 pp.

in which the discs are mounted in a replaceable cartridge, which have capacities of the order of 5,000,000 bytes on-line at any one time. If it is required to operate in a truly random mode, it is of course on-line capacity that matters; but, as we shall see later, a disc file can be used sequentially, when the capacity of an exchangeable disc device, like that of a magnetic-tape transport, is virtually unlimited.

MAJOR AND MINOR DATA UNITS

Records on a disc file are stored in blocks, and nothing less than a complete block is transferred at a time to the computer store. We shall see the reason for this later. However, when we are dealing with disc files, we must recognize a larger natural data unit as well; this is the amount of data that can be read without moving the heads to another position. In the system of Fig. 13.13 it is the amount of data that can be recorded on one track each on ten surfaces. It can be thought of as consisting of ten circular tracks arranged one above the other as if they were on the surface of a cylinder. The entire contents can then be thought of in the form of a series of concentric cylinders. The term *cylinder* has generally been used to denote the major data unit on a disc file; but in one-arm systems, of course, this unit comprises only two tracks, while in systems with more than two heads per arm the unit consists of several cylinders. In this book we shall use the term *volume* to denote the amount of data that can be read without a major movement of the access mechanism, and we shall use this term not only for disc files but also for any other type of random-access device.

ACCESS AND RE-ACCESS

Thus the access time for a particular block is made up of three parts: the head-movement time needed to locate the required volume, the latency while the block moves level with the head, and the actual reading or writing time. With random interrogation we must allow for head movement and latency on every record read; with updating, we must allow for head movement and latency to read the record; but, since the record is actually to be updated *in situ*, we do not have to allow a second head movement for re-writing, though of course there must be a second latency. Consequently it is possible to make a distinction between mean *access* time and mean *re-access* time, where access time is the time needed to locate and read a block at random, whereas re-access time is the time to re-read or re-write the last block read. For most practical purposes we may take the re-access time to be the same as the latency plus the reading time, though, strictly speaking, the mean latency is not quite the same for re-access to the same record as it is for access to another record in the same volume. If the system is organized so that a block consists of a whole track, and if in addition transfers can start at any place in the block, the latency becomes zero, and the reaccess time is simply the block-reading time; otherwise the mean latency on a disc, as on a drum, is half a revolution time.

It is seldom that all the records on a file are moved with the same frequency. One can see this effect very easily in the case of stock control, where some stock items are in frequent demand, while others are wanted only rarely. In fact the same pattern is discernible to a greater or lesser extent with most files, a small proportion of the records accounting for a large proportion of the movements. It therefore follows that if all the most active records are stored in the same volume or in one or two adjacent volumes, the mean head movement can be significantly reduced.

Records are stored on a random-access file, as on a serial file, according to the value of a serial number, or key. The key may be numeric or alphabetic, or it may be a mixture of the two. But, whereas records are stored on a magnetic-tape file strictly according to the *sequence* of their keys, this is not often possible, or even desirable, on a random file. The point is that on a random file a record is referred to not by its key but by the address of the block containing it, which must somehow have been derived from the key. Now unfortunately the keys on a file do not normally form a continuous sequence: even if they happened to start that way, deletions would soon break the sequence, and it is seldom convenient to re-use keys belonging to items that have been deleted. Also it is common for key numbers to have some mnemonic significance, to incorporate within them a code denoting the type of record, or its area of origin—like car registration numbers. Every new motor car registered in Great Britain is given a number consisting of four letters and three digits; the system allows (even after all the rude words have been eliminated) for more than 400,000,000 cars—about seven each for every man, woman, and child in the country. The sequence of car registration numbers contains large gaps.

Here is an example of a sequence of keys that might be found on a file—

MN1467	MP0134	MP1128
MN1469	MP0769	MP1130
MN1570	MP0770	MP1137
MN1571	MP0771	MQ0002
MP0010	MP0772	MQ0003
MP0017	MP1024	MQ0024

Obviously we cannot afford to allot one record space to every key number that *might* appear in a list such as this, for then the greater part of the file would be wasted on non-existent records. Somehow the sequence must be condensed. We could of course store the records in sequential order, putting one in each space until all had been accommodated; but there are two strong objections to such a plan. In the first place, how are new records to be accommodated when they are generated with intermediate key numbers? Remember that a random file cannot, like a tape file, be reorganized on every run. The second objection is, how is a particular record to be located, since there is no necessary connection between the key and the address on the file? Of course a directory or index could be provided, linking keys and addresses—in fact there are systems that work this way—but except in special cases a directory is likely to be rather bulky, and there is still the problem of how to find the desired key in the directory without too much delay.

ADDRESS CALCULATION

Most random files operate by *address calculation.* The idea is that every key should be subjected to an arithmetic, or pseudo-arithmetic, process by which it is transformed into an address within the scope of the file device. Since any such condensing process applied to a random set of keys must generate the same address occasionally from a number of keys, the system is best organized if the records are treated in blocks, all the records in a block having the same generated address, though different primary keys. In mathematical terms, the set of all possible keys is said to be *mapped* on a smaller set of block addresses, the number of records in each block being the number of keys that actually exist out of the subset mapped on that block. The records in the same block may have keys that are close together in the normal sequence, or their keys may be scattered at random, depending on the method of address calculation employed.

The process used for address calculation must satisfy three conditions—

(*a*) it must not generate more addresses than there are blocks available on the file,
(*b*) it must distribute records evenly among the available blocks,
(*c*) it must be as fast as possible.

Naturally it is impossible to devise a process that will put precisely the same number of records into each block. If the keys are randomly distributed, then the addresses derived from them must also be random, provided that the process is not biased. Moreover, it must occasionally happen that the process generates the same address from the keys of more records than a block can accommodate. This means that some records must be accommodated elsewhere—either in adjacent blocks or else in blocks specially reserved for overflow—and a tag must be placed in the home block (the block whose address is given directly by calculation) giving the keys of overflow blocks and the addresses of the blocks where they have been accommodated. If a record has overflowed, then it takes longer to retrieve, since at least two blocks must be read before it can be found, the home block and the overflow block; these two will normally be in the same volume, however.

The simplest form of address calculation is simply to ignore as many digits in the key as are necessary to reduce it to the size of an address. There are two objections to this: in the first place, the address range produced may not accord with the number of blocks available; and in the second place it will produce bias if there is some bias in the distribution of the key digits that are retained. Another approach is to divide the key by the number of blocks, taking the residue as the block address. The best results are usually given by this process when the divisor is a prime. However, on small systems this may conflict with the third of our conditions, since division on small systems is often very slow. It is usually best to use an *ad-hoc* process based on the peculiarities of the key, and designed to yield the desired number of addresses. It is as well to make a statistical analysis of the method chosen, using a sample of the actual keys, in case there should be some peculiarity in the key distribution that gives bias with a particular method of address calculation.

The greater the attempt to make efficient use of a random file device, that is, the greater the mean number of records in a block, the higher the probability of overflow, and consequently the longer it takes to carry out a run. On the other hand, the more space wasted, the faster the run is likely to be. However, the penalty to be paid for overflow is not necessarily very high, particularly in relation to the full access time when the device is being used in a random mode. We might mention here a statistical result that should be fairly obvious: the larger a block is in relation to the size of a record, that is to say, the more records a block will accommodate before it needs to overflow, the lower is the actual probability of overflow. Thus, purely from the standpoint of overflow, it is better to have 100 blocks per volume, each holding up to 30 records, than to have 200 blocks holding only 15 records. On the other hand, larger blocks take longer to read and write; so with only one record moved per block the shorter block might be preferable.

Let us now attempt to crystallize the foregoing with the aid of a worked example. A short while back we gave a sequence of keys consisting of two letters and four digits. There are in fact no fewer than 6,760,000 keys possible on that plan; but let us suppose that the file is not expected to grow longer than 40,000 records in practice. Then we must choose some sort of file device of at least this capacity. Suppose that there is available a disc file that will accommodate up to 60,000 records of the size we are considering; then this would be quite suitable for the job.

We shall suppose that the disc file we have chosen is divided into 150 volumes, that is, the access mechanism is able to take 150 different positions. This means that every volume is large enough to contain 400 records. Similar considerations apply when deciding block size for a disc file as apply when deciding block size for magnetic tape, except that there are fewer degrees of freedom—the block size on a disc file must be a whole track or simple fraction of a whole track. Suppose that we decide to adopt a block size that is one twentieth of a volume (say half a track on a ten-surface device). Then there are 3,000 blocks on the device, and each one has space for up to 20 records. However, some space must be left in each block for a header, and for accommodating tags giving the locations of overflow records, so let us say instead that each block will only accommodate up to 18 records.

The problem now is to devise an address-calculation algorithm that will map keys consisting of two letters and four digits on to 3,000 blocks. Inspection of the keys shows that the first numeral is never greater than 1, and that the second is never greater than 5; these two digits are biased, and should be left out of a simple algorithm. A method that might be employed is—

Ignore the first letter.

Give the second letter its natural value, from 1 to 26, and use it as the first two digits of the block address.

Ignore the next two digits.

Use the last two digits as the last two digits of the block address.

Provided that the letter and digits used are randomly distributed, this scheme should give a random distribution of addresses from 0100 to 2699. The 400 blocks unallocated by this scheme could conveniently be used for overflow records and for system purposes.

We have devised a scheme, then, for storing 40,000 records in 2,600 blocks; so the expected number of records per block is 15·4. In fact, as we have said, each block will accommodate up to 18 records, so the overflow should not be very great. In this case statistical theory tells us that the probability of overflow, that is, the probability of more than 18 keys giving rise to the same block address is about 0·2. This means that some 20 per cent of blocks can be expected to overflow; but this does not mean of course that

20 per cent of records will be placed in overflow locations. From standard statistical theory we can calculate the probability of overflow at each level.*

Number of Overflows	*Proportion of Blocks*	*Number of Records*
1	0·077	200
2	0·059	280
3	0·043	335
4	0·03	312
5	0·02	260
6	0·013	200
7	0·008	145
8	0·005	100
9	0·003	70
10	0·0016	40
11	0·001	30
		and so on

Thus there are some 2,000 records involved in overflow—five per cent of the total.

Finally, let us calculate the time needed to process 3,000 movements on the file we have just designed. Let us suppose that the mean head-movement time is 100 milliseconds, and that the discs rotate at 2,400 r.p.m. The time for one rotation is 25 milliseconds, and if a block is half a track, this will also be the block reading and writing time. Now the operations involved in updating records in home blocks are—

head movement
latency
reading time
latency
writing time

making 200 milliseconds altogether. For records in overflow blocks we must add one more latency and one more reading time, making

* The distribution is Poisson. The proportion of addresses given by precisely N tags is given by—

$$\frac{e^{-m} \cdot m^N}{N!}$$

where m is the mean number of records per block.

250 milliseconds. Therefore the time needed to update 3,000 records is—

$$2850 \times 200 + 150 \times 250 \text{ milliseconds}$$
$$10 \text{ minutes and } 7{\cdot}5 \text{ seconds.}$$

The extra 7·5 seconds is the effect of overflow, which is therefore quite negligible in this case as in most cases.

RANDOM AND SEQUENTIAL OPERATION

We alluded earlier to the possibility of operating on a disc file sequentially. If the file is actually organized randomly, of course, sequential operation is no different from operations with any other arbitrary sequence of input keys; but if the file can be organized sequentially according to keys the process can be speeded up quite considerably. A substantial improvement can be obtained by organizing the file sequentially by volumes, that is, by dividing it into as many sections as there are separate volumes on the device, and recording the records of each section on a separate volume.

The principal difference between sequential processing on a random device and sequential processing on a magnetic tape is that with a magnetic tape *every* block must be read and written, whereas with a random device only those blocks containing moved records need be operated on. If the file in our previous example had been stored sequentially by volumes, we should only need to move the heads 150 times. To update according to 3,000 movements therefore requires—

$$150 \times 100 + 2850 \times 100 + 150 \times 150 \text{ millisec.}$$
$$5 \text{ minutes and } 22{\cdot}5 \text{ seconds.}$$

SERIAL OPERATION

In the last example, every block was read and written once for every moved record within it. If the file has been organized completely sequentially, however, moved records in the same block would be processed at the same time, with a saving in latency and reading and writing time. Unfortunately, as we have already pointed out, completely sequential organization raises problems when new records are created and have to be inserted in their proper place in the sequence. The same effect can be achieved, though, by processing the file *serially* instead of *sequentially*, that is, in order of block addresses instead of keys. For this to be possible, the address calculation must be carried out *before* sorting, and the sorting must be performed on the addresses and not the keys.

HIT RATES

In general, we should expect some blocks to contain one moved record, some two, some three, and so on. There will also in general be blocks that contain no moved records at all, and on very inactive files there may even be whole volumes that can be skipped. The expected number of moved records in a block is of course the ratio of the number of movements to the number of blocks; but what is more important to know is how many blocks contain at least one moved record. This again is a statistical result.* The number of

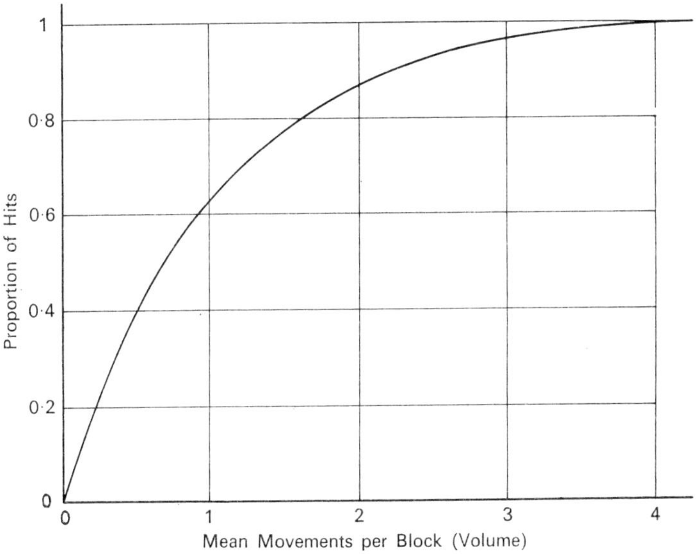

FIG. 13.14. Hit-rate Graph

blocks containing at least one moved record is known as the *block hit rate*, and the number of volumes containing at least one moved record as the *volume hit rate*. We use the following rules to determine them.

(*a*) If the number of movements is less than one third of the number of blocks (volumes) then the number of blocks (volumes) hit is equal to the number of movements.

(*b*) If the number of movements is greater than four times the number of blocks (volumes), then every block (volume) is hit at least once.

* It is, in fact, part of standard sampling theory. What proportion of samples contain at least one marked item? This is Poisson distribution again.

(*c*) If the number of movements is between one third and four times the number of blocks (volumes), then Fig. 13.14 gives the proportion of hits.

The file in our example consisted of 2,600 blocks in 150 volumes. With an input of 3,000 movements, therefore, every volume is hit, and (from Fig. 13.14) 68 per cent of blocks are hit. Thus there will be 150 head movements, 1,618 home-block processing operations, and 150 overflow processing operations, making—

$$150 \times 100 + 1{,}618 \times 100 + 150 \times 100 \text{ millisec.}$$
$$3 \text{ minutes and } 11{\cdot}8 \text{ seconds.}$$

FILE SECURITY

The most difficult problem that arises in connection with random-access files, whether they are being used in a truly random mode or in a sequential or serial mode, is how to ensure file security. It is not possible, as it is with magnetic tape, to prevent writing, since records are updated *in situ*, so there is always a danger that data may be over-written through a program error. The only satisfactory solution that has been found to this problem is to dump the whole file periodically. This can be done on the device itself if it has two separate cartridge drives; but usually, since most mechanisms are not made in this way, the file must be copied out on some other device, such as a magnetic-tape unit. It is quite common to find a cluster of slow, and therefore cheap, magnetic-tape units associated in the same installation with a random-access file.

Dumping is usually performed serially, blocks being dumped in the order of their addresses. It is often combined with a re-organization of the file; random-access files must be reorganized from time to time, particularly if they are sequentially organized, to fill the spaces in home blocks where records have been deleted with records from overflow areas, and, if necessary, to take care of any volume overflow, or overflow from overflow areas.

MAGNETIC-CARD FILES

The only type of random-access device of any importance, other than a disc file, is a card file. In a card file, the data is recorded on magnetic film that is deposited on rectangular pieces of plastic material known as *magnetic cards*. It is recorded along the long dimension of the card in several parallel tracks. The cards are held in magazines, which are generally exchangeable, and of which there may be several on-line at one time. The retrieval mechanism picks out a selected card and transports it rapidly down a track to a drum, around which it is wrapped in order to be read or written on in a similar way to an ordinary drum. In fact, as long as it is only the data on a single card that is being used, a card file can be regarded simply as a special type of small capacity drum; and the same thing can be said to apply in principle if the data is stored sequentially on several cards. A card remains wrapped around the drum until it has to be replaced by another card, when it is returned to its place in the magazine again.

The major access cycle on a card file, equivalent to the head-movement time on a disc file, involves transporting the card from magazine to drum, and is therefore rather slow. The time usually depends on the actual position of the selected magazine: it is generally about a quarter of a second. The minor access cycle, latency plus reading or writing time, may be even shorter than on a disc file. The major data unit, what we have referred to hitherto as a *volume*, is of course one card, which has generally a higher capacity than a disc-file cyclinder. In fact card files are characterized principally by large on-line capacity (of the order of thousands of millions of bytes); but a price is paid in terms of a much longer random-access time. Because of this, card files are not often operated in a random mode when the user file extends over more than one card. However, they can be used sequentially or serially to great advantage. The procedures for determining hit rates and running times are the same as for disc files.

RANDOM-ACCESS HOUSEKEEPING

Like tape files, random-access files can be operated with the aid of housekeeping packages to simplify the task of programming. Most of what has already been said about magnetic-tape housekeeping applies equally to random-file housekeeping. The main features of a housekeeping package are—

file protection,
controlling reading and writing at block level and record level,
scheduling.

The package may even give some aid in address calculation.

Random files, like tape files, must be opened before they can be allocated to programs. The procedures are similar, except that it is the rule rather than the exception for two or more files to be on-line at the same time on a random device. On an exchangeable-disc unit where a file runs to more than one cartridge, the sections must be opened and closed separately, like tape reels.

Reading and writing at block level involves converting block numbers into absolute addresses and operating the access mechanisms appropriately. Writing may also involve reading back as a check. The system will usually also provide a *select* or *search* facility that puts the mechanism into the correct position in advance for reading or writing a particular block. During random processing, a great deal of time can sometimes be saved by using a search facility to overlap operations. A read or write operation on a random device, in contrast to magnetic tape, requires an address to be provided as an extra parameter. Housekeeping subroutines for reading and writing at record level call the block routines to obtain the data if it is not already in the store; they also take care of overflow procedures automatically. They may involve actual transfer of data across the store, or they may simply manipulate modifiers in the appropriate manner.

DUAL ACCESS

Any device with a finite access time is more efficiently used if the operation of the access mechanism can be overlapped with actual processing. This is the principal function of a scheduling routine. Overlap is easy enough to achieve when the device is simply being interrogated; but, because reading and rewriting take place at the same location it is not often possible to overlap updating operations on a random file. To make overlap possible some disc files are availiable with *dual access*, that is, with two separate access mechanisms; one mechanism can then be seeking the next piece of data while the other is waiting to rewrite the current block. A dual access disc file can also be used to provide intercommunication between two separate computers.

SATELLITE SYSTEMS

The devices that we have been dealing with in this chapter are characterized as *fast* devices, that is to say, they are capable of dealing with data at rates of ten thousand bytes per second and upward. One other type of device that must come into the same category, and, though it is not strictly a file device, can conveniently be dealt with in the same chapter, is another computer.

An appreciable part of a computer's time is spent in dealing with peripheral devices. First the commands have to be issued (after checking that the devices are able to receive them), and entries have to be made in various tables recording the new state of the system; then, once the device is in operation, the computer has to hesitate periodically to deal with the data, assembling bytes into words and putting them away in the store; finally, when the transfer has terminated, the Control Program comes in again to check the data, release lockouts, and, if necessary, make a report to the operator. Then there are also various operations to be carried out on the data itself: editing, checking validity, code and radix conversion, and even sorting. Now all these operations involve relatively trivial computation. They consist principally of moving data from place to place in the store, and it is seldom that they involve anything more complex in the way of arithmetic than a straight comparison between two keys. On a cheap processor all this very mundane work would not matter, since it is precisely the sort of thing the machine was designed to do; but, while an expensive machine is performing work of this kind, its fast arithmetic circuits are standing idle. If, however, the fast machine could hand over to a cheap satellite computer the task of dealing with slower peripheral devices and the raw data arising from them, it would be left free to perform the sort of *number-crunching* it had been designed for.

There are several ways in which a fast processor and its satellite can be associated. The simplest is to keep them physically separate and use magnetic tape as an interchange medium. Alternatively they can both be connected permanently on-line to the same cluster of tape transports or, better, to a dual-access disc file. Another way is to build the two into the same set of cabinets, making them communicate either directly or by sharing some or all of the main core store. The commonest way, however, is to connect them together as if they were peripheral devices of each other, using the mechanism that already exists in each for handling fast peripherals. With such a system, commands issued by the one machine become status information when received by the other, so some sort of electronic *black box* must be interposed between the two to turn the interface inside out. The arrangement is easiest to implement if a master-slave relationship is established between the two machines (with the master in this case not necessarily being the larger machine). Where such systems exist, there is normally a software package available to assist the user.

Figure 13.15 shows a typical system using a satellite processor. Of course, there is no reason in principle why a single main processor should not have several satellites, some of them even situated many miles away. One can imagine a computer complex in which a head office keeps a large fast processor that is connected to a number of satellites in area branch offices. The satellites would then perform the day-to-day work of the branches, making reports and returns to head office as required, and passing back also any tasks that involved computation beyond their capabilities. Also, there is no reason in principle why data cannot be exchanged between two processors of the same power, each performing its own tasks and also providing a standby in case of failure of the other. But that is a subject for a later chapter.

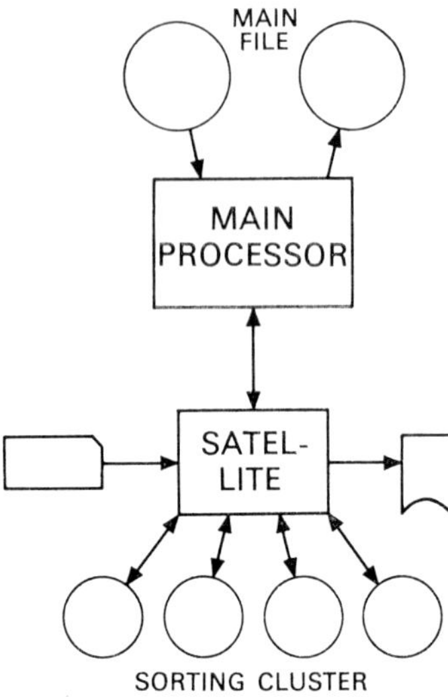

FIG. 13.15. Simple Multi-system

EXERCISES 13

1. Calculate the percentage utilization of magnetic tape recorded with an inter-block gap of 0·7 inches and carrying records of mean length 100 bytes if—

(*a*) recording density is 555 bits per inch and records are not blocked,
(*b*) recording density is 555 bits per inch and records are ten to a block,
(*c*) recording density is 555 bits per inch and records are fifty to a block,
(*d*) recording density is 800 bits per inch and records are ten to a block.

2. An updating run operates on the following tapes—

input file 2,000 feet
main file 3 reels of 2,500 feet
report file (output) 2,500 feet.

Assuming that the transports run at 60 inches per second, find the minimum run time with—

(*a*) one channel,
(*b*) two channels attached to separate clusters,
(*c*) two channels able to be switched to any mechanism.

3. How might the flow diagram of Fig. 13.5 be affected if a working data area were provided as well as separate input and output areas? (Assume lockouts are provided.)

4. How long would it take in the worst case to sort a tape containing data from 24,000 movement cards (all columns punched)—

(*a*) with each card recorded as a separate block,
(*b*) with the cards blocked and pre-sorted in tens?

Assume a recording density of 200 bits per inch, an inter-block gap of 0·7 inch, a tape speed of 60 inches per second, three transports, a single channel, and rewinding speed the same as reading speed.

5. A file-updating run deals with the following items of data—

input file	1,000 feet of magnetic tape
main file	7 reels of tape, 2,400 feet long
output	1,700 printed forms.

Assuming that the tape runs at 120 inches per second, and that the printer produces 60 forms per minute, find the minimum time the run would take with one, two, and three separate tape clusters.

6. A daily tape-processing job is timed as follows—

Punching and verifying cards 5 hours
Input 30 mins
Sorting 10 passes of 1 min. 40 sec. each
Updating and printing 1 hour.

Show how the daily time could be reduced by batching the input. What is the optimum number of batches? (Assume the updating run is tape-limited.)

7. Use a flow diagram to show the working of the system illustrated in Fig. 13.11.

8. Devise an address-calculation algorithm that will reduce an eight-digit decimal key to an address in the range 0 to 2999.

(*a*) assuming that key values are evenly distributed,
(*b*) if the keys are all between 40,000,000 and 70,000,000, with a tendency for the hundred and hundred-thousand digits to be small and the thousand digit to be either 6 or 7.

9. A card file is loaded with magazines containing 512 cards, each card carrying 32 tracks of 2,048 bytes each. If one magazine were used to store a file of 350,000 records of 70 bytes each, what would be the utilization factor? Taking one track per block, suggest a practicable block structure.

10. The file device in the previous example has the following speed parameters—

card-retrieval time	220 millisec.
latency	10 millisec.
track-read time	20 millisec.

Neglecting overflow, calculate the time taken to perform 10,000 interrogations of the file—

(*a*) randomly,
(*b*) serially.

14. Multiprogramming

In earlier chapters we discussed various ways of organizing runs so as to make the most efficient use possible of the equipment available. We have seen how, by providing more data areas in the store, we can reduce to zero, or nearly to zero, the idle time on a peripheral channel. However, in all the examples we have considered so far, the system was limited by one or other of the peripheral devices, and there has always been some idle time left on the processor. The amount of time depended on the number and speeds of the peripheral channels, the activity of the file, and the amount of computation involved in updating a record.

ADVANTAGES

Any time for which a processor is idle represents the waste of an asset. It is waste that could be avoided if it were possible to load another program into the store, and arrange matters so that this second program could come into operation every time the main program was suspended awaiting the termination of a peripheral transfer. A computer that is able to hold two or more programs and switch between them is said to be *multiprogrammed.* Ideally, one would like to have a *mix* of programs that kept all the peripheral devices fully occupied and left no idle time on the processor. In practice it is seldom that such an aim can be achieved, though a skilled system analyst can approach close to it. In most commercial installations, even with multiprogramming, there is still some idle time left on the processor; so sometimes the system is provided with a *base-load* program that uses the processor only, and comes into operation when all the other programs have been suspended. A base-load program might be a mathematical program carrying out some job such as the evaluation of a set of tables, or it might be a test program designed to show up incipient faults in the hardware.

A program sharing a computer cannot be completed in *less* time than if it were the only program present in the store, and it will take longer if it has to wait periodically while another program takes over control. Nevertheless, however long the period between the start and finish of a program, the aggregate time for which it controls the processor is precisely the same as it would have been if it had been the only program present. This follows provided that the amount of work a program has to perform is not affected by multiprogramming, that is, provided that the program can be written without taking cognizance of the fact that it will be run on a multiprogrammed machine. It follows then that provided the elapsed (real) time is not an important consideration, and provided that there are other programs present that can make use of any free time on the processor, a program running in a multiprogrammed environment does not necessarily have to be organized to run particularly efficiently. Multiprogramming relieves programmers of some of the burden of scheduling operations to use the equipment to the best advantage, and it may reduce the sizes of programs in consequence.

PRIORITY

Consider the simple updating program that we discussed in the last chapter. Timing diagrams were given in Fig. 13.10. Even with two tape channels the processor is idle for long periods; this is because the updating, even when it has to wait for the completion of input and output operations, takes less time than it takes to read and write the magnetic tapes. This particular program, then, is very suitable for multiprogramming, provided that a program consisting principally of computation can be found to run with it. Fig. 14.1 shows how the two might match together. The second

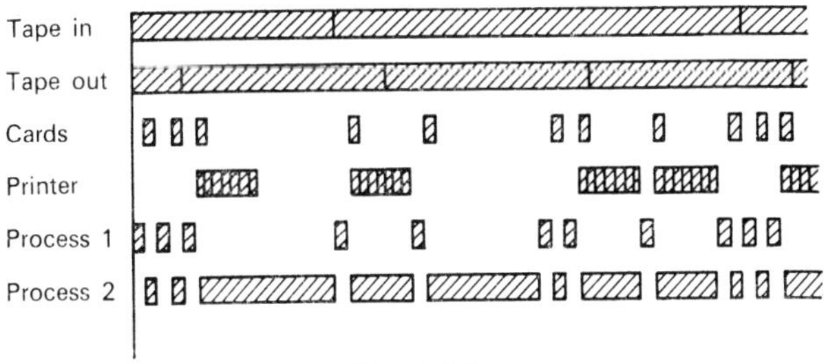

FIG. 14.1.

process comes into operation whenever the first is suspended: but the first process is permitted to interrupt the second whenever external conditions change in such a way that it is able to proceed. In other words, the first process has *priority* over the second.

The idea of priority is fundamental to multiprogramming. When a peripheral transfer finishes, the program that initiated it may be able to proceed. Whether or not it is actually permitted to supersede the program currently in control depends on the relative priorities of the two. Notice that *priority* in the sense we are using the word has no *necessary* connection with the time at which a program is required to be completed. We shall use the term *urgency* to denote this last idea. Program priorities are arranged (unless urgency

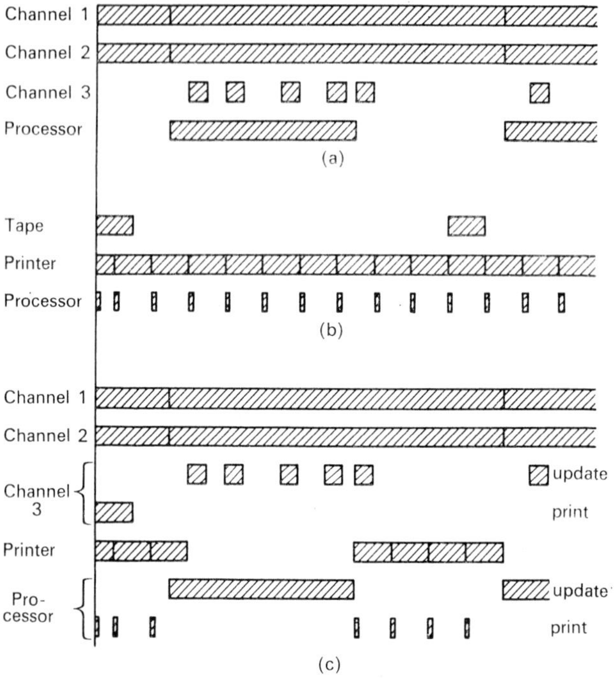

FIG. 14.2.

dictates otherwise) in such a way as to make the most efficient use of all units in the system.

An ordinary file-updating run with printed output is usually limited by the speed of the printer; consequently it is common practice, if the constraints of the office permit, to put data for output on to a spare magnetic tape, and to print it on a separate run. With a multi-programmed machine such an arrangement is particularly attractive, since printing can be concurrent with a run of some other kind—the next day's job, for example. Naturally this is only possible if the organization of the business permits the printing run to be held over until later. Let us take, as an example to show how priorities can affect the running of programs, the case of an updating run sharing the machine with a printing transcription run. We shall assume for simplicity that there are three magnetic-tape channels, and that two store areas are allocated to each stream of data. The first two magnetic-tape channels will be allocated to the old and new main files, and the third will be used for all the detail files, that is, for the input and output of the updating run and for the input to the printing run.

Let us first of all sketch timing diagrams for the two programs as if they were entirely separate. These are shown in Fig. 14.2, with

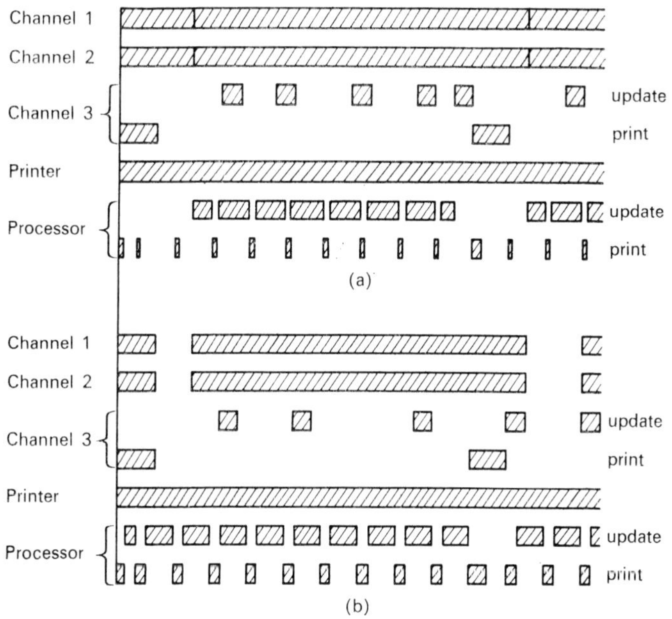

FIG. 14.3.

the updating program at (*a*), and the transcription program at (*b*). The transcription program is printer-limited, so the printer is running continuously. The processor comes into operation for short bursts when it is necessary to prepare the next line, and the tape is brought into operation whenever the current data area is exhausted.

Now let us put the two programs together in the same computer and, since we probably regard the updating program as the more important, let us give that the higher priority. The result is as shown in Fig. 14.2 (*c*). The transcription program takes over the processor when the updating program can no longer use it. Unfortunately this scheme confines the use of the printer mechanism to these periods as well, so the actual time of the printing run is more than doubled. Obviously this will not do; so let us reverse the priorities so that the transcription program comes at the top. The result is shown in Fig. 14.3 (*a*). The printer is now kept busy the whole time, but without causing any delay to the updating program. This result is typical: a multiprogrammed system is generally used most efficiently when the program whose limiting device has the shortest cycle is given the highest priority.

In the foregoing example we have assumed that the system is still peripheral-limited even when multi-programmed. This need not necessarily be so. Two or more programs that separately use only a proportion of processor time can, when running together, occupy it all. If the proportions used by the separate programs added together come to more than one hundred per cent, a situation develops like that shown in Fig. 14.3 (*b*). This represents a machine shared, as before, by an updating program and a printing program; but the amount of editing required before printing has been doubled, and the activity of the file has been increased. As before, the transcription program has been given the higher priority; but now the file channels have to stop periodically to allow the processor to catch up. Fig. 14.3 (*b*) illustrates another point as well: there is still a little unused processor time. Obviously a simple priority system does not quite meet the bill in this situation; but fortunately most commercial jobs are so heavily limited by peripheral speeds that a situation like this seldom arises.

Provided that all the parameters are known—quantities of data, speeds of peripherals, and proportion of time spent on processing—it is possible to analyse any multiprogramming mix and determine the best order of priority. However, it is very much easier to do this experimentally, adjusting priorities until the desired result is obtained, that is, until the peripheral devices are all running at top speed, or until the most urgent program is running as fast as it will go. Any multiprogramming system should therefore provide some means whereby priorities can be changed while programs are running; this might be done by means of console messages from the operator. A form of message might be provided giving a new priority list to replace the old one; but a better system is one in which every program is given a priority number that determines its position in the table. To alter a program's priority, it is then only necessary to alter its priority number by means of a message such as—

@ PRI UPDATE 56

which would change the priority number of UPDATE to 56. If its previous number was 50, it would move up to a position above any programs with numbers in the range 51 to 55.

ON-LINE MAINTENANCE

One further advantage of multiprogramming must be mentioned—its convenience to a maintenance crew. The maintenance of a computer generally consists of two parts: servicing the mechanical parts of the system (adjustment, oiling, cleaning etc.), and running test programs. On a single-program machine, test programs must be run during a special maintenance shift, usually at the beginning of the day. On a multiprogramming system, on the other hand, test programs can be run at the same time as production programs, testing devices that are temporarily not required. This is known as *on-line maintenance*; in this way the whole working day becomes available for production runs.

The form of multiprogramming we have described is the commonest; but it is not the only one. Multiprogramming can also be organized by time multiplexing. We introduced the idea of a multiplexer in Chapter 12, a device that makes it possible to service several units on the same channel by switching to each one in turn. The same principle can be used to service several programs concurrently by allowing each in turn to take control. The arrangement can involve several instruction registers or only one, and it may run asynchronously, with each program being allowed as much time as necessary to obey a single instruction, or synchronously, with each being allowed a fixed time slot in which to do as much work as it can. Since a processor is usually store limited, with the store actively engaged in reading or writing nearly all the time, a multiprogrammed system operating in this way is practically equivalent to a system in which several processors are permitted access to a single storage device in turn. For this reason a single processor, multiprogrammed by time-multiplexing, is sometimes called a multiprocessor.

PROGRAM RELOCATION

A program that is to run on a multiprogrammed machine must be relocatable, that is to say, it must be written and assembled in such a way that it can be obeyed from any part of the store. If this were not done, programs would have to be loaded into particular areas of the store, and two programs might be prevented from running concurrently by the accident that their store areas happened to overlap. With modern methods of program assembly, programs are normally assembled in relocatable form. This is because assemblers do not allocate absolute addresses but provide instructions with addresses relative to one or more datum or base addresses. In some systems it is the loader routine that makes addresses absolute by adding the appropriate datum or base. Programs loaded in this way are said to be *statically relocatable*, since they can be moved to another part of the store only by loading them a second time.

A system becomes much more flexible if programs or program segments are *dynamically relocatable*, that is, if they can be moved from place to place while the program is actually being obeyed. Naturally a program must be suspended while this is done; moreover, current peripheral transfers related to it must be allowed to terminate before a program can be moved, otherwise part of the transfer will be to the wrong part of the store. Dynamic relocatability confers upon a system the power to accept a new program at any time, provided that there is enough storage space to accommodate it, even if the spare storage does not happen to be initially in blocks the right size (see Fig. 6.1, page 91).

However, not all programming systems can be made relocatable. For a program to be dynamically relocatable, it must not contain any absolute addresses at all. One can well imagine the chaos that would ensue if a program were moved from one place in the store to another between planting an absolute link and obeying it. Addresses in a dynamically relocatable program must remain relative right up to the moment when they are referred to, when the datum or base can be added to them. (In the case of replaced addresses, of course, the datum has to be added in turn to each address.) Thus the datum value has to be used in just the same way as a modifier. Indeed a system that provides for modification of addresses can generally be organized in such a way that programs become dynamically relocatable. All that is needed is for the assembler to convert every symbolic name into a modifier *and* a displacement; the displacement is put into the instruction as a relative address, together with a number specifying the index register containing the base modifier. Modifier (datum) values must be allocated initially by the loader, which determines the initial location of the program; and they must be altered later by the Control Program if the object program, or part of it, has to be shifted elsewhere during the run.

When an ordinary modifier is used as a datum for a relocatable program or segment, the programmer cannot use it freely for general modification; but this is not such a drawback as it might seem—at least not in commercial programming. Modifiers are usually only indexed in programs that run sequentially through sets of data. Mathematical programs do this to a very high degree; but commercial programs tend to operate on the items in a set quite randomly, using the modifier unchanged to point to the datum or base of the set. In mathematical programs, the loss of a modifying facility is a serious handicap; consequently some languages provide for double modification in those instructions most commonly used in mathematical work (binary arithmetic, floating point, etc.), the intention being that one modifier can be used, if desired, to define the base of a relocatable segment, while the other is used for normal modification. Whether or not the programmer is *compelled* to use modifiers in this way depends first on how much of the relocating system is built into the hardware, and second on what assemblers and loaders are available. It is possible, at least in theory, to have both static and dynamic relocatability on the same system, though the practical problems of organization would seem to preclude such a way of working.

FRAGMENTATION

Relocatable programs are treated either as single blocks or as sets of separately relocatable *fragments*, depending whether the system enables one or several datum addresses to be handled at one time. The fragments need not correspond to actual segments or sets in the program, though it is generally preferable if the program can be fragmented in a way that relates to its natural structure, if this is at all possible. A fragmented program is easier to handle than a single-block program: less movement of data is necessary when making space in the store for it, and it can be permitted to grow or diminish in size in accordance with changing needs (generally by the addition or deletion of complete fragments). A further advantage of fragmentation is that only one copy of a subroutine used by two or more programs need be kept at one time—provided, of course, that the system permits fragments to be held in common by two or more programs. With a single-block system, each program must incorporate its own copy of every subroutine it uses within the body of the block, and several copies of certain segments of peripheral-control packages may be found in the store at the same time. It must be mentioned, however, that subroutines shared between two or more programs must not be allowed to contain variable data. The reason for this is that a program may be suspended while obeying a subroutine; a subsequent program calling the same subroutine would then find the data with wrong initial values, and would generate incorrect results; moreover the earlier values would be lost when the original program came to use them. Subroutines containing only instructions and fixed data are known as *pure procedures*. They may be read from but not written to. They are sometimes also known as *re-entrant* subroutines, since they can call themselves if need be.

PROTECTION

Programs sharing the same store must be protected from one another. While it is natural to expect a fault in a program to cause that program itself to fail, if a fault in one program were allowed to affect other programs in the same store, an anarchic situation would develop that would be practically impossible to resolve. Some means must be provided, therefore, in a multiprogramming machine, to frustrate any attempt to address registers outside the region or regions of store allocated to the current program. Trouble might arise, for example, if a programmer wrote an address larger than the scope of the program or segment; or if he permitted a modifier to increase beyond the limit of its domain. The simplest way to provide protection is to confine each program within, say, one quarter of the store; and make sure all addresses are within the correct quarter by using the hardware to force their most significant two bits automatically to 00, 01, 10, or 11, according to the program in control, no matter what values these two bits have been given by the programmer or might have taken up after modification.

Such a simple scheme is not, unfortunately, very practicable; it restricts the maximum size of programs to one quarter of the store, and wastes space if programs are shorter than this, or if fewer than four programs are available for multiprogramming. Several refinements to the scheme are possible, however; a program could, for example, be permitted to use two, or three, quarters of the store if necessary; alternatively the store could be divided into eight or sixteen parts, and the programs allotted space according to their needs. Even so, the amount of store space left unoccupied could be quite appreciable.

The smaller the sections into which a store is divided, the better use can be made of the space available. In Chapter 12 we mentioned a scheme for organizing a store divided into a number of fixed-length blocks, and we showed how blocks in communication with peripheral units could be locked out temporarily. We said that a short binary key could be associated with every block, and held in a special auxiliary store, from which it would be retrieved automatically whenever that block was referred to. One of the values that the key could take, it was suggested, was a lockout code, which would cause the program to be suspended if it was detected. The same idea can be extended to provide protection in a multiprogrammed computer. A different key code is allocated to each program, and any attempt on the part of one program to use a block with a key belonging to another leads to suspension. There should also be at least one universal key, for use with blocks containing shared subroutines.

Another way of detecting when addresses go out of bounds is to associate a limit address with every datum address. With this arrangement, every address must be checked against the limit before it is permitted to refer to the store, thus ensuring that it is within the delimited region. Now it will sometimes happen with such a scheme that an incorrect address added to the datum gives rise to an absolute address beyond the range of the whole store. For instance, if the store consists of 65,536 words, and the datum of a program is 40,000, then a relative address of value 27,000 would give rise to an absolute address 67,000, beyond the end of the store. If the address register could contain this address, no harm would be done; the address would be detected as out of range, and the program would be suspended. On the other hand, if the address register could accommodate no number greater than 65,535 that is, if it were only 16 bits long, the number 67,000 would be truncated, leaving a residual address of 1464. This is below the limit, and therefore apparently legitimate; but it is not in fact legitimate, since it comes below the datum as well. Consequently a limit test alone is not enough to test the validity of an address: it must be supplemented either by a test for overflow, or better still by a test against the datum. The second is preferable since it does not preclude the use of negative modifiers—represented by their complements with respect to the absolute range of the addressing mechanism.

THE CONTROL PROGRAM

In Chapter 7 we described a simple operating system suitable for a single-program machine. Everything that was said then applies with equal force in a multiprogrammed machine. At the same time, we mentioned the need for a *Control Program*, or Monitor Program, which is permanently present in the store; and we mentioned then and have mentioned later several functions that this program must perform. Here they are again—

- loading programs and controlling their running,
- interpreting the operator's commands and carrying them out,
- reporting exceptions to the operator,
- interpreting steering information and scheduling runs,
- controlling peripheral devices as required by the program,
- allocating peripheral devices to programs and releasing them,
- suspending a program if it cannot proceed further, and releasing the suspension when the inhibition has been removed.

There are other functions that are provided in some systems by the Control Program, and in others by optional library routines—for instance, tracing facilities, and file checking. There may also be some system subroutines that are not directly connected with the operation of peripheral devices, but are included for convenience with the Control Program.

To the functions just listed we may now add others pertaining to multiprogramming—

suspending and re-activating programs according to priority,
ensuring a continuous flow of programs organized so as to make the best use of the equipment,
calculating each program's use of the equipment, for purposes of costing,
controlling subprogramming (see below),
making the operator's task as easy as possible.

In a sense, any computer with a Control Program can be said to be multiprogrammed since the Control Program and the user program run concurrently, with the former having the higher priority. Also, of course, some mechanism must have been provided to protect the Control Program from the consequences of errors in the user program. The Control Program comes into play whenever the current user program is interrupted, which may be the result of any one of several possible incidents, either in the program itself or on a peripheral device. Program incidents may be voluntary or involuntary, that is to say, they may arise from a deliberate call of a system subroutine (for example by a TFER instruction) or as a result of an unintentional error or a reference to a part of the store that is locked out.

The commonest peripheral incident is the termination of a transfer. Now it will often happen that a program has been suspended pending the termination of a transfer, either because the program wants to use the peripheral device again or because it is locked out of the part of the store the device is using. When a transfer terminates, therefore, there is usually some program that is made free to continue; it will continue, however, only if it has the highest priority of the programs that are able to go.

Figure 14.4 shows the skeleton of a Control Program for a multiprogrammed machine. However, it must be emphasized that not all Control Programs are like this, and that it must be taken as an illustration rather than a definitive model. The diagram refers to a priority list; this is a list of programs usually arranged in the order in which they were loaded, giving their priorities, whether they are suspended or free, and, if suspended, the reason for suspension.

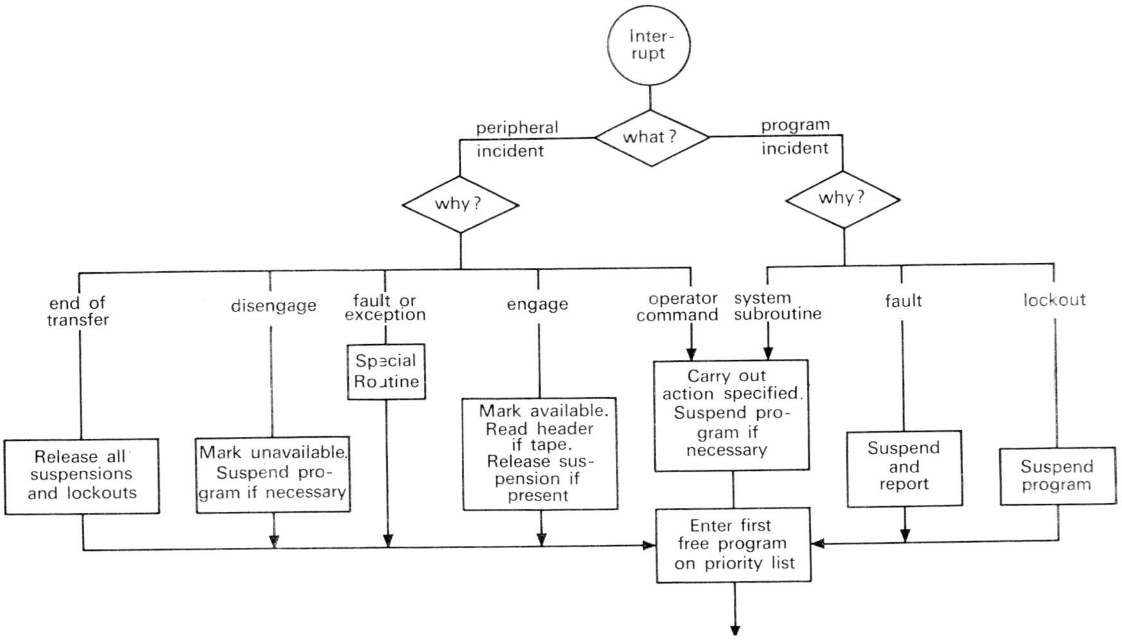

FIG. 14.4. Skeleton of Control Program

The information in such a table would of course be coded; but it might be interpreted, for example, as—

Priority	*Program name*	*Suspended or free*	*Reason for suspension*	*Peripheral*
5	BASELOAD	F		
1	PRINTING	S	lockout	printer
3	UPDATE	F		
2	SORT	S	unavailable	tape 1 tape 2
4	STATISTICS	S	failure	

In this example, the program in control is UPDATE. The program with the highest priority, PRINTING, is locked out while a line is being printed, and the next highest, SORT, is suspended because two tape units are unavailable (probably rewinding). Before SORT can be freed, both units must become available.

The priority list is not the only list that the Control Program must consult and keep up to date. Each peripheral device has its own list, giving information about which program it is allocated to, whether it is available for use or not, and the name of the document or file occupying it. Such tables may be very complex: for instance, a random-access device may carry several files at the same time allocated to different programs. The limiting addresses of each file on a multi-file device must be given in the list, and should be checked every time a block is read. Some files may also be protected from writing. Of course, not all the information on a file will necessarily be in the same table. It must be said once more that Control Programs differ widely in the way they are organized: the jobs that have to be done are the same; but the way they are carried out leaves a deal of room for choice.

Peripheral faults are shown in Fig. 14.4 as leading to a block marked *special routine*. Of course the actual procedure varies not only from device to device but also between two similar devices if they are being used in different ways by the system. Some devices are able to repeat an instruction that has failed; others cannot. Fig. 14.5 shows the flow of a fault routine for magnetic tape. Notice that more repetitions are permitted for reading than for writing; this is because too many attempts to write over a faulty patch of tape might result eventually in a block being accepted in spite of error—no checking system can be one hundred per cent effective. Another point to notice is that an arrangement like this requires the last instruction on every device to be stored away somewhere in the Control

Program: it is no good referring back to the initiating program for it, since the instruction will by then have been surpassed, and modifiers associated with it may have changed their values.

A fault on some devices must be reported straight away to the operator, who will then investigate and attempt to rectify it. A fault on a card reader, for example, may involve a *card wreck*, that is a card that has jammed in the track and been torn. In a case

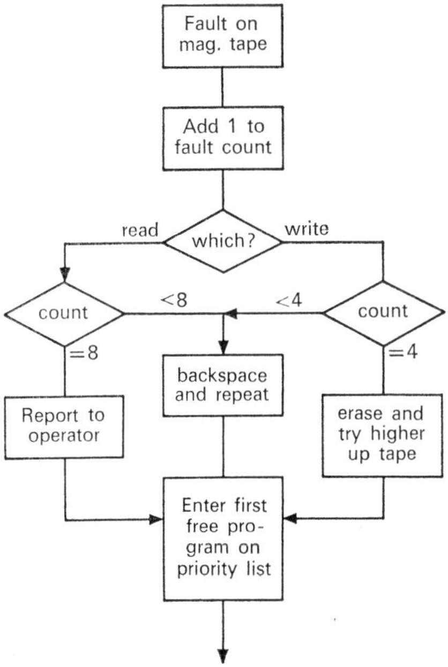

FIG. 14.5. Magnetic-tape Fault Routine

like this, the wreck must be cleared first of all. What happens then depends on particular circumstances: it may be possible to carry on without the card; if not, a new card has to be punched to replace it.

In a previous chapter we suggested several different sets of rules that a Control Program might apply to the suspension of programs—

(*a*) a program is suspended whenever it initiates a peripheral transfer, or

(*b*) a program is suspended if it tries to use a peripheral device that is busy, or if it encounters an instruction specifying suspension, or (*c*) as (*b*) but the program is also suspended if it is locked out of an area of store that is communicating with a peripheral device.

The first choice is the simplest; but it increases the elapsed time of a program, since it does not allow any overlap between peripheral devices and the processor. The second choice avoids this; but it puts an additional burden upon the programmer. The third choice is the best from the standpoint of the user; but it requires a lockout mechanism to be provided.

Once there is a lockout mechanism in a machine, a fourth arrangement becomes possible—

(*d*) A program is still suspended in the event of a lockout; but if it tries to use a busy peripheral device the instruction is placed in a queue, from which it is obeyed as soon as the instruction preceding it has been obeyed. The program is suspended only if it tries to use a device whose queue is full.

A queueing arrangement is particularly valuable in cases where either the supply of data tends to be sporadic, or the amount of computation performed on each item of data varies wildly. In a queueing system, several storage areas must be provided for holding data; then, during periods when the rate of processing exceeds the rate of supply of data, the program has a reserve of data to draw on. The ability to queue instructions is particularly valuable when several peripheral devices have to make use of the same channel, which might happen on a multiprogramming machine with only one or two magnetic-tape channels, or when several files used concurrently are written in the same device, as might happen on a multiprogramming system with a single random-access mechanism.

CHARGING FOR TIME

Computer installations offering time for hire, and data-processing departments that are not treated as overheads but expected to be self-accounting, must have some basis on which to charge their clients. With a single-program machine the basis is simple: the user is charged for the amount of time the system is occupied with his program, and he may be asked to pay an additional charge for the use of peripheral devices. (This, of course, is on top of what he pays for the preparation of data.)

With multiprogrammed computers the basis of charging must be rather more complicated to be fair, since the time a machine is occupied on a particular job is only a part of the time the job is actually in the machine. The charge must be made up of at least four separate elements—

(*a*) the amount of time the processor is actually under the control of the job (what is sometimes called the Mill time),
(*b*) the amount of storc occupied,
(*c*) the peripheral requirements,
(*d*) a surcharge for urgency.

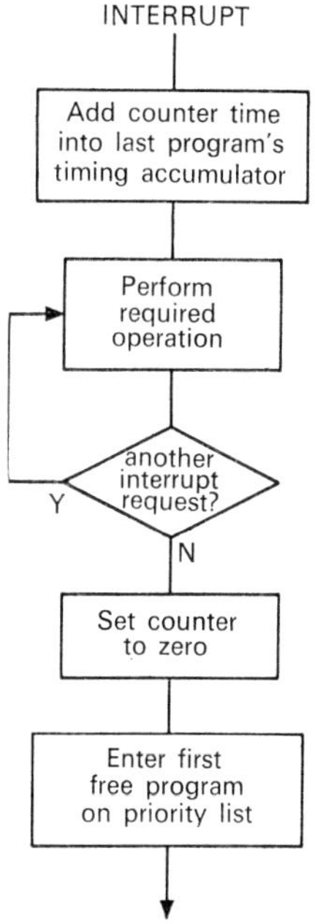

FIG. 14.6. Timing Programs

It would be most inequitable to charge the user of a shared installation for the time that his program was actually in the machine, since a job that took a short time if processed alone might, because of low priority, spend a much longer time in a shared store. If necessary, the charge for the use of storage can be weighted by the Mill time, and the peripheral charge by the time they are actually allocated to the program. The last weighting might encourage users to write programs so that they relinquish peripheral units as soon as they are no longer needed. It does not so much matter if the basis of charging is a bit involved, since a computer is available, after all, to carry out whatever calculations are necessary.

For the Control Program to be able to assess the Mill time, it must be provided with some sort of timing device. This could simply be a binary counter stepping at equal intervals, or it could be a clock with a digital output, or again it could combine the two functions. A clock is needed in any case if time checks are to be given on the console typewriter as was suggested in Chapter 7. If the timing device incorporates a counter, it should be used in the manner shown in Fig. 14.6. Every time the Control Program is entered, the content of the counter is added into a running total associated with the last user program to have been active. Before control is passed back again to another (or the same) user program, the counter is reset again to zero. In this way, no user can be charged with time spent in the Control Program. The timing device can be connected as a peripheral unit; but it is generally better if it can be integrated with the system centre, so that it can be interrogated as rapidly as the store. Another function of the device would be to assist in keeping a log of computer operations.

SUBPROGRAMMING

Once a mechanism has been provided for multiprogramming, the possibility arises of using it to provide subprogramming. The idea of subprogramming is to allow a program to be split into two or more branches, which can then proceed independently, performing their own separate parts of the job, until they have all finished their tasks, when they can be united once more into a single stream of instructions. It is usual to treat one of the branches as the main program and the others as subprograms. The arrangement is shown in Fig. 14.7. It is not absolutely necessary for a machine to be a multiprogrammed system for it to provide subprogramming; but the requirements for subprogramming are very similar to those for multiprogramming. In the first place, subprograms must be subject to an order of priorities (and it is not always the main program that comes first on the list). In the second place, subprograms are turned on and off by the Control Program in much the same way as separate multiprogrammed jobs. Notice that terminating a subprogram is something akin to abolishing a program; it is equivalent to removing the subprogram from the priority list (though in practice it would probably be left there and just tagged as unusable); it is not the same as suspension, which implies that a program is to be re-entered later at the place where it was abandoned. Initiation and termination are system sub-routines provided as part of the Control Program. Subprograms may be protected from one another; but they must have some means of intercommunication, such as holding common data areas. The easiest arrangement is not to raise any protective barriers at all between them, permitting one to damage the other if it is faulty. In this case there is no need for a separate reuniting operation as shown in Fig. 14.7, since the two segments will never really have been disunited.

One of the chief uses of subprogramming is in jobs whose operating speed can be limited in either of two ways. For instance, consider an updating program in which an occasional item arises

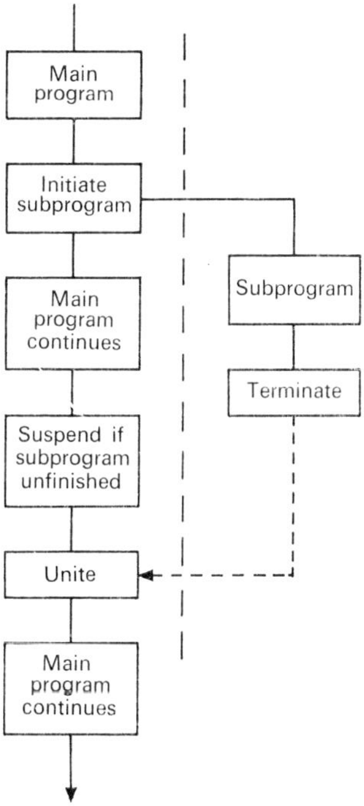

FIG. 14.7. Subprogramming

requiring lengthy analytical treatment. The process is illustrated in Fig. 14.8 (*a*). It is normally limited by the file device; but, when an analysis has to be carried out, it becomes Mill-limited for a time. On the simple scheme, the file device must wait until the analysis is finished before it can carry out the next transfer. It does not help in this case to provide extra data areas, since it is the actual transfer instruction that is delayed. One solution would be to scatter read instructions and update-write routines (or jumps to a single routine) at suitable intervals throughout the analysis; but subprogramming, if it is available, provides a more elegant solution. This is shown in Fig. 14.8 (*b*). The subprogram, since it is pure computation, is given a lower priority than the main program (denoted by the figures attached to the outputs of the *activate* block). Whenever the main program is suspended pending the end of a file transfer, the subprogram can carry on with the analysis of the last record presented to it. Should the main program ever overtake the subprogram and

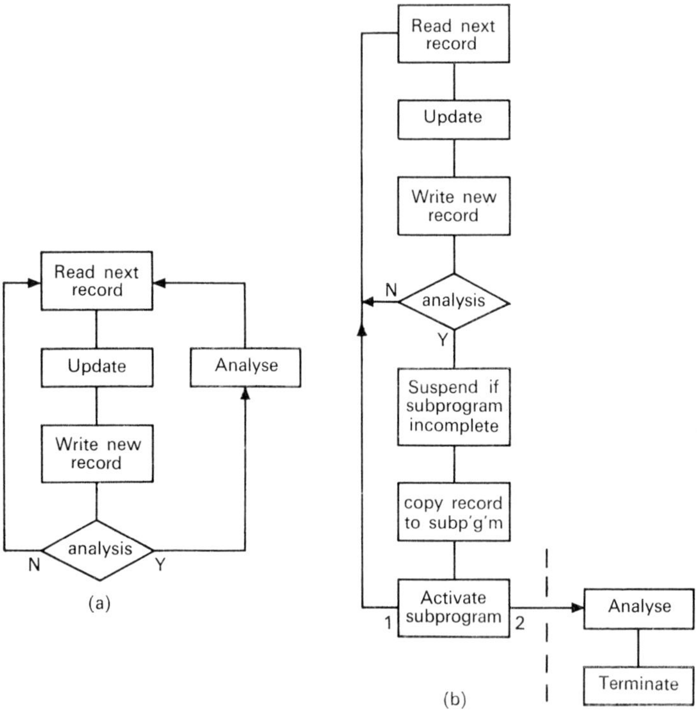

FIG. 14.8.

require a new record to be analysed before the previous analysis is complete, it is then suspended.

A similar approach can be used for a program whose speed can be limited by either of two different peripheral devices, for instance an updating program that produces an occasional demand for exception printing, and becomes printer-limited for a short period in consequence. Another case arises when the supply of data is sporadic. We suggested earlier that such a situation could be conveniently dealt with by queueing instructions. If a machine has no built-in facilities for queueing, however, subprogramming can be used to provide them. The queue is built up in a subprogram, which is given a higher priority than the main program. As soon as one transfer terminates, the subprogram is activated and issues the next instruction in the queue. The main program can then carry on with its work, adding an instruction to the queue whenever it encounters one and suspending itself if the queue is either full or empty.

It is not normally possible for two different programs to use the same file; but there is no objection to two subprograms of the same program doing so. Consider a case in which a random-access file is

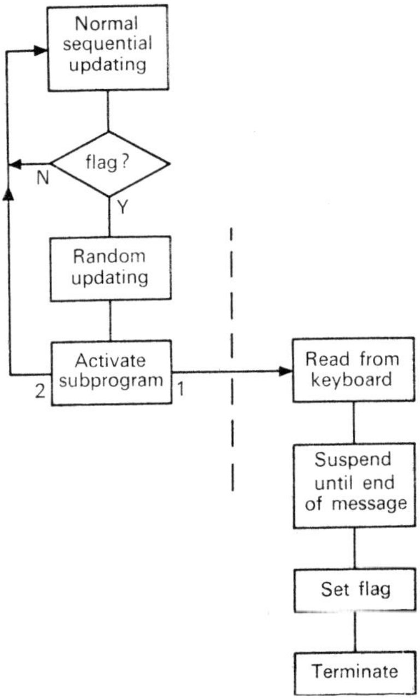

FIG. 14.9.

being updated sequentially or serially by movements read from magnetic tape, and at the same time is being updated at random by movements entered manually on a keyboard. We may imagine the serial movements to constitute the normal daily input and the random movements to be urgent business that arrived too late to be included with the normal daily input. There are several possible ways of organizing this as a subprogrammed activity: one is shown in Fig. 14.9. Because the supply of information to it is out of the system's control, a keyboard must be kept permanently in the reading condition. Here it is being dealt with by the subprogram, which must consequently have the higher priority; as a result, there is no necessity for the main program to be suspended while the subprogram is active.

OPERATING SYSTEMS

In the simplest form of organization, every peripheral device is either unallocated or else allocated to a particular program or job. The allocation may have been brought about in one of several ways: by means of a special ALLOCATE instruction or an OPEN-FILE instruction, by a console message, by the details on a steering input, or by a header or sentinel attached to the document. The device remains allocated until the program releases it, either with a special RELEASE instruction or by closing the file or by implication when the program terminates. Closure may be in one of several modes according to whether the program wishes to relinquish the device or retain it for use by a subsequent file, or whether the file is to be dismounted or handed over to another program.

TRANSFERS THROUGH THE CONTROL PROGRAM

Some systems are organized in such a way that transfers to or from certain peripheral devices take place not directly to or from areas in the user program's store area, but via store areas accessible only to the Control Program. There are several reasons why such an arrangement may be desirable: the Control Program may be required to process the data in some way—there may be some conversion to perform; or the program may have initiated the transfer by calling a system subroutine that performs an editing function; or it may be processing records logically, leaving blocking and unblocking to the Control Program. Keeping transfers under system control may also obviate the need for a lockout mechanism; the suspension test need only be made on the instruction that transfers the data from the Control Program's area to the user program's area, and not on any arbitrary reference to store. In some systems, all transfers to or from keyboard devices are made through the medium of the Control Program. This is because keyboard devices are rather difficult to program because of having to be kept in a permanently reading condition, since the supply of data is out of the control of the system. This method of working is particularly convenient if the device is fitted with a *delete* button which is intended to make the system ignore the last message.

A system subroutine controlling peripheral transfers in which data is passed through an area in the Control Program, would need a general structure like that shown in Fig. 14.10. For outward transfers, the Control Program can accept data and start writing it immediately: for inward transfers, if delays are to be avoided, the Control Program should keep one item of data in hand, which it passes to the object program on demand, provided that the peripheral transfer is complete. The operation of transferring data may in fact involve physical transference; on the other hand, it may simply involve manipulating modifiers.

WELL SYSTEMS

It is generally only the slower peripheral devices, (those used for input and output) that are operated in this way. But the idea could be taken a stage further yet. Data might be accepted by the Control Program even *before* the object program that is to use it has been

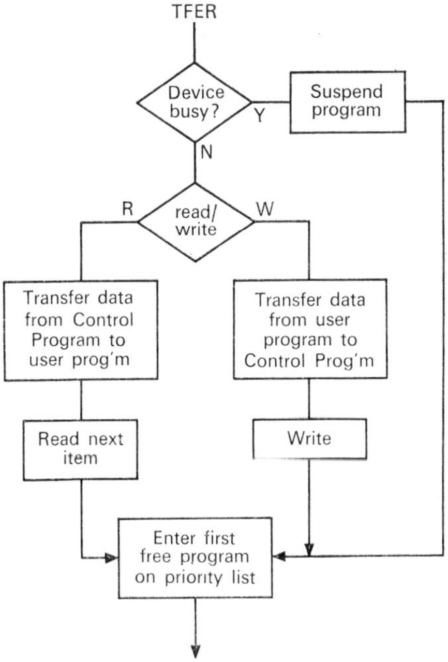

FIG. 14.10. Transfers via Control Program

loaded into the machine, and kept on some sort of fast storage device until it is actually called for. Here we have the elements of a powerful and flexible operating system. This is how it works. Every job starts off as a number of *documents:* there is the program text, the steering information that specifies how it is to be compiled and run, and the various pieces of data it is to use. Every document is preceded by a header or sentinel giving its name and, perhaps but not necessarily, the program it belongs to. The sentinel takes the form of a card placed on top of a pack or a leader of paper tape spliced on to the beginning of a reel. It might, for convenience, have a different colour from the rest of the document. Somewhere too, there must be an extra document listing all the documents germane to the job, though this could of course be incorporated with the steering document.

Documents are loaded into appropriate peripheral devices just as they arrive, or as the devices become available. Some documents may even be entered on keyboards. They are all read by the Control Program in the order in which they arrive, on a backing store (usually a drum or disc file) in what is called a *well*. When all the documents for a particular job have been received—some may already be stored in the system from a previous job—the program is ready to go. But it is not necessarily started immediately; it may have to wait for enough store space to accommodate it, or for a particular type of file device to be freed, or for an operator to load a file, or it may simply be held up because it is not particularly urgent and because it does not mix well with the current set of programs. Eventually it is started and begins to generate output. Here again the concept of a well is useful. The appropriate type of output device may not be available—besides, most programs generate data faster than most output devices can absorb it. Consequently, output data is also placed in a well, to be fed to an appropriate device when it is convenient. The job can be abolished as soon as it finishes its work, and storage space become immediately available to accommodate a new job if necessary.

The type of operating system that makes use of wells has two enormous advantages. In the first place, it take a great deal of the burden of running the installation efficiently away from the operator. The operators do not have to deal with the documents in any particular order, nor do they have to decide when a job is ready to start; they do not have to remember which device is allocated to which program, since all the slow devices are operated by the Control Program, and they do not have to check that documents are present and loaded. The other advantage is that the throughput of the system is increased by a substantial factor. The flow of jobs is smooth, and there are no unscheduled delays due to mistakes on the part of the operators or to document queues waiting for a particular device to become free. The scheduling is all done by the Control Program, which, provided that it is given a good algorithm to apply, can do the job faster and more effectively than a human operator, allocating priorities and ensuring that all the peripheral devices are kept busy. A well system is particularly valuable when an installation is required to deal with a number of short jobs, when the operators could not be expected to keep a proper account of all the documents involved.

With a simple operating system, a peripheral device is operated by the program for which the document it carries is destined, and which has been written with a knowledge of the form taken by the data. With a well system, on the other hand, every document is read by the same general-purpose routine, which must therefore be given some information on the structure of the document and the way it is to be read. This is done by the header, which must therefore be read as soon as possible after the device has been loaded; this of course means that the system must be informed whenever a new document is loaded, either by a console message or, better, by means of a special *engage* button on the peripheral device. Notice that the procedure is slightly different when a continuation document is loaded (for example, the residue of a stack of cards too large for the hopper), since the system already has a link to the correct reading routine.

ON-LINE PROGRAMMING

Most computer installations are operated on what is known as the *closed-shop* principle. The programmer need never even see the machine. He delivers his program text and data, together with a set of operating instructions, to the operating staff, who, in due course return to him either the results he wants or else the post-mortem and trace information that will enable him to find and correct a fault. The arrangement is convenient, in that the only people in direct contact with the machine are those specifically trained in operating it, and it avoids having too many cooks tripping over each other's heels in the computer room. Unfortunately it can lead to inordinate delays. Look at the following typical sequence of events—

Programmer sends manuscript program for punching.

Cards received duly punched.

Programmer checks punching and sends cards to computer room for compilation.

Programmer receives cards back together with a list of syntactic errors.

Corrects errors and sends corrections for re-punching (or else does the job himself).

Sends program (now syntactically correct) to computer room together with test data.

Program fails. Trace and/or post-mortem information returned to programmer.

Programmer locates error, has correction cards punched, sends corrected program to computer room.

Program fails. Trace and/or post-mortem information returned to programmer.

And so on . . .

Considering the turn-around time required for each of these activities, and adding time for weekends, holidays, sickness, and so on, one can easily see that even quite a short program can take a month or more before it is developed.

One rather unsatisfactory solution is to relax the strict *closed-shop* rule; and this is done to a greater or lesser extent in most installations. A far better solution would be to put the programmer on-line, that is, in communication with the machine by means of a direct data link terminating in a typewriter. A programmer with access to an on-line terminal can enter his program direct without having to use a punch operator as an intermediary. The assembler or compiler can check each statement for syntactic accuracy as it is typed, and errors can be corrected as they arise. Once the program has been compiled, it can be kept on a backing file, from which it can be retrieved at any time at the behest of its originator. When the program fails, a limited amount of trace information can be transmitted straight back to the programmer, who, if he is able, can make the necessary corrections; if the error proves to be hard to locate, the programmer can request more information and, if necessary, sign off and retire to his desk to think. Moreover, on-line programming offers the possibility of using single-shot methods of program development, that is, of working through parts of the program, statement by statement, stopping periodically to investigate the effect that the last group of statements has had.

When a program is finally running productively, its results, if they are not too bulky, can be transmitted back direct to the originator at his typewriter. Moreover, the possibility arises of the user's being able to steer the program as he wishes, altering parameters to change its mode of working so that, for instance, it may perform its work more rapidly or alter its degree of accuracy. This idea can be extended still further in the case of a simulation program providing a model of some real-life situation. An on-line programmer can manipulate the model, testing it under several different conditions, and generally treating it as he might treat an experiment on the bench.

What are the characteristics that a computer must have if it is to be suitable for on-line programming? In the first place, obviously, it must be multiprogrammed. Secondly, it must be a big machine, big enough to accommodate the complex Control Program required by an on-line installation as well as the various user programs. The store will also have to hold an assembler and possibly several compilers and a trace program at the same time. Another requirement is for plenty of backing storage, since the machine must be able to retain all data and programs (both productive and under development) that are likely to be called for by on-line users.

An on-line machine must have an efficient system for organizing the main store, for deleting programs that have finished and for making space available in suitably sized blocks to accommodate new programs. The system must be able to reorganize the store rapidly, since it will have to do it often; consequently it is practically obligatory for the programming system to permit some sort of fragmentation of programs, since less data need be moved to accommodate a new (fragmented) program. Moreover, as we have already pointed out, fragmentation permits the use of routines common to two or more programs: an essential requirement where several programs are continually demanding access to the same assemblers and compilers, and where storage space is liable to be the main limiting factor.

Compilation in an on-line system ceases to be what it is in a more conventional system, a single run at the start of the job. The compiler is liable to be called in at any time to compile a new statement or redefine a piece of data. The object program, the compiler, and the user can be thought of as comprising a sub-system working to produce a particular result. Among the first of the duties the user has to perform is to identify himself; this is to prevent unauthorized use of the system and also, if necessary, to indicate who is to be charged for the time used. To prevent fraud—one user identifying himself as another—it is common practice for every user to be given a password known only to himself and to the controller of the security system. Having identified himself, the user then identifies his job and proceeds to develop or run his program. This leads to an exchange of messages between himself and the machine, the machine reporting the occurrence of exceptional conditions, and replying to queries, the user correcting errors, and requesting further information. All this requires a number of conventions to have been established for the exchange of information; in other words it requires the development of a special type of conversational man-machine language.

We began this chapter by showing how multiprogramming can lead to a more efficient use of computer hardware: we have finished it by describing a type of multiprogramming system in which the hardware is in fact used less efficiently, but in relation to which human beings (rather more valuable capital assets) are used more efficiently. The less efficient the use of the machine, the more efficient the use of people. If the machine has to service a restricted number of terminals, it can keep them all busy; but there will then be periods for which it is under-used. On the other hand, if the number of terminals is increased until the machine is kept fully occupied, a queue situation develops, and the machine's responses may be delayed. It may even happen that some potential users may have to be turned away, or may have to be asked to wait until the machine can accept their work. In such circumstances users can be given precedence according to seniority, or the urgency of their work, or the rates they are prepared to pay, or some other criterion.

EXERCISES 14

1. How might the flow diagram of Fig. 14.4 be affected if the system were able to queue up to four instructions on any peripheral device?
2. Show with the aid of a flow diagram how a Control Program might deal with an end-of-tape marker. Assume that the presence of the marker is signalled at the end of a transfer, and that *no* further blocks can be written on the tape.
3. Sketch timing diagrams to correspond to the flow diagrams of Figs. 14.8 (*a*) and (*b*). Assume that there are ten records per block.
4. Sketch a flow diagram to show how subprogramming can be used to organize a queue of instructions.
5. A disc file is used to couple two computers in a multiple system. Although it is not able to store an instruction, the disc file can be reserved when it is busy, in which case, at the termination of the transfer it will interrupt the computer that reserved it and present itself as busy to the other computer. Suggest by a flow diagram how the Control Program might implement a transfer instruction involving this device.

15. *The Architecture of a Range*

COMPATIBILITY

All the major computer manufacturers offer compatible ranges of machines, that is, they offer a number of machines at different prices but capable of accepting programs written in the same assembly language. Manufacturers have been forced to make their products *compatible* by the increasing quantities of standard software they have been obliged to supply with their machines—an elaborate Control Program, an assembler, compilers for several languages, utility subroutines, housekeeping packages, input-output packages, tracing and diagnostic aids, etc. It became impossible for manufacturers to provide the necessary amount of software separately for every machine they wished to offer unless some items at least could be shared between several machines. The simplest way to do this was to design all the machines with the same instruction code; then all of them would at least be able to obey the same programs and routines, even if some of the programs ran more efficiently at one end of the range than at the other.

What applies to the manufacturer's software applies with the same force to the user's software; consequently, anyone who buys or hires a machine from a compatible range knows that should he decide later to enlarge his installation, he can change to the next larger machine in the range without having to rewrite any of his programs.

The term *compatibility* as applied to computers is open to some misinterpretation. Obviously no manufacturer is going to claim that every system he sells or hires is going to be able to accept every program written for every other system, since systems have different amounts of store and different peripheral configurations. Fortunately, the normal requirement is for a system that will grow, not for one that will shrink; consequently the normal user wants *upward compatibility*, or the ability to carry programs on to a larger system, provided that the appropriate peripheral devices are present. This is not to say that it would not be possible to rewrite a program to run more efficiently on the larger machine; but the fact that it will run at all is of enormous benefit.

If compatibility is to be understood fully in this sense, it must extend beyond the mere user language and embrace the whole operating system; for the way programs are written is conditioned by the way they must eventually be run, that is, by the conventions that are to be used for headings, operator commands, and so on. This does not mean, by the way, that all programmers must know in detail how the computer is operated; but they must write their programs in accordance with a set of rules and specifications based on the conventions of the operating system. Operating systems, then, must be in some sense compatible throughout a computer range or, to be precise, they must be compatible upward throughout the range, since it should go without saying that the larger a machine, the more operating flexibility it must have.

Compatible operating systems demand compatible peripheral devices. Apart, though, from considerations of compatibility, it is to a manufacturer's advantage to make as many as possible of his peripheral units usable with as many as possible of his computers. Naturally some fast devices are too fast for the smaller processors, and some of the smaller devices may be inappropriate to the larger systems; but, by and large, devices should be interchangeable. Ideally, a user wishing to expand his computing capacity should be able to retain all his old peripheral units and merely expand or replace the system centre.

STANDARD PERIPHERALS

Standard peripheral units do not necessarily imply a standard peripheral interface. Indeed the provision of a range tends to make a standard design of interface more difficult to achieve, since it must, at one and the same time, be simple enough to be implemented on cheap devices and cheap computers, and yet powerful enough to handle data at the rates of the fastest files on the fastest computers. In fact, what is often done is to provide two standard interfaces, one for use with the slower units (input and output), the other for the faster file devices. Another approach is to provide what in effect are standard subsets of a conceptual comprehensive interface. This means that it is not possible in general to plug any device into any socket on any computer in a range. But who wants to! The real requirement is for it to be possible to provide any computer with a peripheral configuration suitable for the job it is to do.

The master plan that covers all the systems in a compatible range is known as the *architecture* of the range. It must follow the principle of trading speed for cheapness at the bottom of the range and economy for power at the top. In fact this sort of trading is heavily weighted in favour of the big machine. It is well known that the power of a computer system is proportional not to its cost but roughly to the square of its cost. Why this should be so is not properly understood; nor is it known whether the relationship arises from the nature of computers or from the nature of the markets in which they are sold. But the point is that the square law works—at least so long as it is not treated as much more than a rough rule of thumb. In spite of the fact that larger computers offer better value for money, though, there is still a big demand for small and medium systems. Users seem to prefer to have a small computer of their own rather than to club together to buy a larger system.

The idea of a compatible computer range is fairly new, and so far no manufacturer has succeeded in providing a set of completely compatible machines covering the whole marketable range. In fact any range must have a centre of balance, a band of prices over which the architectural concepts are ideally suited to the hardware and to the internal organization of the machines. Towards the two extremities of the range, some efficiency has to be sacrificed to compatibility, and machines at the extremities are less efficient than they might have been had they been specifically designed to meet a particular price without the need for compatibility. Fortunately different manufacturers seem to have concentrated on different sections of the marketable range, so that a prospective user can select the machine that meets his present needs from a range that seems to cover his future needs as well. Furthermore, he can rest secure in the knowledge that technological advances will in time make it possible for any range to be extended upward beyond its present upper limit.

PROBLEMS OF STORE ORGANIZATION

One of the chief problems to be solved in planning a compatible range is how to organize the store so that it is used as efficiently as possible in every machine. A small system may require no more than a few thousand bytes of storage, while the machine at the top end of the range, which may have to accommodate several on-line users, needs several million bytes. If the compatible instruction code is to have addresses long enough to suit the large system (the Control Program, if not the individual user programs, must be able to address the whole store) the smallest machine is going to be burdened with addresses and instructions far longer than it really needs. One solution is to make the machines compatible at some level of language higher than machine code—at the level of the symbolic assembly language, for instance. This means of course that programmers cannot presume upon a particular format for data or instructions, which forbids them several short-cut techniques.

An alternative approach is to use modification for increasing the length of addresses at the top of the range. The instruction is furnished with a comparatively short address—long enough to cover the whole store in the smallest group of systems. The architecture also provides a method of modification capable of generating addresses long enough to cover the largest store likely to be fitted. Of course modification increases the time taken by an instruction; but it is usually possible to overlap modification with some other activity in the organization of a large system. An extension of this idea is the detached address: the instruction does not address store locations directly, but addresses a group of registers holding detached addresses referring to the store. The instruction length is then not dependent on the maximum size of the store, while the length of the detached-address registers can be tailored to fit the system into which they are incorporated.

Generally, each processor in a range is offered with a choice of store sizes, and it is normally possible to increase the storage capacity of a system even after it has been in operation for some time on the user's premises. Unfortunately, this means that the coupling between the store and the processing units must be flexible in both a mechanical, and an organizational, sense. It is not possible to do this without adding somewhat to the time taken to interrogate the store.

TRADING SPEED FOR COST

Because electrical signals take a finite time to travel from place to place, there is a conflict between the sheer physical size of large computers and the speed they are expected to operate at. This conflict is particularly marked in the field of core stores. High-speed stores must be fairly small; this is partly to keep the lengths of the internal wires, and consequently the propagation times of signals, as short as possible, and partly because larger stores require more powerful, and consequently slower, circuits. High-speed stores must therefore be made up of relatively small blocks (say sixteen thousand bytes). Now this raises the possibility of overlapping their cycles to gain a higher effective speed still; but overlapping requires co-ordination, which in turn requires time, particularly if there is an appreciable distance between the co-ordinating unit and the store blocks. There comes a point at which extra complexity yields a less than proportionate gain in speed*—the point at which the maximum practicable computer size has been

* In terms of the economist, marginal yield falls with increasing investment.

reached with a given technology. This will not of course be the maximum *possible* size: any speed limitation can be overcome at this level; but the cost of overcoming it is not always worth paying.

OVERLAP

The system centre increases in complexity upwards throughout a range of machines. At the bottom end, the machine organization is as simple as possible, and no particular care is taken to make sure that all the functional units are being kept as busy as they might be. Further up the range, more and more operations are overlapped so that all the units are employed more efficiently. The simplest form of overlapping is parallel working, treating all the bits in a word at the same time. Thus it might be possible to find the smallest computers in a range operating in a serial mode, whilst higher up, data is processed a byte at a time, and higher up still a word at a time. As with everything else, parallelism has its limit; this is the point where it takes longer to propagate *carry* from one end of the parallel unit to the other than it takes to add or subtract the actual bits. The propagation of carry is by nature a serial activity. Where precisely this point comes in a particular range depends on the nature of the circuit elements used. With some circuit families it is worth while operating in a fully parallel mode: with others, eight bits in parallel may be as fast as sixteen.

The faster the internal operation of a computer, particularly the speed of its store, the more peripheral units it can handle at one time. Peripheral units generally transmit one byte at a time, while most stores are arranged to read or write whole words. Consequently, if peripheral transfers are not to take up a disproportionate amount of the time of the system centre, some device must be interposed between the peripheral and the store for assembling bytes into words or, for outward transfers, for breaking words into individual bytes. Such a device might appear only on the medium and larger systems of a range, either as part of the system or as an option; and it could exist in several versions to suit different sizes of machine.

HARDWARE

It is always possible to trade speed for cheapness in a computer system by employing a cheaper, slower set of hardware, that is, by using cheaper transistors and slower circuits. But there is a point beyond which it is not worth while taking things, a point where further savings in cost are no longer worth the fall in speed. Costs depend primarily upon the quantities of an item that are produced; as a consequence, the fastest transistor or integrated circuit in full-scale production costs very little more than the slowest, and must *ceteris paribus* be preferred. Besides, the production of a range of machines is much easier to organize if the same family of circuits can be used in all the machines in the range—or at least in several of them. There is also a minimum speed of store below which it is not worth while to fall. There is probably little to be gained by using core stores with cycle times less than about two microseconds; far better to cut the cost of a store in some other way—by making it narrower for instance, that is, by making it yield only a small number of bits (say one byte) on each cycle. By the same token, the speed at the top end of a range can be enhanced by using a store with a width of two words or more.

SUBSET CODES

Another way of making small computer systems cheaper is to supply them with only a subset of the full instruction repertoire. Some instructions are inappropriate on small machines anyway—floating-point instructions for instance. Even multiplication and division of integers can be dispensed with and replaced, on the rare occasions when they are unavoidable, by subroutines. Better still, multiplication and division, and perhaps a few other costly functions, can be supplied as system subroutines; then, when they are needed they can be written just as if they had been implemented in hardware, since system subroutines are called by writing normal function mnemonics. As system subroutines they would of course be slow; but they would be performed at full speed if the program were transferred to a larger machine with a full built-in function repertoire. Sometimes a group of functions, or some other feature, is offered as an option at extra cost. In fact it happens not infrequently that a feature that is wholly absent from the smallest machines of a range is offered as an option in mid-range and supplied obligatorily with the largest machines. It nearly always happens, though, that something is sacrified, usually speed, by making a feature into an option.

OPERATING SYSTEMS

Another variant over a range of machines is the operating system. The more flexible it is, the more software needed to implement it, and the more store space it occupies. Consequently, the smallest systems can have only a very simple operating system, providing perhaps only one obligatory mode of running programs, and with the operator's controls reduced to a few switches. Further up the range it might be possible to provide a console typewriter giving a choice of a number of ways of working. Above this comes multiprogramming, first of all in a restricted sense, providing for one big program and one or two small transcription programs to run concurrently; then, still further up the range, in a general sense complete with subprogramming. At the top of the range come the big powerful operating systems: well systems for ease of operation, and on-line systems for rapid program development. At this stage the Control Program might occupy as many as a hundred thousand bytes or more, though normally some part of it would be lying on a backing store.

MULTIPROCESSORS

The upper limit of a computer range can be extended by yoking two or more separate machines together to make what is known as a *multiprocessor*. In fact there are several reasons other than power why computers are coupled together—one is to provide standby. There are applications where it is particularly important to avoid complete breakdown, even if it is likely to last only a few seconds. By coupling two machines together it is possible to make sure that there is computing power available even if one of them should fail. However, duplicating whole hardware units in this way is not necessarily the best way to increase the reliability of a system, since not only are the least reliable elements duplicated but money is wasted in duplicating also those elements that are least likely to fail. Another type of multiprocessor is the master-slave system, which was dealt with in Chapter 9. There is an added advantage to the user if the master and slave are machines from the same range, since then only one programming system need be learned, and programs can be off-loaded from one machine to the other (if need be) to balance their loads. The term *multiprocessor* has been used for systems in which processors are coupled together through a peripheral device or a data link; but it should strictly be applied only when the method of coupling is to give all the units access to the same store, or to parts of the same store complex.

FORWARD COMPATIBILITY

We have said that a user will wish his new computer to be compatible in an upward sense. He will also wish it to be compatible in a backward and forward sense, that is to say, he will want to be able to run the programs that are already operating on his present machine, and he will want an assurance from the manufacturer that any new programs he writes will run on any future machine he may buy from him. Moreover, he will want his programs to run on a new machine at least no slower than they used to run on the old machine.

It is sometimes alleged that the solution to the problem of forward compatibility, is to settle once and for all on a standard machine language. But this would stultify further advances in computer engineering. It would become in time like trying to organize a modern complex industrial society using the tongue of Chaucer.

TRANSLATION

When once we accept that there must be new computer languages for some time yet, possibly a few new ones for every new generation of machines, we have to devise some means of carrying forward programs written in outdated languages. The first solution that

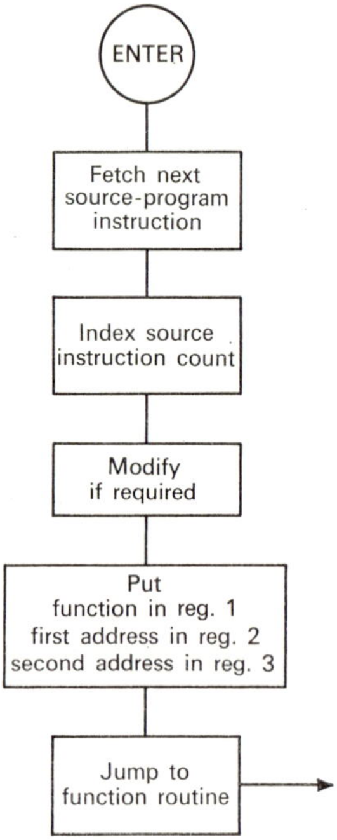

FIG. 15.1.

suggests itself is to translate programs from one language into another. Unfortunately, except in special circumstances, it is not really practicable to do this. The trouble is that it is not possible to tell from the textual form of a program just what the writer's intention was; consequently, every instruction in the source language has to be copied exactly in the target language, generally with a substantial subroutine. The result is that the translated program is many times longer than it was in the original language, and simply will not fit into the store of the computer that is intended to run it. Machine languages are tailored to fit the internal shapes of the machines they are designed for—in contrast to languages like FORTRAN, which have been designed from the start to be easy to translate.

SIMULATION

Since translation is not often possible, the program in the source language must be stored in the target machine in its original form, and obeyed from there. This is done by means of a program in the language of the target machine, which examines in turn each instruction and performs the operation specified by it. This process is known as *interpretation*, or *simulation*. It is no faster to simulate a program than to run it in translated form—indeed it may be slower—but a simulated program needs far less store. Only the simulator program and the source program in its original language have to be accommodated. Fig. 15.1 shows a flow diagram typical of the central routine of a program simulator.

EMULATION

The speed of a simulator can be greatly improved by providing special instructions designed specifically for its use, to perform the operations that occur most frequently in it. These are first and foremost the operations detailed in Fig. 15.1—fetching the next instruction, modifying it, and separating its fields. To provide special instructions in a machine with the fixed-store form of microprogram simply involves augmenting the fixed store to the extent of a few more micro-routines; moreover, such a facility can be made an optional feature and supplied at extra cost only to those users who are likely to make use of it. A further improvement in simulator speed can be achieved by supplying extra registers with special dataflow routes to match the exact needs of the special instructions used by the simulator. Simulation, aided by extra hardware, is referred to as *emulation*.

EXERCISES 15

1. A computer has a 48-bit word with an instruction format—

F	X	Y	Z
6	14	14	14

where F is a function, X and Y operand addresses, and Z the address of a modifier 48 bits long that is to be added to the whole instruction before it is obeyed. Suggest with a flow diagram how the central routine of a simulator for this computer might be organized on a 32-bit machine. Why would it be impossible to use a translation technique for this particular language?

2. Code the flow diagram which you worked out for the last exercise.
3. What additional functions might be helpful in simulating the language given in question 1?

MODEL ANSWERS TO EXERCISES

CHAPTER 1

1.

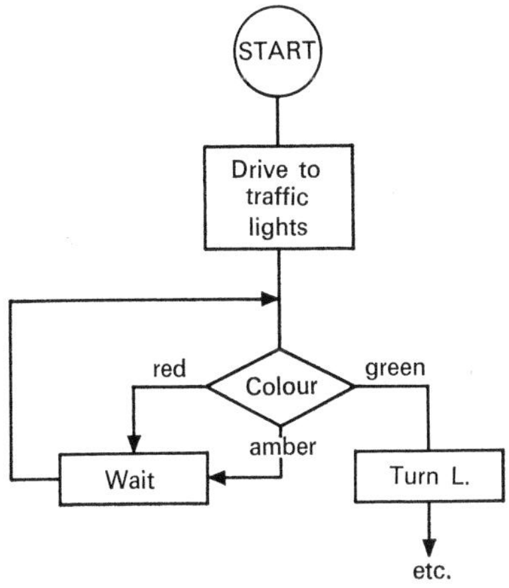

2.

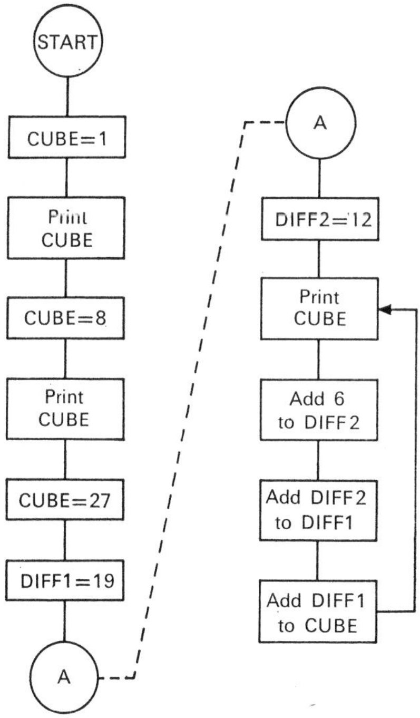

3.

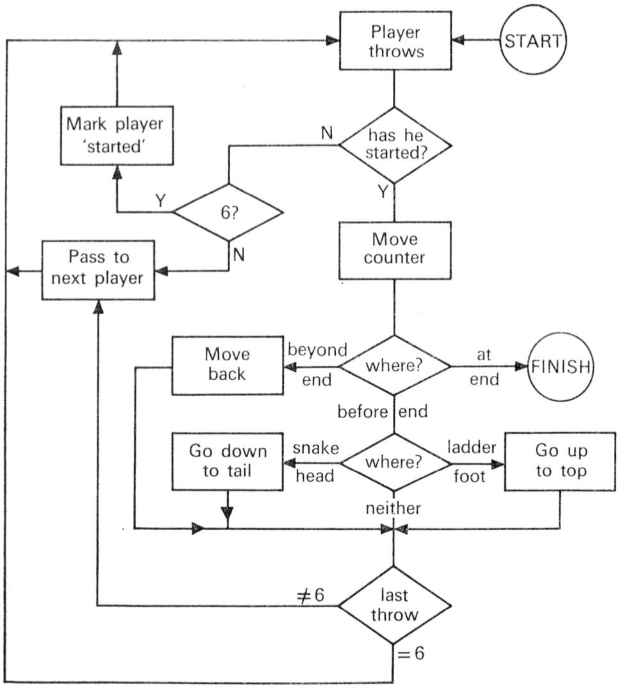

4. Keep one transport for standby.
   Load scratch tape.
      Start transcription.
   Load two more scratch tapes.
      Start sort.
   Load two reels of main file.
      Start update.

When first reel of old and new file have been run, replace with third reel of main file and a scratch tape respectively.

Demount second and third reels of old and new main file when finished.

5.

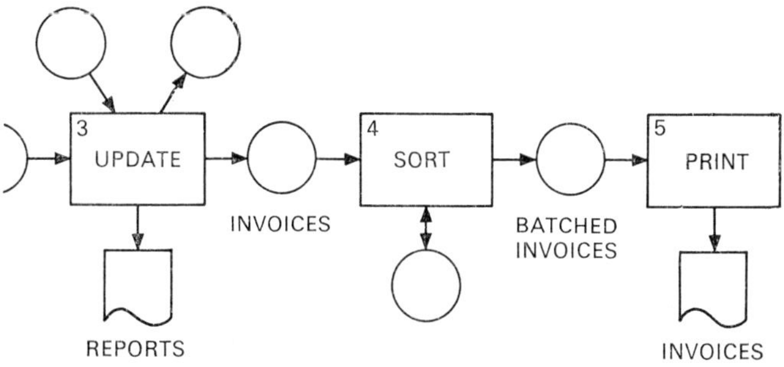

The minimum number of decks is four. Six would give faster processing, since main-file reels could then be mounted in advance of requirements.

6.

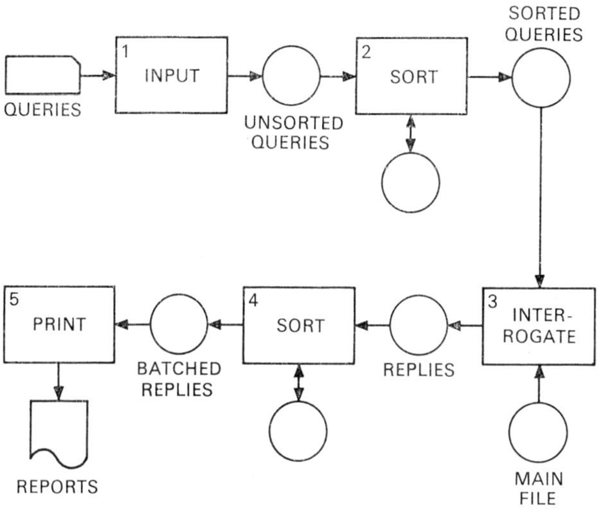

CHAPTER 2

1. For 1 to 9 see p. 16.

10	1010	100	1100100
20	10100	200	11001000
30	11110	300	100101100
40	101000	400	110010000
50	110010	500	111110100
60	111100	600	1001011000
70	1000110	700	1010111100
80	1010000	800	1100100000
90	1011010	900	1110000100

1000	1111101000
2000	11111010000
3000	101110111000
4000	111110100000
5000	1001110001000
6000	1011101110000
7000	1101101011000
8000	1111101000000
9000	10001100101000

981 = 1111010101
7654 = 1110111100110
4096 = 1000000000000

2. Octal
981 = 1725
7654 = 16744
4096 = 10000
Hexadecimal
981 = 3 $\overline{\mathrm{D}}$ 5
7654 = 1 $\overline{\mathrm{D}}$ $\overline{\mathrm{E}}$ 4
4096 = 1000

3. Add together all the even bits and all the odd bits. Subtract one from the other. If the difference is zero or a multiple of three, the whole number is divisible by three.

Add together even pairs of bits and odd pairs of bits, treating them as digits in radix four. Subtract one from the other. If the difference is zero or a multiple of five, the whole number is divisible by five.

4. (*a*) 12, 14, 16, 18.
(*b*) 2, 4, 6, 8, 10, 20, 22, 24, 26, 28, 29, 31, 33, 35.
(*c*) 11, 12, 13, 14, 15, 16, 17, 18, 29, 30, 31, 32, 33, 34, 35, 36.
(*d*) 1, 2, 3, 4, 5, 6, 7, 8, 9, 10.
(*e*) 11, 13, 15, 17, 19, 21, 23, 25, 27, 30, 32, 34, 36.
(*f*) none.

5.

a	0011
b	0101
a ∨ b	0111
ā	1100
$\bar{b}$	1010
ā & $\bar{b}$	1000

The other proof follows by substituting $\bar{a}$ for a and $\bar{b}$ for b in the table above.

6.

$$a \vee b = (aNb)N(aNb)$$
$$a \,\&\, b = (aNa)N(bNb)$$
$$a \equiv b = [aN(bNb)]N[(aNa)Nb]$$
$$a \not\equiv b = [(aNa)N(bNb)]N(aNb)$$

a	0011
b	0101
aNb	1000

CHAPTER 3

1. (*a*)

ZERO	J	'2'
POS	J	'7'

(*b*)

DIFF	MOVE	B
DIFF	SUB	A
POS	J	'3'
DIFF	MOVE	A
DIFF	SUB	B

2.

SECOND	MOVE	'O'
THIRD	MOVE	'1'
OUT	CBD	THIRD
LP	TFER	OUT
FIRST	MOVE	SECOND
SECOND	MOVE	THIRD
THIRD	ADD	FIRST
	J	'– 5'

3.

CUBE	MOVE	'1'
OUT	CBD	CUBE
LP	TFER	OUT
CUBE	MOVE	'8'
OUT	CBD	CUBE
LP	TFER	OUT
CUBE	MOVE	'27'
DIFF1	MOVE	'19'
DIFF2	MOVE	'12'
OUT	CBD	CUBE
LP	TFER	OUT
DIFF2	ADD	'6'
DIFF1	ADD	DIFF2
CUBE	ADD	DIFF1
	J	'– 5'

4.

PAY	SDIV	'5'
DIM1	ADD	PAY
PAY	MOVE	PAY + 1
PAY	SDIV	'2'
DIM5	ADD	PAY
PAY	MOVE	PAY + 1
PAY	SDIV	'5'
DOL	ADD	PAY

```
PAY        MOVE   PAY + 1
PAY        SDIV   '2'
DOL5       ADD    PAY
DOL10      ADD    PAY + 1
```

5.

```
LOWER      MOVE   PRICE
LOWER      AND    '65535'
UPPER      MOVE   PRICE
UPPER      SH     '- 1'
UPPER      SH     '17'
ORDER      SDIV   '12'
PRICE      MOVE   PRICE
POS        J      '5'
ORDER      MOVE   ORDER
NZERO      J      ERROR
ORDER      MOVE   ORDER + 1
ORDER      SDIV   '12'
PROD       MOVE   ORDER
PROD       MLT    UPPER
COST       MOVE   PROD
PROD       MOVE   ORDER + 1
PROD       MLT    LOWER
COST       ADD    PROD
```

6.

```
NUMB       MOVE   '0'
WS         MOVE   STATS
WS         NEQ    STATS + 1
WS         NEQ    STATS + 2
STATS      AND    STATS + 1
STATS      AND    STATS + 2
WS         SUB    STATS
NEG        J      '4'
WS         SH     '- 1'
ZERO       J      '4'
POS        J      '- 2'
NUMBER     ADD    '1'
           J      '- 4'
           STOP
```

CHAPTER 4

1.

```
3          MOVE   '0'
4          MOVE   '135'
LEAST      MOVE   LIST(3)
LEAST      TSUB   LIST(3)
NEG        J      '2'
LEAST      MOVE   LIST(3)
3          CTJ    '- 3'
           STOP
```

2. K X V M C N O P H Q R S Z Y I J A D L E G W B U F T
The same sequence of instructions as for enciphering.

3.

```
4            MOVE    '0'
6            MOVE    TEXT(4)
6            SUB     '32'
ZERO         J       '7'
6            SUB     '10'
ZERO         J       '7'
6            SUB     '4'
ZERO         J       '3'
6            SUB     '17'
TEXT(4)      MOVE    KEY(6)
4            ADD     '1'
             J       '– 10'
             STOP
```

4. (*a*)

```
6            MOVE    '0'
WS           MOVE    STRING(6)
NZERO        J       '4'
STRING(6)    MOVE    '32'
6            ADD     '1'
             J       '– 4'
             STOP
```

(*b*)

```
6            MOVE    '0'
STRING(6)    TSUB    '32'
ZERO         J       '3'
6            ADD     '1'
             J       '– 3'
6            SUB     '1'
STRING(6)    MOVE    STRING(6)
NZERO        J       '3'
STRING(6)    MOVE    '32'
             J       '– 4'
             STOP
```

5.

```
3            MOVE    '0'
HIGH         MOVE    '135'
LOW          MOVE    3
3            ADD     HIGH
3            SH      1          divide by 2
3            TSUB    HIGH
ZERO         J       '9'
LIST(3)      TSUB    VALUE
ZERO         J       FOUND
NEG          J       '– 7'
HIGH         MOVE    3
3            ADD     LOW
3            SH      1
3            TSUB    LOW
NZERO        J       '– 7'
             STOP
```

6.

```
COUNT     MOVE   '0'
3         MOVE   'ARRAY'
4         MOVE   '20'
0(3)      MOVE   0(3)
NZERO     J      '2'
COUNT     ADD    '1'
3         ADD    '20'
3         CTJ    '− 4'
          STOP
```

CHAPTER 5

1.

```
2(7)      MOVE   2(7)
ZERO      J      '7'
WS        MOVE   0(7)
O(7)      MLT    WS
OVR       J      1(1)
2(7)      SUB    '1'
NZERO     J      '− 3'
          J      0(1)
--------------------------
0(7)      MOVE   '1'
1(7)      MOVE   '0'
          J      0(1)
```

This subroutine raises a number to any power, including zero. In case of overflow it returns to the address after the link. Link in 1, parameter-list address in 7. Number is first parameter; power is third parameter. Double-length result left in first and second parameter locations with third empty.

2. (a) Parameter list made up in sequence of PAY, PAY + 1, DIM1, DIM5, DOL, DOL5, DOL10. Then sequence of instructions is the same but with names replaced by 0(*x*), 1(*x*), etc., where *x* contains address of parameter list. Terminate with link jump.

(*b*) Parameter list made up of PAY, PAY+1, and COIN, where COIN is the name of a list consisting of DIM1 to DOL10. In the subroutine, an index register (3 say) must be dumped, and loaded with COIN. Then names PAY and PAY+1 are replaced by 0(*x*) and 1(*x*); but DIM1 etc. are replaced by 0(3) etc. Terminate by replacing content of 3 and jump to link. (Alternatively use replacement addressing for DIM1 etc. and avoid dumping—if facilities are available on the machine.)

3. Parameter list: 0 and 1, data;
2, result.

List address in 7; link in 1.

```
HCF:   0(7)      SUB    1(7)
       ZERO      J      '8'
       POS       J      '− 2'
       0(7)      ADD    1(7)
       1(7)      SUB    0(7)
       ZERO      J      '6'
       POS       J      '− 2'
                 J      '− 8'
       --------------------------
       2(7)      MOVE   1(7)
                 J      0(7)
       --------------------------
       2(7)      MOVE   0(7)
                 J      0(1)
```

4.

```
        CARD        TFER    CR
        3           MOVE    CARD
        3           SUB     '65'
                    J       SW(3)
```

5. (*a*)

```
SZERO:  0(6)        MOVE    0(6)
        NZERO       J       0(1)
        0(6)        MOVE    '32'
                    J       1(1)
```

(*b*) Stack pointer in 7, link in 1; stack is used for passing parameter on input.

```
SZDEC:  1(7)        MOVE    6
        6           MOVE    0(7)
        2(7)        MOVE    1
        7           ADD     '2'
        1           J       SZERO
                    J       '3'
        6           ADD     '1'
                    J       '- 3'
        ---------------------------
        7           SUB     '2'
        1           MOVE    2(7)
        6           MOVE    1(7)
                    J       0(1)
```

Calling sequence:

```
        1(7)        MOVE    1
        2(7)        MOVE    'STRING'
        7           ADD     '2'
        1           J       SZDEC
        7           SUB     '2'
        1           MOVE    1(7)
```

6.

```
SZFRAC: 1(7)        MOVE    6
        6           MOVE    0(7)
        0(6)        TSUB    '32'
        ZERO        J       '3'
        6           ADD     1
                    J       '- 3'
        ---------------------------
        2(7)        MOVE    1
        7           ADD     '2'
        6           SUB     '1'
        1           J       SZERO
                    J       2'
                    J       '- 3'
        ---------------------------
        7           SUB     '2'
        1           MOVE    2(7)
        6           MOVE    1(7)
                    J       0(1)
```

CHAPTER 6

1.

```
@NAME
CARDSELECT
@DATA
TEXT 'CARDS STARTING WITH £'
@SPACE
CARD (80/)
CARD1 (4/)
@PROGRAM
LP              TFER    TEXT
CARD1           TFER    CR
2               MOVE    '0'
3               MOVE    '4'
CARD1 (2)       SUB     '48'
@COMMENT
NUMERALS HAVE CODES 48 TO 57
@PROGRAM
2               CTJ     '– 1'
3               CDB     CARD1
CARD            TFER    CR
CARD            TSUB    '36'
NZERO           J       '2'
LP              TFER    CARD
2               CTJ     '– 4'
                STOP
@END
```

2.

```
         @NAME
         SEGCARDSELECT
         @GLOBAL
         HEAD, OUTPUT, INPUT, CARD
         @SEGMENT
         @NUMERIC
         COUNT '100'
         @SPACE
         CARD (80/)
         @PROGRAM
         1               J       HEAD
         1               J       INPUT
         CARD            TSUB    '36'
         NZERO           J       '2'
         1               J       OUTPUT
         COUNT           SUB     '1'
         NZERO           J       '– 5'
                         STOP
         @SEGMENT
         @DATA
         HEADING 'CARDS STARTING WITH £'
         @PROGRAM
HEAD:    LP              TFER    HEADING
                         J       0(1)
OUTPUT:  LP              TFER    CARD
                         J       0(1)
         @SEGMENT
         @PROGRAM
```

```
INPUT:   CARD          TFER   CR
                       J      0(1)
         @END

3.       @NAME
         ALPHACOUNT
         @SPACE
         DATA (80/)
         CLIST (26)
         PRINT (4/)
         @PROGRAM
         2             MOVE   '100'
         DATA          TFER   CR
         4             MOVE   '0'
         5             MOVE   '80'
         3             MOVE   DATA(4)
         3             SUB    '65'
         CLIST(3)      ADD    '1'
         4             CTJ    '- 3'
         1             CTJ    '- 7'
         @COMMENT
         COUNTING COMPLETE. NOW PRINT
         @PROGRAM
         1             MOVE   '0'
         2             MOVE   '26'
         PRINT         CBD    CLIST(1)
         LP            TFER   PRINT
         1             CTJ    '- 2'
                       STOP
         @END

4.       @SEGMENT
         @DATA
         KEY 'QWERTYUIOPASDFGHJKLZXCVBNM'
         @SPACE
         TEXT (text length/)
         @PROGRAM
```

TEXT is global, KEY need not be. At least one global label is necessary.

```
5.       @MACRO
         (JSYM, X, N, A, S, L)
         X             MOVE   A
         X + 1         MOVE   N
         0(X)          TSUB   S
         ZERO          J      L
         X             CTJ    '- 2'
         @COMMENT
         THIS MACRO JUMPS TO L WHEN THE SYMBOL
         S IS FOUND IN A STRING OF N ITEMS
         STARTING AT ADDRESS GIVEN IN A. IT
         USES INDEX X LEAVING IT POINTING AT
         LAST ITEM TESTED AND X + 1 FOR COUNT
         LEAVING IT WITH ONE MORE THAN NO OF
         ITEMS NOT YET TESTED.
```

6.

```
        SIZE     MOVE   '120'
        6        JSYM   SIZE, TEXT, 32, REPL
                 STOP
REPL:   O(6)     MOVE   '45'
        TEXT     MOVE   6
        TEXT     ADD    '1'
        SIZE     MOVE   7
        SIZE     SUB    '1'
                 J      '– 7'
```

CHAPTER 7

1.

```
@LOAD SORT
OK 9.00.00
SORT LOADED 9.01.30
@GO SORT
OK 9.02.15
@FIND UPDATE
OK 9.02.32
SORT FINISHED 9.06.15
@LOAD UPDATE
OK 9.06.29
UPDATE LOADED 9.06.33
@GO UPDATE
OK 9.06.45
UPDATE FILE ON MT2 9.33.59
UPDATE FINISHED 9.34.01
```

2.

```
@LOAD SORT
@GO SORT
@LOAD UPDATE
@GO UPDATE
@FINISH
```

3. (*a*)

Load program-library tape
Load cards DATA
Load two scratch tapes
Load program SORT and go
While sorting load magnetic tape MAINFILE,
  load invoice forms in printer, find UPDATE
At end of SORT load UPDATE and go
At end of UPDATE label and date new MAINFILE
Return old and new main files to tape library.

(*b*)

Load program-library tape
Load steering cards ahead of DATA cards
Steer
Load MAINFILE, invoice forms in printer
At end of UPDATE label and date new MAINFILE
Return old and new main files to tape library.

4.

```
@LOAD REPGEN
OK 14.34.05
REPGEN LOADED 14.34.47
```

```
@GO REPGEN
OK 14.35.16
REPGEN FINISHED 14.41.06
@LOAD REPORT
OK 14.42.21
REPORT LOADED 14.42.39
@GO REPORT
OK 14.43.17
REPORT FILE1 ON MT2 14.52.23
REPORT FINISHED 14.52.26
```

5. after OK 14.35.16
insert CR FIX 14.35.18
then all times delayed by, say, 3 minutes until
OK 14.43.17
becomes OK 14.46.17
then LP FIX 14.46.27
then times delayed by a further 4 minutes, say, giving

```
REPORT TYPE 14.47.31
LOAD FILE NEXT REEL
REPORT FILE1 ON MT2 14.59.23
REPORT FINISHED 14.59.26
```

6.

```
CARD        TSUB   '48'
NEG         J      ERROR
CARD        TSUB   '53'
POS         J      ERROR
2           MOVE   '1'
3           MOVE   '4'
CARD(2)     TSUB   '48'
NEG         J      ERROR
CARD(2)     TSUB   '58'
POS         J      ERROR
2           CTJ    '– 4'
3           MOVE   '20'
CARD(2)     TSUB   '32'
ZERO        J      '5'
CARD(2)     TSUB   '65'
NEG         J      ERROR
CARD(2)     TSUB   '91'
POS         J      ERROR
2           CTJ    '– 6'
3           MOVE   '10'
CARD(2)     TSUB   '48'
NEG         J      ERROR
CARD(2)     TSUB   '58'
NEG         J      '5'
CARD(2)     TSUB   '65'
NEG         J      ERROR
CARD(2)     TSUB   '91'
POS         J      ERROR
2           CTJ    '– 8'
```

CHAPTER 8

1.

	1	$1\frac{1}{2}$	2	3
(*a*)	MOVE A	X MOVE A	B MOVE A	B MOVE A
	STORE B	X STORE B		
(*b*)	MOVE B	4 MOVE B	4 MOVE B	4 ADD A, B
	ADD A	4 ADD A	4 ADD A	
	STORE 4			
(*c*)	MOVE A	X1 MOVE A	WS MOVE A	WS MOVE A
	STORE WS	X2 MOVE B	A MOVE B	A MOVE B
	MOVE B	X1 STORE B	B MOVE WS	B MOVE WS
	STORE A	X2 STORE A		
	MOVE WS			
	STORE B			
(*d*)	MOVE A	X MOVE A	A MOVE A	ZERO J A, B
	TEST ZERO	ZERO J B	ZERO J B	
	J B			

2. (*a*) Read store at A
add '27' (from instruction reg.)
write back to A from Mill.

(*b*) Read X
add to B
read A
rewrite
read B(X)
set Mill to subtract
write difference back to B(X).

(*c*) Read A
rewrite
read B
rewrite
read (B)
rewrite
read (A)
add to (B)
write sum back to (A)

For (*b*) and (*c*) a second address register is needed, since one address must be preserved while the store is being read at the other.

3. ab ac bc $\overline{a}\overline{b}$ $\overline{a}\overline{c}$ $\overline{b}\overline{c}$

first three activated by combination 111 last one activated alone by 100.

4. read control word
read store at address in control word
insert new byte
rewrite store
add 1 to byte address
subtract 1 from count
if count = 0 initiate interrupt.

5. (*a*) $0{\cdot}6 + 0{\cdot}8 + 1{\cdot}2 + 72 = 74{\cdot}6\%$

   (*b*) $0{\cdot}6 + 0{\cdot}8 + 1{\cdot}2 + 48 = 50{\cdot}6\%$

   (*c*) $0{\cdot}6 + 0{\cdot}8 + 1{\cdot}2 + 18 = 20{\cdot}6\%$

6. (*a*) crisis time = 42 microsec.
   42 − 30 = 12, which is less than 20, so only one channel

   (*b*) crisis time = 167 microsec.
   167 − 30 = 137, which is just below seven times 20, so 7 channels are possible.

CHAPTER 9

1.

	machine 1	72·84 microsec.
	machine 2	9·52
	machine 3	3·94

2. The formula to use is

$$\frac{1000}{T} = AP + h$$

where T is throughput and A is activity, *p* is P.O. unit and *h* is hesitation time.

(*a*)	2-channel	for T = 66·6	A = 1·4
	1-channel	for T = 33·3	A = 2·9
(*b*)	2-channel	for A = 2	T = 47·6
	1-channel	T is limited at 33·3 by the equipment	
(*c*)	1-channel	for T = 33·3	A = 2·9
		for T = 16·6	A = 5·9

CHAPTER 10

1.

	0·56789E–3	0·2468E8	0·314159E1
	0·876543E3	0·20000003E8	0·234E254

2.

	468E20	87654E107
	87742E107	9E107
	53343E–54	103087E22

3.

	0·1235E3	0·1001E–6
	0·7823E6	0·8136E0
	0·25E–17	0·2052E10

4.

0·110000011001E011
0·111100010000E100
0·011011001011E110
0·000100000010E110

5.

1	MOVE	X + 1
1	SUB	Y + 1
NEG	J	'9'
2	MOVE	Y
2	SH	'0'(1)
X	ADD	2
OVR	J	'2'
	J	'9'

X	SH	'1'
X + 1	ADD	'1'
	J	'7'

1	MOVE	Y + 1
1	SUB	X + 1
X + 1	MOVE	Y + 1
X	SH	'0'(1)
X	ADD	Y
OVR	J	'– 8'

6. (*a*)

2	MOVE	SIZE
1	MOVE	'0'
	FLOD	A(1)
	FADD	B(1)
	FSTO	C(1)
1	CTJ	'– 3'

(*b*)

2	MOVE	SIZE
1	MOVE	'0'
	FLOD	A(1)
	FMLT	B(1)
	FADD	P
	FSTO	P
1	CTJ	'– 4'

CHAPTER 11

1.

1	MOVE	'8'
2	MOVE	'20'
SUM	MOVE	'0'
SUM	ADD	ARRAY(1)

2.

FLD	F	FADD	C
FMLT	F	FMLT	D
FMLT	E	FSUB	A
FSTO	A	FDIV	G
FLD	B	FSTO	A

3. (*a*) Put value in 2358;
in 1245 replace 0 by 1251.
in 1251 put 0/2358.

(*b*) In 1234 replace 1247 by etc.;
in 1247 replace etc. by 1234;
change previous item in main list to refer to 1247 instead of 1234.

(*c*) In 1235 replace 1236 by 1238;
in 1240 replace 0 by 1241;
add 1236, 1237, 2346 to list of available space.

(*d*) In 1241 replace 1246 by 0;
in 1245 replace 0 by 1246.

4. (*a*) A B C * + D E F * − *
(*b*) A B − C D * − E F G + * +
(*c*) A B C − D * − E F * + G +

5.

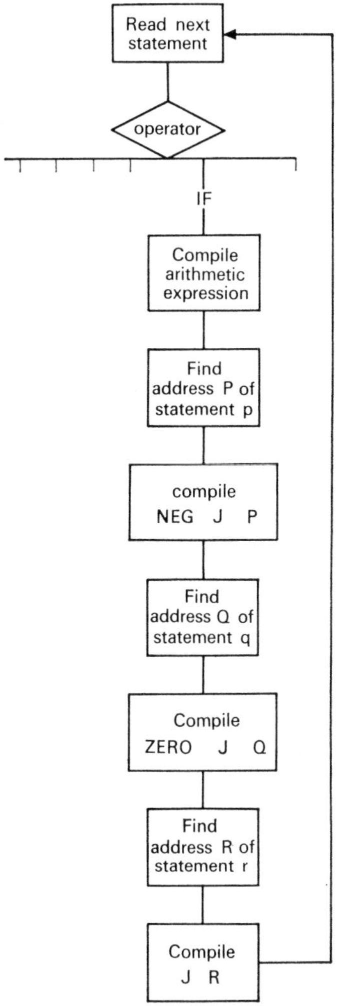

6. (*a*) ⟨operator⟩ ::= +| − | * |/
   (*b*) ⟨identifier⟩ ::= ⟨letter⟩|⟨identifier⟩ ⟨letter⟩| ⟨identifier⟩ ⟨digit⟩
   (*c*) ⟨variable argument⟩ ::= ⟨identifier⟩|⟨integer⟩
   ⟨argument⟩ ::= ⟨variable argument⟩| '⟨variable argument⟩'

CHAPTER 12

1. (*a*) 1600
   (*b*) 400
   (*c*) 2000 (on the assumption that spacing is controlled by the transmission of space characters in the appropriate places).

2. (*a*) 40 forms per min.
   (*b*) 40 forms per min.

3. 2 hours 19 min.

4. Reduced to 1 hr. 55 min.
   90 cards per min.

5. (*a*)

LP	TFER	HEADING
2	MOVE	COUNT
CARD	TFER	CR
CARD	TSUB	'36'
NZERO	J	'3'
PRINT	TFER	CARD
LP	TFER	PRINT
1	CTJ	'− 5'

(*b*)

LP	TFER	HEADING
2	MOVE	COUNT
CARD	TFER	CR
WORK	TFER	CARD
CARD	TFER	CR
WORK	TSUB	'36'
NZERO	J	'3'
PRINT	TFER	WORK
LP	TFER	PRINT
1	CTJ	'− 6'

(*c*)

LP	TFER	HEADING
2	MOVE	COUNT
CARD1	TFER	CR
3	MOVE	'CARD1'
4	MOVE	'CARD2'
5	MOVE	'PRINT1'
6	MOVE	'PRINT2'
(4)	TFER	CR
(3)	TSUB	'36'
NZERO	J	'6'
(5)	TFER	(3)
LP	TFER	(5)
WS	MOVE	5

5	MOVE	6
6	MOVE	WS
WS	MOVE	3
3	MOVE	4
4	MOVE	WS
1	CTJ	'– 11'

6.

00100010	01100001
00100011	01100011
00100001	01100010
00100000	01100110
01100000	01100111

CHAPTER 13

1. (*a*) 20·5% (*b*) 72% (*c*) 93% (*d*) 64%

2. (*a*) 65 min. (*b*) 33 min. 20 sec. (*c*) 32 min. 30 sec.

3.

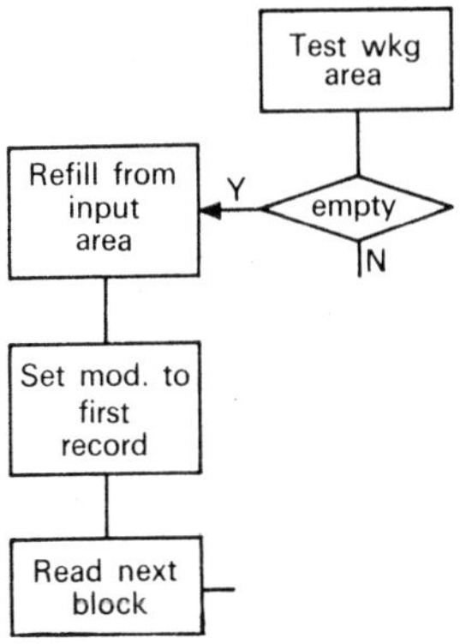

4. (*a*) 15 passes of 14 mins. 40 sec., with rewinding, 330 mins.
   (*b*) 12 passes of 6 mins. 16 secs., with rewinding, 112 mins. 48 sec.

5. (*a*) 57 mins. 40 secs.
   (*b*) 29 mins. 40 secs.
   (*c*) 28 mins. 20 secs. (printer-limited).

6. With a single batch, job time—

$$= 300 + 30 + 16/40 + 60$$
$$= 406 \text{ min. } 40 \text{ sec.}$$

With three batches, job time—

$$= 100 + 100 + 100 + 10 + 15 + 60$$
$$= 385 \text{ min.}$$

This is the optimum; with more batches, processing takes longer than punching.

7.

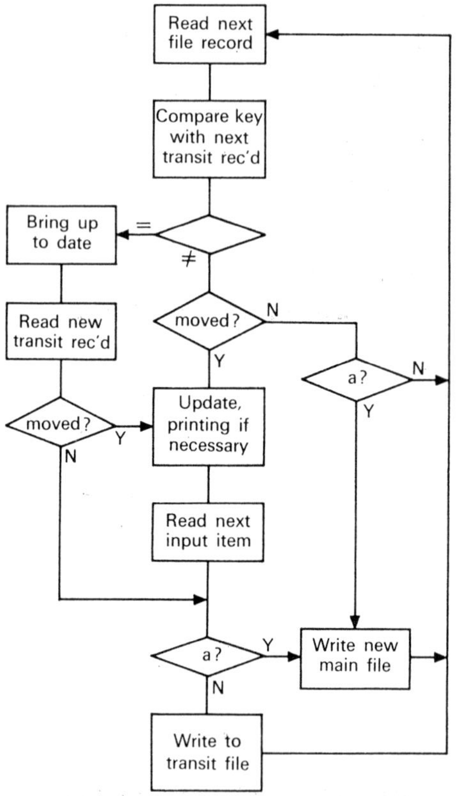

8. (*a*) Multiply key by 3 (or add three times) and use first four digits of product to give address.

(*b*) Subtract 40,000,000 and take digits 1, 2, 7 and 8 of the result to give address.

9. Utilization = 73%

Allow 88 bytes for overflow tags and store up to 28 records to each track.

10. (*a*) Time = 250 × 10 sec. = 41 min. 40 sec.

(*b*) Block hit rate = 0·46 (from graph)

Time = 512 × 0·22 + 16384 × 0·46 × 0·03 sec.
= 5 min. 39 sec.

CHAPTER 14

1.

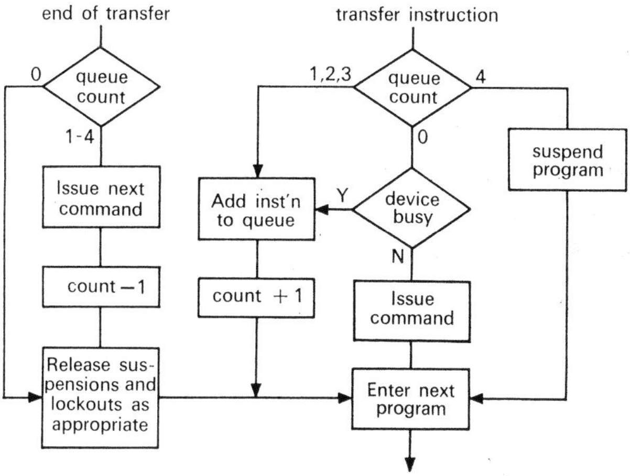

2.

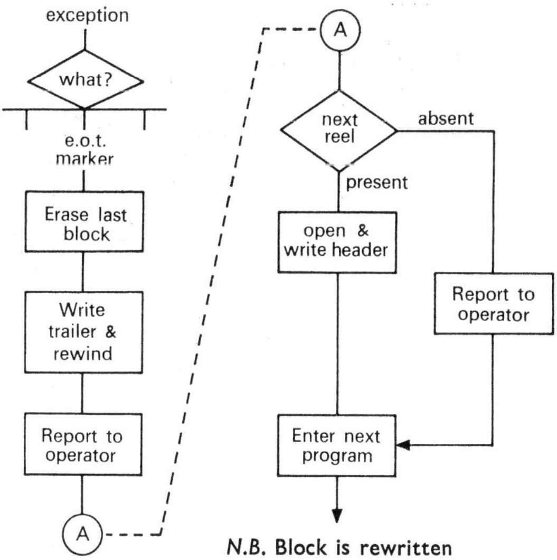

N.B. Block is rewritten on next entry to C.P. (end of header). Suspensions, lockouts are not released until after this.

3.

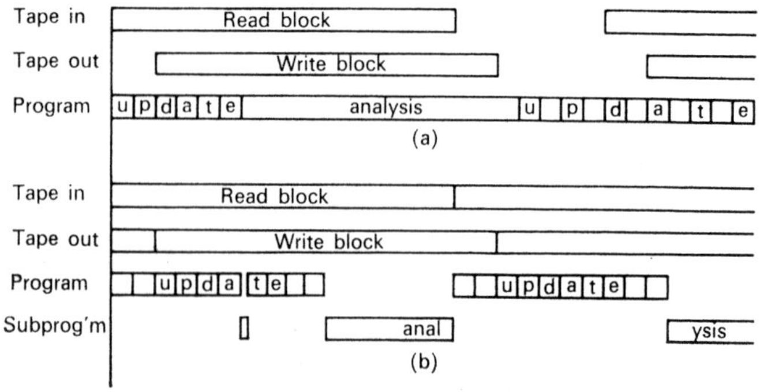
Tape in
Read block
Tape out
Write block
Program
update
analysis
(a)
Tape in
Read block
Tape out
Write block
Program
update
Subprog'm
anal
ysis
(b)

4.

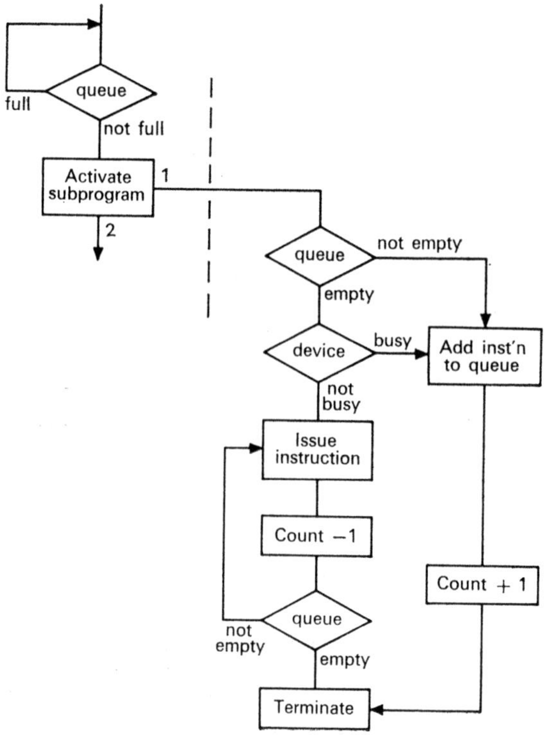
queue
full
not full
Activate subprogram
1
2
queue
not empty
empty
device
busy
Add inst'n to queue
not busy
Issue instruction
Count −1
Count + 1
queue
not empty
empty
Terminate

5.

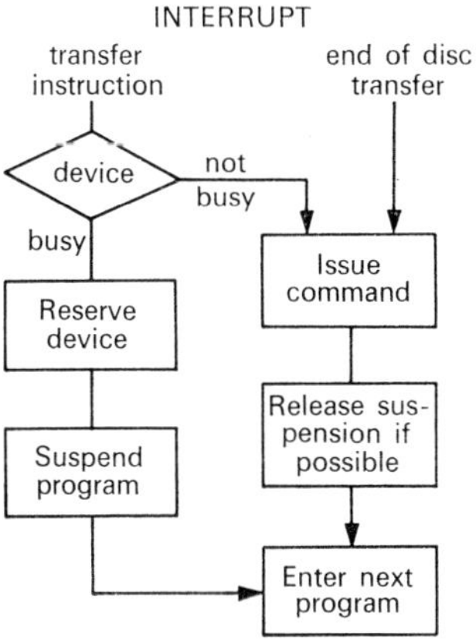

CHAPTER 15

1.

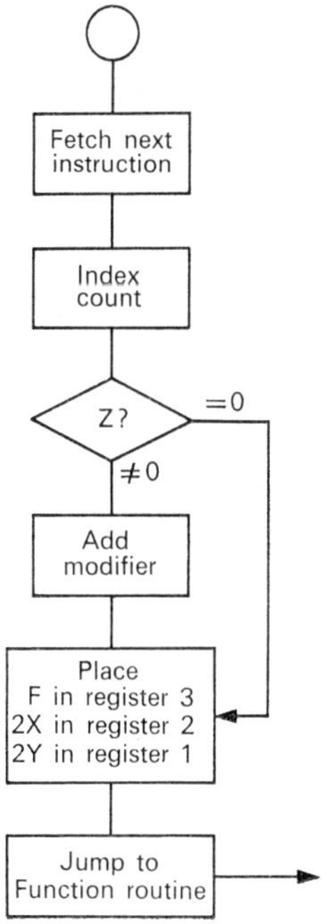

Translation cannot be used in this case because the function can be altered by modification, rendering the translation incorrect.

2. Assume that the instruction is stored in the top 49 bits of a 64-bit double-length word, with the sign bit of the lower half kept at zero. OBPROG is the base address of the object program (content of this and next address are zero). Instruction count is in 7, and 4 is used for linking.

FETCH:	1	MOVE	OBPROG(7)
	7	ADD	'1'
	2	MOVE	OBPROG(7)
	7	ADD	'1'
	3	MOVE	1
	3	SH	'14'
	3	AND	'32766'
	1	ADD	OBPROG(3)
	POS	J	'3'
	1	SUB	'sign bit'
	2	ADD	'1'
	2	ADD	OBPROG + 1(3)
	1	SH	'28'
	3	MOVE	2
	3	SH	'− 3'
	1	ADD	6
	1	AND	'32766'
	3	MOVE	2
	3	SH	'26'
	2	SH	'11'
	2	AND	'32766'
	4	J	SWITCH(3)

3. (i) An instruction that will put

6 most significant bits of Y in X,
next 14 bits in $X-1$
next 12 bits together with bits 1 and 2 (sign bit is bit 0) of $Y+1$ in $X-2$
next 14 bits in $X-3$

(ii) A double-length ADD instruction (a double-length instruction for subtraction and a double-length MOVE instruction would also be useful in this application).

APPENDIX I

Table of Powers of Two

n	2^n	n	2^n
0	1	16	65,536
1	2	17	131,072
2	4	18	262,144
3	8	19	524,288
4	16	20	1,048,576
5	32	21	2,097,152
6	64	22	4,194,304
7	128	23	8,388,608
8	256	24	16,777,216
9	512	25	33,554,432
10	1,024	26	67,108,864
11	2,048	27	134,217,728
12	4,096	28	268,435,456
13	8,192	29	536,870,912
14	16,384	30	1,073,741,824
15	32,768	31	2,147,483,648

APPENDIX II

Standard Seven-bit Code

BIN	HEX	0 000	1 001	2 010	3 011	4 100	5 101	6 110	7 111
0000	0	Null	TC$_7$	space	0	—	P	@	p
0001	1	TC$_1$	DC$_1$	!	1	A	Q	a	q
0010	2	TC$_2$	DC$_2$	"	2	B	R	b	r
0011	3	TC$_3$	DC$_3$	#	3	C	S	c	s
0100	4	TC$_4$	Stop	£	4	D	T	d	t
0101	5	TC$_5$	TC$_8$	%	5	E	U	e	u
0110	6	TC$_6$	TC$_9$	&	6	F	V	f	v
0111	7	bell	TC$_{10}$	'	7	G	W	g	w
1000	8	FE$_0$	cancel	(	8	H	X	h	x
1001	9	FE$_1$	end	)	9	I	Y	i	y
1010	*A*	newline	SS	*	:	J	Z	j	z
1011	*B*	linefeed	escape	+	;	K	[	k	NC$_1$
1100	*C*	FE$_4$	IS$_4$	,	<	L	$	l	NC$_2$
1101	*D*	FE$_5$	IS$_3$	−	=	M	]	m	NC$_3$
1110	*E*	SO	IS$_2$	.	>	N	^	n	NC$_4$
1111	*F*	SI	IS$_1$	/	?	O	↑	o	delete

TC = transmission control
FE = format effector
DC = device control
SO = shift out
SI = shift in
IS = item separator
SS = special sequence
NC = national character.

£ and $ may be replaced by national currency signs.

APPENDIX III

Typical Card Code

rows	*symbol*	*rows*	*symbol*	*rows*	*symbol*	*rows*	*symbol*
none	space	10	&	11	–		
0	0	10/0	&	11/0	″		
1	1	10/1	A	11/1	J	0/1	/
2	2	10/2	B	11/2	K	0/2	S
3	3	10/3	C	11/3	L	0/3	T
4	4	10/4	D	11/4	M	0/4	U
5	4	10/5	E	11/5	N	0/5	V
6	6	10/6	F	11/6	O	0/6	W
7	7	10/7	G	11/7	P	0/7	X
8	8	10/8	H	11/8	Q	0/8	Y
9	9	10/9	I	11/9	R	0/9	Z
		8/10/2	+	8/11/2	[	8/0/2	£
8/3	#	8/10/3	.	8/11/3	$	8/0/3	,
8/4	@	8/10/4	;	8/11/4	*	8/0/4	%
8/5	(	8/10/5	:	8/11/5	>	8/0/5	?
8/6	)	8/10/6	′	8/11/6	<	8/0/6	=
8/7	]	8/10/7	!				

APPENDIX IV

Multiplication, Division, and Radix Conversion

Multiplication

Multiplication in binary radix is quite analogous to multiplication in decimal radix. Partial products are formed by multiplying the multiplicand by all the digits of the multiplier in turn, and these are summed to give the full product. In binary radix, of course, the multiplier digits can only have the values 0 and 1, so the partial products are either zero or identical to the multiplicand. Also, in a computer, the partial products are added one by one into a running total as soon as they are formed. For example, to multiply 1001100101 by 1100010110 we should proceed as follows—

```
          1001100101
         ×1100010110
         -----------
         10011001010
       +1001100101
        ------------
        111001011110
     +1001100101
      --------------
      11010010101110
 +1001100101
  ------------------
  101001100110101110
+1001100101
 -------------------
 1110110001110101110
```

The process requires only three registers, since the growing product can be allowed to displace the multiplier bits after they have been dealt with. Although we have not shown the addition of zero in the example given above, the operation has to be performed in the simplest system, which therefore takes as many cycles as there are bits in the multiplier. The algorithm may start at the less significant end as shown here, or it may start at the more significant end, whichever happens to be the more convenient.

The same algorithm can be expressed in a different way as a series of successive halving and doubling. In this form the two numbers are written side by side, and the multiplier is successively halved, neglecting the residues, until it has been reduced to zero. The multiplicand is then doubled as many times, and values corresponding with even quantities in the halving column are deleted, the rest being added to give the desired product. For instance, we can multiply 567 by 234 as follows:

halving	doubling
234	(567)
117	1134
58	(2268)
29	4536
14	(9072)
7	18144
3	36288
1	72576
	132678

The halving process of course is equivalent to converting the number to binary radix. Thus if we scan the halving column from bottom to top, putting 1 for every odd quantity and 0 for every even quantity, we get 11101010, which is the binary form of 234. The other column consists of the normal partial products. Multiplication by halving and doubling is known as Russian multiplication, on account of its use by ignorant peasants in that country before the days of Soviet enlightenment. However, it is much older, and is said to have been used by the ancient Egyptians.

Negative numbers represent a special case. We have said that the quantity $-x$ is normally represented by $(2^n - x)$, where 2^n is one greater than the largest number that a register will hold. Now without its sign bit, the representation of $-x$ is—

$$2^n - 2^{n-1} - x \text{ or } 2^{n-1} - x$$

Consequently just before the sign bit is dealt with in multiplying y by $-x$, the accrued product is—

$$(2^{n-1}; - x)\, y \text{ or } 2^{n-1}y - xy$$

Therefore, by subtracting y in the significance 2^{n-1}, that is in the significance of the sign bit, we can obtain the desired result $-xy$, or to be more precise $2^{2n} - xy$, since it is double length. All this means simply that the sign bit must be dealt with by subtraction instead of addition.

In the simplest multipliers there is only one adder; but the process can be speeded up by providing two, three, or even more adders, when the system can be said to be operating in radix four, eight, or higher. It is possible to operate in radix four, and consequently to double the speed of multiplication, by providing one adder-subtractor instead of two adders (that is, by providing just what is ordinarily provided in a computer's arithmetic unit). We note first that the residues in radix 4 are 0, 1, 2, and 3, and that 3 is $4 - 1$, which means that it can be dealt with by subtracting the multiplicand and adding it again in the next significance (radix-4), that is, on the next cycle. This means that the following algorithm can be applied—

Examine next two bits of multiplier and—

for 00 do nothing,
for 01 add multiplicand,
for 10 add twice multiplicand (shift and add)
for 11 subtract multiplicand and raise flag.

When the flag is raised, the algorithm becomes—

for 00 add multiplicand and lower flag,
for 01 add twice multiplicand and lower flag,
for 10 subtract multiplicand,
for 11 do nothing.

The procedure is a bit different when it comes to the sign bit, of course; but the reader will probably be able to work that out for himself.

It is possible to work in radix 8 using one adder and one adder-subtractor. The algorithm is based on the following identities—

$$3 = 2 + 1 \qquad 6 = 4 + 2 \text{ or } 8 - 2$$
$$5 = 4 + 1 \qquad 7 = 8 - 1$$

As before, a flag is set after subtraction, and the operation in the next cycle is modified accordingly. Again the procedure is slightly different when the sign bit is being dealt with.

Division

Binary division is of two kinds—*restoring* and *non-restoring*. Restoring division is analogous to ordinary long division. Take for instance the product that was formed in the previous example—

```
                     1100010110
           ______________________
1001100101 ) 1110110001110101110
           – 1001100101
             ----------
              1010011001
            – 1001100101
              ----------
                1101001010
               –1001100101
                -----------
                 1110010111
                –1001100101
                 ----------
                   1001100101
                  –1011100101
                   ----------
                   . . . . .
```

In this example we have not shown the steps leading to zero, quotient bits. In a computer, however, the subtraction must be performed at every stage and, if the result changes sign, the original value of the dividend must be restored by adding the divisor again in the same significance—hence the name restoring division. Thus the full division process may need one subtraction cycle for every one in the quotient, and two cycles—one subtraction and one addition—for every nought in the quotient.

In non-restoring division, as its name implies, the dividend is not restored after a change of sign: instead the operation changes sign on the next cycle. To take the same example once again—

```
                      1100010...
           ______________________
1001100101 ) 1110110001110101110
            –1001100101
             -----------
             01010011001
            –1001100101
             -----------
              00001101001
             –1001100101
              -----------
               10000001000 negative
              +1001100101
               -----------
                10011011011 negative
               +1001100101
                -----------
                 11010000000 negative
                +1001100101
                 -----------
                  00111001011 positive
                 –1001100101
                  -----------
                   11011001101 neg.
                 + etc.
```

Here the third subtraction produces a negative result—indicated by a one in the most significant place; a nought is therefore entered in the quotient and the process changes to adding. Noughts are added as long as the result remains negative. When the sign changes again, a one is entered and the next operation is subtractive. Non-restoring division requires one cycle for every bit in the quotient, regardless of its value. Both restoring and non-restoring division require only three registers, since the growing quotient can be allowed to displace the contracting dividend.

Division is characterized by the fact that it is not possible to know what operation to perform in the next cycle until the sign of the result of the present cycle is known, that is, until it is completely finished. Because of this it is not possible to devise a faster algorithm than the foregoing. However there are several methods by which the algorithm can be speeded up—by doing both addition and subtraction, for instance, and selecting the correct result at the end, or working in radix four and providing facilities for 'trying' one, two, or three times the divisor. All these methods, however, require a great deal of equipment in relation to the frequency of division instructions.

Radix conversion

Conversion from decimal to binary radix is a straightforward process. Each cycle consists in multiplying the binary result formed so far by ten and adding the next binary-coded decimal digit. Negative numbers are best dealt with by complementing after conversion. To illustrate the process, let us consider the conversion of the decimal number 1234.

Take 1,	0001
multiply by ten	1010
add 2	1100
multiply by ten	1111000
add 3	1111011
multiply by ten	10011001110
add 4	10011010010

Conversion in the opposite sense can be performed by successively dividing by ten and entering the residues in the result, starting at the less significant end. But, as we have seen, division is a slow process and ought to be avoided as far as possible. A better method is to perform one division only, dividing the binary number by whatever power of ten converts it to a proper fraction. The decimal digits can then be evolved by successive multiplications by ten, the integral parts of the resulting numbers being the required digits. For example, the binary number formed in the previous example is converted back to decimal radix as follows—

Take binary number	10011010010
divide by ten thousand	0·00011111100101111
multiply by ten	1·0011101111101011
remove integral part 1	
multiply by ten	10·010101110010111
remove integral part 12	
multiply by ten	11·01100111110011
remove integral part 123	
multiply by ten	100·0000110111111
remove integral part 1234	

Notice that the fraction must be held to an accuracy of several more bits than the original integer. The reader will be able to verify for himself that fewer bits than we have shown here would not have given the correct result.

APPENDIX V

The City and Guilds Mnemonic Code

The City and Guilds Mnemonic Code is a single-address code that uses a mnemonic function and a numeric address. It is designed for simplicity, particularly simplicity of assembly, since it is intended that it should be available on any computer to which access is made by students working on the City and Guilds syllabus. Because it is implemented on a number of different machines, it cannot be defined precisely in every respect, and examination must of necessity be confined to those aspects that can be rigorously defined. The code is currently undergoing some extension; but, since the extensions have not been announced at the time of writing, this appendix has had to be based on the original form of the code. Nothing that is said here will be invalidated, of course, by the revision of the code, though it may prove possible to shorten some of the instruction sequences by using the new functions.

Instructions are of the form—

$$\mathrm{F} \quad \mathrm{Q} \quad n \quad m$$

where F is a function in mnemonic or numeric form, n the address, m an index register used for modification, and Q a qualifier digit used to control tracing or in any other manner determined by the implementation. In machine representation, F is a two-digit number, n an address between 0 and 999, and m and Q single digits.

Numbers are held to a precision of seven decimal digits. They may be integral, fractional or mixed, and positive or negative. Their exact representation depends on the form of implementation.

The code assumes a store of 1000 locations that can accommodate either numbers or instructions. The first ten have special significance as follows—

0 is always empty,
1 is the accumulator (symbol A),
2 and 3 are normal index registers,
4 is used for planting a link.

The indexing facilities associated with the first ten registers are determined by the form of implementation; for the purposes of this appendix, only registers 2 and 3 will be used for modification. It is probable that special features will be attached to registers 5 to 9 in the extended version of the code.

The syllabus specifies a minimum function set, though the set may be augmented by the implementer. The set will probably also be increased by the extensions currently under discussion, though throughout this appendix it is only the original minimum set that will be used. This is divided into seven groups.

In the first group, n is treated as an address modified by m.

Numeric	*Mnemonic*	*Operation*
00	LDA	load operand into accumulator
01	ADD	add operand into accumulator
02	SUB	subtract operand from accumulator
03	MLT	multiply accumulator by operand
04	DIV	divide accumulator by operand (quotient only, no residue)

The second group is similar, except that the operand n is to be regarded as an integer literal. There is no modification.

Numeric	*Mnemonic*	*Operation*
10	LDAN	load literal
11	ADDN	add literal
12	SUBN	subtract literal
13	MLTN	multiply by literal
14	DIVN	divide by literal

There is only one function in the third group. The argument is a modified address—

20	STA	store accumulator in address specified.

The fourth group consists of jumps. The argument is a modified address to which the jump is to be made if the condition is satisfied. There is no facility for labelling instructions—

30	JUN	jump unconditionally
31	JGR	jump if content of accumulator is positive or zero
32	JEQ	jump if content of accumulator is zero
33	JSR	jump unconditionally, planting a link in register 4
34	JST	stop until operator intervention, then jump

The fifth group is made up of standard functions of the type normally provided as system subroutines or library subroutines. The operand in every case is the content of the accumulator, which is overwritten by the result. The address, which is not modified, provides an escape jump in case the operand is out of the operable range (e.g. negative argument for square root)—

40	SQT	square root
41	EXP	exponential
42	LGN	natural logarithm
43	SIN	
44	COS	
45	ARC	arctan
46	ENT	integral part

The sixth group is at present concerned with input and output on punched tape, though it is possible that it may be modified by the extensions to the code. In any case, it is probable that the functions will still be available in their current form in some manner whatever happens. The character code used depends on the implementor, but within the machine alpha characters are stored as their decimal values at the least significant ends of registers. Numbers should not contain more than seven decimal digits, should be opened by a decimal digit or sign and terminated by a newline. The functions are—

50	RCT	read one character from tape to specified (modified) address
51	PCT	punch one character from specified address
52	RNT	read number into accumulator, converting it to normal internal form. Address gives escape jump in case of error
53	PNT	punch number in accumulator as signed decimal with *n* integral and *m* fractional digits
54	PNL	punch newline symbol

The last group provides for punched-card input and output. Again, much depends on the implementation, and details may be extended in the near future.

A whole card is read or punched at a time, and the details of the operations are similar to those in the previous group—

60	RCC	read 80 characters
61	PCC	punch 80 characters
62	RNC	read number into accumulator
63	PNC	punch number in accumulator

Four assembly directives are provided. They are distinguished by being enclosed in brackets—

(STORE *n*)	introduces program text and constants, which are to be stored sequentially starting at location *n*
(WAIT)	stop assembling until operator intervention
(EXECUTE *n*)	start obeying program at instruction in location *n*
(TITLE)	transfer characters direct from input to output medium up to next newline

EXAMPLES

In the examples that follow, it is assumed (unless the contrary is explicitly stated) that assembly commences in location 100. Data will be stored from location 10 onwards, and the address of a parameter list will be handed over in register 3. It is also assumed that there is no difference in form between numbers and modifiers.

CHAPTER 3

BALANCING A LEDGER (*PAGE 44*)

Data locations: 10 credit total
11 debit total
12 credit balance
13 debit balance

```
100 LDA   10          STA   13
    SUB   11          JST      exit
    JGR   109     109 STA   12
    LDAN   0          LDAN   0
    STA   12          STA   13
    LDA   11          JST      exit
    SUB   10
```

HIGHEST COMMON FACTOR (*PAGE 46*)

Data: 10 A
11 B
12 HCF

```
100 LDA   10          ADD   10
    SUB   11          STA   11
    JEQ   113         JUN   100
    JGR   101     113 LDA   11
    ADD   11          STA   12
    STA   10          JST      exit
    LDA   11
    SUB   10
    JEQ   113
    JGR   107
```

STATE PENSION SCHEME (PAGE 47)

Data: 10 age
11 sex (0 female, 1 male)
12 married state (0 div., 1 single, 2 married)
13 husband's age

Jump to 300 if pension entitlement; jump to 200 if not.

```
LDA    11        JUN    200
JEQ   106        LDA     12
LDA    10        JEQ    200
SUBN   95        SUBN     1
JGR   300        JEQ    300
JUN   200        LDA     13
JUN   103
LDA    10
SUBN   90
JGR   110
```

TAX EXAMPLE (PAGE 52)

Data: 10 pay in dims
11 tax in dims

```
LDA    10        STA     11
DIVN   10        LDA     10
STA    10        SUBN   500
SUBN  200        JGR    121
JGR   108        JST
LDAN    0        MLTN     2
STA    11        ADD     11
JST              STA     11
MLTN    3        LDA     10
STA    11        SUBN   800
LDA    10        JGR    128
SUBN  300        JST
JGR   114        MLTN     2
JST              ADD     11
MLTN    2        STA     11
ADD    11        JST
```

TRIVIAL INPUT-OUTPUT EXAMPLE (PAGE 55)

Output on paper tape instead of printer. Error subroutine starts at location 200—

```
RNT   200
STA    10
RNT   200
ADD    10
PNT   n, m
```

It is not possible to perform any of the packing and unpacking examples in the City and Guilds Code.

CHAPTER 4

There is at present no count-and-jump facility in the code. Also, collation arrangements depend on the form of implementation, so it might prove to be misleading to give any of the examples on character codes here.

SUM LIST OF 135 NUMBERS (PAGE 63)

List starts at location 500. The sum is to be placed in location 10. The modifier is in 2.

```
LDAN   1          ADDN    1
STA    2          STA     2
LDA    500        SUBN  135
ADD    500,2      JEQ   111
STA    10         JUN   103
LDA    2          JST
```

SORTING 135 NUMBERS (PAGE 68)

Data:
- 10 flag (0 down, 1 up)
- 11 working space
- 2 & 3 modifiers
- numbers for sorting in 500 to 634.

```
LDAN   0          LDAN    1
STA    10         STA    10
STA    2          LDA     3
ADDN   1          STA     2
STA    3          ADDN    1
LDA    500,2      STA     3
SUB    500,3      SUBN  135
JGR    116        JEQ   123
LDA    500,2      JUN   105
STA    11         LDA    11
LDA    500,3      JEQ   126
STA    500,2      JUN   100
LDA    11         JST
STA    500,3
```

DEBITING AN ACCOUNT AND TESTING OVERDRAFT (PAGE 69)

Data:
- 2 modifier
- 10 DEBIT
- 200 jump destination if limit exceeded
- 500 start of account with balance in 504 and limit in 516

```
LDAN  500
STA     2
LDA     4,2
SUB    10
STA     4,2
SUB    16,2
JGR   108
JUN   200
```

LARGEST ELEMENT IN FIRST COLUMN OF 10 × 20 *ARRAY* (*PAGE 71*)

```
Data:     2      modifier
         10      largest value
        500          start of array

        LDAN    0              LDA      2
        STA    10              ADDN    20
        STA     2              STA      2
        LDA    10              SUBN   200
        SUB   500,2            JEQ    114
        JGR   108              JUN    103
        LDA   500,2            JST
        STA    10
```

REPLACE FIRST COLUMN OF ARRAY BY ROW SUMS (*PAGE 71*)

```
Data:   2 & 3    modifiers
        10       working space
         5       counter

        LDAN    0              LDA      5
        STA     2              SUBN     1
        ADDN    1              STA      5
        STA     3              JEQ    117
        LDAN   19              JUN    106
        STA     5              LDA      3
        LDA   500,2            SUBN   200
        ADD   500,3            JEQ    122
        STA   500,2            LDA      3
        LDA     3              JUN    101
        ADDN    1              JST
        STA     3
```

CHAPTER 5

GENERALIZED LISTING SUBROUTINE (*PAGE 78*)

```
Data:    200   start of subroutine
           2   modifier
           3   address of parameter list
                     0 address of first item to be summed
                     1 number of items
                     2 cleared to receive sum

     200 LDA      2            STA      2
         STA    216            SUB      1,3
         LDA      0,3          JEQ    213
         STA      2            JUN    204
         LDA      2,3          LDA    216
         ADD      0,2          STA      2
         STA      2,3          JUN      0,4
         LDA      2            dump for reg. 2
         ADDN     1
```

CALLING SEQUENCE FOR ABOVE SUBROUTINE (PAGE 78)

Data: parameters in 150, 151, 152
subroutine starts at 200

Calls for summation of 135 numbers starting at address 500.

```
LDAN 150          STA    1,3
STA    3          LDAN   0
LDAN 500          STA    2,3
STA    0,3        JSR  200
LDAN 135
```

TRIAL BALANCE (PAGE 80)

Data: subroutine starts at 200
3 gives address of parameter list
0 start of account
1 accumulated credit balance
2 accumulated debit balance

```
200 LDA    2          SUB    0,2
    STA  218          STA    2,3
    LDA    0,3        JUN  215
    STA    2          ADD    1,3
    LDA    0,2        STA    1,3
    ADD    0,3        LDA  218
    STA    2          STA    2
    LDA    0,2        JUN    0,4
    JGR  213          dump for reg. 2
    LDA    2,3
```

There is no replacement facility in the code.

SWITCH JUMP (PAGE 82)

The sequence switches to one of four subroutines in 214, 237, 200 and 249 according to the value of the fifth word of a record starting in location 500. It is assumed that there is no difference between the forms of modifiers and ordinary numbers.

```
100 LDA  504
    STA    2
    JSR  103,2
    JUN  214
    JUN  237
    JUN  200
    JUN  249
```

The subroutines exit with—

```
    JUN    4,4
```

CHAPTER 6

CARD-SELECT PROGRAM (PAGE 94)

The nearest equivalent to this would be a program for reading 100 cards and punching copies of all those starting with the letter L. It is assumed that L is stored as the number 12. There are no facilities for inserting comments, nor, with no alphabetic names, is there any need for directives to define them. The program might be

```
(TITLE) CARDS STARTING WITH L
(STORE 100)
LDAN  100
STA     5
RCC   500
LDA   500
SUBN   12
JEQ   111
LDA     5
SUBN    1
JEQ   113
STA     5
JUN   102
PCC   500
JUN   106
JST
(WAIT)
(EXECUTE 100)
```

Segmentation is not possible, so the next example has no equivalent.

MACRO (PAGE 100)

There are no facilities for writing macros in the code; the nearest equivalent is an ordinary subroutine. Assume a parameter list with its address in 3. The parameters are—

0 start of list to be scanned
1 number of items
2 location to receive largest item

Suppose that the subroutine starts in location 200.

```
200 LDA   0,3        SUBN    1
    STA   2          STA   1,3
    LDA   0,2        JEQ   0,4
    STA   2,3        LDA   2,3
    LDA   2          SUB   0,2
    ADDN  1          JGR   204
    STA   2          JUN   202
    LDA   1,3
```

APPENDIX VI

Suggestions for Further Reading

Introductory

HOLLINGDALE and TOOTHILL, *Electronic Computers* (Penguin).
McRAE, *Introduction to Business Computer Programming* (Gee).

Programming

CHAPIN, *Programming Computers for Business Applications* (McGraw-Hill).
DAVISON, *Programming for Digital Computers* (Business Publications).

Automatic Programming

HIGMAN, *A Comparative Study of Programming Languages* (Macdonald).
McCRACKEN, *A Guide to* FORTRAN *Programming* (Wiley).
McCRACKEN, *A Guide to* COBOL *Programming* (Wiley).

Hardware

FLORES, *Computer Logic* (Prentice Hall).

Systems

FISHER and SWINDLE, *Computer Programming Systems.*
GREGORY and VAN HORN, *Automatic Data-Processing Systems* (Chatto & Windus).
WEGNER *et al.*, *Introduction to System Programming* (Academic Press).

Management

I.C.L., *Techniques of Computer Management* (I.C.L.).
McCRAE, *The Impact of Computers on Accounting* (Wiley).

Index

(Note: *the letter* "f" *following a page reference denotes that the item indexed is referred to in a footnote on that page.*)